Global

Please find a Facebook page for *Global Issues*, which features updates on many of the subjects discussed in this book. Please feel welcome to visit, like, comment, and share: https://www.facebook.com/GlobalIssuesHiteSeitz

Global Issues
An Introduction

SIXTH EDITION

Kristen A. Hite and John L. Seitz

WILEY Blackwell

This sixth edition first published 2021
© 2021 John Wiley & Sons Ltd

Edition History
Blackwell Publishers Ltd (1e, 1995); Blackwell Publishing Ltd (2e, 2002 and 3e, 2008);
John Wiley & Sons Ltd (4e, 2012 and 5e, 2016)

The right of Kristen A. Hite and John L. Seitz to be identified as the authors of this work has been asserted in accordance with law.

Registered Offices
John Wiley & Sons, Inc., 111 River Street, Hoboken, NJ 07030, USA
John Wiley & Sons Ltd, The Atrium, Southern Gate, Chichester, West Sussex, PO19 8SQ, UK

Editorial Office
9600 Garsington Road, Oxford, OX4 2DQ, UK

For details of our global editorial offices, customer services, and more information about Wiley products visit us at www.wiley.com.

Wiley also publishes its books in a variety of electronic formats and by print-on-demand. Some content that appears in standard print versions of this book may not be available in other formats.

Library of Congress Cataloging-in-Publication Data
Names: Hite, Kristen A., author. | Seitz, John L., 1931- author.
Title: Global issues : an introduction / Kristen A. Hite and John L. Seitz.
Description: Sixth edition. | Hoboken, NJ : Wiley-Blackwell, 2020. |
    Includes bibliographical references and index.
Identifiers: LCCN 2020012767 (print) | LCCN 2020012768 (ebook) | ISBN
    9781119538509 (Paperback) | ISBN 9781119538523 (Adobe PDF) | ISBN
    9781119538486 (epub)
Subjects: LCSH: Economic development. | Developing countries–Economic
    policy. | Developing countries–Economic conditions. | Economic
    history–1945–
Classification: LCC HD82 .H528 2020 (print) | LCC HD82 (ebook) | DDC
    338.9–dc23
LC record available at https://lccn.loc.gov/2020012767
LC ebook record available at https://lccn.loc.gov/2020012768

Cover Design: Wiley
Cover Image: © David Malan/Photographer's Choice RF/Getty Images

Set in 10.5/13pt Minion Pro by SPi Global, Pondicherry, India

*To those who serve the needs of others – humans, animals, and plants,
all essential parts of our lovely but endangered planet*

Contents

List of Plates

List of Figures, Maps, and Tables

Figures

Maps

Tables

Tables

Acknowledgements

This edition benefited from the substantial research contributions of Brian Farrell (Wealth and Poverty), Monika Shepard (Population), Jason Farr (Food), Carlos Saavedra (Energy), Katherine Liljestrand (Natural Resources and Pollution), and Liz Schmitt (Technology and Sustainable Futures).

We would like to thank the following reviewers who made useful suggestions for improving this edition: Dr Laté Lawson-Lartego, Amanda Davis Edwards, Ed.D. Brian Farrell, Justin Vaughan, Merryl Le Roux, Liz Wingett, Caroline McPherson, and Rajalakshmi Nadarajan.

We would also like to thank Wofford College, both for providing author John Seitz with an office and for supporting the development and teaching of Global Issues as a semester-long course, which enabled author Kristen Hite to take the class from Dr Seitz in the late 1990s and orient towards the subjects covered in this book.

Introduction

The Creation of Global Issues

What causes an issue to become a "global issue"? Are "global issues" the same as international affairs – the interactions that governments, private organizations, and peoples from different countries have with each other? Or is something new happening in the world? Are there now concerns and issues that are increasingly being recognized as global in nature? It is the thesis of this book that something new is indeed happening in the world as nations become more interdependent. While their well-being is still largely dependent upon how they run their internal affairs, increasingly nations are facing issues that they alone cannot solve, issues that are so important that the failure to solve them will adversely affect the lives of many people on this planet. In fact, some of these issues are so important that they can affect how suitable this planet will be in the future for supporting life.

The issues dramatize our increasing interdependence. The communications and transportation revolutions that we are experiencing are giving people knowledge of many new parts of the globe. We see that what is happening in far-off places can affect, or is affecting, our lives. For example, instability in the oil-rich Middle East affects the price of oil around the world, and since many countries are dependent on oil as their main source of energy, the politics of oil becomes a global concern.

Many nations in the world are now dependent on other nations to buy their products and supply the natural resources and goods they need to purchase in order to maintain a certain standard of living. An economic downturn in any part of the world that affects the supply and demand for products will affect the economic status of many other nations. This is an important part of globalization that will be discussed in Chapter 2.

Global Issues: An Introduction, Sixth Edition. Kristen A. Hite and John L. Seitz.
© 2021 John Wiley & Sons Ltd. Published 2021 by John Wiley & Sons Ltd.

Even a global issue such as world hunger illustrates our increasing interdependence. A person might say that starving or malnourished people in Africa don't affect people in the rich countries, but even here there is a dependency. Our very nature and character depend on how we respond to human suffering. Some rich nations such as the Scandinavian nations in northern Europe give a significantly higher portion of their national wealth to poor nations for development purposes than do other rich nations such as the United States and Japan.

Global issues are often seen as being interrelated. One issue affects other issues. For example, climate change (an environmental issue) is related to an energy issue (our reliance on fossil fuels), the population issue (more people produce more greenhouse gases), the wealth and poverty issue (wealthy countries produce the most gases that cause climate change), the technology issue (technology can help us create alternative energy sources that produce less or no greenhouse gases), and the future issue (will the changes we are making in the Earth's climate seriously harm life on this planet?). As we recognize these interrelationships, we realize that usually there are no simple solutions.

Interdisciplinary knowledge is required to successfully deal with the issues. The student or adult learner reading this book will be receiving information from multiple disciplines such as biology, economics, political science, environmental science, chemistry, and others. Neither the social sciences nor the physical sciences have the answers on their own. Feel good about yourself, reader, because you are engaged in the noble task of trying to understand how the world really works. Complicated? Yes, of course. Impossible to discover? Certainly not. Just read seriously and carefully. It takes effort and you can keep learning throughout your life.

Perhaps, global issues were born on the day, several decades ago, when the Earth, for the first time, had its picture taken. The first photograph of Earth, which was transmitted by a spacecraft, showed our planet surrounded by a sea of blackness. Many people seeing that photograph realized that the blackness was a hostile environment, devoid of life, and that life on Earth was vulnerable and precious. No national boundaries could be seen from space. That photograph showed us our home – one world – and called for us to have a global perspective in addition to our natural, and desirable, more local and national perspectives.

This book discusses *some* of the main current global issues of our time. The reader can probably identify others. During the reader's lifetime, humanity will have to face new global issues that will continue to surface. It is a characteristic of the world in which we live. Maybe our growing ability to identify such issues, and our increasing knowledge of how to deal with them, will enable us to handle the new issues better than we are doing with the present ones.

Chapter 1

What is Development?

Developing Toward What?

When we talk about global issues, "development" can be a confusing term. Development, as used in this book, is the ways in which economies progress through their societies to improve well-being. This requires us to consider how to measure progress as a society at the global level. Cultures across the world have very different ideas of how to define progress. Many define it by material wealth. But not all, by any means. Bhutan, for example, has a national happiness indicator in addition to measuring national wealth by the more conventional means of domestic production (gross domestic product – GDP).

This inevitably causes us to wonder *what we are developing toward?* In other words, what is the end goal? More stuff? Longer lives? Better health? Smarter people? Better relationships? Greater happiness? That answer is not an easy one: embedded in it are many different assumptions that vary based on different cultures and values.

Global Issues: An Introduction, Sixth Edition. Kristen A. Hite and John L. Seitz.
© 2021 John Wiley & Sons Ltd. Published 2021 by John Wiley & Sons Ltd.

The United Nations defines human development as the enlarging of human capabilities and choices; in a yearly publication it ranks nations on a human development index, which tries to measure national differences of income, educational attainment, and life expectancy.[1] The United Nations has suggested the purpose of development to be the creation of an environment in which people can lead long, healthy, and creative lives. But for most of the last century, most of development was geared towards increasing national incomes, on the assumption that developing towards wealth could lead to other benefits. Let's explore further what twentieth-century development looked like, and then consider what it means for an increasingly interdependent world with finite resources.

Twentieth-Century Approach: Development as Economic Growth

For roughly the past century, "development" has been viewed primarily through the lens of economic growth plus the social changes caused by or accompanying that economic growth.[2] Economists have traditionally used gross national product (GNP) or a country's average per capita income as the measures of economic development. Some organizations, such as the World Bank, also divide countries according to their level of income, and consider low- and middle-income countries to be "developing" and high-income countries to be "developed." High-income countries were early adopters of intensive manufacturing. They amassed large amounts of wealth that lifted many of their citizens out of poverty; economists referred to these "industrialized" nations as "developed" nations. Most of them are located in the northern hemisphere, so they are also sometimes called "the North."

If we accept the vision of development as building wealth, it makes sense that the overwhelming priority is to transition from economies of subsistence (prioritizing getting households the basic resources on which to live) to economies of consumption (prioritizing getting households greater incomes to rapidly increase consumption and further stimulate the economy). This approach typically leads first to a transition towards industrialized economies, and then, as machines replace workers, to a second transition towards economies based on goods and services.

In the 1950s and 1960s, it was common to think of development only in economic terms. It was, of course, economic growth with the agricultural and industrial revolutions that created the increased food and higher standards of living that permitted more human beings to inhabit the planet. The development that took place in Europe and the United States as they industrialized led to an increase in the average family's income, and this meant more money to buy goods, including food.

In the second half of the twentieth century, nations generally took one of two approaches to development. The first approach was to develop government policies focused on creating jobs and providing social services to meet basic needs.[3] The other approach, encouraged by international development institutions like the World Bank, re-evaluated the role of government in economic development and focused on minimizing government influence on market prices by gearing public policies away from regulation, encouraging the private sector to provide social services (also known as "market-based solutions").[4] This market approach became known as the "Washington Consensus," focusing on economic efficiency and fiscal discipline. Much foreign assistance in the twentieth century certainly encouraged nations along this route. The market approach in particular assumed that economic growth was functionally synonymous with "development."

Unprecedented economic growth and material prosperity took place in a handful of countries like the United States during the twentieth century, and this was made possible, in large part, by cheap energy and abundant access to resources, often exported from other countries. The desire to achieve the high living standards of the Northwest by following the route taken by the United States and other wealthier nations – both capitalist and communist in the past – with their emphasis on industrialization has been attractive to many governments as a seemingly clear development path towards poverty reduction.

Mostly by default, this became the "model" for development, where individual lifestyles and modes of industrial production were based on converting raw materials to more expensive and useful productions, utilizing plentiful, inexpensive, polluting energy – a model that has driven climate change and placed the future of our planet in jeopardy. For example, in the 1990s, the Chinese economy grew at an amazing 10 percent a year, lifting millions of people out of poverty. And with this new wealth came a massive need for increased energy production as well as a tidal wave of demand for the increased production of consumer goods.

But does this kind of development work for everyone? Results have been mixed, and you can use this book to help make your own assessment. Some of those working in international development recognized that this development strategy was a gamble, that maybe benefits would not trickle down to the poor, but the alternative of trying to work directly with the millions of rural poor did not seem viable. Poverty rates dropped substantially in a number of industrialized countries – although in some places, national incomes went up more than poverty rates went down. The Washington Consensus led on one hand to increases in the GDPs of many countries but also to cuts in social spending – and as a result some of the poorest became even worse off.[5] By some estimates, only 20 percent of development assistance reached rural populations, even though the clear majority of people lived in rural areas.[6]

The process of creating wealth has also created negative impacts to the environment. Countries are slowly realizing that the effects of economic activity on the environment should not be ignored. But awareness is not high in countries, especially ones that are still in the early stages of industrialization. This helps explain why some countries have welcomed polluting industries, such as factories that manufacture asbestos, since jobs today are often prioritized over a vague worry that workers may contract cancer in 20 to 30 years. But also, a slowly growing number of people realize that if the economic activity that gives jobs to people harms the environment, future costs resulting from that economic activity may become substantial.

Twenty-First-Century Approach: Developing towards Sustainability

At first, global discussions about development, environment, and social issues occurred on very separate tracks. The 1972 Stockholm Conference on Human Environment was seen by many poor countries as an effort by rich countries to constrain the development of the rest of the world under the auspices of environmental protection. The view at that time was that environmental protection was a luxury that could only be afforded once a country had developed. Besides, countries argued, most of the environmental problems were located in the handful of countries that had been able to accumulate wealth as they industrialized without the controls. But as environmental problems became more widespread, so did discussions about how they related to the development process itself.

In the 1970s an awareness grew – in both the "less developed" nations and the "developed" industrialized nations – that some of the social and environmental changes which were coming with economic growth were undesirable. More people were coming to understand that for economic development to result in happier human beings, attention would have to be paid to the effects that economic growth was having on social and environmental factors. Were an adequate number of satisfying and challenging jobs being created? Were adequate housing, healthcare, and education available? Did women have equal opportunities? Were people living and working in a healthy and pleasant environment? Did people have enough nutritious food to eat? Every country is deficient in some of these factors and, in this context, is still "developing" in some capacity.

By the 1980s, concerns were mounting about the social and environmental implications of more and more countries following a development model based on ever increasing rates of production and consumption. By 1987, the concept of "sustainable development" emerged in a landmark report by the Brundtland Commission called *Our Common Future*. The term means that economic growth in the present should not take place in such a manner that it reduces the ability of future generations to meet their own needs. Economic growth and efforts to improve the living standards of the few or the many should be sustainable; in other words, they should be able to be continued without undermining the conditions that permit life on Earth, thus making future development impossible or much more difficult. The term represents an effort to tie economic growth, the protection of the environment, and social development together, a recognition that future economic growth is possible only if the basic systems that make life possible on Earth are not harmed. It also implies a recognition that the economy, the environment, and social conditions are all important, that economic development and the reduction of poverty are essential to the protection of the environment.

The United Nations environment conference in Rio de Janeiro in 1992 made the term "sustainable development" widely known around the world. Sustainable development was endorsed by the conference and a new organization – the Commission on Sustainable Development – was set up under the United Nations to monitor the progress nations are making to achieve it. But it still was not a mainstream concept for the development community.

Meanwhile, the social dimensions of development were becoming more acute. The elevated profile of the "Right to Development" from its introduction in 1981[7] made it clear that development needed to be inclusive, not just economically lucrative in the context of raising a country's average GNP. The Fourth World Conference on Women in Beijing elevated gender issues to a new level. The International Labor Organization saw a proliferation of global labor agreements to address some of the workforce challenges of industrialized economic growth. The World Bank and other multilateral development banks began adopting new policies and procedures to address unacceptable impacts to communities caught in the crosshairs of well-intentioned development projects. And amid all of this, poverty remained persistent and pervasive, even as the twentieth-century development model continued to churn out ever-increasing rates of production and consumption.

Wave of Hope: The Millennium Development Goals (2000–2015)

As the challenges of inclusive development became more acute, in 2000, the nations of the world historically committed themselves to work toward helping the neediest when they endorsed the Millennium Declaration and adopted the Millennium Development Goals (MDGs), which refocused development on the "basic needs" approach, recognizing that market-based solutions alone could not solve widespread poverty and that governments needed to support effective social policies such as healthcare and education to avoid marginalizing the poor.[8] Between 2000 and 2010, natural resource shortages contributed significantly to food and energy crises, in turn challenging traditional notions of economic development based on the once dominant Washington Consensus model.[9]

Continuing to focus on positive developments, one can find many reasons to feel optimistic. In 2000, representatives of 189 nations met in a conference sponsored by the United Nations and adopted eight goals they would work toward achieving in the new century. Each goal, which was stated in general terms, had specific targets to help measure progress in reaching the goal. This is significant in that development was broken down into more elements and indicators than the twentieth-century model focused on GNP. Education, gender equality, child and maternal health, infectious diseases, and hunger were all incorporated into the development goals. And significantly, one of the goals (MDG # 7) was focused on environmental protection, with a notable goal of integrating the principles of sustainable development into country policies and programs. Finally, the last goal was focused on addressing some of the structural problems of the twentieth-century development model, with the aim of improving the global financial system, addressing countries' mounting debt load, and offering special considerations for the poorest and other specially situated countries.

By 2014, several targets of the Millennium Development Goals had been met, including halving hunger rates as well as the extreme poverty rate: by 2010, 700 million fewer people lived on $1.25 per day than in 1990.[10] Advances in malaria and tuberculosis treatment saved an estimated 25.3 million lives by 2012, and 2.3 billion people gained access to drinking water from an improved source.[11] Development aid had increased by 66 percent.[12]

At the beginning of the MDG period, the concept of "sustainability" was a small part of the development dialogue. At that time, "sustainability" was mostly a popular buzzword for those who wanted to be seen as pro-environmental but who did not really intend to change their behavior. It became a public relations term, an attempt to be seen as abreast with the latest thinking of what we must do to save our planet from widespread harm. But within a decade or so, governments, industries, educational institutions, and organizations started to incorporate "sustainable development" in a more serious manner.

A number of large corporations appointed corporate officers for sustainability. Not only were these officials interested in how their companies could profit by producing "green" products, but they were often given the task of making the company more efficient by reducing wastes and pollution and by reducing its carbon emissions. Many colleges and universities adopted sustainability as a legitimate academic subject and something to be practiced by the institution. Many nonprofit organizations added the promotion of sustainability to their agendas. This all set the stage for a more formal convergence of the UN's environmental and development agendas.

As sustainable development gained momentum, the "Washington Consensus" of the twentieth century began to erode. Nancy Birdsall and Francis Fukuyama of the Center for Global Development argued that the global recession driven by the United States at the end of the first decade of the twenty-first century changed the model for global development and that now the focus is much more on the ability of governments to help the poor and provide social protections.[13] They predicted that many mid-and lower-income countries would reject the free-market approach and adopt a basic needs approach while increasing domestic industrial production. "In fact," they explained, "development has never been something that the rich bestowed on the poor but rather something the poor achieved for themselves."

Sustainable Development Goals (2015–2030)

In 2015, the United Nations adopted Sustainable Development Goals for 2015–2030 to replace its mainstream Millennium Development Goals in place from 2000–2015. While the sustainable development agenda from the 1992 Rio Earth Summit factored in clearly to some of the individual goals, the overall focus was still on poverty alleviation through the historic paradigm of economic development. During that same period of implementation, countries began to embrace sustainable development as a key pathway to creating an economy that can provide for the population without undercutting the people and planet that form the basis of that very economy.

In 2012, countries met again in Rio for a new global summit on sustainable development. By this time, it was clear the development and environment agendas were becoming more aligned. Countries shared progress they had made towards sustainable development and discussed challenges going forward, but largely diverted conversations about targets. There were questions about how to best integrate economic and social development with environmental considerations, and governments began focusing on high-level efforts to merge development and environment, building from the Millennium Development Goals and Rio summits on Sustainable Development. There are two ways to view this development: one is that countries have found environmental problems challenging and wish to avoid taking on new, high-profile commitments. The other is that the concept of "sustainable development" has become so mainstream that environmental considerations have become integrated into the broader development dialogue.

In the second decade of the twenty-first century, countries began developing a broad set of "sustainable development goals" intended to help the United Nations develop new targets after the Millennium Development Goals had run their course by 2015. By integrating these sustainable development goals with conventional, high-level development discussions at the UN, countries made it clear that the concept of sustainability is fundamental to development.

In September 2015, to a standing ovation from many world leaders, 193 nations unanimously adopted the UN Sustainable Development Agenda as a "blueprint for development." UN Secretary-General Ban Ki-moon welcomed the decision, calling it "an agenda for people, to end poverty in all its forms ... It is an agenda for shared prosperity, peace and partnership (that) conveys the urgency of climate action (and) is rooted in gender equality and respect for the rights of all. Above all, it pledges to leave no one behind." This agenda sets forth 169 targets supporting 17 Goals for 2030. As the next step beyond the Millennium Development Goals, these Sustainable Development Goals reflect a concerted global effort to provide for the growing number of people on the planet by alleviating poverty, improving livelihoods, and sustaining the ecosystems necessary to maintain all of the Earth's inhabitants in the coming decades. We have included these goals below, as they are relevant to every chapter in this book. As you think about where "development" is headed, consider what actions governments will need to take to realize all of these goals and how different the world might look if some or all of the goals are achieved.

United Nations Sustainable Development Goals:

1   End poverty in all its forms everywhere.
2   End hunger, achieve food security and improved nutrition, and promote sustainable agriculture.
3   Ensure healthy lives and promote well-being for all at all ages.
4   Ensure inclusive and equitable quality education and promote lifelong learning opportunities for all.
5   Achieve gender equality and empower all women and girls.
6   Ensure availability and sustainable management of water and sanitation for all.
7   Ensure access to affordable, reliable, sustainable, and modern energy for all.
8   Promote sustained, inclusive, and sustainable economic growth, full and productive employment and decent work for all.
9   Build resilient infrastructure, promote inclusive and sustainable industrialization, and foster innovation.
10 Reduce inequality within and among countries.
11 Make cities and human settlements inclusive, safe, resilient, and sustainable.
12 Ensure sustainable consumption and production patterns.
13 Take urgent action to combat climate change and its impacts.
14 Conserve and sustainably use the oceans, seas, and marine resources for sustainable development.
15 Protect, restore, and promote sustainable use of terrestrial ecosystems, sustainably manage forests, combat desertification, halt and reverse land degradation, and halt biodiversity loss.
16 Promote peaceful and inclusive societies for sustainable development, provide access to justice for all, and build effective, accountable, and inclusive institutions at all levels.
17 Strengthen the means of implementation and revitalize the global partnership for sustainable development.

Now sustainable development is more integrated and global development goals are increasingly focused on the social and environmental basis of well-being in addition to conventional economic indicators. Countries have adopted ambitious targets and indicators, and the world is watching to see what kind of progress can be made in the coming years to meaningfully advance towards these goals – including whether wealthy nations will step up financial and other assistance to help achieve these goals.

Development Assistance and Foreign Aid

It's one thing to have development plans; it's another thing to make it happen. Planning and building a more sustainable world is not cheap or easy. The United Nations has set an aid target for the rich countries to contribute 0.7 percent of their wealth (as determined by their GNP) towards official development assistance ("ODA") for developing countries. As of 2017, US \$135 billion flowed through official development assistance channels.

Foreign aid is used regularly to help donor nations achieve their political objectives and can include military aid as well as economic assistance. Development assistance is usually given with the objective of helping a nation develop, often in exchange for the recipient country making changes or promises to use the money a certain way. More than two thirds of ODA (\$98 billion in 2016) flows bilaterally, that is from a specific donor country directly to a specific recipient country. The remaining tens of billions flow multilaterally through international institutions and funds that help channel money for specific development purposes.

Multilateral institutions that control the biggest flows of development finance include the World Bank and regional public financial institutions such as the Asian, African, and Inter-American Development Banks. The Global Environment Facility, established during the 1922 Rio Earth Summit and headquartered at the World Bank, helps administer development assistance to support the environment. UN institutions such as the United Nations Development Programme also have specific rules for administering development projects across the world. More specialized funds, such as the Green Climate Fund and Global Fund to Fight AIDS, Tuberculosis and Malaria, help channel funding flows in support of specific issues like fighting infectious diseases and climate change.

Curiously, even though the overall development model has moved past the focus on national incomes, the "developed" and "developing" country divide continues to be officially based on average per capita incomes. As of 2018, some 150 countries were considered "developing countries" (the vast majority of countries in the world) based on per capita incomes below US \$12,276.[14] Note that climate finance is seen as separate and additional to official development aid, as politically countries view climate finance as obligatory payments by wealthy historic emitters for the costs of coping with climate impacts caused by their emissions. Adding to the already complicated picture of development assistance, some island nations have been deemed ineligible due to inequality: one or two billionaires on a small island can raise the average GDP beyond the average income threshold, even though many countries on the list had not yet met the Millennium Development Goals.[15]

Speaking of billionaires, while it is primarily countries who command the billions for official development assistance, private actors and philanthropy are increasingly significant players. Perhaps most substantial is "The Giving Pledge," a most unusual effort by two American billionaires – Bill Gates and Warren Buffett – to get other billionaires around the world to give at least half of their wealth to charities, as they are doing.[16] As of 2018, 187 billionaires from 22 countries had signed the pledge.[17] While many are private about their total net worth, by one report, estimates are that the Giving Pledge reflects a total giving commitment of at least US \$600 billion.[18]

While private philanthropists have great latitude in how they spend their money, countries have carefully negotiated a set of rules and processes for official development assistance. For example, countries track relevant funds against sustainability markers ("Rio markers" as well as the Sustainable Development Goals. The Organisation for Economic Co-operation and Development ("OECD") evaluates all official development aid based on its efforts to deliver on the Sustainable Development Goals.[19] It also evaluates how much additional private funding gets leveraged from the spending of official development aid, finding in 2018 that 77 percent of all leveraged private funding went to middle income countries, and not to those most in need. [20]

Part of this also involves making sure funds are both programmed and spent effectively, a concern in many countries. In 2014, a report by the ONE Campaign estimated that corruption deprived countries' economies of 1 trillion dollars (that's $1,000,000,000,000).[21] To give perspective, this sum would be enough to provide about 165 million vaccines or educate 10 million children per year.[22]

Experiences with foreign aid: a personal account
by John Seitz

The unanticipated consequences of the use of technology (discussed in more detail in the Technology Chapter 9) can be seen in a situation of which I (Seitz) have some personal knowledge. When I was in Iran in the late 1950s with the US foreign aid program, one of our projects was to modernize the police force of the monarch, the Shah of Iran. We gave the national police new communications equipment so that police messages could be sent throughout the country quickly and efficiently. The United States gave this kind of assistance to the Shah to bolster his regime and help him to maintain public order in Iran while development programs were being initiated. All fine and good, except for the fact that the Shah used his efficient police – and especially his secret police, which the US Central Intelligence Agency helped train – not just to catch criminals and those who were trying to violently overthrow his government, but to suppress all opponents of his regime. His secret police, SAVAK, soon earned a worldwide reputation for being very efficient – and ruthless. Such ruthlessness, which often involved torturing suspected opponents of the Shah, was one of the reasons why the Shah became very unpopular in Iran and was eventually overthrown in 1979 by the Ayatollah Khomeini, a person who had deep anti-American feelings.

For a fuller discussion of the unanticipated consequences of American aid to the Shah, see John L. Seitz, "The Failure of US Technical Assistance in Public Administration: The Iranian Case," in Eric Otenyo and Nancy Lind (eds), *Comparative Public Administration: The Essential Readings* (Oxford: Elsevier, 2006), pp. 321–34.

Part of the way donor governments address concerns about effectiveness of funding is to cherry pick what they spend and where they spend it, and as a result some of the neediest causes remain unfunded. For a more global approach, donor governments channel money to development institutions with relatively strong policies governing how the money gets spent. Multilateral development banks maintain specific policies and procedures that not only require careful management and accounting of funding, but also which help avoid unacceptable social and environmental harms. What is interesting is that these institutions originally started out after World War II by lending money in support of the twentieth-century development approach, but the results were so disastrous for communities and for the environment that they had to change their policies to constrain lending towards sustainability, refusing to fund projects with unacceptable social and environmental harms. These social and environmental safeguards have now become the norm for international finance, both public and private.

The amount of foreign aid that wealthy nations have contributed in relation to the donors' wealth fell rather dramatically in the second half of the twentieth century. There was a slight upturn at the end of the century, but the aid was still far below the United Nations' target. From 2000–2014, official development assistance increased 66 percent; however, bilateral aid dropped considerably during this same time period. While the United States gives the largest amount of aid, in relation to its wealth as measured as a percentage of gross national income, it is near the bottom of aid donors.

Plate 1.1   Street children in Nepal

Source: Ab Abercrombie.

Culture and Development

There are about 15,000 nations on our planet and about 200 nation-states. The nation-states are the political entities, what are commonly referred to as countries. They are often made up of several or many individual nations, or different cultures. The nation is a group of people that share a common history, a common ancestry, and usually a common language and a common religion. They often have common traditions, common ways of doing certain things and of interacting with each other and toward outsiders. Because of these similar features that make them different from other peoples, each nation's people see the world and their place in it differently than others, approach problems differently, and have arrived at different solutions to situations humans face. The unique language of the culture is used to pass the common history and traditions down to the young. The United Nations now estimates that of the approximately 7,000 languages in the world, by the end of this century about 90 percent of them will be endangered.[23] The term "endangered language" means that the group that speaks the language – which is often unwritten – is becoming so small that there is a real possibility the group will die out or become absorbed by the larger dominant culture around it and will disappear forever.

For most of the twentieth century, "development" was associated with certain economic policies and associated consumption culture, particularly in the United States. The United States has been one of the largest producer of goods and services and its culture is closely associated with material wealth. Because of the worldwide popularity of US movies, music, fast food, and clothes, and of the English language, it is common to read that the American culture is replacing local cultures in many countries. But some recent studies indicate that only some rather superficial aspects of the American culture are being adopted, such as Coca-Cola and Big Macs, while more important values are not.

Social integration is proceeding at such a rapid pace that one can say that there is the beginning of a world culture. Much of this culture is exported from the United States, but it is also truly international as foods, music, dances, and fashions come from various countries. Many European cultures place a higher value on leisure and government social services than did the dominant twentieth-century culture in the United States, which emphasized earning higher income so people could acquire more material objects. The degree to which people seem to be happy to trade income for more leisure to enjoy life varies across the globe, and, maybe not surprisingly, those who do may have a higher "satisfaction with their lives" than those who prioritize primarily material gain.[24]

What will be lost if a culture dies out? Cultures represent the amazing variety of human life on Earth that reflect the different ways members of one species – the human species – have decided to live. A culture represents the accumulated knowledge of one group, knowledge that is available to others to pick and choose from, so they can improve their own lives (some would call this "development"). In addition, the multitude of cultures makes life on Earth extremely rich and varied. The discovery of that variety often leaves an observer with a sense of awe and with a realization that the loss of any culture leaves life less wonderful.

The Yanomami

In the Amazon region of Brazil live the Yanomami. It is believed that the people have lived in this region for thousands of years. The approximately 9,000 Yanomami represent the largest group of indigenous people living in the Americas who still follow hunter-gatherer methods.[25] Although they had very limited contact with other cultures for many years, this changed in the late 1980s when gold was discovered in the Brazilian Amazon region. Thousands of miners flew into the area where the Yanomami lived. The miners brought with them diseases to which the Yanomami had no natural immunity. Amnesty International estimates that from 1988 to 1990 about 1,500 Yanomami died.[26] In addition to the malaria that killed many, some Yanomami died from mercury poisoning, which came from eating fish poisoned by the mercury the miners had used in the streams to sift for gold. Others were killed by armed attack. Amnesty International reported: "These attacks are often carried out by private agents, including gunmen hired by land claimants, timber merchants or mining interests. They have gone almost entirely unpunished – in fact, state-level authorities have even colluded with them."[27]

The Yanomamis' situation became known throughout Brazil and around the world as mining problems persisted. Responding to pressures within Brazil and from some foreign countries (the attention given to Brazil because of the upcoming UN environmental conference probably played a role), the Brazilian government in 1991 set aside for the Yanomami about 36,000 square miles of land. When added to that set aside by Venezuela, which was slightly smaller than the Brazilian grant, this was an amount of land equal to the size of Portugal and the amount anthropologists said the Yanomami needed in order to survive. In 1990, the agency in charge of Indian affairs in the Brazilian government announced that it was forcibly removing all miners from Yanomami lands.[28] In 1993, Brazil used its police and military force to forcibly remove 3,000 miners who were still in Yanomami lands. But more recently, mining pressures have resurfaced, with over 10,000 miners invading Yanomami territories in 2019.

What will be the fate of the Yanomami? No one knows, of course, but if history is a guide, one would have to say that their prospects of surviving are not bright. While the actions by the Brazilian and Venezuelan governments to reserve a large amount of land for the use of these people is a hopeful step, disturbing signs exist. The presence of gold in their lands increased tension. Despite some success removing miners in the early parts of this century, by 2011, the nonprofit organization Survival International reported that about 1,000 gold miners were illegally working on Yanomami land. In 2002 the Brazilian army began building more bases along its largely undefended northern border, which crosses Yanomami lands. Some of the soldiers got Yanomami women pregnant and brought venereal diseases.[29] In 2009 swine flu hit the Yanomami as did Covid-19 in 2020. In 2012, Survival International reported a "massacre" of up to 80 Yanomami individuals.[30] And in 2018, a measles epidemic further devastated the Yanomami population.[31]

There is abundant research showing that many indigenous cultures confronted with modern development pressures increasingly find it challenging to preserve their traditional knowledge – such as specialized farming techniques, natural cycles, and natural healing methods and medicines. This can present a threat to their traditional livelihoods and increases dependencies on modern goods, which may have significant cultural, social, and environmental impacts.[32] In some cases, when outside companies show up and alter the economic and cultural landscape of traditional cultures, alcoholism and suicide rates and have increased dramatically.

Some people are giving a new respect to previously marginalized cultures of indigenous and tribal peoples. There is a growing recognition that these traditional cultures may have knowledge that humans need if they are going to survive – such as an ability to live in harmony with nature, a concern for future generations, and a knowledge of how to foster a sense of community. Indigenous and tribal peoples in tropical forests have been recognized as possessors of important knowledge regarding medicinal plants and of skills that have enabled them to live in the forests without destroying them. There is also a growing recognition that if we want to preserve the world's forests and the multitude of species they harbor, we must make it possible for those living in them to survive and thrive without cutting down the trees. If these peoples cannot survive, probably the forests cannot either. If these peoples do survive, they can help protect the forests that are their homes.

Conclusion

If we take in all of the information in this chapter, we begin to have a much more complete vision of development going forward, one better suited to this century and more focused on sustainability than purely on economic growth. The Millennium Development Goals already represented a big departure from the post-World War II model focused almost exclusively on increasing production and consumption as a means to increase incomes. The twentieth century model assumed more money could get the things desired by development, and it discounted the social and environmental costs of doing so. The Sustainable Development Goals allow for different pathways to get there, and recognize that not every path towards income generation is beneficial for inclusive and sustainable development. Under these goals, sustainable development means everyone has their basic needs met while resources and ecosystems remain intact – a tall order but also quite a necessary one.

Throughout this book, we explore the different dimensions and approaches to development. Because the very notion of development is evolving, and because a diversity of cultures and nations have different visions for progress, we try to minimize the use of terms like "developed" and "developing." Given how much development has been conflated with GDP growth, we often refer to countries by their wealth classification as opposed to "developed" and "developing," because those terms are more accurate than assuming development equities to a country's wealth classification, which is an idea rooted in the last century's development model.

The term "developing countries" is typically understood to be those countries in which agriculture or mineral resources have a large role in the economy while industrialization, manufacturing and services have a lesser role. The infrastructure (transportation, education, health, and other social services) of these countries is usually less adequate for their needs than infrastructure of the wealthiest 20 percent of countries (aka "developed nations"). At the same time, some of the countries classified as "least developed" (i.e. have the lowest average incomes per capita) are highly developed in culture and many such regions of the world had ancient civilizations with architecture, religion, and philosophy that we still admire, which brings us back to the question of what are we developing towards? And if the answer to this question varies, perhaps we should avoid assuming that 80 percent of the world wants to follow the twentieth century approach for "developing" inequitably and unsustainably. Since many of the less (economically) developed nations are in the southern hemisphere, they are at times referred to as "the South" instead of "developing."

Even though institutions like the World Bank use wealth to differentiate between "developed" and "developing" countries, they also agree that development is more than economic growth. "Development" can also include the social and environmental changes that are caused by or accompany economic growth, some of which are positive and thus may be negative. Awareness has grown – and continues to grow – that the question of how economic growth is affecting people and the planet needs to be addressed. Countries are slowly learning that it is cheaper and causes much less suffering to try to reduce the harmful effects of an economic activity or project at the beginning, when it is planned, than after the damage appears. To do this is not easy and is always imperfect. But an awareness of the need for such an effort indicates a greater understanding and moral concern than did the previous widespread attitude that focused only on creating new products and services.

This book combines the economic, environmental, and the social components into the concept of development. We use the neutral and expanded definition of development because economic development alone has sometimes led to negative social and environmental consequences that rival in scale the economic benefits generated. We have chosen this definition because there is no widespread agreement on what these desirable and undesirable features are.

In this book we will look at some of the most important current issues related to development. The well-being of people depends on how governments and individuals deal with these issues. We will first look at issues related to wealth and poverty, then turn to population, food, and energy. We'll then turn to the environmental impacts: climate change, natural resources, and pollution. In the last two chapters, we consider the role of technology and then conclude with a consideration of what the future holds. As you read this book, consider for yourself: If the goal is "development," what are we developing toward? And how do we manage the interdependent relationships between societies, the environment, and a globalized economy? The way we answer these questions informs how we address global issues.

Notes

1 United Nations Development Programme (UNDP), *Human Development Report 2004* (New York: UNDP, 2004), p. 127.

2 See, generally, Wolfgang Sachs, *The Development Dictionary: A Guide to Knowledge as Power* (Johannesburg: Witwatersrand University Press, 2003).

3 United Nations Department of Economic and Social Affairs (UN DESA), *World Economic and Social Survey 2010: Retooling Global Development* (New York: United Nations, 2010).

4 Ibid.

5 Nancy Birdsall and Francis Fukuyama, "The Post-Washington Consensus: Development after the Crisis," *Foreign Affairs* (March/April 2011); UN DESA, *World Economic and Social Survey 2010*.

6 Barbara Ward, *Progress for a Small Planet* (New York: W. W. Norton, 1979).

7 African Charter on Human and Peoples Rights, Art. 22 (1982).

8 Birdsall and Fukuyama, "The Post-Washington Consensus." ("The global food, energy and financial crises that exposed the systemic flaws inherent in the functioning of deregulated global markets required governments to step in to address those crises – and in ways that dealt a blow to the conventional wisdom underpinning the Washington Consensus.")

9 Ibid.

10 United Nations, *The Millennium Development Goals Report 2014*, p. 4, at http://www.un.org/millenniumgoals/2014%20MDG%20report/MDG%202014%20English%20web.pdf (accessed July 2015).

11 Ibid.

12 United Nations, Millennium Development Goals website, at http://www.un.org/millenniumgoals/global.shtml (accessed December 2018).

13 Birdsall and Fukuyama, "The Post-Washington Consensus."

14 See, generally, Organisation for Economic Co-operation and Development, Development Assistance Committee website, at https://data.oecd.org/oda/net-oda.htm (accessed December 2018).

15 Compton Bourne, Financing for Development Challenges in Caribbean SIDS: A Case for Review of Eligibility Criteria for Access to Concessional Financing. United Nations Development Programme (2015).

16 See, generally, The Giving Pledge website, at www.givingpledge.org (last accessed December 2018); see also Stephanie Strom, "Billionaires' Pledge to Give Away Half Gains Followers," *New York Times* (August 5, 2010), p. A15.

17 The Giving Pledge website, at www.givingpledge.org (last accessed December 2018).

18 Peter Koteki, "The billionaire 'Giving Pledge' signed by Bill Gates and Elon Musk could soon be worth up to $600 billion." *Business Insider* (July 18, 2018), at https://www.

businessinsider.com/bill-gates-elon-musk-giving-pledge-may-reach-600-billion-2018-7/ (last visited December 2018) (citing the 2017 Wealth X Billionaire Census).

19   OECD, Development Co-operation Report 2018: Joining Forces to Leave No One Behind, p. 33.

20   Ibid., p. 40.

21   ONE Campaign, *The Trillion-Dollar Scandal* (2014), at https://s3.amazonaws.com/one. org/pdfs/Trillion_Dollar_Scandal_report_EN.pdf (accessed July 2015).

22   Ibid.

23   UN Department of Economic and Social Affairs, SEcretariat of the Permanent Forum on Indigenous Issues, *State of the World's Indigenous Peoples*, document ST/ESA/328 (2010), p1, at http://un.org/esa/socdev/unpfii/documents/SOWIP/en/SOWIP_web.pdf

24   Minority rights Group International, *World Directory of Minorities and Indigenous Peoples – Brazil, Yanomami* (2008).

25   James Brooke, "Brazil Evicting Miners in Amazon to Reclaim Land for the Indians," *New York Times* (March 8, 1993), p. A4.

26   Ibid.

27   James Brooke, "In an Almost Untouched Jungle Gold Miners Threaten Indian Ways," *New York Times* (September 18, 1990), p. B6.

28   Larry Rohter, "A New Intrusion Threatens a Tribe in Amazon: Soldiers," *New York Times* (October 1, 2002), p. A1.

29   "Yanomami "Massacred" by Goldminers in Venezuela," *Survival International* (August 30, 2012), at https://dissidentvoice.org/2012/08/yanomami-massacred-by-goldminers-in-venezuela/ (accessed November 2018).

30   "Deadly measles epidemic hits isolated Yanomami tribe," *Survival International* (June 28, 2018), https://survivalinternational.org/news/11967 (accessed November 2018).

31   One encouraging sign is that when Western scientists seek information from the medicine men of indigenous peoples about natural drugs and health cures, the medicine men are given new respect. This new respect might help encourage some of their youth to study under them. But, all too often today, when the medicine men die, the knowledge they have acquired dies with them. See Daniel Goleman, "Shamans and Their Longtime Lore May Vanish with the Forests," *New York Times*, June 11, 1991, p. B5. As an example of a study showing the harmful effects Western contact can have on the culture of indigenous peoples, see Katharine Milton, "Civilization and Its Discontents," *Natural History* (March 1992), pp. 37–43.

32   As one author has written: "[indigenous peoples] may offer living examples of cultural patterns that can help revive ancient values for everyone: devotion to future generations, ethical regard for nature, and commitment ot community among people." Alan Durning, "Supporting Indigenous Peoples," in Lester R. Brown et al., *State of the World 1993* (New York: W.W. Norton, 1993), p. 100.

Further Reading

World Bank, The 2018 Atlas of Sustainable Development Goals: an all-new visual guide to data and development. World Bank Data Team 05/24/2018 http://blogs.worldbank.org/ opendata/2018-atlas-sustainable-development-goals-all-new-visual-guide-data-and-development?cid=ECR_LI_worldbank_EN_EXT (accessed December 2018).

United Nations Sustainable Development Goals Website: www.un.org/sustainabledevelopment/sustainable-development-goals/ (accessed October 13, 2015).

United Nations Sustainable Development Goals website containing the text of all 17 Sustainable Development Goals, expandable by topic: https://sustainabledevelopment.un.org/topics/ (accessed October 13, 2015).

United Nations Press Release, Historic New Sustainable Development Agenda Unanimously Adopted by 193 UN Members, at http://www.un.org/sustainabledevelopment/blog/2015/09/historic-new-sustainable-development-agenda-unanimously-adopted-by-193-un-members/ (accessed October 13, 2015).

Chapter 2

Wealth and Poverty[1]

The mere fact that opposing visions of economic development have grown to shape the international agenda is in one sense merely an indication that development concerns are receiving attention on a global scale for the first time in history.

Lynn Miller, *Global Order* (1985)

---

1 Brian Farrell contributed substantially to the research and updates reflected in this edition. Please reflect his contribution in any direct citation to this chapter.

Global Issues: An Introduction, Sixth Edition. Kristen A. Hite and John L. Seitz.
© 2020 John Wiley & Sons Ltd. Published 2020 by John Wiley & Sons Ltd.

For most of history, human beings have lacked material wealth. A few individuals in many societies had a higher standard of living than their fellow humans, but the vast majority of people on Earth have shared a common condition focused on meeting their daily needs. The Industrial Revolution brought a fundamental change. Through a fundamentally faster rate of production and consumption, new wealth was created in the industrializing nations in Europe and eventually larger numbers of people prospered. And the differences between the rich and the poor countries and people amplified. A few industrialized countries achieved higher living standards and pulled away from the rest of the world.

Before the Industrial Revolution, the difference between the per capita incomes of the richest and poorest countries was 3 to 1 in 1820.[1] In the twentieth century, the disparity between the richest and poorest countries intensified: the gap grew to 11 to 1 1913; it reached 35 to 1 in 1950, 44 to 1 in 1973, then 72 to 1 in 1992.

The trend continued into the twenty-first century. In 2009, the richest countries had a 76 to 1 margin of wealth advantage in terms of gross domestic product (GDP).[2] In 2017, the difference raised to over 90 times the wealth of low income countries.[3]

Another way to show this trend is through differences in real (i.e. controlling for inflation) per capita incomes. From 1970 to 1995, the richest one-third of countries increased real per capita incomes nearly 2 percent annually. The middle third of countries increased only about 0.5 percent annually. The poorest third had no increase in incomes.[4] After that period, a more positive trend emerged for the poorer countries. Gross national incomes (GNI) more than doubled in low and middle income countries from 1998 to 2008 – a significant increase from the previous decade – and increased again by approximately 30 percent from 2009 to 2015.[5]

Despite notable periods of income growth for low to middle income countries, the gaps between rich and poor *within* countries also continued to increase. A 2018 study of the United States economy following 2008–2009 economic crisis found that "the U.S. experienced a widely-shared recession followed by a deeply fractured recovery."[6] The study states, "it took under five years for prosperous communities to replace lost jobs while distressed ones are unlikely to ever recover on current trend lines."[7] One more way to demonstrate that the gap between the richest and poorest is increasing is the following: in 1960, the richest 20 percent of the world's population had 30 times more income than the lowest 20 percent of the world's people. By 2009, the richest 20 percent had now more than 75 times the income of the poorest.[8] And less than a decade later – in 2016 – the richest 62 people on the planet people claimed as much wealth as half of the world's population.[9]

Not only is the gap between the richer and poorer nations growing, but the gap between the rich and the poor *within* countries is also growing. For example, a 2015 United Nations International Labor Organization report found the gap between the rich and poor had increased markedly in Spain and the United States.[10] According to one 2017 study, in 2016 the top 1 percent wealthiest people in the United States accounted for 40 percent of the national wealth, higher than at any time since 1962.[11] While these figures are notable, this trend of concentrating wealth in the hands of the wealthy is not uncommon: in 2017, just over 2000 of China's wealthiest people claimed a total wealth of $2.6 trillion, roughly equivalent to the GPD of the United Kingdom.[12]

By the way, don't let all these numbers make your head ache. You don't have to remember them all to understand the subject. But read them carefully as they illustrate the points being made. For example, do the numbers show that the rich are getting richer and the poor poorer? It's much more complicated than that. The data demonstrates that global initiatives to combat extreme poverty based on income levels have been largely successful, but inequality is still a problem. Some people are getting poorer, but not the majority in low-to-middle income countries or the rich countries. Taking in the overall data, we could say the poor are getting richer, and the rich are getting richer faster. But it would not be accurate to simply say the poor are getting poorer.

The growing gap between the rich and the poor is only one part of the picture of worldwide economic conditions. As we explored in the first chapter, metrics such as GDP and GNI per capita are important indicators but they do not tell the full story about development. Having an international standard to discuss extreme poverty, such as earning US $1.90/day, is a helpful rubric working on solutions that affect the world's poorest populations, but it is not a perfect indicator of extreme poverty. And even if the standard is met universally, does it mean that poverty has actually been eradicated? Can everyone become middle class? Can everyone become rich? Let's take a quick look at the middle class from the global perspective.

Homi Kharas of the Brookings Institution offered a definition of middle class as follows: "People who have enough money to cover basics needs, such as food, clothing and shelter, and still have enough left over for a few luxuries, such as fancy food, a television, a motorbike, home improvements or higher education."[13] According to Kharas, the middle class earn approximately $11 to $110 per day per capita. Kharas argues that a family of four earning $12,000 per year would struggle in the United States, but the income would qualify as middle class in many countries, including Indonesia. Kharas estimates that about 3.7 billion people in the world are middle class by international standards. In some wealthier nations, and particularly in areas with high costs of living and low opportunities for economic mobility, people who attain over $40,000 per year may genuinely describe their economic circumstances as impoverished. While the economic experience of their struggle is very much real, Kharas has argued that that they have met the threshold of the global middle class, even as they may materially have less than others in the world with far lower incomes. What this fails to answer is whether it is a reasonable goal – or even possible – for everyone to be middle class.

Can We Eradicate Poverty?

Which are you – an optimist, or a pessimist? When one thinks about the living standards of the world's people there are figures that support both positions.

Here's the **optimistic view:** on the positive side, the total GDP (gross domestic product) of low-to-middle income countries nearly doubled from 2009 to 2017, up from approximately $3.5 trillion to $6.5 trillion.[14] The growth rate of per capita income in developing countries was relatively high in the 1960s and 1970s but stagnated in the 1980s. In the early 1990s, rapid growth began again, especially in East Asia (from Indonesia to South Korea), but a financial crisis in the late 1990s stopped that growth. Overall the decade of the 1990s was one of impressive economic growth for some countries, such as China and India, while other nations became poorer.[15] In the first half of the first decade in the twenty-first century there was strong economic growth in much of the world that reduced the number of people living in extreme poverty from 1.8 billion in 1990 to 1.4 billion in 2005.[16] Note that the international standard for extreme poverty is based on the number of people below a daily income threshold: less than $1.25 a day until 2015, and then $1.90 after that.

This improvement ended with the very serious economic crisis that occurred in the United States and spread to Europe and many other countries in 2008–2009. The crisis led to abrupt declines in exports from resource rich yet economically poor countries and a lowering of the prices they received for their commodities (mainly minerals and agricultural products). Trade and foreign investments declined. The World Bank estimates the crisis left an additional 50 million people in extreme poverty in 2009.[17]

Despite the global financial hardship, in 2010, the UN's Millennium Development Goal of reducing global poverty by one-half of the 1990 poverty level was achieved.[18] Figure 2.1 shows the overall reduction in extreme poverty in developing countries during the final decades of the twentieth century.

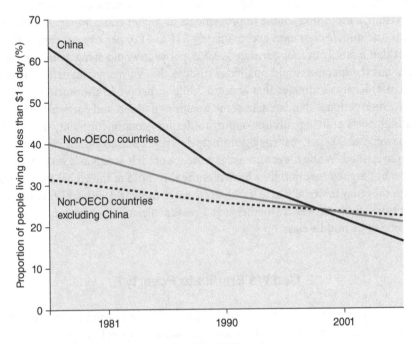

Figure 2.1 Global extreme poverty rate, 1980–2000

Source: World Bank, *World Development Indicators*, 2005.

Table 2.1   Global extreme poverty rate

Poverty at the International Poverty Line of $1.90/day (in 2011 purchasing power parity)

Region	Headcount ratio (%)		No. poor (millions)	
	2013	*2015*	*2013*	*2015*
East Asia and Pacific	3.6	2.3	73.1	47.2
Europe and Central Asia	1.6	1.5	7.7	7.1
Latin America and the Caribbean	4.6	4.1	28.0	25.9
Middle East and North Africa	2.6	5.0	9.5	18.6
South Asia	16.2	12.4	274.5	216.4
Sub-Saharan Africa	42.5	41.1	405.1	413.3
World Total	**11.2**	**10.0**	**804.2**	**735.9**

Source: World Bank, *World Development Indicators*, 2018.

Table 2.1 gives a closer look at the progress made from 2013 to 2015 in reducing the number of people in poor countries living in extreme poverty, i.e. living daily on $1.90 or less. In the last 25 years, based on daily income statistics, one billion fewer people are living in extreme poverty, and by 2018, the global poverty rate was at its lowest historic levels, according to World Bank president Jim Kim.[19]

Note that much of that progress took place in East Asia and South Asia, where China and India are located. By their sheer population size, overall increases in income of the poorest people in these two countries has significantly improved the global poverty rate. The impressive economic growth that both nations experienced in the late twentieth century, especially China, came after they introduced new economic policies that spurred foreign investments. At the beginning of the 1980s, China was one of the poorest countries in the world with about 60 percent of its people living in extreme poverty. Between 1981 and 2012, China more than halved the number of people living on less than $1.25 per day (reduced by 660 million).[20] Poverty rates fell from 51 percent in 1990 to about 24 percent in 2015.[21] By 2017, the rate of extreme poverty (people living on less than $1.90) in China had fallen dramatically: down to 0.7 percent of the population.[22] The unprecedented reduction of extreme poverty in China and India are shown in Figures 2.2 and 2.3 respectively. Figure 2.4 demonstrates the global trend in poverty reduction.

Overall, the global growth in wealth last century corresponded to marked increases in well-being, as illustrated in this excerpt from a report by the United Nations Development Programme (UNDP):

> Progress in human development during the twentieth century was dramatic and unprecedented. Between 1960 and 2000 life expectancy in developing countries increased from 46 to 63 years. Mortality rates for children under five were more than halved. Between 1975, when one of every two adults could not read, and 2000 the share of illiterate people was almost halved. Real per capita incomes more than doubled from $2,000 to $4,200.[23]

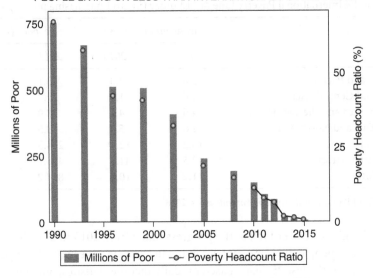

Figure 2.2 Poverty trend (by International Standards: $1.90 USD): China

Source: World Bank, Poverty and Equity Database and PovcalNnet, 2018.

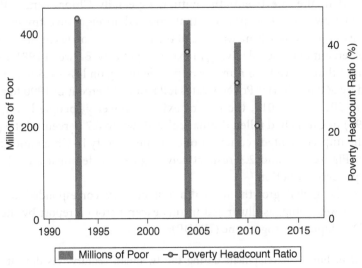

Figure 2.3 Poverty trend (by International Standards: $1.90 USD): India

Source: World Bank, Poverty and Equity Database and PovcalNet, 2018.

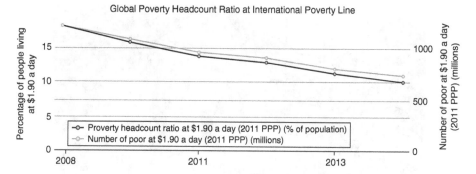

Figure 2.4 Percent of the global population living in poverty on less than $1.90 USD a day: International Poverty Line ($1.90)

Source: World Bank, Poverty and Equity Database and Povcalanet, 2018.

Mainstreaming Sustainable Development

Continuing to focus on positive developments, one can find many reasons to feel optimistic. As discussed in Chapter 1, in 2000, representatives of 189 nations met in a conference sponsored by the United Nations and adopted eight goals they would work to achieve in the new century. Each goal, which applied from 2000 to 2015, had specific targets to help measure progress in reaching the goal. To address poverty, the United Nations set a target of reducing by half the number of people living on the equivalent of less than $1 a day by 2015. This poverty goal was successful, leading to a new and more ambitious goal for the 2015–2030 period under the Sustainable Development Goals.

How did the world do in achieving the first Millennium Development Goal – a goal, by the way, unprecedented in the world's history? As we have seen from the information presented above, China and India are doing quite well, but the same cannot be said for many other countries. Take the time to read the following paragraph from the *Millennium Development Goals Report 2015* by the United Nations, as it presents a good summary of the world's progress up to that date in achieving this goal:

> The world economy continues to grow at a modest pace. Growth of world gross product is projected to accelerate slightly from 2.6 per cent in 2014 to 2.8 per cent in 2015—a downward revision by 0.3 percentage points from the forecast presented in the World Economic Situation and Prospects 2015 in January. In 2016, global growth is forecast to improve to 3.1 per cent. There are still considerable downside risks to the baseline forecast, related to the upcoming move towards monetary policy normalization

Plate 2.1   Poverty in Indonesia

Source: World Bank.

in the United States, ongoing uncertainties in the euro area, potential spillovers from geopolitical conflicts and persistent vulnerabilities in emerging economies. The overall subdued performance of the world economy since the global financial crisis has raised concerns of a "new normal" of lower growth, especially in view of a broad-based weakness in investment.

The downward revision in global growth for 2015 reflects mainly a deteriorating outlook in the economies in transition and several large developing countries, especially in South America. Gross domestic product (GDP) in the economies in transition is projected to contract by 2 per cent this year, while average growth in developing countries is expected to remain at 4.4 per cent, about 3 percentage points below the pre-crisis pace. The growth divergence between the various regions is widening in 2015. This can be partly attributed to the differing impacts from the recent drop in the prices of oil and other commodities.[24]

By 2014, the Millennium Development Goal of halving the extreme poverty rate had been met: by 2010, 700 million fewer people lived on $1.25 per day than in 1990.[25] While much of the world still lives in extreme poverty and hunger, this successful reduction can point to a glass-half-full outlook.

Then in 2015, nations adopted a new and more ambitious 15-year target under the United Nations Sustainable Development Goals: ending poverty by 2030. Optimists cite the information above as reasons to believe this is achievable; however, pessimists question whether this goal is genuinely achievable.

A Pessimistic View: The Persistence of Poverty

Now, here's some information for the pessimist. The United Nations claimed in 2014 that about 1 in 8 people in the world, or 827 million people, endured chronic hunger between 2011 and 2013, and 1 in 4 children, or about 160 million, suffered from chronic undernutrition in 2012.[26] In 2018, the United Nations reported that chronic hunger rose to approximately 1 in 9 people in the world.[27] We review this in more detail in Chapter 4.

Plate 2.2   The weight of poverty falls heavily on children in poorer nations
Source: United Nations.

As illustrated in Figure 2.5, over 700 million people still live in extreme poverty.[28] From 2012 to 2014, 11 percent of the global population, or about 770 million, still lacked clean drinking water and 2.5 billion lacked adequate sanitation (Goal 6 of the Sustainable Development Goals).[29] About 1.2 billion had no electricity.[30] (We return to discussions on clean drinking water, electricity, and sanitation in subsequent chapters of the book.) In 2015, about 47.18 million people living in East Asia and the Pacific lived in extreme poverty, as did about 7.15 million in Europe and Central Asia, 25.90 million in Latin America and the Caribbean, 18.64 million in the Middle East and North Africa, and 413.25 million in sub-Saharan Africa. In 2013, about 274.49 million in South Asia lived in extreme poverty.[31]

Regional aggregation using 2011 PPP and \$1.9/day poverty line

2015

Region	Pov.line(PPP$/day)	Headcount(%)	Pov. gap(%)	Squaredpov. gap	Num of poor (mil.)
East Asia and Pacific	1.90	2.32	0.46	0.16	47.18
Europe and Central Asia	1.90	1.47	0.40	0.18	7.15
Latin America and the Caribbean	1.90	4.13	1.54	0.92	25.90
Middle East and North Africa	1.90	5.01	1.28	0.50	18.64
Other high Income	1.90	0.68	0.49	0.42	7.32
Sonth Asia	Survey data coverage is too low, the result is suppressed				
Sub-Saharan Africa	1.90	41.10	15.79	8.24	413.25
World Total	1.90	10.00	3.10	1.49	735.86
World less Other High Income	1.90	11.62	3.55	1.67	728.54

2013

Region	Pov.line(PPP$/day)	Headcount(%)	Pov. gap(%)	Squaredpov. gap	Num of poor (mil.)
East Asia and Pacific	1.90	3.64	0.69	0.23	73.14
Enrope and Central Asia	1.90	1.59	0.42	0.18	7.67
Latin America and the Caribbean	1.90	4.57	1.76	1.07	27.98
Middle East and North Africa	1.90	2.64	0.52	0.17	9.45
Other high Income	1.90	0.60	0.44	0.38	6.39
South Asia	1.90	16.15	3.03	0.87	274.49
Sub-Saharan Africa	1.90	42.54	16.56	8.70	405.10
World Total	1.90	11.20	3.38	1.59	804.23
World less Other High Income	1.90	13.05	3.89	1.80	797.83

Figure 2.5 Number of extremely poor individuals by region

Source: The World Bank. "http://iresearch.worldbank.org/PovcalNet/povDuplicateWB.aspx

A depressing number of countries (46) actually became poorer in the 1990s.[32] Many of these were in Africa and a few were in Latin America and in Europe and Central Asia. In Africa many of the countries growing poorer are in sub-Saharan Africa and are being hit by an HIV/AIDS epidemic, among other problems, while in Europe and Central Asia parts of the former Soviet Union found the transition to becoming an independent country difficult. For many the path from a planned, state-managed economy to a freer economy was filled with obstacles.

Where are the world's poor? Figure 2.5 shows that the world's poor are concentrated in Africa, East Asia, and South Asia, with a particularly high concentration in sub-Saharan Africa. Within regions and countries, the poor tend to be concentrated in rural areas with a high density of population, such as on the Ganges plain in India and on the island of Java in Indonesia. Although urban poverty is a growing problem due to demographic migration toward cities, 76 percent of extreme poverty occurred in the rural areas of the poorer countries as of 2013.[33] Part of this is due to how poverty is defined, part is due to differences between rural and urban livelihoods, and part is due to disparities in economic opportunities.

Figures 2.6 and 2.7 show an interesting contrast in the poverty situation. From 1990 to 2015, the proportion of those in two of the poorest regions in the world – sub-Saharan Africa and South Asia – who were living in extreme poverty actually

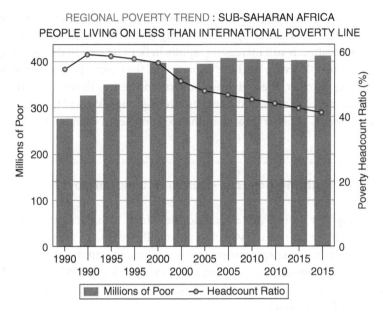

Figure 2.6 People living on less than International Poverty Line ($1.90 USD): Sub-Saharan Africa

Source: The World Bank. http://povertydata.worldbank.org/poverty/region/EAS

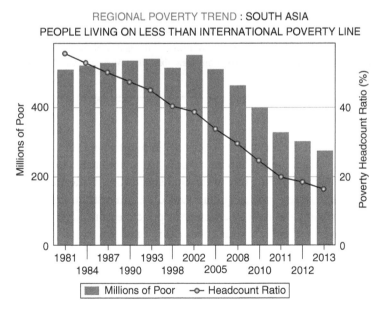

Figure 2.7 People living on less than International Poverty Line ($1.90 USD): South Asia

Source: The World Bank. http://povertydata.worldbank.org/poverty/region/EAS

decreased, while at the same time the number of people in both regions living in extreme poverty increased. Do you know why it was this way? As we will see in Chapter 3, population is still increasing rapidly in both regions of the world so there are now more people living in these regions and thus more people at the bottom economic rung. Further, the weight of poverty in the less developed nations falls heaviest on women, children, and minority ethnic groups. We will take a closer look at the repercussions of poverty for marginalized peoples in Chapter 3.

Fighting poverty – can an individual do it?

Is there any way an individual can aid the efforts to reduce poverty in our world? Yes, there are ways. If you can't personally work with the poor, you can give some funds to an organization that is working to improve the lives of the poor. Here are a few of those we donate to annually: Doctors Without Borders, Grameen Foundation, International Rescue Committee, and Oxfam (where author Hite has worked).

But you might ask: How can I be sure the organizations I give my money to will not waste my money? Several reputable organizations evaluate other organizations for this very characteristic. One of the best is the American Institute of Philanthropy, called by the *New York Times* "the pit bull of watchdogs."

Note: If you are one of those rare individuals who wants to personally aid those who are poverty-stricken, read the following article to learn how others are doing this: Nicholas D. Kristof, "The D.I.Y. [Do It Yourself] Foreign Aid Revolution," *New York Times Magazine*, October 24, 2010, pp. 49–53.

How much are the richer nations doing at present to help the poorest nations? Over the past several decades, there have been some agreements to reduce the debt of poorer nations, but other economic challenges (like trade barriers) remain. Nontariff trade measures, such as quotas, subsidies, and restrictions on exports, are increasingly prevalent and may be enacted for policy reasons having nothing to do with trade. However, they have a discriminatory effect on exports from countries that lack the resources to comply with requirements of nontariff measures imposed by rich nations.[34] For example, the huge subsidies that wealthy nations give to their farmers make it very difficult for farmers in the rest of the world to compete with them. Another example would be domestic health or safety regulations, which, though not specifically targeting imports, could impose significant costs on foreign manufacturers seeking to conform to the importer's market. Industries in developing markets may have more difficulty absorbing these additional costs.[35] See below for further discussion on trade.

Systematic Approaches

Now that we have made a brief examination of poverty and international efforts to help alleviate it, let's focus on another question: why are some countries rich and some poor? There is no agreement on the answer to that question, but various views have been presented over the years. Although vast differences among the nations of the world make generalizations hazardous, it can be useful to consider some of the most widely accepted approaches or views of economic development: the first is a relatively purely market-driven approach, in which the primary function of the state (if any) is to enable and govern the physical, infrastructural, social, and political conditions which allow free market transactions to occur. These conditions may range from transportation networks (though there are some who argue that even these should be privatized) to legal systems enabling enforcement by the state of private property contract rights that facilitate commercial transactions between relative strangers. The second approach envisions a more active role for the state, which has historically ranged from direct central control of production and labor by the state as described by Karl Marx and his intellectual descendants, to more indirect means of guiding or influencing market forces through direct government purchase and expenditure, regulation, subsidies, and/or incentives, as described in part by John Maynard Keynes and implemented in the US in the form of an economic stimulus package in response to the "Great Recession" in the first decade of the twenty-first century.[36] In both cases, it is important to consider inclusive governance in order to help address inequality and enable civil society to meaningfully participate in economic activities and benefit from development.[37] The third approach we describe is a blended approach.

A Market Approach

A decentralized, market-driven approach holds that nations can acquire wealth by following four basic rules: (1) the means of production – those things required to produce goods and services such as labor, natural resources, technology, and capital (buildings, machinery, and money that can be used to purchase these) – must be owned and controlled by private individuals or firms; (2) markets must exist in which the means of production and the goods and services produced are freely bought and sold; (3) trade at the local, national, and international levels must be unrestricted; and (4) a state-enforced system of law must exist to guarantee business contracts so as to ensure safe commercial relations between unrelated individuals.

Adam Smith, the eighteenth-century Scottish political economist sometimes credited as founder of the market approach, believed that the operations of labor are the key to increasing production. He argued that it is much more efficient for workers to specialize in their work, focusing on one product rather than making many different products. If workers do this, and if they are brought together in one location so their labor can be supervised; increased production will result. Smith also presented the idea that, if the owners of the means of production are allowed to freely sell their services or goods at the most advantageous price they can obtain, the largest amount of products and services will be produced and everyone will benefit. It is the prices in the markets that suggest to the businessman or businesswoman new profitable investment opportunities and more efficient production processes. (For example, when oil prices rose dramatically in the 1970s, new investments occurred in alternative energy sources and some industries came up with ways to reduce the amount of oil they needed to buy. Some business people saw the alternative energy investments as a way for them to make money in the energy field, and some industries cut their costs, thus increasing their profits, by becoming more efficient in their use of energy.)

Plate 2.3 The market approach is followed on the streets in many countries

Source: Mark Olenski.

Smith did not focus on the role of the entrepreneur, but later market theorists did, making the entrepreneur – the one who brought the means of production together in a way to produce goods and services – a key component in this approach. Finally, Smith and other market theorists emphasized the importance of open trade. David

Ricardo earned a place in economic history for positing that if a nation concentrates on producing those products in which it has a comparative advantage over other nations – advantages that climate, natural resources, cheap labor, or technology give it – and if it trades with other nations that are also concentrating on those products that *they* have the greatest advantage in producing, then all will benefit.

A market approach holds that government has a crucial but limited role in maintaining an environment in which economic transactions can flourish. Under this approach, government would confine its activities to providing for domestic tranquility that would ensure that private property is protected and contracts are secure; providing certain services, such as defense; enforcing private contracts; and helping to maintain a stable supply of money and credit. The reason some nations are poor, according to the market approach, is that they have not been successful in competing with other countries within the bounds of the basic rules listed above.

Advocates of the market approach point to the wealth of the United States and Western Europe as evidence of the correctness of their view. Even Karl Marx said that the hundred years of rule by capitalists were the most productive in the history of the world. And although an uneven distribution of income occurred in Western Europe during its early period of industrialization, the distribution of income later became much less uneven. This indicated that the new wealth was being shared by more and more people.

Nations such as Japan and West Germany, which came back from the devastation of World War II to create extremely strong economies by following the basic principles of the market approach, are also cited as evidence of the validity of the approach. Examples can also be found among non-western countries that have achieved such impressive economic growth by following the principles of this approach that they have moved into a separate category of the economic development: the newly industrializing countries. Many of these economies, such as China, South Korea, Taiwan, and Singapore, achieved their high economic growth at first mainly by exporting light manufactured products to the developed nations.

Finally, advocates of the market approach point to the decisions of Eastern Europe and other countries, during the 1980s, to adopt at least some market mechanisms in their efforts to reform their economies. Even China – the largest remaining communist government – has adopted many important aspects of the market approach, which is widely believed to contribute substantially to China's impressive economic growth.

Critics of the market approach point to the high rates of unemployment that have existed at times in Western Europe and the United States. At the present time, high unemployment rates are still found in a number of nations that have followed the market approach, despite impressive increases in their GNP. Much of the industry that has come to the South has been capital intensive; that is, it uses large amounts of financial and physical capital but employs relatively few workers. The more recent economic shocks resulting from the global pandemic have also exposed the inequalities and fragilities of market-based economies.

There is evidence from Brazil, which has basically followed the market approach for the past several decades, that the distribution of income within growing economies became more unequal during the period when the countries were experiencing high rates of growth. The same thing happened in China in the 1990s. The rich got a larger proportion of the total income produced in these countries than they had before the growth began. And even worse than this is the evidence that the poor in these countries, such as Brazil, probably became absolutely poorer during the period of high growth, in part because of the high inflation which often accompanied the growth.[38] (High inflation usually hurts the poor more than the rich because the poor are least able to increase their income to cope with the rising prices of goods.) The economic growth that came to some nations following the market approach failed to trickle down to the poor and, in fact, may have made their lives worse. High inflation was halted in Brazil in the 1990s, as was the trend for income inequality to worsen. At the end of the century the distribution of incomes in Brazil continued to be highly unequal. The poorest 20 percent of the population received about 3 percent of the income in the country, and the richest 20 percent received about 62 percent.

Critics of the market approach have also pointed out that prices for goods and services set by a free market often do not reflect the true costs of producing those goods and services. Damage to the environment or to people's health that occurs in the production and disposal of a product is often a hidden cost, which is not covered by the price of the product. The market treats the atmosphere, oceans, rivers, and lakes as "free goods," or as a global commons, and, unless prohibited from doing so by the state, it transfers the costs that arise because of their pollution to the broader community. In the language of economics this is called a "negative externality," a term rarely discussed in public. Some critics believe this flaw in the market system is what is really responsible for our changing the climate on Earth, to be discussed in detail in Chapter 6.

And finally, critics point to the cycles of positive and low or negative growth that are a normal part of the market approach. An extreme case of this was seen as recently as 2008/2009 when a near collapse of market economies started in the United States and spread to Europe and other parts of the world. A major recession occurred in the United States, which was only prevented from turning into a depression by major intervention by the state. Many economic analysts attributed this failure of the market system in the United States to a lack of regulation by the government or state.

The State as Economic Actor

Approaches to economic development that envision a role for the state beyond that described in the previous section vary widely. Advocates of Marxist-Leninist thought in early twentieth-century Russia built a communist state, the Soviet Union, which functioned as the *only* economic actor, overseeing a centrally planned economy and directing the production and distribution of all goods, services, and labor. In a socialist country most of the means of production – land, resources, and capital – are publicly controlled to ensure that the value obtained from the production of goods and services is used to benefit the nation as a whole. The prohibition on the private control or ownership of these so-called factors of production leads, according to this approach, to a relatively equal distribution of income, as everyone, not just a few individuals, benefits from the economic activity. Central planners set prices and invest capital in areas that are needed to benefit the society.

Some state-focused approaches to economic development envision a strong role for the state beyond direct central planning. With respect to the global distribution of wealth, one explanation popular among those who take a state-based approach to economic development attributes the causes of poverty in the world to international trade. According to the state approach, the root of the present international economic system, where a few nations are rich and the majority of nations remain poor, lies in the trade patterns developed in the sixteenth century by Western Europe. ("Dependency theory" is the name given to this part of the state approach, popularized by Immanuel Wallerstein.[39]) First Spain and Portugal and then Great Britain, Holland, and France gained colonies – many of them in the southern hemisphere – to trade with. The imperialistic European nations in the northern hemisphere developed a trade pattern that one can still see clear signs of today. The mother countries in "the core" became the manufacturing and commercial centers, and their colonies in "the periphery" became the suppliers of food and minerals. Railroads were built in the colonies to connect the plantations and mines to the ports. This transportation system, along with the discouragement of local manufacturing competing with manufacturing in the mother countries, prevented the economic development of the colonies. The terms of trade – what one can obtain from one's export – favored the European nations, since the prices of the primary products from the colonies remained low while the prices of the manufactured products sent back to the colonies continually increased. It was the political power of the "core" that determined the global economic structure, rather than the economic "laws" of the market.

When most of the colonies gained their independence after World War II, this trade pattern continued. Many resource rich yet economically poor countries still produce food and minerals for the world market and primarily trade with their former colonial powers. The world demand for the products from the poorer nations fluctuates greatly, and the prices of these products remain depressed. The political and social systems that developed in the former colonies also serve to keep the majority within these nations poor. A local elite, which grew up when these countries were under colonial domination, learned to benefit from the domination by the Western countries. In a sense, two societies were created in these countries: one, relatively modern and prosperous, revolved around the export sector; while the other consisted of the rest of the people, who remained in the traditional system and were poor. The local elite, which became the governing elite upon independence, acquired a taste for Western products, which the industrial nations were happy to sell them at a good price.

The present vehicle of this economic domination by the North of the South is the multinational corporation. Tens of thousands of these exist today. In 2009, 140 of the

500 richest corporations in the world had headquarters in the United States, while many others were headquartered in Europe and Japan.[40] In 2018, the figure reduced to about 130.[41] These corporations squeeze out smaller local firms in the developing nations, evade local taxes through numerous devices, send large profits back to their headquarters, and create relatively fewer jobs than their local counterpart when the manufacturing firms they set up utilize the same capital-intensive technology that is common in the industrialized countries. Also, they advertise their products extensively, thus increasing demands for things such as Coca-Cola and mobile technology while many people in the countries in which they operate still do not have enough to eat.[42]

Advocates for a state approach point to the adverse terms of trade that many poorer countries face today. There is general agreement that there has been a long-term decline in the terms of trade for many of the agricultural and mineral products that these resource rich nations export. There has also been great volatility in the prices of some of these products, with a change of 25 percent or more from one year to the next not uncommon for some products. Such fluctuations make economic planning very difficult. There is also clear evidence that the industrialized countries, while primarily trading among themselves, are highly dependent on other countries for many crucial raw materials, including chromium, manganese, cobalt, bauxite, tin, and, of course, oil.

Although international trade is still far from being the most important component of the US economy, it is a very important factor for many of the wealthiest corporations. In the early 1980s about one-half of the 500 wealthiest corporations listed in *Fortune* magazine obtained over 40 percent of their profits from their foreign operations.[43] Some multinational corporations have financial resources larger than those of many nations.

Finally, the defenders of a state approach argue that there is little chance for many poor nations to achieve as fair a distribution of income as that achieved by Europe after it industrialized. This situation has evolved because controlling elites have repressive tools at their disposal (such as sophisticated police surveillance devices and powerful weapons) that the European elites did not have. This allows them to deal with pressures from the "have-nots" in a way the Europeans never resorted to.

Critics of a state approach point to the breakup of the Soviet empire in Eastern Europe in the late 1980s, and to the collapse of communism in the former Soviet Union and the breakup of that country in the early 1990s, as support for their view that the state approach cannot efficiently produce wealth. In fact, it was the dissatisfaction of Eastern Europeans with their economic conditions that played a large role in their massive opposition to the existing communist governments and their eventual overthrow. Dissatisfaction with economic conditions also played a large role in the overthrow of the Soviet government, a startling rejection of the state approach by a people who had lived under it for 70 years.

Critics of the state approach also point to the suppression of individual liberties in the former Soviet Union, China, and other communist states as evidence that the socialist model for development has costs that many people are not willing to pay. In

Plate 2.4 The state approach to development struggles to survive the collapse of communist regimes in Europe, as can be seen in the posters of a Communist Party conference in Nepal

Source: Ab Abercrombie.

fact, most revolutions have huge costs, leading to much suffering and economic deterioration before any improvement in conditions is seen; even after improvements occur, oppressive political and social controls are used by leaders to maintain power.

Some critics say that central planning has proven to be an inefficient allocator of resources wherever it has been followed. Without prices from the free market to indicate the real costs of goods and services, the central planners cannot make good decisions. And if efficient central planning has proven to be impossible in a country such as the former Soviet Union, it has proven to be even worse in nations where governmental administrative capability is weak. A final criticism of central planning is that it always leads to a large, inefficient governmental bureaucracy.

Even less invasive forms of state involvement in the economy tend to provoke similar criticisms. The state, lacking a profit motive or the threat of bankruptcy, is going to be less responsive to changes in economic conditions that may necessitate a change in policy. Further, that excessive government involvement in the economy means the state is "picking winners and losers," a process that virtually invites corruption. And finally, that the state cannot become involved in the economy without making value choices that are better left to individual consumers.

Additionally, some argue that the state approach generates less wealth than the free market approach. Multinational corporations have created more wealth, especially in richer economies. They have brought new technologies; and they have helped the balance of payments problems of those nations by bringing in scarce capital and by helping develop export industries that earn much-needed foreign exchange. These advantages help explain why multinational corporations are welcomed by many countries.

Finally, the critics of a state approach argue that political elites have used dependency theory, especially in Latin America where the theory is popular, to gain local political support among the bureaucracy, military, and the masses. To blame the industrial nations for their poverty frees them from taking responsibility for their own development and excuses their lack of progress. It also frees them from having to clean their own houses of governmental corruption and incompetence and stop following misguided economic development approaches. According to some critics, the newly industrializing countries have shown that when market principles are followed, economic progress can be made even by nations that have a dense population and few, if any, natural resources.

A Blended Approach

In practice, most countries blend state and market approaches to tailor them toward the political and economic priorities for a given country (or at least for those who hold much of the power). Friedrich List, a German political and economic theorist who began his career in 1817, posited (in contrast to those who push always for freer and more open trade) that in relatively underdeveloped economies, nascent industries may need state protection from foreign competitors in order to allow them to grow to the point where the country could truly exploit its competitive advantage in a given economic endeavor.[44] Some have even credited Friedrich List with first proposing the concept now known as "human capital,"[45] a concept often used by those who argue that states with less developed economies need to invest in their citizens, to ensure a healthy and educated workforce that can participate meaningfully in the economy.

Decentralized regulation: a catalyst for technological innovation?

In evaluating why the United States pioneered innovation in fracking technologies, Dan Merrill concluded that decentralized regulation was key to enabling innovation. In the article "Four Questions about Fracking," Merrill considers how governance structures impact innovation:

> Why does decentralized regulation promote innovation? The theory that explains this might go as follows. All regulators tend to be risk averse. If things go well, they get no credit. If things go badly, they get blamed. But the degree of risk aversion of regulators falls along a spectrum. Some are more risk averse than others. Where

regulation is decentralized, a new technology like fracking can find at least one or two states where it is allowed to get going. This sets in motion a natural experiment. If the results are good, and the risks do not seem too great, then risk-averse regulators in other states will give it the green light to go ahead there, too. If the results are not so good, or the risks seem too large, then the regulators in other states will throw up roadblocks to the new technology, and the experiment will wither away. In a more centralized regulatory environment, which tends to be the norm in other parts of the world, the experiment is less likely to get off the ground in the first place. This is because the median regulator is risk averse. And being the only regulatory game in town, the risk aversion of the median regulator is likely to translate into hostility to technological innovation.

Please see Chapter 9 later in this book for more discussions on the role of technology in development.

Source: Case Western Reserve Law Review, 63 (4) (2013) (internal citations omitted).

One relatively modern example of this blended approach is South Korea. From the 1960s through at least the 1980s, South Korean economic growth was predicated on massive government investment in its infrastructure and citizens, as well as heavy government intervention in the economy (through regulation, subsidies, and government-granted monopolies) that allowed certain family-controlled firms, such as Hyundai and Samsung, to become economic powerhouses that could drive the national economy.[46] While South Korea has now adopted a much more market-oriented approach, these nationally prioritized firms benefited directly from the state approach.

Trade and Global Economic Interdependence

After the killing in World War II ended in 1945, a number of world leaders asked, "What should be done to prevent a person like Adolf Hitler coming to power again?" One of the answers given was to prevent an international economic collapse, such as the Great Depression, which created the conditions that led to the rise of Hitler. With that idea in mind, it was agreed that trade among nations should be encouraged so that, it was hoped, prosperity would spread and economies would become more interdependent. In 1947, under the sponsorship of the United Nations, the General Agreement on Tariffs and Trade (GATT) was signed by about 20 countries. These countries, later joined by about a hundred others, conducted a series of negotiations to promote free trade by reducing tariffs and other barriers to trade such as import quotas.

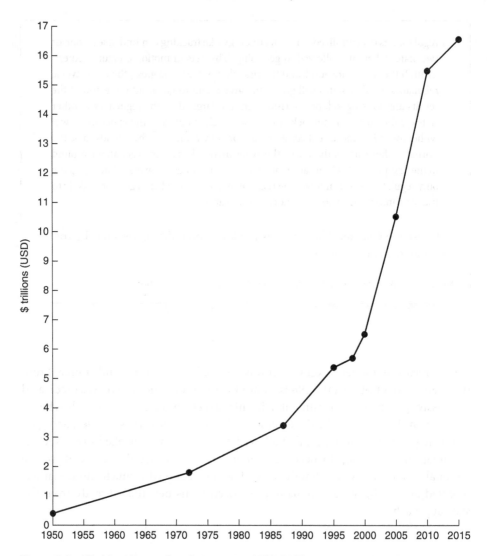

Figure 2.8   World trade: merchandise exports, 1950–2015

Source: Based on data from World Trade Organization.

The success of these efforts is clearly shown in Figure 2.8, which shows that from 1950 to the turn of the century world trade rose from about $500 billion to nearly $6 trillion, then more than doubled in just ten years. By 2017 exports had risen to US $17.73 trillion, while trade in services reached US $5.28 trillion.[47]

In 1995, GATT evolved into the World Trade Organization (WTO). The WTO was given the task of implementing the many agreements reached under the GATT negotiations and of setting up an arbitration mechanism to resolve trade disputes among its members.

The great expansion of international trade has created a highly interdependent world economy. That integration of the economies of many nations, combined with the proliferation of communication technologies that transcend national borders, and other factors, has been the main force in creating a new situation in the world called globalization. Globalization is mainly fueled by economic forces and sustained by new political, social, and technical integrative forces in the world today. Politically, international governmental organizations such as the United Nations, the International Monetary Fund, and the World Bank, along with regional organizations and agreements such as the European Union and the US-Mexico-Canada trade agreement, are playing an increasingly important role in global governance.

In 2000, part of the package of the adoption of the Millennium Development Goals included a need for rich countries to help poorer countries by reducing tariffs and quotas on the poor country's exports. This push for "freer" trade was viewed as an opportunity to increase the extraction and production of materials, thereby increasing GDP.

Global Interdependence

The global economy is leading to the growing interdependence of the world's people. Like many things, if not most things in life, it has positive and negative aspects and a critical reader should appreciate the implications of both.[48]

Positive aspects

The global economy has brought more wealth to both rich and poor nations. Although all nations have not benefited from the liberalization of international trade, "since 1950 there has been a close correlation between a country's domestic economic performance and its participation in the world's economy."[49] The United States had an unprecedentedly long period of economic growth and non-Western countries and areas such as China, the Republic of Korea, Taiwan, and Singapore that also embraced global trade as an economic development opportunity have obtained relatively high levels of prosperity.

The formation of a global community has started. Nations around the world now face common problems, both economic and environmental, that they are working together to solve. More and more individuals are taking advantage of the new communication and transportation technologies to learn about and enjoy the whole planet.

As nations prosper in a global economy, economic interdependence helps promote peaceful societies (war can be disruptive to most forms of trade aside from weapons). New ideas and more international contacts could even lead to an improvement of human rights in some countries, especially those with a poor track records on human rights. It previously had this effect in some formerly communist states.

If trade helps grow an economy in an inclusive way, hunger and crime rates are typically lowered and poverty is reduced.[50]

New products are available and often at a lower price than if they had been produced locally. New jobs are created, not just in the industrialized countries but also in many less industrialized nations. Jobs lead to the reduction of poverty. The World Bank reports that "there are almost no examples of countries experiencing significant growth without reducing poverty."[51]

Negative aspects

The ease of transportation, of both people and goods, makes the transmission of diseases throughout the world easier than before. This became acutely obvious during the global pandemic associated with Covid-19, which also illustrated the fragility of economies more dependent on steady streams of commerce through global supply chains. In the same way, rapid electronic communications and the huge number of people and goods moving through the world make criminal and terror activities more difficult to control.

Although it is true that increased production can cause more pollution, many argue that once nations become richer and reduce their poverty, they tend to clean up their environments.

A number of jobs are lost in rich countries when multinational corporations move some of their production or service facilities to less industrialized nations where labor costs are lower. It is true that many new jobs are still being created in the United States, fewer in Europe and Japan, but the type of available jobs may be changing and it is not easy for certain (particularly older) workers who have been laid off to qualify for them.

Some have argued that corporations are moving facilities to nations with less protective laws to escape the necessity of complying with stricter environmental and labor laws in their home countries. Rapid economic growth in countries such as China and India has led to major pollution of air, water, and land.

Cultural imperialism by the United States, with its corresponding undermining of local cultures, is increasing. A world traveler can frequent many cities and dine on Big Macs, fries, and shakes in any of them. The largest single export industry in the United States is not aircraft or automobiles but entertainment, especially Hollywood films.

The gap between rich and poor nations is growing. Some poor nations are being left behind economically and technologically. The shift to knowledge-based industries is accelerating and creating an even greater gap. From 2010 to 2014, about 87 percent of people in the United States had access to the internet, whereas only about 18 percent of Indians did, and even fewer in Pakistan and Bangladesh.[52] In 2014, 4.4 billion people still did not have any access to the internet – a quarter of these lacked any access to electricity.[53]

Because nations' economies are so tied together today, an economic problem in one can spread to others extremely quickly. We saw that happening in the late 1990s when a financial crisis hit Thailand, Indonesia, Malaysia, the Republic of Korea, and other countries. Economic recessions and depressions also come with the dominance of the market. Capitalism has always had its cycles, and a "down" cycle can mean high unemployment and human suffering. Many of the fastest growing economies are tied to that of the US. If the United States goes into a period of slow or no growth it will affect many other countries whose wealth comes mainly from exports to the United States. We saw this very thing happening in the world recessions of 2008–2009 and the economic shocks from Covid-19.

We are also seeing an increase in nationalism and protectionist measures. Many nations are not so happy about losing some of their national autonomy to multilateral institutions such as the International Monetary Fund, World Trade Organization, World Bank, and regional trade organizations. While the world has enjoyed an unprecedented era of economic growth fueled by aggressively expanding the volume of goods and services traded as well as development finance that supports enhanced trading infrastructure, we are also seeing some backlash. By the end of 2018, there had been a big uptick in protectionist measures.[54] Several free trade agreement negotiations had either fallen apart or got renegotiated. And the United States and China had taken significant measures against each other's exports.

Geography and Wealth, Geography and Poverty

Adam Smith had a second theory of why some nations are rich and some poor. Modern economists usually ignore this part of Smith's writings. Not only did Smith believe that a free market economy would lead to wealth, but he also believed that nations bordering a sea would usually be richer than inland, landlocked countries. Recent research shows that geography does matter. Nations with access to the sea by coastal ports or by navigable rivers and those in the temperate climate zone have historically been the wealthiest nations. Those nations landlocked and in the tropical zone or mainly desert or mountainous have had less access to trade routes and perhaps not surprisingly have had lower GNPs on average.[55]

Why does geography matter? The reasons are not hard to discover. First, shipping and receiving goods by sea is cheaper than shipping by land or air. For example, shipping a container to a major coastal city can cost only a fraction of the cost of shipping to a remote landlocked area (for example it might cost $3,000 to ship a container to the Ivory Coast and $10,000 more to send a similarly sized container to landlocked Central African Republic). Also, people and new ideas often arrive in coastal areas first. Second, tropical climates are plagued by infectious diseases, such as malaria, which debilitate the workforce. An estimated hundreds of millions of new cases of malaria occur each year, nearly all of them in the tropics. Winter is the great natural controller of many diseases. In tropical countries many diseases flourish all year long, making them difficult to control. And recognizing the economic wealth in many tropical countries is relatively limited, thereby limiting opportunities to profit commercially, pharmaceutical firms have tended to prioritize economically lucrative conditions such as erectile dysfunction over more critical health needs such as malaria.

Agricultural production is also usually higher in temperate and subtropical climates than in tropical climates. For example, a hectare of land in the temperate zone produces about 6 tons of corn or maize, while the same amount of land in the tropics produces about 2 tons. Rich countries spend much more on research to help their farmers in the temperate zone increase production than on research that would better serve many of the world's poorest and most vulnerable farmers, who are more concentrated in poorer tropical countries.

Geography alone does not explain why some countries are wealthier than others. While nearly all the wealthiest countries are in the temperate zone, such as North America, Western Europe, and Northeast Asia, the economic system they follow is also important. For example, the former Soviet Union and Eastern Europe are still struggling economically to overcome their socialist pasts. This fact is shown even more dramatically by looking at present and past countries with the same geographical characteristics, but which have or had different economic systems and vastly different wealth: South Korea and North Korea, West and East Germany (before unification), Austria and the Czech Republic, and Finland and Estonia. In each case the first-mentioned state in the comparison followed a market system and greatly outperformed the second, originally socialist state.[56]

In addition to the difficulties caused by climate and lack of access to the sea, many landlocked countries face economic difficulties caused by borders with their neighbors that restrict the easy flow of goods, capital, and people.

According to Ricardo Hausmann, professor of the practice of economic development at the John F. Kennedy School of Government at Harvard University: "If current trends persist, countries that face high transportation costs and a high dependence on tropical agriculture will be left far behind, mired in poverty and income inequality. Will the rest of the world find this outcome morally acceptable?" Hausmann believes that the world has tried to help these countries, but its efforts have been insufficient, as shown by the widening gap between the rich and poor. He calls for more "globalized governance." By this he means more international agreements to make borders less of a barrier to people, goods, and capital. He also calls for international support for development projects that improve the transportation systems within and between countries, and, lastly, he calls for international aid in health and agricultural technology that benefits the tropical world.[57]

Conclusions

The market approach to development places emphasis on the seemingly strong motivation individuals have to acquire more material goods and services. When people are freed from external restraints, the market allows them to use their initiative to better their lives. The release of creative energy that comes with the market approach is impressive. At the beginning of the twenty-first century most countries throughout the world were following it, at least to some degree, as the Western capitalist countries became the models to imitate. While the economic recession at the end of the first decade of 2000 has caused many countries to question a complete market approach, the model nevertheless is employed by many nations today.

With the collapse of communism and the breakup of the former Soviet Union, the state approach to development received a serious blow. The reliance on the state to create wealth was discredited. Yet in no country of the world is a state without some significant state functions relating to the economy. Within the capitalist world there is a debate among nations regarding how much involvement government should have in directing and guiding the economy. Traditionally, Japanese and European capitalism relied on more government involvement than did capitalism in the United States.

This debate became of upmost importance in 2008 when the US market system nearly collapsed and a depression in the United States was prevented only by massive financial support by the national government of parts of the banking and insurance industries and automobile corporations. Alan Greenspan, the head of the Federal Reserve that monitored the economy and that had been given credit for the unprecedentedly long period of economic growth the United States had gone through, admitted to Congress that the model of the market economy he was following had an unknown flaw in it. This admission was rather shocking. If the chief "overseer" of the US economy didn't really understand how it worked, who did? Greenspan, who had favored loose government regulation of the economy, went from being a laissez faire economist to one who now called for much tighter government regulation of the economy. As mentioned in this chapter, the unprecedentedly deep recession in the United States spread throughout the world and slowed the efforts to help millions of people escape from extreme poverty. Yet as the chapter's section on the UN's Millennium Development Goals shows, economic growth was still strong enough in the developing world to enable the United Nations to meet the goal of halving extreme poverty to 15 percent by the year 2015.

Even after the seemingly total victory of the market approach over the state approach in the 1990s, the state approach is not dead; what is dead is the total or near total reliance on it as the best way to create wealth. But the economic crisis of 2008–2009 indicated that the world is still struggling to find the right balance between the market and state systems.

Today's globalization is still driven by market forces focusing on economic growth. That growth has done much to reduce world poverty. But large and vocal protests at international meetings dealing with aspects of globalization have drawn attention to some of the negative aspects of globalization. More emphasis on human governance appears to be needed. The United Nations Development Programme stated the need as follows: "When the market goes too far in dominating social and political outcomes, the opportunities and rewards of globalization spread unequally and inequitably – concentrating power and wealth in a select group of people, nations, and corporations, marginalizing the others." The UNDP believes that markets should continue to expand but that more governance is needed: "The challenge is to find the rules and institutions for stronger governance – local, national, regional and global – to preserve the advantages of global markets and competition, but also to provide enough space for human, community, and environmental resources to ensure that globalization works for people – not just for profits."[58]

There are dangerous signs that all is not well. Economic growth is reducing poverty and the market approach has produced that reduction better than the state or blended approaches. The reduction of extreme poverty is universally praised, as it should be. No human being should have to live as the very poor live today. As the poor obtain new wealth, they tend to consume more goods and services. (The growing middle class in China is a good example of this with its desire for automobiles.) But rich nations historically have relied on fossil fuels to provide the energy needed to make their goods and provide their services. We now know how that kind of energy is placing a tremendous strain on our world; it is changing our planet in ways that will seriously hurt much of the life on the planet, both in rich and poor nations alike. This will be discussed more in our chapter on climate change.

The bottom line is that while achieving a certain level of economic wealth unquestionably affords critical opportunities to improve livelihoods, we cannot presume that economic wealth alone will lead to the development outcomes we desire. The classical use of the term "development" has defined progress by the increased growth of material goods by any means possible and this purely production-based notion of "development" is increasingly seen as not viable. It is for that reason that we focus in this book on sustainable development pathways that direct our attention toward human well-being, while considering both the costs and benefits of the growth of material goods and services.

Notes

1   United Nations Development Programme (UNDP), *Human Development Report 1999* (New York: Oxford University Press, 1999), p. 38. The 2010 number comparing the richest countries as a group with the poorest countries as a group is from the World Development Indicators database, World Bank, July 1, 2011, at http://siteresources.worldbank.org/DATASTATISTICS/Resources/GNIPC.pdf (accessed July 2015).

2   UNDP, *Human Development Report 1999*, p. 38. The 2010 number comparing the richest countries as a group with the poorest countries as a group is from the World Development Indicators database, World Bank, July 1, 2011, at http://siteresources.worldbank.org/DATASTATISTICS/Resources/GNIPC.pdf (accessed July 2015).

3   According to the World Bank, rich countries had about USD $51,500,000 million while low income countries had approximately USD $550,000 million. World Development Indicators database, December 17, 2018 revision, at https://data.worldbank.org/indicator/NY.GDP.MKTP.CD?end=2017&start=2017 (accessed December 2018).

4   Bruce Scott, "The Great Divide in the Global Village," *Foreign Affairs* (January/February 2001), pp. 162–3.

5   According to the World Bank, low-and-middle income countries had about USD $6,900 gross national income per capita, (2011 Purchase Power Parity) in 2009 and USD $10,843 in 2017. World Development Indicators database, World Bank, at https: //data. worldbank.org/indicator/NY.GNP.PCAP.PP.CD?start=2009 (accessed December 2018).

6   C.K. "The gap between poor and rich neighbourhoods is growing" *The Economist* (November 13, 2018) at https://www.economist.com/democracy-in-america/2018/11/13/the-gap-between-poor-and-rich-neighbourhoods-is-growing (accessed December 2018).

7   Ibid.

8   World Bank Development Indicators Database, April 19, 2010 revision.

9   Alex Whiting, "Richest 62 People Own Same as Half of World's Population: Oxfam," *Reuters* (January 18, 2016) at https://af.reuters.com/article/topNews/idAFKCN0UW0DQ?fbclid=IwAR3HHRmVm6CJLRHbqAMQN7372gzokSnq-9TAJ9PHYVXEL0Bnxp6ZBVOvV6E (accessed December 2018).

10 International Labour Organization, Global Wage Report 2014/2015: Wages and Income Inequality, section 7.2, p. 23, at http://www.ilo.org/wcmsp5/groups/public/—dgreports/—dcomm/—publ/documents/publication/wcms_324678.pdf (accessed July 2015).

11 Christopher Ingraham "The Richest 1 Percent Now Owns more of the Country's Wealth than at any Time in the past 50 Years" *The Washington Post* (December 6, 2017) at https://www.washingtonpost.com/news/wonk/wp/2017/12/06/the-richest-1-percent-now-owns-more-of-the-countrys-wealth-than-at-any-time-in-the-past-50-years/ (accessed December 2018).

12 Porsha Pan "Hurun Report Releases China Rich List 2017 in Association with 36G" The Hurun Research Institute (October 12, 2017) at http://www.hurun.net/EN/Article/Details?num=5A320E03FD31 (accessed December 2018).

13 Heather Long and Leslie Shapiro. "Does $60,000 make you Middle-class or Wealthy on Planet Earth?" *The Washington Post* (August 20, 2018) at https://www.washingtonpost.com/business/2018/08/20/does-make-you-middle-class-or-wealthy-planet-earth/ (accessed December 2018).

14 World Bank Development Indicators Database, December 17, 2018 revision.

15 China increased its per capita GDP about tenfold from $440 in 1980 to $4,475 in 2002 (in international prices), while India's per capita GDP rose from $670 in 1980 to $2,570 in 2002. World Bank, *World Development Report 2005* (New York: World Bank and Oxford University Press, 2005), p. 27.

16 United Nations, *The Millennium Development Goals Report 2010* (New York: United Nations, 2010), p. 6.

17 Ibid., p. 7.

18   United Nations, *The Millennium Development Goals Report 2014*, p. 4, at http://www.
      un.org/millenniumgoals/2014%20MDG%20report/MDG%202014%20English%20
      web.pdf (accessed July 2015).

19   The World Bank "Decline of Global Extreme Poverty Continues but Has Slowed: World
      Bank" (September 19, 2018) at https://www.worldbank.org/en/news/press-release/2018/09/
      19/decline-of-global-extreme-poverty-continues-but-has-slowed-world-bank ("Over the
      last 25 years, more than a billion people have lifted themselves out of extreme poverty, and
      the global poverty rate is now lower than it has ever been in recorded history. This is one of
      the greatest human achievements of our time.").

20   "Global Poverty: A Fall to Cheer", *The Economist*, (March 3, 2012), at http://www.
      economist.com/node/21548963 (accessed July 2015).

21   United Nations, *The Millennium Development Goals Report 2010*, p. 7

22   The World Bank "Poverty & Equity Data Portal" at http://povertydata.worldbank.org/
      poverty/country/CHN (accessed December 2018).

23   UNDP, *Human Development Report 2004* (New York: Oxford University Press, 2004),
      p. 129.

24   United Nations, "World Economic Situation and Prospects 2015, Update as of
      mid-2015*" (May 19, 2015) at http://www.un.org/en/development/desa/policy/wesp/
      wesp_archive/2015wesp_myu_en.pdf (accessed December 2018).

25   United Nations, *The Millennium Development Goals Report 2014*, p. 4, at http://www.
      un.org/millenniumgoals/2014%20MDG%20report/MDG%202014%20English%20
      web.pdf (accessed July 2015).

26   Ibid., pp. 5, 12.

27   World Health Organization, "Global hunger continues to rise, new UN report says 821 mil-
      lion people now hungry and over 150 million children stunted, putting hunger eradication
      goal at risk," (September 11, 2018) at https://www.who.int/news-room/detail/11-09-2018-
      global-hunger-continues-to-rise---new-un-report-says (accessed December 2018).

28   World Bank, *World Development Report 2014: Risk and Opportunity* (Washington, DC:
      World Bank, 2014), p. 5.

29   United Nations, *The Millennium Development Goals Report 2014*, pp. 4–5; UN
      Department of Social and Economic Affairs, Population Division, *World Population
      Prospects: The 2012 Revision*, at http://esa.un.org/unpd/wpp/unpp/panel_population.
      htm; World Bank, "Energy," at http://www.worldbank.org/en/topic/energy (both
      accessed July 2015); World Bank, *World Development Report 2010* (Washington, DC:
      World Bank, 2010), p. xx.

30   United Nations, *The Millennium Development Goals Report 2014*, pp. 4–5; UN
      Department of Social and Economic Affairs, Population Division, World Population
      Prospects: The 2012 Revision, at http://esa.un.org/unpd/wpp/unpp/panel_population.
      htm; World Bank, "Energy," at http://www.worldbank.org/en/topic/energy (both
      accessed July 2015); World Bank, *World Development Report 2010* (Washington, DC:
      World Bank, 2010), p. xx.

31   World Development Indicators database, December 17, 2018 revision at http://iresearch.
      worldbank.org/PovcalNet/povDuplicateWB.aspx (accessed December 2018).

32   UNDP, *Human Development Report 2004*, p. 132.

33   The World Bank and the International Monetary Fund, "Rural-Urban Disparities and
      Dynamics and the Millennium Development Goals," *Global Monitoring Report 2013* (2013) at

https://siteresources.worldbank.org/INTPROSPECTS/Resources/334934-1327948020811/
8401693-1355753354515/8980448-1366123749799/GMR_2013_Full_Report.pdf   p85
(accessed December 2018).

34 UN Conference on Trade and Development (UNCTAD), "Non-Tariff Measures to
Trade: Economic and Policy Issues for Developing Countries" (2013), pp. vii–viii, at
http://unctad.org/en/PublicationsLibrary/ditctab20121_en.pdf (accessed July 2015).

35 Ibid.

36 See, e.g., the American Recovery and Reinvestment Act webpage at http://www.recovery.
gov/arra/About/Pages/The_Act.aspx (accessed July 2015).

37 This framework derives from Alan Wolfe's classification of the three main views of
development. He presented his ideas in a paper titled "Three Paths to Development:
Market, State, and Civil Society," which was prepared for the International Meeting of
Nongovernmental Organizations (NGOs) and United Nations System Agencies held in
1991 in Rio de Janeiro. Some of his views on this subject are contained in his book
Whose Keeper? Social Science and Moral Obligation (Berkeley: University of California
Press, 1989). In this book, we have adapted Wolfe's framework as Market, State, and a
Blended Approach.

38 Censuses in Brazil have revealed that the percentage of national income going to the top
10 percent of the population was 40 percent in 1960, 47 percent in 1970, and 51 percent
in 1980. During the same period the poorest 50 percent of the population received 17
percent of the national income in 1960, 15 percent in 1970, and 13 percent in 1980.
Thomas E. Skidmore and Peter H. Smith, *Modern Latin America*, 2nd edn (New York:
Oxford University Press, 1989), p. 180. In Latin America as a whole in the 1980s the
poorest 10 percent suffered a 15 percent drop in their share of income. See UNDP,
Human Development Report 1999, p. 39.

39 For a fuller discussion of dependency theory see Bruce Russett and Harvey Starr, *World
Politics: The Menu for Choice*, 2nd edn (New York: W. H. Freeman, 1985), ch. 16; and
John T. Rourke, *International Politics on the World Stage*, 7th edn (New York: Dushkin/
McGraw-Hill, 1999), p. 400.

40 "Global 500," *Fortune Magazine* (July 20, 2009). Stacy VanDeveer, "Consuming
Environments: Options and Choices for 21st Century Citizens," in *Beyond Rio+20:
Governance for a Green Economy* (Boston: Boston University, 2011), pp. 43–51.

41 "Global 500," *Fortune Data Store* (2018) at http://fortune.com/global500/list/filtered?non-
us-cos-y-n=true (accessed December 2018). "FAQ: How many U.S. companies are in the
FORTUNE Global 500 List? There are approximately 130 U.S. companies that appear in
the FORTUNE Global 500 List. Most of these companies also appear in the FORTUNE
500 List."

42 While it does not deal with the areas of the world described as "developing nations,"
Victoria de Grazia's *Irresistible Empire: America's Advance through 20th Century Europe*
(Cambridge, MA: Harvard University Press, 2005) explores how US political and
commercial power combined to create and export new consumer habits in Europe,
and is an enlightening look at how cultural, commercial, and economic power can
interact.

43 Frederic S. Pearson and J. Martin Rochester, *International Relations: The Global
Condition in the Twenty-First Century*, 4th edn (New York: Random House, 1998),
p. 499.

44   See, e.g., H. Dunning, "Governments and the Macro-Organization of Economic Activity: An Historical and Spatial Perspective," *Review of International Political Economy*, 4 (1) (1997), p. 45.

45   See, e.g., David Levi-Faur, "Friedrich List and the Political Economy of the Nation-State," *Review of International Political Economy*, 4 (1) (1997), pp. 154–78.

46   Marcus Noland, "Six Markets to Watch: South Korea," *Foreign Affairs* (January/February 2014), at https://www.foreignaffairs.com/articles/south-korea/2013-12-06/six-markets-watch-south-korea (accessed July 2015). World Trade Statistical Review 2018, p27, at https://www.wto.org/english/res_e/statis_e/wts2018_e/wts2018_e.pdf (accessed December 2018).

47   For a good discussion of the potential for globalization doing good or harm see "Overview: Globalization with a Human Face," in UNDP, *Human Development Report 1999*, pp. 1–13.

48   Peter F. Drucker, "Trade Lessons from the World Economy," *Foreign Affairs* (January/February 1994), p. 104.

49   UNDP, *Human Development Report 2003* (New York: Oxford University Press, 2003), p. 6. For example, many types of crime dropped in the United States during its recent long period of economic growth, and during the decade of the 1990s "the number of hungry people [in the world] fell by nearly 20 million.

50   World Bank, *World Development Report 2005*, p. 31.

51   World Bank data, "Internet Users (per 100 people)," at http://data.worldbank.org/indicator/IT.NET.USER.P2 (accessed July 2015).

52   Roberto A. Ferdman, "4.4 Billion People around the World still don't have Internet. Here's Where they Live," *The Washington Post* (October 2, 2014), at https://www.washingtonpost.com/news/wonk/wp/2014/10/02/4-4-billion-people-around-the-world-still-dont-have-internet-heres-where-they-live/ (accessed January 2020)

53   World Trade Organization, Report shows sharp rise in the coverage of trade-restrictive measures from WTO members (December 11, 2018), at https://www.wto.org/english/news_e/news18_e/trdev_11dec18_e.htm (accessed December 2018).

54   Katherine Bennhold, "Love of Leisure, and Europe's Reasons," *New York Times* (July 29, 2004), p.A8.

55   Jeffrey Sachs, Andrew Mellinger, and John Gallup, "The Geography of Poverty and Wealth," *Scientific American*, 284 (March 2001), p. 74.

56   Most of the analysis on the relationship between geography and wealth and poverty is taken from Ibid., pp. 70–5; and Ricardo Hausmann, "Prisoners of Geography," *Foreign Affairs* (January/February 2001), pp. 45–53.

57   Hausmann, "Prisoners of Geography," p. 53.

58   UNDP, *Human Development Report 1999*, p. 2.

Further Reading

Bardhan, Pranab, "Does Globalization Help or Hurt the World's Poor?" *Scientific American*, 294 (April 2006), pp. 84–91. The answer according to this short article is that it does both. Bardhan discusses how to maximize the help and minimize the hurt.

Bhagwati, Jagdish, *In Defense of Globalization* (Oxford: Oxford University Press, 2004). The argument of this economics professor at Columbia University is that globalization has been overwhelmingly a good thing and its few downsides can be mitigated. His thesis that globalization leads to economic growth and economic growth leads to the reduction of poverty is the foundation for his belief that poor nations are not hurt by globalization but actually need more of it.

Chua, Amy, *World on Fire: How Exporting Free Market Democracy Breeds Ethnic Hatred and Global Instability* (New York: Anchor Books, 2003). A professor of law at Yale University, the author, who is a friend of globalization, argues that as the market and democracy have spread into the less developed nations, ethnic hatred and violence have increased, along with anti-Americanism. Chua explains why and identifies the urgent need for a greater sharing of the economic wealth that globalization has brought to various minorities.

Collier, Paul, *The Bottom Billion: Why the Poorest Countries Are Failing and What Can Be Done About It* (Oxford: Oxford University Press, 2007). Focusing mainly on Africa, where Collier states 70 percent of the world's poor live, he focuses on what he sees as the four main causes of poverty: civil war, the curse of rich resources, a landlocked location, and bad government.

Collins, Daryl, Jonathan Morduch, Stuart Rutherford, and Orlanda Ruthven, *Portfolios of the Poor: How the World's Poor Live on $2 a Day* (Princeton: Princeton University Press, 2009). The authors visited 100 households twice a month over a year in Bangladesh, India, and South Africa to record poor people's income, much of it from the informal economy. The authors also examine many microcredit operations.

Farmer, Paul, *Pathologies of Power: Health, Human Rights and the New War on the Poor* (Berkeley: University of California Press, 2003). Farmer presents case studies to support his three main points: the poor are not responsible for their situation, but have been hurt by their circumstances; the poor can be successfully treated and cured of disease, even those in the most dire conditions; good health is a human right, for without it all other human rights are meaningless.

McKibben, Bill, "Reversal of Fortune," *Mother Jones* (March/April 2007), pp. 33–43, 87–8. McKibben attacks the central concept of market economics: economic growth. Here, in his own words, is his justification for a position most people consider radical: "Growth no longer makes most people wealthier but instead generates inequality and insecurity. Growth is bumping up against physical limits so profound – like climate change and peak oil – that trying to expand the economy may be not just impossible but also dangerous."

Sachs, Jeffrey D., *The End of Poverty: Economic Possibilities for Our Time* (New York: Penguin Press, 2005). Sachs presents a plan to rid the world of extreme poverty by 2025. He does not dismiss the effectiveness of the market approach but believes that it is incomplete by itself. Poor countries that are weighed down by harmful geography, an inadequate healthcare system, and weak infrastructure (e.g., roads, ports, power, and communication facilities) cannot improve without significant, wisely given, foreign aid.

Singer, Peter, *One World: The Ethics of Globalization* (New Haven, CT: Yale University Press, 2002). Called one of the most provocative philosophers of our time, Singer writes, "How well we come through the era of globalization (perhaps whether we

come through it at all) will depend on how we respond ethically to the idea that we
live in one world."

United Nations Development Programme, United Nations Environment Programme, World
Bank, and World Resources Institute, *World Resources 2005: The Wealth of the Poor:
Managing Ecosystems to Fight Poverty* (Washington, DC: World Resources Institute,
2005). An attractive, easy-to-read reference source giving environmental, social, and
economic trends of about 150 nations. In this volume the focus is on how the natural
world can be utilized in a sustainable manner to benefit the rural poor.

Chapter 3

Population[1]

---

1   Monika Shepard contributed substantially to the research and updates reflected in this edition. Please reflect her contribution in any direct citation to this chapter.

Global Issues: An Introduction, Sixth Edition. Kristen A. Hite and John L. Seitz.
© 2021 John Wiley & Sons Ltd. Published 2021 by John Wiley & Sons Ltd.

Population

Prudent men should judge of future events by what has taken place in the past, and what is taking place in the present.

Miguel de Cervantes (1547–1616), *Persiles and Sigismunda*

The Changing Population of the World

The population of the world is growing. No one will be startled by that sentence, but what is startling is the rate of growth, and the fact that the present growth of population is unprecedented in human history. The best historical evidence we have today indicates that there were about 5 million people in the world in about 8000 BCE. By 1 CE there were about 200 million, and by 1650 the population had grown to about 500 million. The world reached its first billion people in about 1800. While it took thousands of years for the global population to reach 1 billion, it only took a little over a century for the population to reach the next billion: the second billion came about 1930. The third billion was reached about 1960, the fourth about 1974, and the fifth about 1987. The sixth came in 1999 and the seventh in 2011. Prior to the advent of Covid-19, the population was projected to exceed eight billion by 2023.[1] These figures indicate how rapidly the population is increasing. Table 3.1 shows how long it took the world to add each billion of its total population. A projection is also given for the next billion.

How can we explain this dramatic increase in population growth? Development gains over the last two centuries have seen major improvements in health conditions for many and the overall lowering of the death rate, dramatically and rapidly reducing rates of early death by disease. With this great success came a population explosion, the rapid increase of the number of humans on the planet that we are facing today, with significant impacts for the Earth's resources. Population growth rates are starting to stabilize in many places, while the UN expects over half the growth in the

Table 3.1 Time taken to add each billion to the world population, 1800–2046 (projection)

Date	Estimated world population (billions)	Years to add 1 billion people
1800	1	2,000,000
1930	2	130
1960	3	30
1974	4	14
1987	5	13
1999	6	12
2011	7	12
2023 (projected)	8	13
2037 (projected)	9	14

Source: Data from UN Department of Economic and Social Affairs, Population Division, *World Population Prospects: The 2012 Revision*; 2017. The 2017 Revision, custom data acquired via website (accessed November 27, 2018).

coming decades to be concentrated in just nine countries.[2] Overall, the total number of people on the planet continues to increase while natural resources continue to decline. This chapter explores the complex situation of the global population in the context of development, and later chapters explore the relationships between population, wealth, food, energy, climate, and the environment.

There is another way to look at population growth, one that helps us understand the uniqueness of our situation and its staggering implications for life on this planet. Because most people born can have children of their own, the human population can – until certain limits are reached – grow exponentially: 1 to 2; 2 to 4; 4 to 8; 8 to 16; 16 to 32; 32 to 64; 64 to 128; and so on. When something grows exponentially, there is hardly discernible growth in the early stages and then the numbers shoot up. The French have a riddle they use to help teach the nature of exponential growth to children. It goes like this: if you have a pond with one lily in it that doubles its size every day, and which will completely cover the pond in 30 days, on what day will the lily cover half the pond? The answer is the twenty-ninth day. What this riddle tells you is that if you wait until the lily covers half the pond before cutting it back, you will have only one day to do this – the twenty-ninth day – because it will cover the whole pond the next day.

If you plot on a graph anything that has an exponential growth, you get a J-curve. For a long time there is not much growth but when the bend of the curve in the J is reached, the growth becomes dramatic. Figure 3.1 shows what Earth's population growth curve looks like.

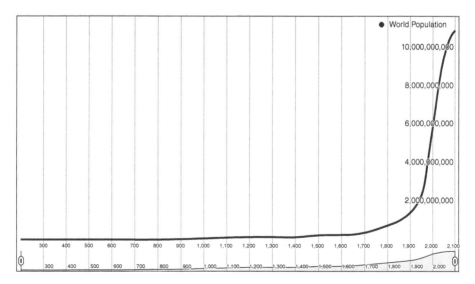

Figure 3.1 Population growth and projection from 8000 BCE to 2100 CE

Source: **Worldometers** (www.Worldometers.info), based on data from United Nations, Department of Economic and Social Affairs, Population Division. World Population Prospects: The 2017 Revision. (Medium-fertility variant).

The growth of the Earth's population has been compared to a long fuse on a bomb: once the fuse is lit, it sputters along for a long while and then suddenly the bomb explodes. This is what is meant by the phrases "population explosion" and "population bomb." The analogy is not a bad one. The world's population has passed the bend of the J-curve and is now rapidly expanding. The United Nations estimates that the world's population reached 7 billion in 2011, adding 5 billion people in less than one century. But recent estimates indicate that while the population will grow substantially – especially in Africa – over the coming decades, the population is growing at a slower rate than before: women throughout the world now have on average fewer than three children per woman whereas in the 1950s they had five; further, human sperm counts in wealthy countries have decreased by half over the past several decades.[3] But an average of slightly less than three children per woman still means the population is growing dramatically.

Figure 3.2 shows that the largest growth in the future will be in the less wealthy countries, with India, China, and some nations in Africa leading the way. In 1950 about one-third of the world's people lived in economically wealthy countries. At the end of the twentieth century that total reduced to about 20 percent living in countries with relatively rich economies. During the present century, nearly all of the growth in population will occur outside of these historically wealthy countries, particularly in urban areas in parts of Africa and Asia.[4] An ever larger percentage of the world's population will be relatively poor, with increased displacement and migration

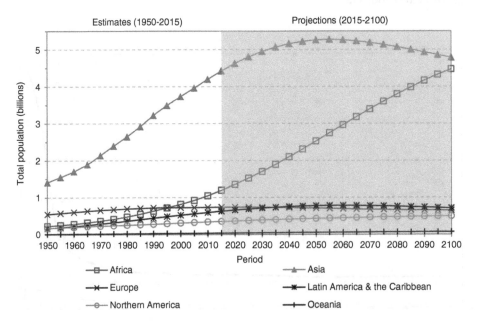

Figure 3.2   Population by region: estimates, 1950–2015, and medium variant projection, 2015–2100

Source: United Nations, Department of Economic and Social Affairs. Population Division (2017). *World Population Prospects: The 2017 Review*. New York: United Nations.

across the globe due in large part to climate impacts, conflict, and economic distress (already almost 1 percent of the globe is displaced in some form).[5] The United Nations projects that by 2050 about 86 percent of the Earth's population will be residing in the world's poorer nations.[6]

Because no one knows for sure what the size of Earth's population will be in the future, the United Nations gives three projections: a high, medium, and low one, based on the possible number of children the average woman will have. Projections are educated guesses. The United Nations believes the middle projection is the most likely, rising from the current estimate of 7.5 billion to 8.6 billion by 2030, 9.8 billion by 2050, and 11.2 billion by 2100.[7] The population in high income countries is expected to slowly grow to 1.287 billion in 2050,[8] with migration from poorer countries accounting for most population growth.[9] The vast majority of the global population will be in less wealthy countries (especially middle income), which are expected to increase from 6.1 billion people in 2015 to 8.47 billion in 2050.[10] From 2018 to 2100 about one-half of the annual growth is expected to occur in nine countries: India, Nigeria, Democratic Republic of the Congo, Pakistan, Ethiopia, Tanzania, United States, Uganda, and Indonesia.[11] The largest growth is expected in India, which is likely to pass China as the largest country in the world by 2028, with 1.4 billion people.[12] At that time India and China will account for about one-third of the world's population. Figure 3.3 shows the different variants of population projections by the United Nations for the world population up to 2050.

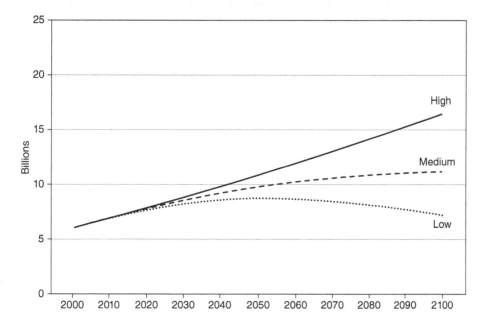

Figure 3.3 World population projections to 2100: three scenarios

Source: Based on data from UN Department of Economic and Social Affairs, Population Division, *World Population Prospects: The 2017 Revision*; Max Roser, "Future Population Growth," The History Database of the Global Environment (HYDE) (2018), https://ourworldindata.org/future-population-growth.

Covid-19 and other pandemics: impacts on global populations

As of November 2020, the coronavirus pandemic of 2019-2020 (Covid-19) had caused over one million confirmed deaths worldwide, with the total number of Covid-related deaths substantially higher yet difficult to document. The highest documented Covid-related death rates generally occurred in the Americas and Europe, ranging from 50-100 additional deaths per 100,000 people by November 2020. In the United States for example, the national death rate was estimated to be over 10% higher due to Covid-19. In 2020, Covid-19 proved particularly lethal to more vulnerable populations, including those over age 60, living in poverty, and with other underlying health conditions.

What will Covid-19's impact be on the overall global population? At the time this book went to print, it was not yet known. However, we do know more about how other pandemics have affected global populations in the past. For example, a particularly bad strain of the flu in 1918-1919 was estimated to have killed between 50-100 million people globally, yielding a significant impact on the global population. In that time roughly 100 years preceding Covid-19, the global population was only about 25% of what it is today and infectious diseases were still the leading cause of death. Over the near term, experts think life expectancies increased likely due to the fact that more people with underlying health conditions died, and birth rates also increased in the years following – though at least some of this was attributed more to the end of the first world war.

While it may be premature to speculate on the lasting population effects of Covid-19 at the global level, we have seen in at least some countries, death rates spiked substantially as the coronavirus disease spread. While advances in medicine and other technologies mean that infectious diseases are no longer the leading cause of death globally, Covid-19 demonstrates that global pandemics remain a significant global issue – not only due to death rates but also due to associated effects such as economic impacts and food shortages.

Sources: Johns Hopkins Coronavirus Resource Center, Mortality Analyses: Mortality in the Most Affected Countries, at https://coronavirus.jhu.edu/data/mortality (visited Nov 10, 2020); Kate Whitnig, A science journalist explains how the Spanish flu changed the world, World Economic Forum (2020), at https://www.weforum.org/agenda/2020/04/covid-19-how-spanish-flu-changed-world/ (visited Nov 2020); Jeffery Taubenberger & David Morens, 1918 Influenza: the Mother of All Pandemics, Emerging Infectious Diseases 12(1):15–22 (2006); Donald Fricker Jr., 279,700 extra deaths in the US so far in this pandemic year, The Conversation, at https://theconversation.com/279-700-extra-deaths-in-the-us-so-far-in-this-pandemic-year-147887 (visited Nov 2020).

Shifting Demographics: Rural to Urban

Another major change occurring in the world's population is the movement of people from rural areas to urban areas. Although this is happening throughout the world, the trend is especially dramatic in poorer countries, where a significant portion of rural youth are fleeing to cities with hopes of a better life. But all too often good paying jobs are not as available in the cities as hoped, pushing many rural migrants into poorer areas such as slums on the edges of big cities. In 2012, roughly one-third of the urban population in poor countries lived in informal settlements.[13]

As of 2014, more than half the world's population lived in urban areas and it is projected by 2050 that over two-thirds will reside in urban areas. Although Africa and Asia were home to 90 percent of the world's rural population in 2014, by 2050 Africa could become 56 percent urban, and Asia could be 64 percent urban. Further, three countries combined – India, China and Nigeria – are expected to account for more than one third of the world's urban population growth between 2014 and 2050.

Table 3.2 lists the world's ten largest cities in 1990 and 2014 and the projected ten largest for the year 2030 and 2050.

Note the trend in the growth of cities in countries with economies that have been rapidly growing. It is hard to imagine a city like Calcutta getting any bigger. In 1950, it had a population of about 4 million, with many thousands of people living permanently on the streets; in 1990 it had a population around 10 million and an estimated

Plate 3.1 Many migrants move to informal settlements in urban areas

Source: United Nations.

Table 3.2   Ten largest cities in the world, 1990, 2014, 2050 (projection)

Population in 1990 (millions)		Population in 2014 (millions)		Population in 2050 (projected millions)	
Tokyo, Japan	32	Tokyo, Japan	37	Mumbai (Bombay), India	42
Kinki M.M.A. (Osaka), Japan	18	Delhi, India	24	Delhi, India	36
New York-Newark, USA	16	Shanghai, China	22	Dhaka, Bangladesh	35
Mexico City, Mexico	15	Mexico City, Mexico	20	Kinshasa, Democratic Republic of the Congo	35
São Paulo, Brazil	14	São Paulo, Brazil	20	Kolkata (Calcutta), India	33
Mumbai, India	12	Mumbai, India	20	Lagos, Nigeria	32
Kolkata (Calcutta), India	10	Kinki M.M.A. (Osaka), Japan	20	Tokyo, Japan	32
Los Angeles, USA	10	Beijing, China	19	Karachi, Pakistan	31
Seoul, Republic of Korea	10	New York-Newark, USA	18	New York City-Newark, USA	24
Buenos Aires, Argentina	10	Cairo, Egypt	18	Mexico City, Mexico	24

Source: Based on data from UN Department of Economic and Social Affairs, Population Division, *World Urbanization Prospects: The 2009 Revision*; *World Urbanization Prospects: The 2014 Revision, Highlights*. 2050 data based on Daniel Hoornweg and Kevin Pope "Socioeconomic Pathways and Regional Distribution of the World's 101 Largest Cities," *Global Cities Institute Working Paper No. 04 2014*. Accessible here: https://sites.uoit.ca/sustainabilitytoday/urban-and-energy-systems/Worlds-largest-cities/population-projections/city-population-2050.php.

400,000 lived on the streets.[14] If the present rate of growth continues, it will have a population of about 33 million by 2050.[15]

Note also the increased size of the cities, as illustrated in Figure 3.5. Cities with over 5–10 million people are sometimes called "megacities."[16] In 1990, there were only ten cities with more than 10 million people. By 2014 there were 28 cities in the world with populations over 10 million people, the majority of these in emerging economies.[17] It is projected by 2030 there will be 41 megacities. Figure 3.5 shows the breakdown of the total number of cities by size for 1990, 2014 and 2030 (projected).[18] Many of these cities had vast areas of substandard housing and serious urban pollution, and many of their residents lived without sanitation facilities, safe drinking water, or adequate healthcare facilities.

With respect to urbanization, although countries differ on their definitions of "urban" (the United States defines urban as places of 2,500 or more, Japan uses 50,000, and Iceland 200), by 2018, 55 percent of the global population lived in urban areas (Figure 3.6 and 3.7).[24] There has been a particular trend toward increased urbanization in poorer nations: in 1950 only about 20 percent of their population

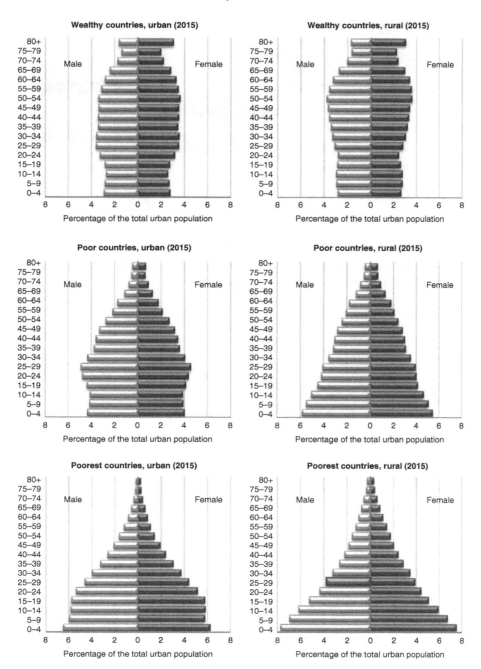

Figure 3.4 Percentage of the population by age for urban and rural areas of countries in three groups, 2015

Source: United Nations Department of Economic and Social Affairs Population Division, "Changing population age structures and sustainable development: A Concise Report." United Nations (New York, 2017), p.7; *Urban and rural population by age and sex*, version 3 (2014). p. 7.

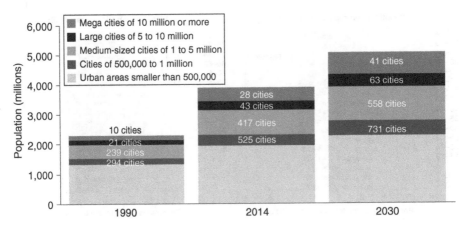

Figure 3.5 Global urban population growth by city size

United Nations, Department of Economic and Social Affairs, Population Division (2014). *World Urbanization Prospects: The 2014 Revision, Highlights (ST/ESA/SER.A/352).*

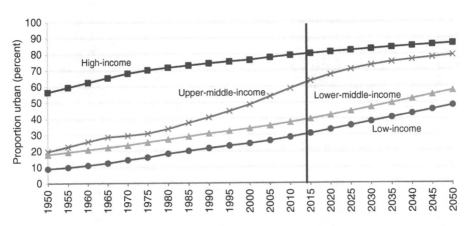

Figure 3.6 Percentage of urban by income group, 1950–2050

Source: United Nations, Department of Economic and Social Affairs, Population Division (2015). *World Urbanization Prospects: The 2014 Revision, (ST/ESA/SER.A/366)* p. 12.

was urban, but that increased to 40 percent in 2000. In 2009, for the first time in human history, more people lived in urban areas in the world than in rural areas, and by 2014 about 25 percent of the global urban population resided in wealthy countries.[14] Of the projected urban population growth at 2.5 billion people by 2050, 90 percent of this growth will be happening in Asia and Africa.[25] Nevertheless, 60 percent of the population in Africa and 52 percent in Asia still live in rural areas.[26] The trend is toward more urbanization as megacities and other cities continue to grow. The United Nations expects nearly all the world's population growth in the future will be in the urban areas of less wealthy nations.

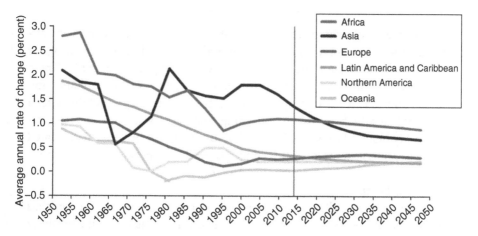

Figure 3.7 Average annual rate of change of the percentage of urban residents by major area, 1950–2050

Source: United Nations, Department of Economic and Social Affairs, Population Division (2014), *World Urbanization Prospects: The 2014 Revision, Highlights* (ST/ESA/SER.A/352), p. 10.

Innovative sustainable cities[19]

Shenzhen, China

In 2014, Shenzhen won the City Climate Leadership Award for Urban Transportation, sponsored by Siemens and the C40 Cities Climate Leadership Group. Known around the world as a leader in developing electric vehicles, this was the first city in the world to convert all of its 16,000 public buses.[20] However, what sets Shenzhen apart from other cities is its push to start infusing public transportation sectors, such as buses and taxis, with hybrid and electric vehicles. The city's leadership collaborated with public and private actors to add over 3,000 new energy buses and 850 pure electric taxis to the city's general transportation circuit by late 2013. This project has already led to a reduction of 160,000 tons of carbon pollution between 2009 and 2013. By 2015, the absolute carbon emission of units included for control in Shenzhen had declined by 5.31 million tons since 2010, with the carbon intensity down by as much as 41.8 percent, far exceeding the 21 percent reduction target issued by China to Shenzhen during the 12th Five-year Plan period.[21]

Buenos Aires, Argentina

Buenos Aires, another 2014 recipient of the City Climate Leadership Award, was honored for its Solid Urban Waste Reduction Project. The city has been working to become a Zero Waste city through the combination of a Zero Waste Law, increased recycling, public education, and infrastructure development; for example, within the city center the government is installing a series of underground waste disposal units, within parks and plazas there has been a major effort to add public recycling facilities called Green Stations or Puntos Verdes, and installation of new treatment plants and modernization of existing ones.[22] Thirty-two public parks contain "Green Stations," at which residents may bring recyclable waste for sorting, and every city block has a waste disposal bin. By 2014, this initiative had created 4,500 urban recoverer jobs and reduced overall landfill waste by 44 percent.

Curitiba, Brazil

Curitiba has been called the most innovative city in the world. City officials from around the world visit Curitiba to learn how this city, with relatively limited funds, has been tackling urban problems. By using imaginative, low-cost solutions and low technology, Curitiba has become a prosperous city with an urban life that many cities in the more developed nations have yet to achieve. Here is how the city achieved this.

Transportation The city made public transportation attractive, affordable, and efficient. Instead of building a subway, which the city could not afford, it established a system of extended, high-speed buses, some carrying as many as 275 passengers on express routes, connecting the city center with outlying areas. Many people own cars in Curitiba, but 85 percent of the commuters use public transportation. This has reduced traffic congestion and air pollution. There are 30 percent fewer cars on city streets than you would expect from the number of cars owned by its residents. Curitiba moves over 2,700,000 passengers per day, which is more people than live in the city.[23]

Trash collection The city's "garbage that is not garbage" initiative encourages residents to exchange their trash for goods like food, bus tickets, and school supplies. This program has led to the recycling of 70 percent of trash.

Education Small libraries have been built throughout the city in the shape of a lighthouse.

Health Curitiba has more health clinics – that are open 24 hours a day – per person than any other city in Brazil.

Environmental education The Free University for the Environment was built out of recycled old utility poles next to a lake made from an old quarry. Short courses on how to make better use of the environment are broadly offered. Taxi drivers are required to take a course there in order to get licensed.

Governmental services Colorful, covered Citizenship Streets have been built throughout the city to bring government offices to where the people live and shop. Here people can pay their utility bills, file a police complaint, go to night court, and get a marriage license. Vocational courses are subsidized to help provide accessible classes to all residents.

The main credit for this innovative city has been given to its former mayor Jaime Lerner, an architect and planner. He served three terms as mayor of the city and later served two terms as governor of the state.

Causes of the Population Explosion

Although it is easy to illustrate that the human population has grown exponentially, it is not so easy to explain why we are in a situation at present of rapidly expanding population. Exponential growth is only one of many factors that determine population size. Other factors influence how much time will pass before the doublings – found in exponential growth – take place. Still other factors influence how long the exponential growth will continue and how it might be stopped. We will consider these last two matters later in the chapter, but we will first look at some of the factors that drastically reduced the amount of time it took for the world's population to double in size (Figure 3.8).

The agricultural revolution, which began about 8000 BCE, was the first major event that gave population growth a boost. When humans learned how to domesticate plants and animals for food, they greatly increased their food supply. For the next 10,000 years until the industrial revolution, there was a gradually accelerating rate of population growth, but overall the rate of growth was still low because of high death rates, caused mainly by diseases and malnutrition. As the industrial revolution picked up momentum in the eighteenth and nineteenth centuries, population growth was given another boost: advances in sanitation, health, industry, agriculture, and transportation improved the living conditions of the average person. Population was growing exponentially, but the periods between the doublings were still long because of continued high death rates. This situation changed drastically after 1945. Lester Brown explains why that happened:

> The burst of scientific innovation and economic activity that began during the forties substantially enhanced the Earth's food-producing capacity and led to dramatic improvements in disease control. The resulting marked reduction in death rates created an unprecedented imbalance between births and deaths and an explosive rate of population growth. Thus, while world population increased at 2 to 5 percent *per century* during the first fifteen centuries of the Christian era, the rate in some countries (in the late 1970s) is between 3 and 4 percent *per year*.[17]

It was primarily improvements in life expectancies around the world after World War II that gave the most recent boost to population growth. The spreading of public health measures, including the use of vaccines, across the globe enabled countries to control diseases such as smallpox, tuberculosis, yellow fever, and cholera. Children and the elderly are especially vulnerable to infectious diseases; thus,

2018	CHINA 1,394	INDIA 1,371	UNITED STATES 328	INDONESIA 265	BRAZIL 209	PAKISTAN 201	NIGERIA 196	BANGLADESH 166	RUSSIA 147	MEXICO 131
2050	INDIA 1,680	CHINA 1,344	NIGERIA 411	UNITED STATES 390	INDONESIA 320	PAKISTAN 307	BRAZIL 231	CONGO, DEM. REP. 216	BANGLADESH 202	ETHIOPIA 191

Figure 3.8 Most populous countries by millions.

Source: Population Reference Bureau. *The World Population Data Sheet 2018*. worldpopdata.org (accessed November 28, 2018).

the conquering of these diseases allowed more children to live and bear children themselves.

While life expectancies around the world increased rapidly, birth rates generally remained higher than death rates. Birth rates have been high throughout human history. If this had not been true, you and I might not be here today since high birth rates were needed to replace the many people who died at birth or at an early age. (If you walk through an old cemetery, you can see evidence of this fact for yourself as you pass the family plots with markers for the many children who died in infancy and through adolescence.) Birth rates remained high right up until the late 1960s, which was the beginning of a gradual lowering of birth rates around the world.

Demographic transitions: population and development

The demographic transition, as shown in Figure 3.9, has four basic stages. In the first stage, which is often characteristic of preindustrial societies, there are high birth rates and high death rates that lead to a stable or slowly growing population. Death rates are high because of harsh living conditions and poor health. In the second stage, there is a decline in the death rate as modern medicine and sanitation measures are adopted and living conditions improve. Birth rates continue to be high in this stage as social attitudes favoring large families take longer to change, even as technology, health, and economic conditions evolve. This situation ignites what is known as the population explosion. In the third stage, birth rates become more aligned with the lower death rate. Population growth remains high during the early part of the third stage but falls to near zero during the latter part. Most industrial nations passed through the second and third stages from about the mid-1800s to the mid-1900s. In the final and fourth stage, both the death and birth rates are low, and they fluctuate at a low level. As in the first stage, there is a stable or slowly growing population.

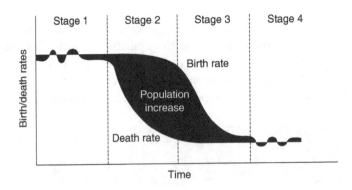

Figure 3.9 The classic stages of demographic transitions

Source: Joseph A. McFalls Jr, "Population: A Lively Introduction," *Population Bulletin*, 53 (3) (September 1998), Figure 12, p. 39.

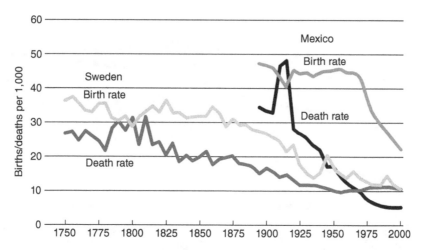

Figure 3.10 Demographic transition in Sweden and Mexico

Source: B. R. Mitchell, *European Historical Statistics 1750-1970* (1976), Table B6, Council of Europe, *Recent Demographic Developments in Europe 2001* (2001), Tables T3.1 and T4.1; Centro Latinamericano y Caribeño de Demografía, *Boletín Demográfico*, 69 (2002), Tables 4 and 7; Francisco Alba-Hernández, *La población de México* (1976), p.14; UN Department of Economic and Social Affairs Population Division, *World Population Prospects: The 2002 Revision* (2003), p.326. As presented in "Transitions in World Population," *Population Bulletin*, 59 (March 2004), p. 7.

Most wealthy nations are already in the fourth stage of the demographic transition, but globally most countries are still in the second stage or the early parts of the third stage. There have been some significant differences between countries with regard to the second and third stages. For those nations that were early adopters of industrialization, the reduction in the death rate was gradual as modern medicines were slowly developed and the knowledge of germs gradually spread. The birth rate dropped sharply, but only after a delay that caused the population to expand. For the rest of the world, increase in life expectancy has been sharper than it was for the developed nations as antibiotics were quickly adopted, but poverty still lingered for many and the reduction in the birth rate has lagged. Both of these facts have caused a much larger increase in the population of the less wealthy nations than had occurred in the nations that shifted to industrialized economies in the nineteenth century. The difference in this transition can be seen in Figure 3.10, which compares the demographic transitions of Sweden and Mexico.

The differences in the experiences of many nations have led many demographers to change the opinion they had in the 1950s that economic development would cause less wealthy nations to go through the same demographic transition as wealthy ones, and thus achieve lower population growth (Figure 3.11). There are obviously important differences between the experience of countries that industrialized early and that of the rest of the world. Probably as important as the fact that death rates dropped much faster last century than those prior is the fact that the industrialization that is taking place in emerging economies today is not providing many jobs and as such is not necessarily benefiting the vast majority of people in those regions.

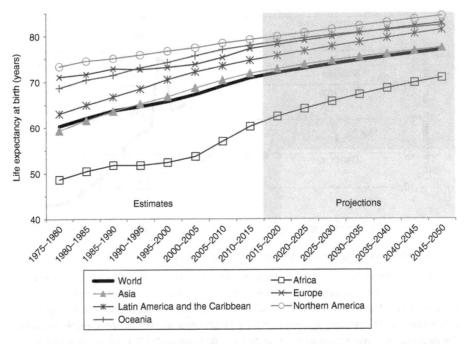

Figure 3.11 Life expectancy at birth (years) by region: estimates 1975–2015 and projections 2015–2050.

Source: United Nations, Department of Economic and Social Affairs. Population Division (2017). *World Population Projects: The 2017 Review.* New York: United Nations.

A relatively small, modern sector *is* benefiting from this economic development and the birth rate of this group is generally declining, but for the vast majority in the rural areas and in poor urban areas, high birth rates continue.

In the coming decades, high growth rates are expected in the less wealthy countries because a larger percentage of their population consists of children under the age of 15 who will be growing older and having children themselves.[27] Consider Figure 3.12: If we plot the number of people in a country according to their ages, we can see clearly the difference between rapidly growing populations, which less wealthy nations tend to have, and relatively stable or slowly growing populations, which tend to occur in wealthier nations.

Sons preferred in India[28]

Sons are preferred in many countries. This has been particularly notable in India, where there are a number of places where a strong preference for sons has increased the ratio of men to women over the past century. Between 2015 and 2020, the ratio of male births per female births is estimated at 1.106,[29] which is about 89 percent women to men. This has led to 37 million more men than women according to the most recent census – and if current trends continue, these numbers will only grow as India is poised to soon become the world's most populous nation.[30] Girls are more likely than boys to be neglected or mistreated, and India has a history of higher death rates and lower life expectancy for women than for men. Additionally, medical technology enables expectant parents to abort female fetuses, which has pushed the sex ratio at birth well above 105 boys to 100 girls, the normal ratio throughout the world. In the state of Haryana, just to the northwest of New Delhi, for example, a 2011 survey found that for children age 0–6, there were only 834 girls for every 1,000 boys.

Many families in India (and also China, Korea, and a number of other countries) value sons in past because they may live with their parents after marriage and contribute to family income. Sons provide vital financial support to elderly or ill parents, who often have no other source of income. Traditionally daughters move away at marriage and transfer their allegiance to their husband's family. At least historically, parents would therefore expect less financial or emotional support from daughters after they leave home.

In many parts of India, daughters can mean an additional cost to parents – the obligation of paying her prospective husband's family a large dowry. Dowries often require parents to go into debt, and the amount families must pay has been increasing over the years. A 2018 study found that dowries were contributing heavily to India's gender imbalance. Specifically, a 1 percent increase in the price of gold led to an extra 33,00 "missing" female births each year, attributed largely to anticipated future dowry obligations.[31]

The financial and social disadvantages of having a daughter prompt some women to abort their pregnancies if they are carrying a daughter. Pregnant women can determine the sex of their fetus through ultrasound and other examinations. As this technology becomes more widely available, more parents are using it to choose the number and sex of their children. Nearly all aborted fetuses in Indian hospitals are female. The national government has passed laws prohibiting sex-selective abortion, as have many Indian states, but these laws are difficult to regulate.

Birth rates have dropped close to or below replacement rates in wealthier nations but remain high in most other countries. Countries with steep declines in birth rates and are disproportionately concentrated in Eastern Europe: Bosnia and Herzegovina, Bulgaria, Croatia, Hungary, Japan, Latvia, Lithuania, Republic of Moldova, Romania, Serbia, and Ukraine all have projected declines of more than 15 percent by 2050.

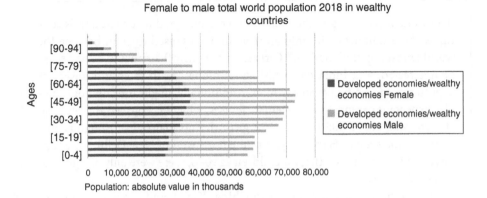

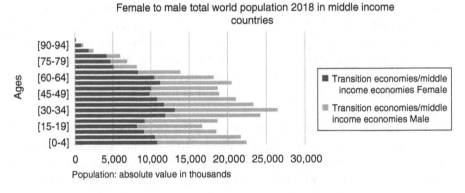

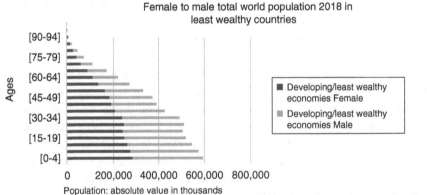

Figure 3.12   Population structure by gender and age-group, annual 2018

Source: United Nations Conference on Trade and Development. *Population structure by gender and age-group, annual, 1950-2050*, illustration by Monika Shepard. http://unctadstat.unctad.org/wds/ TableViewer/tableView.aspx?ReportId=134160 (accessed December 23, 2018).

Birth rate and fertility in all European countries are below the required level for replacement.[32]

There are several reasons for these substantial differences in birth rates. First, many people want to have many children. If many children die in infancy, as they still do in countries with relatively high infant mortality rates, more births are needed to replace the number of people surviving into adulthood. In many families, particularly in rural areas, children are tasked with helping with domestic and agricultural work, sometimes at the expense of their education. Before child labor laws severely restricted the use of children in factories in the United States and Europe, it was common for children to take paying jobs to help the family gain income. Additionally, the expectation is often that children (and specifically males in many cultures) are needed to ensure that the parents have someone to take care of them when they are old and can no longer work, which becomes a particularly acute need in the many countries where pensions or other assistance are unavailable.

Other reasons for continued high birth rates include tradition and religion. Cultural and religious norms are strong, and one does not break with these norms easily. Tradition is very important in many societies, and traditionally families have been large in rural settings. Also, religion is a powerful force in rural societies and some religions either advocate for large families or against birth control. The unavailability or unacceptance of birth control options is a particularly significant factor for higher birth rates in some places. By 2015, more than 142 million women had an unmet need for contraceptives – and this is a conservative estimate, limited to only married or in-union women of reproductive age.[33]

Plate 3.2   Children take care of children in many situations, as this girl is doing in Mexico

Source: Mark Olencki.

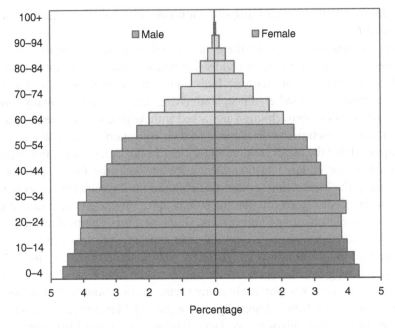

Figure 3.13   Distribution of the world's population by age and sex, 2017

Sources: United Nations, Department of Economic and Social Affairs, Population Division (2017).
World Population Prospects: The 2017 Revision. New York: United Nations.

How Population Growth Affects Development

How does population growth affect development? While there is no easy answer to the question of what is "too large" or "too small" a population for a country – a question we will return to in the final section of this chapter – we can identify some obvious negative features of a rapidly growing population, a situation which would apply to many less developed countries today.

Rapid growth

Let's look at the age distribution of the population in Figures 3.4 and 3.13. It is striking that a large percentage of people in both rural and urban areas are below the age of 15. This means that a large proportion of the population in these countries is mainly nonproductive. Food, education, and healthcare must be provided for children and youth until they become independent. Obviously, if a nation has a large portion of its population in the under-15 age group, its economy will be faced with a significant burden to provide for its younger members.

A rapidly growing population also puts a great strain on the resources of the country. Use of the country's resources at rates that exceed replenishment compromises ecosystems from renewing themselves. This can lead to the land becoming less fertile and the forests being destroyed. An example of this is the making of patties out of cow droppings and straw by women in India and Pakistan. These patties are allowed to dry in the sun and are then used for fuel. In fact, dung patties are the only fuel many families have for cooking their food. But the use of animal droppings for fuel prevents essential nutrients from returning to the soil, thus reducing the soil's ability to support vegetation.

In the years ahead, around two billion children will turn 5 with more than 1.2 billion young people transitioning into adulthood and beginning to look for a job. A large concentration of these people will be in African countries such as Burundi, Mali, and Niger.[34] A large population of young people also means that there will be a terrific demand for jobs when these children grow old enough to join the labor force – jobs that are unlikely to exist. The ranks of the unemployed and underemployed will grow in many poorer nations, and this can easily lead to political and social unrest. As we saw earlier in this chapter, people from the rapidly growing rural areas of the global South are heading for the cities hoping to find work. What they find, though, is a scarcity of jobs, undoubtedly a contributing factor in the high rates of urban crime.

A rapidly growing population also puts a tremendous strain on the ability of a nation to ensure adequate living conditions for everyone. The poor condition of much of the housing available to the poor is something that makes a lasting impression on

Plate 3.3 Growing cities in less developed nations often have a mixture of modern and substandard housing

Source: United Nations.

foreign visitors to these countries – that is, if they venture beyond the Western-style hotels where they sometimes stay. A shortage of affordable housing can lead to over-crowding, which may be exacerbated by a rapidly growing population, impacting privacy and individual rights.

Urban crime: a personal experience by John L. Seitz

An experience in that country helped me to understand that urban areas are often less safe than rural areas. I lived at different times in Monrovia, the capital city of that country, and in a small village in a rural area. Once while I was in Monrovia, a thief entered my bedroom and stole my wallet and watch from under my pillow, which was under my sleeping head at the time. Such an event was unheard of in the rural areas, but was not that uncommon in the city. After the theft happened, I was happy to return to my "primitive" village, where I felt much safer.

Slow growth

Because it impacts the labor force, a slow population growth rate has the potential to impede a country's productive capacity, and therefore also its economic growth. Partly because of low birth rates, a number of European countries welcomed immi-grants during the 1950s and 1960s from Turkey, southern Italy, and other relatively poor areas of Europe and North Africa. For some in the business world, a growing population signifies more consumers of products. But a number of the industrial countries have shown in the post-World War II period that a high level of economic growth is possible even when population growth is low.

Japan is a good example to look at. The country has experienced impressive eco-nomic growth in recent decades, and its population is projected to decline, dipping below 100 million by 2065[35] down to 84 million by 2100.[36] However, the decreasing population has enabled the country's modest economic growth of recent years to trigger increased per capita income.[37] The healthcare advances that have enabled the people of Japan to reach an average lifespan of 84 years have also allowed for a healthier population that spends less on medical care.[38] Additionally, long-term benefits of reduced population pressure include greater availability of food, housing, and land.

An aging population and low birth rates

We saw earlier the types of problems that are created when a country has a large share of its population aged 15 or under.

But other countries (mostly wealthier ones at present) face a different situation: a rapidly aging population, both in urban and rural areas as seen from Figure 3.4. New challenges arise when the proportion of a population that is over 65 starts to expand. As of 2017, the world's population aged 65 years or over will more than double by 2050; in Asia, Latin America, and Africa the population will likely more than triple. [39] While the global total is projected to increase from 608 million to over 1.5 billion in 2050, Asia could see its population rise from 330 million to 956 million. [40]

In Chapter 1 we discussed that part of the benefits of development include improved healthcare. When this is combined with a reduction in national birth rates (which then reduces the workforce population), the ratio of working-age people to retired people declines and can put a strain on social safety nets to support elderly persons no longer working.

With a decrease in birth rates and an increased older population, countries in this situation are facing a population conundrum: who will take care of these older generations and what is the best way to support government programs such as pensions, healthcare and other social programs that are paid based on the number of people working? In countries like the United States which have a national social security system, it is the payments from the current workers that provide money for those not working, which can become stressed when there are fewer workers and more recipients in need of assistance. Some proposals are looking into how people can remain in the workforce longer and/or get some benefits for volunteering their time. [41]

There are also increased healthcare costs as a population ages. More government funds are needed to care for the medical and social needs of the aged since the expectation in many countries is that families should not bear the exclusive burden to pay for these services. This is a common concern in Europe, where by the year 2050 it is expected that about 34 percent of its people will be 65 or older, as compared to 23 percent in 2013. [42] At the beginning of the twenty-first century only about 15 percent were of that age. Also of concern in Europe is the more than doubling of the number of people 80 or over, from 4.5 percent in 2013 to 9.5 percent in 2050 (Figure 3.14). [43]

Caring for the aged is a universal concern and is particularly acute in areas with a large percentage of aging populations, which are mostly concentrated in wealthy countries. It certainly is for Japan. In 2013, 32.3 percent of the population was 60 or older, and by 2050 it is expected that this group will increase to about 42.7 percent in a population that will probably be smaller than it was in 2000. [44] More countries, such as China, will also face an aging problem in the twenty-first century. Mainly because of the dramatic reduction in its birth rate, the percentage of people aged 60 or over in China is expected to increase from 13.9 percent in 2013 to 32.8 percent by mid-century. [45] By contrast, because of immigration and a relatively higher birth rate, in 2013 19.7 percent of the population in the United States was 60 or older and that group will grow to about 27 percent by 2050 (Figure 3.15). [46]

Projections are that about 50 countries, most of them wealthy, will experience population declines between now and 2050. Germany is expected to go from 82 million

Population

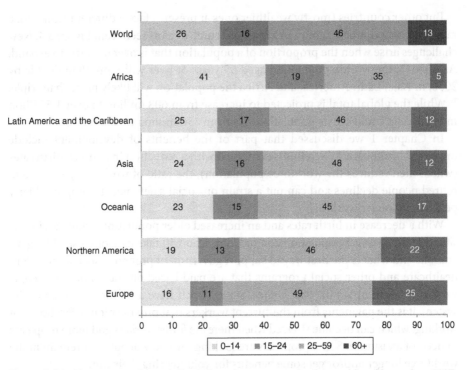

Figure 3.14 Percentage of population in broad age groups for the world and by region, 2017

Source: United Nations, Department of Economic and Social Affairs, Population Division (2017), *World Population Projects: The 2017 Revision*. New York: United Nations.

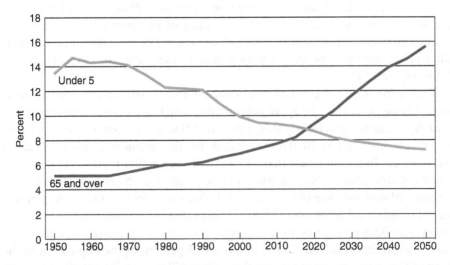

Figure 3.15 Young children and older people as a percentage of global population: 1950 to 2050.

Source: Wan He, Daniel Goodkind, and Paul Kowal, *An Aging World: 2015*. U.S. Census Bureau, International Population Reports (Washington, 2016).

to 74 million, Japan from 126 million to 107 million, and the Russian Federation from 142 million to 128 million.[47] The United States would also face a declining population in the twenty-first century were it not for its high immigration levels. Declining populations raise fears about loss of national power, economic growth, and even national identities by some people in these countries. But most population experts believe that if population decline is gradual, the negative social and economic consequences can be handled. Much more difficult to manage, they believe, are situations where the decline is rapid.[48] It is possible that some nations will find a smaller population easier to maintain in a sustainable manner, a concept which will be discussed in the final chapter.

When a country has a low birth rate, and the number of young people entering the labor market is reduced – a situation now common throughout Europe and Japan – this can lead to conflict over immigration policies. Hostility to foreign workers by extreme nationalists in Germany in the early 1990s led to fatal attacks on some foreigners in the country. Japan, a country that traditionally has been culturally insular, is also managing conflicts about having to rely on foreign workers. (The Japanese government has been concerned that a shrinking workforce will be unable to support the increasing healthcare costs and welfare costs of an aging population.)

A number of European nations and Japan had such low birth rates in the mid-1990s that their populations had started to decline or would soon do so. Declining populations became common in Russia and the former Eastern European satellites, no doubt because of the harsh economic conditions these countries were facing as they tried to replace their planned economies with market economies. Long-term decline in population for most of Europe appears inevitable. In the first half of this century, the population of Europe is expected to decline from about 730 million to 645 million by 2100.[49]

Some governments have tried different measures to encourage families to have more children – such as direct financial payments for additional children, tax benefits, subsidized housing preferences, longer maternity and paternity leave, childcare, and efforts to promote gender equality in employment – but these policies have had only modest effects in authoritarian states and minimal effects in more liberal democracies such as France and Sweden.[50]

How Development Affects Population Growth

How does development affect the growth rate of population? There is no easy answer to that question, but population experts strongly suspect that there *is* a relationship, since the West had a fairly rapid decline in its population growth rate after it industrialized. In the nineteenth century, Europe began to go through the demographic transition, discussed earlier in this chapter. Overall, we can ask how economic growth leading to increased wealth in a country is affecting society and population policies. For example, is some of the increased wealth being used to provide more services to the majority of people, such as medical clinics for the rural poor who have the high birth rates, and family planning services that will help rural women receive contraceptives and help them plan their families; or is the wealth mainly benefiting the rich and urban class? Are basic costs of living and childcare proving cost-prohibitive for families that would otherwise desire larger families? Are increased education levels reducing birth rates? All of these questions and others need to be answered when analyzing the type of development a country has.

Factors lowering birth rates

What factors cause birth rates to decline? As the West industrialized, it became more urban, and living space in urban societies is scarcer and more expensive than it was in rural societies. The availability of goods and services increased, which led to families increasing their consumption of these rather than spending their income on raising more children. Women now had job opportunities in urban areas that hadn't existed in the rural areas and now could contribute to the family's wealth.

Certainly, better healthcare and better nutrition, both of which lower infant mortality and thus raise a family's expectations of how many children will survive, are important factors. Another factor tending to lower birth rates is the changing role of women. Women with years of education are more likely to use some sort of contraception than are those women with little or no education.[51] Education for women tends to be associated with delayed marriage, increased knowledge about contraceptives, increased employment opportunities, and evolving views of their role in society.

As Western nations industrialized, child labor laws, compulsory education for children, and old age pension laws reduced some of the economic incentives for having many children. These laws made it more difficult for children to be viewed as producers on the farms and in the early factories; instead, they were considered consumers at some economic cost to their families. Traditional religious beliefs, which often support large families, also tended to decline.

There is little debate today that economic growth, especially if it benefits the many and not just the few, can lead to lower birth rates. There is also ample evidence that improving the social and economic status of women can lead to lower birth rates, even in areas which remain very poor – such as in the southern state of Kerala in India, where birth rates are significantly lower than in the rest of India. But there is also evidence that birth rates can decrease and are decreasing in poor countries – even in some where there has been little or no economic growth and where the education and social status of women remains very low, such as in Bangladesh – where an effective family planning program exists and modern contraceptives are available.[52] (Fertility rates dropped in Bangladesh from 6.36 births per woman in 1955 to 2.14 births per woman in about 2018.[53])

In the past several decades, fertility has declined significantly in the world, although as Figure 3.16 shows, the decline has been much greater in some regions than in others. Note that Europe is below replacement level, which is generally considered to be an average of 2.1 children per woman (the extra one-tenth compensates for the death of some girls and women before the end of their child-bearing years). Also note that Africa still has high fertility.

The conclusion of some researchers who have reviewed the results of fertility studies conducted in various countries is that "although development and social change create conditions that encourage smaller family size, contraceptives are the best contraceptive."[54] These researchers found that three factors are mainly responsible for the impressive decline in birth rates that has occurred in many countries since the mid-1960s: more influential and more effective family planning programs;

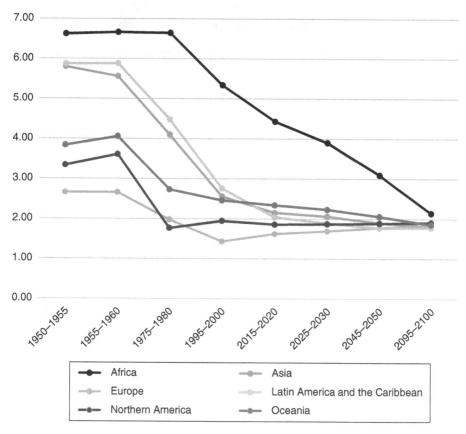

Figure 3.16 Fertility decline in world regions in terms of number of children per woman by region from 1950 to 2100 (projected)

Source: Created by Monika Shepard, derived from custom data acquired from United Nations, Department of Economic and Social Affairs, Population Division (2017). *World Population Prospects: The 2017 Revision*, at https://population.un.org/wpp/DataQuery/(accessed December 20, 2018).

Plate 3.4   Breast-feeding can delay a woman's ability to conceive and provides the most healthful food for a baby

Source: United Nations.

new contraceptive technology; and the use of the mass media to educate women and men about birth control.[55]

International Conferences on Population

The first international conference on population was held in 1974 in Romania under the sponsorship of the United Nations. It was anticipated that this conference would dramatize the need for population control programs in the less developed countries, but instead a debate took place between rich and poor countries over what was causing poverty: population growth or underdevelopment. The United States and other wealthy nations argued for the need for birth control measures in the Global South, while a number of the poorer countries argued that what they needed was more economic development. Some developing countries called for a new international economic order to support their development. They advocated more foreign aid from the richer countries, and more equitable trade and investment practices. The conference ended with what seemed to be an implicit compromise: that what was needed was both economic development and policies to manage population growth, and that an emphasis on only one factor and a disregard of the other would not work to reduce poverty.

In 1984, the United Nations held its second world population conference in Mexico City. The question of the relationship between economic growth and population growth was raised again. The United States argued that economic growth produced by the private enterprise system was the best way to reduce population growth. The United States did not share the sense of urgency that others felt at the conference concerning the need to reduce the world's increasing population. It announced that it was cutting off its aid to organizations that promoted the use of abortion as a birth control technique. (Subsequently the United States stopped contributing funds to the United Nations Fund for Population Activities and the International Planned Parenthood Federation, two of the largest and most effective organizations concerned with population issues.[56]) The United States stood nearly alone in its rejection of the idea that the world faced a global population crisis, as well as in its advocacy of economic growth as the main population management mechanism. The conference endorsed the conclusion reached at the first conference ten years earlier that *both* birth control measures *and* efforts to reduce poverty were needed to reduce the rapidly expanding global population.

In 1992, the United Nations Conference on the Environment and Development – the so-called Earth Summit held at Rio de Janeiro, Brazil, which will be discussed in detail in Chapter 6 – did not directly address population policies. The Rio Declaration says only that "states should ... promote appropriate demographic policies," and Agenda 21, the action plan to carry out the broad goals stated in the declaration, does not mention family planning. The light treatment of the population issue by this conference was, in part, the result of North–South conflicts over whether the poor or the rich were mainly responsible for the destruction of the environment. (When the population issue was raised, attention was focused on the harm to the environment that large numbers of poor people in the South could inflict, whereas the South held that overconsumption by the North caused most of the pollution that was harming the environment.) The rejection of any explicit connection between rapid population growth and environmental damage was also a result of opposition by the Vatican to any declarations which could be used to support the use of contraceptives and abortion to control population growth, practices that the Catholic Church has opposed. Also, some countries with conservative social traditions were opposed to raising any issue that could bring up the status of women in their countries.

While there was no explicit reference to population issues in its formal statements, the Rio conference, and the multitude of meetings around the world held to prepare for it, did cause increased attention to be placed on population, especially bringing to the forefront the perspectives of women.

The United Nations held its third conference on population – formally called the International Conference on Population and Development – in Cairo, Egypt in 1994. Although the Vatican and conservative Islamic governments made abortion and sexual mores the topic of discussion in the early days of the conference, the conference broke new ground in agreeing that women must be given more control over their lives if population growth was to be controlled. The conference approved a 20-year plan of action whose aim was to stabilize the world's population at about 7.3 billion by 2015. The plan called for new emphasis to be placed on the education of girls, providing a large range of family planning methods, health services, and economic opportunities for women. The action plan called for both rich and poor nations to increase the amount they spent on population-related activities to an aggregate of $17 billion by the year 2000, a significant increase over the $5 billion that was then being spent.

Five years after the Cairo conference, the United Nations found new approaches to managing populations had been initiated around the world, but that scarce resources and many needs led to population programs not receiving top priority in all nations. It found also that pledges of aid from donor nations were seriously underfunded.[57]

In 2003, the United Nations General Assembly voted to end the automatic holding of international conferences. Because of their large expense of funds and human energy and the danger that they were becoming routine, the United Nations decided that the decision to hold an international conference should be made on a case-by-case basis when there was a special need for international cooperation.

Governmental Population Policies

Managing growth

Many governments today have some policies that try to control the growth of their populations, but this is a very recent trend. Traditionally, governments have sought to increase their populations, either through encouraging immigration (as the United States did in its early years) or through tax and other economic assistance to those families with many children. As late as the mid-1970s, many governments rejected putting programs in place to help manage population levels. A survey taken in conjunction with the 1974 United Nations population conference found that, out of 110 developing countries, about 30 had population control programs, another 30 had information and social welfare programs, and about 50 had no population management programs at all.[58] This United Nations conference ended with no explicit consensus among the participants that there was a world population "problem" at all. The delegates at the conference did pass a resolution stating that all families have the right to plan their families and that it is the responsibility of governments to make sure all families have the ability to do so.

The ability to control the number and timing of children a couple has is called family planning. Family planning services provide healthcare and information on contraceptives. The expansion of family planning services around the world in the past 40 years has been truly revolutionary. By 2015, about 64 percent of married couples worldwide were using contraceptives, a dramatic increase from the approximately 10 percent in the 1960s.[59] The average number of children per woman dropped from more than five in 1950 to less than three by 2012, still more than needed for a population to stabilize.[60] In the poorest countries, the average number

Plate 3.5 Advertisement for contraceptives in Costa Rica

Source: George Shiflet.

of children per woman was still over four.[61] Most wealthy countries and a few rapidly industrializing countries maintain a birth rate at or below two children per couple, the replacement level.

Although more than half of married women worldwide used contraceptives in 2015, the rate among countries varied greatly. In sub-Saharan countries, the contraceptive rate among married women was about 28 percent, while in Mexico and Thailand the use was closer to 73 percent and 79 percent respectively.[62] Wealthier countries had a contraceptive use rate of about 70 percent at this time.[63] As mentioned before in this chapter, at the beginning of the twenty-first century about 143 million women of reproductive age in the poor nations wanted no further children but were not using contraceptives. They are considered to be potential family planning users if the services were made available to them. Figure 3.17 depicts increases in contraceptive use in selected countries.

Requests by countries for foreign aid to help them manage their population rates now exceed the international assistance available for this activity. It was calculated in 2012 that providing family planning services to the estimated 222 million women whose potential demand remained unmet would cost an estimated $3 billion annually. While this seems like a huge amount, relative to other expenditures being made at present, it is not. (The cost of one modern submarine in the United States is over $2 billion.) Despite some controversial policies (see discussion earlier in this chapter about US policy in the 1980s), the US government has historically been the largest single donor of aid for population and family planning activities in the developing world. However, as we discuss in Chapter 1, its development assistance, which includes population assistance, is far below the recommended level.

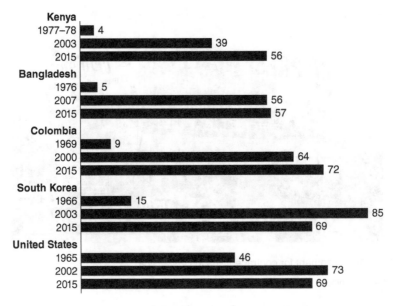

Figure 3.17 Increases in modern contraceptive use in selected countries, by percentage of women

Sources: Based on data from UN Department of Economic and Social Affairs, Population Division, *Levels and Trends in Contraceptive Use,* 2015, 2009, and 1998 editions; C. Haub and B. Herstad, *Family Planning Worldwide* (2002); ORC Macro, Demographic and Health Survey data. As presented in "Transitions in World Population," *Population Bulletin,* 59 (March 2004), p. 8. Modern contraceptives include sterilization, oral contraceptives, IUDs, condoms, diaphragms, implants, injectables, and other barrier and chemical methods.

Recognizing that many Member States were not on track to meeting their commitments pursuant to the 1994 International Conference on Population and Development (ICPD) and its Programme of Action, which had been set to expire in 2014, the UN General Assembly extended the Programme of Action by resolution in 2010 and the Commission on Population and Development adopted a resolution reaffirming the Programme of Action and its central implementation provisions in 2014.[64] However, the international assistance provided continued to fall below the cost of population assistance: in 2011 the total assistance provided for population programs amounted to $11 billion, while the ICPD estimated that global costs for that year were close to $67 billion.[65]

Mexico   Mexico is a country that has had rather dramatic success with its family planning program. The government began this program only in 1972, when it had one of the highest rates of population growth in the world. In the early 1970s, the annual population growth rate was estimated to be above 3 percent, while in 2010 it was estimated to be down to about 1.4 percent.[66] The average number of children per woman in Mexico dropped from about 7 in 1965 to about 2.26 in 2018.[67]

Plate 3.6 Family planning class

Source: United Nations.

In 1972, Mexico's President Luis Echeverria Alvarez announced a reversal of governmental policy on the population issue. His decision to support a strong effort to control the rapid growth of the Mexican population led the government to use Mexfam, the local affiliate of the International Planned Parenthood Federation, to set up family planning clinics throughout the country. (By the early 1990s Mexfam had set up 200 of these clinics.) Besides making contraceptives readily available, the government and Mexfam mounted a large propaganda campaign using television soap operas, popular songs, billboards, posters on buses and in subway stations, and spot announcements on radio and television. The leaders of the Catholic Church in Mexico did not oppose the government's efforts.

But if the present birth rate continues, Mexico's population will increase by 15 percent by 2050. To increase the use of contraceptives, the National Population Council began focusing its efforts on the rural population, adolescents, and men. Men are an especially important target since the rate of contraceptive use by men in Mexico is low and social and economic conditions have evolved such that men have become more receptive to intentionally planning their family size.

A few countries have adopted more forceful measures than family planning to try to reduce their population growth. Japan drastically reduced its population growth by legalizing abortion after World War II, by some accounts in order to reduce the number of Japanese children fathered by American military men stationed in Japan.

Lowering fertility rates drastically in just 10–15 years – can it be done?

The answer is yes, it can be done. We know it can because countries such as
Iran, Tunisia, and Algeria have done it under a four-part strategy:
1   Promote child survival.
2   Promote girls' education and gender equality.
3   Promote availability of contraceptives and family planning, especially for
    the poor who cannot afford them.
4   Raise productivity on the farm, enabling more women to earn income.

Source: Jeffrey D. Sachs, "Lower Fertility: A Wise Investment," *Scientific American*, 295 (September
2006), p. 42.

India   India did not see significant changes with its voluntary family planning
programs, so enacted more forceful measures in the mid-1970s, such as the
compulsory sterilization of some government workers with more than two children.
Several states in India passed laws requiring sterilization and/or imprisonment for
those couples who bore more than two or three children. A male vasectomy program
was also vigorously pursued, with transistor radios and money being given as an
incentive to those agreeing to have the sterilization operation. Public resentment
against these policies mounted and helped lead to the defeat of Prime Minister
Indira Gandhi's government in 1977. Birth control efforts slackened after that event.
Fertility has declined substantially in India from about five children per woman in
1970 to about two children in 2015.[68] In 2016, the government updated its policies
to provide free injectable contraceptives as an alternative to the previously promoted
method of female sterilization.[69] Even with this decline, population is now increasing
by about 15 million a year, an increase which leads the world. India now has about
18 percent of the world's population on only 2.5 percent of the world's land, and is
poised to soon become the most populous country on the planet.[70]

China   China has about 19 percent of the world's population but only about 7 percent
of its arable land, and has implemented vigorous programs to limit its population
growth and has drastically reduced its birth rate.[71] For many years the communist
government, under the leadership of Mao Zedong, encouraged the growth of the
population, believing that there was strength in numbers. The policy was eventually
reversed and the average number of children per woman dropped from about six in
1970 to about two in the year 2000. In 2015 China's population was about 1.4 billion,
and the population is expected to remain steady or slightly decline through 2075.[72]
    China employed a wide assortment of measures to limit the growth. These
included broadly promoting contraceptives, encouraging sterilization, and making

abortions readily available. The government, through extensive publicity efforts, promoted the one-child family as the ideal, encouraging late marriages and providing employment and housing incentives to one-child couples.

Partly because of a concern that there will not be enough adult children to care for their aging parents, the one-child policy is being moderated. It has been widely enforced in the urban areas, but in rural areas, where about 60 percent of the people still live, couples were usually allowed to have a second child if the first child was a female. The one-child policy was also not applied to ethnic groups in the country, partly because many of them live in strategic border areas and the government did not want to cause resentment among them. There is evidence that there was widespread disregard of the policy in some rural areas where it was not uncommon at the turn of the century to find families with three, four, five, or even more children.[73]

China's birth control policies have been both admired and criticized in other countries. Admiration has been given for the spectacular accomplishment, for producing one of the fastest, if not the fastest, demographic transitions in history. The policy has been credited with having prevented the birth of an additional 400 million children.[74] The one-child policy was criticized because of the means used to enforce it, which included the use of abortions as a backup to contraceptives – sometimes on women who strongly preferred not to have one. The use of the coercive techniques of the past has mainly ended and emphasis shifted to education and "family planning fees" for women who have "unapproved" children.[75]

Concerns also emerged at unnaturally low numbers of female births being reported. A male child was strongly desired in many areas to carry on the family name, to take care of his parents when they get old (an old age social security system still does not exist in the rural areas), and to help with agricultural work.[76] Because of stringent family planning policies and a social preference for having a male child, there is speculation that many couples resorted to measures such as aborting pregnancies if the fetus was female – ultrasound equipment has become widespread to indicate the sex of the fetus.[77]

Population-related challenges in China's future include an aging population because of low fertility; fewer children to take care of aging parents; single children with no siblings, aunts or uncles; and a shortage of females for males to marry. Dissatisfaction is also spreading in parts of the country because of the increasing social and financial inequality that has come with China's increasing economic prosperity as it follows the market approach. Also, as the population continues to grow in tandem with consumption and industrialization expansion, there will be increasing stress on the environment.

Promoting growth

Although most countries now recognize a need to limit population growth, a few have openly favored increasing their populations, among them the military governments that ruled in Argentina and Brazil in the 1960s and 1970s. Both countries have large areas that are still sparsely populated. A few Brazilian military officers even advocated encouraging population growth so that Brazil could pass the United States in size and become the dominant nation in the Western hemisphere. It is doubtful that a larger population alone could ever put a country in this position.

Aside from some pro-growth statements, the Brazilian military governments did not effectively promote population growth. They became basically neutral on the issue of population and gradually made it possible for the main nongovernmental family planning organization to operate in the country. After the military left power in Brazil in the mid-1980s, a new constitution acknowledged the right of women to family planning. This provision had the tacit approval of the Brazilian Catholic Church. By the mid-1990s about 75 percent of Brazilian women were using some form of contraception.[78] From 1960 to 2005, the average number of children born to a Brazilian woman dropped from about six to about two. Despite legal limitations, abortions have not been uncommon. One estimate is that there were about 1.4 million abortions performed annually in Brazil in the mid-2000s.[79]

Other countries, such as Mongolia and some in sub-Saharan Africa, have at times advocated larger populations both for strategic reasons and because of the belief that a large population is necessary for economic development. Even the US government, which generally recognizes the need for a check on population growth, has some policies that promote large families, such as income tax laws that allow

---

Romania: a disastrous pro-birth policy

Romania is an example of a country that tried to promote the growth of its population. After World War II, the birth rate there fell so sharply that within a few years the population of the country would actually have started declining. In the mid-1960s the communist government, headed by Nicolae Ceauşescu, decided to try to reverse this trend, not only to ward off a possible decline of population but to actually increase the number of people. Ceauşescu believed that a large population would improve Romania's economic position and preserve its culture, since Romania was surrounded by countries with different cultures. "A great nation needs a great population," said Ceauşescu. He called on all women of childbearing age to have five children. Monthly – and in some places, even weekly – gynecological exams were given to all working women 20 to 30 years old. If a woman was found to be pregnant, a "demographic command body" was called in to monitor her pregnancy to make sure she did not interrupt it. A special tax was placed on those who were childless.

The main techniques the government used to promote its pro-growth policy were to outlaw abortion, which was one of the main methods couples had used in the postwar period to limit the size of their families, and to ban the importation and sale of contraceptives. The birth rate immediately shot up, but within a few years it was nearly back to its previous low as couples found other means to limit their families. One of the means was secret abortions, and many women either died or ended up in hospital after abortions were performed or attempted by incompetent personnel. Another tragic result of Ceauşescu's pro-birth policy (as well as of his failed economic policies) was the abandoning of unwanted children. Tens of thousands of these children ended up in understaffed and ill-equipped orphanages (there are photo essays of Romania's orphanages in the sources below). Many babies were even sold for hard currency to infertile Western couples. The pro-growth policy ended in 1989 with the overthrow of the Ceauşescu regime and with his execution.

Sources: James Nachtwey, "Romania's Lost Children," *New York Times Magazine*, June 24, 1990, pp. 28–33; and Jane Perlez and Ettore Malanca, "Romania's Lost Boys," *New York Times Magazine*, May 10, 1998, pp. 26–9.

deductions for children. Many nations have contradictory policies, some encouraging population growth while others discourage it.

A generalization one can make about governmental policies that are aimed at influencing population growth is that, aside from drastic measures, governmental policies have not been very successful in either promoting or limiting birth rates very much if these policies are out of line with what the population desires. One can also generalize that matters pertaining to reproduction are still considered to be private decisions and not matters for public policy to control.

A growing number of industrialized countries are increasingly faced with a rapidly expanding retirement-age population and a shrinking labor force that will have to support its elderly citizens. Some of these countries, such as Sweden, Hungary, South Korea, and Japan, have tried various policies to encourage women to have more children. The policies have included paid maternity and paternity leave, free childcare, tax breaks for large families, family housing allowances, and even cash paid to parents raising a child. At the start of this century, a study of these efforts concluded that as we enter the next century, a growing number of countries will have near-zero growth or will decline in size. Experience in Europe, Japan, and other countries suggests that governments can encourage people to have more children, but at a high price and not enough to affect long-term trends.[80]

The Future

The growth of the world's population

In 2015, the world's population was estimated to be about 7 billion. The United Nations projects that the world's population will continue to grow to about 10 billion by 2050 and 11.2 billion by 2100,[81] depending on the seventy of global diseases and the success of family planning measures. The most likely total, according to the United Nations, is between 9 and 10 billion. The United Nations bases its projection on the assumption that the world's population growth rates, while still above their replacement rates, will continue the decline that started in the late 1960s.[82]

Unusual for a wealthy country, the population of the United States is expected to continue to grow significantly, increasing from about 300 million in 2010 to about 400 million around 2050. Rather atypical of Northern Europe, the United Kingdom's population is projected to grow from about 62 million in 2010 to about 75 million in 2050.[83]

The carrying capacity of the Earth

Will the Earth be able to support a population of 9 to 10 billion, 2–3 billion more than the present size, or will catastrophe prevent that figure from being reached? (The world was 2 billion when one of your authors (Seitz) was born. Now it is more than three times that size, a remarkable change in just a single lifetime.) Understanding the concept of "carrying capacity" will help answer the question of potential catastrophe. Carrying capacity is the number of individuals of a certain species that can be sustained indefinitely in a particular area. Carrying capacity can change over time, making a larger or smaller population possible. Human ingenuity has greatly increased the carrying capacity of Earth to support human beings, for example, by increasing the production of food. (This was unforeseen by Thomas Malthus, who wrote about the dangers of overpopulation in the late 1700s.) But carrying capacity can also change so that fewer members of the species can live. A change in the climate might do this. Care must be exercised when using the concept of carrying capacity because, in the past, its definition implied a balance of nature. Many ecologists no longer use the concept of balance of nature because numerous studies have shown that nature is much more often in a state of change than in a balance. Populations of different forms of life on Earth are usually in a state of flux as fires, wind storms, disease, changing climate, new or decreasing predators, and other forces make for changing conditions and thus changing carrying capacity.

There are four basic relationships that can exist between a growing population and the carrying capacity of the environment in which it exists. A simplified

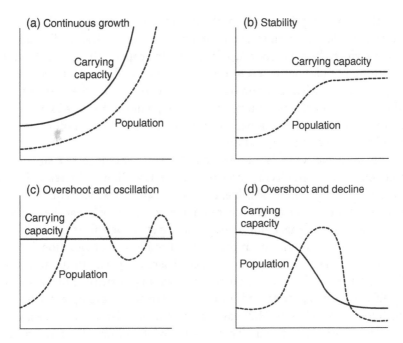

Figure 3.18 A growing population and carrying capacity

depiction of these is given in Figure 3.18. Graph (a) illustrates a continuously grow-ing carrying capacity and population. Although human ingenuity as seen in the agricul-tural revolution (to be discussed in Chapter 4) and in the industrial/scientific revolution has greatly increased the capacity of the Earth to support a larger number of human beings, it is doubtful the human population can continue to expand indef-initely. A basic ecological law is that the size of a population is limited by the short supply of a resource needed for survival. The scarcity of only one of the essential resources for humans – which would include air, energy, food, space, nonrenewable resources, heat, and water – would be enough to put a limit on its population growth. It is unknown how much farther the carrying capacity can be expanded before one of the limits is reached, or whether the global population has already overshot its limit.

Graph (b) of Figure 3.18 illustrates a population that has stabilized somewhat below the carrying capacity. (In actuality the population may fluctuate slightly above and below the carrying capacity, but the carrying capacity remains basi-cally unchanged.) Examples of this can be seen in relatively undisturbed tropical rain-forests where many species are relatively stable in an environment where average temperature and rainfall vary little.[84] Graph (c) portrays a situation where the population has overshot the carrying capacity of the environment and then oscillates above and below it. An example of this situation may be the relation-ship between the great gray owls and their prey, lemmings and voles, in northern forests. Lemmings and voles are an important food source for the owls. Their pop-ulations rapidly increase over a period of four to six years and then, as predators increase their consumption of them, their numbers crash catastrophically, caus-ing the owls to flee the area to escape mass starvation.[85] Graph (d) illustrates a situation in which the overshooting of the carrying capacity leads to a precipitous decline in the population, or even to its extinction, and also to a decline in the carrying capacity. Such a situation has occurred with deer on the north rim of the Grand Canyon in the United States, and with elephants in Kenya's Tsavo National Park.[86] In both cases, the number of animals increased to a point where they destroyed the vegetation they fed upon.

The human species with its unique mental powers, could create a situation that combines elements of graphs (a) and (b), and use its abilities to increase the carry-ing capacity of Earth, where possible, that policies and practices equitably enable the least amount of suffering. But there are many indications that the species has not yet recognized its danger and is not yet taking effective efforts to prevent either situation (c) – which would mean the death of millions – or situation (d), which could lead to the decline of the human race. There are places in the world where population expansion has already passed the carrying capacity of the land and the land itself is now being destroyed; in parts of Africa, for example, fertile land is turning into desert and in the Himalayan mountain area, land is being destroyed by human-made erosion and floods. There are many other examples of the reduction of the carrying capacity of the Earth that is taking place at unprecedented rates today around the world – the result of uncontrolled overgrazing, overfishing, over-planting, overcutting of forests, and the overproduction of waste which leads to pollution. (Some of this reduction of carrying capacity is being caused by popula-tion pressures and some by economic forces, for example the desire to increase short-term profits.) This deterioration has led many ecologists to believe that unless there is a rapid and dramatic change in many governmental policies, the human species may indeed be headed for the situations depicted in either the oscil-lation or decline graphs in Figure 3.18.

"Optimum" size of the Earth's population

What is the "optimum" size of the Earth's population? That question, like others we have asked in this chapter, is not going to be easy to answer, but it is worth asking.

There is one other aspect of the carrying capacity concept that demonstrates some of the trade-offs in evaluating the global carrying capacity for humans: what quality of life should the population enjoy? Joel Cohen, a distinguished biologist, head of the Laboratory of Populations at Rockefeller University and Columbia University and author of the influential book *How Many People Can the Earth Support?*, persuasively argues that when asking the question "How many people can the Earth support?" an attempt must be made to answer ques-tions such as the following:

- *How many at what average level of well-being?* What type of diet, transportation, and health system will be provided?

- *How many with what distribution of well-being?* If we are content to have a few rich and a large number poor, the Earth can probably support more than if the income distribution is fairly equal.
- *How many with what physical, chemical, and biological environments?* How much clean air, water, and wilderness do we want?
- *How many with what kinds of domestic and international political institutions?* How will conflicts be settled at home and internationally?
- *How many with what technology?* How food and goods and services are produced affects the Earth's carrying capacity.
- *How many with what values, tastes, and fashions?* Are we vegetarians or meat eaters? Do we commute to work by car, mass transport, or bicycle?
- *How many for how long?* How long can that number of people be supported?[87]

The concept "sustainable development," which will be discussed in Chapter 9, is related to carrying capacity and is now being used more frequently than carrying capacity to convey some of the same concerns.

Paul Ehrlich, professor of population studies and of biology at Stanford University, defines the optimum size of the Earth's population as that "below which well-being per person is increased by further growth and above which well-being per person is decreased by further growth." What does "well-being" mean? Ehrlich explains what he believes it means:

> The physical necessities – food, water, clothing, shelter, a healthful environment – are indispensable ingredients of well-being. A population too large and too poor to be supplied adequately with them has exceeded the optimum, regardless of whatever other aspects of well-being might, in theory, be enhanced by further growth. Similarly, a population so large that it can be supplied with physical necessities only by the rapid consumption of nonrenewable resources or by activities that irreversibly degrade the environment has also exceeded the optimum, for it is reducing Earth's carrying capacity for future generations.[88]

Ehrlich believes that, given the present patterns of human behavior – behavior that includes the grossly unequal distribution of essential commodities such as food and the misuse of the environment – and the present level of technology, we have already passed the optimum size of population for this planet.

Julian Simon, author of *The Ultimate Resource*, believed that the ultimate resource on Earth is the human mind. The more human minds there are, said Simon, the more solutions there will be to human problems. Simon admitted that population growth in poor countries could lead to short-term problems since more children will have to be fed. But in the long run these children will become producers, so the Earth will benefit from their presence. Simon agreed that rapid population growth could harm development prospects in poor nations, but he was not disturbed by moderate growth in these countries. According to Simon, larger populations make economies of scale possible; cheaper products can be made if there are many potential consumers. Also, services can improve, as seen by the development of efficient mass transportation in Japan and Europe in areas of dense population.[89]

Simon's views won favor in the Reagan and Bush administrations (father and son) in the United States and were used to give academic support to a new US policy on population – popularly called the Mexico City policy. This policy basically saw the effect of population growth as a "neutral phenomenon ... not necessarily good or ill," a position which Marxist ideology also held.[90] While many economists in the United States do not share Simon's view that "more is better," many do share his view that human ingenuity, especially new technology and resource management practices, can increase the carrying capacity of the Earth as it has in the past.[91]

Joel Cohen believes there is no way to estimate the optimum size of the human population on Earth because no scientifically based answers have been given to the questions he presented above. In simpler terms, no one has answered the fundamental question: "How many people can the Earth support with what quality of life?" Obviously the Earth can support a large number of people if they are all living at a subsistence level – with barely enough to eat – or if a relatively few are rich and the rest poor, or if they accept frequent risks of violent storms and droughts. But Cohen believes that even without an agreed-upon "optimum number," the many things that governments and individuals can do to improve conditions for the present generation and future generations are worth doing.[92]

Population-related challenges in our future

At the time this book went to print, it was too early to tell what impact the Covid-19 pandemic would have on populations at the global level. What do you think?

Throughout this book we are also going to be looking at many current problems related to population rates increasing in tandem with consumption. Here we mention a few of the most important ones. Hunger is an obvious problem in which population plays a key role, and the number of hungry people is huge. The news media are used to dramatizing this problem only when there are many children with bloated bellies to be photographed, but much more common than the starving child today, and probably in the future, will be the child or adult who is permanently debilitated or who dies because of malnutrition-related disease. Pollution and the depletion of nonrenewable resources will increase as the world's population grows. Migration of people to places that both do and do not welcome them will increase significantly in the future, and this can cause tension. According to UN estimates, by 2018, nearly 1 percent of the global population had expressed an intent to migrate, with an estimated 258 million people already migrating internationally across borders, compared to about 173 million in 2000, and 102 million in 1980.[93] Climate change is becoming the lead driver of migration, in connection with an increased frequency of weather-related disasters.[94]

In Assam, India, several thousand "unwelcome" immigrants were massacred in 1983. Wars have taken place in the past in which population played an important role and they will probably occur in the future. In the 1960s, a border war broke out between El Salvador and Honduras over "unwelcome"

Salvadorians in Honduras. In the 1990s, numerous brutal civil wars occurred in Africa. While we cannot identify population issues as the main cause of these conflicts, it is likely that increasing resource pressures made the ethnic conflicts more likely.

There are growing numbers of people in places facing increased populations competition and conflict over the scarce water. The most critical areas are the Middle East and North Africa, where the population more than tripled between 1960 and 2010, thus but the amount of water available per person did not. About 1 billion people today, mostly in rural areas, do not have access to safe drinking water. According to the United Nations, 700 million people in 43 countries already face severe water shortages.[95] In some of these regions, droughts have been common throughout history. What is not common in these regions is the population density that is present and projected. While water scarcity can obviously promote conflict, it also has the potential of promoting cooperation as nations are forced to devise ways to conserve and share scarce water. It is projected that by 2050, 1.5 billion people will still be living in areas with water scarcity, while one-half of the global population will live in water-stressed areas.[96]

Climate-fueled disasters are also affecting populations, which will be discussed in Chapter 6. An increase in the average global temperature could intensify the water cycle. There could be more rain in some locations but also more droughts.

Plate 3.7   A crowded train in Bangladesh

Source: World Bank.

One bright development is that the industrialized countries are learning to con-serve water and to use it more efficiently. Water use in the United States has actually declined about 20 percent since 1980. This decline came because of new water-saving technologies and practices such as less wasteful irrigation techniques and water-stingy toilets. (In the United States, toilets used about 6 gallons of water per flush. After a law passed by Congress in 1992 set new standards, new toilets now use 1.5 gallons per flush, a big reduction.) Japan has made major reductions in water use in its industry. Some of these water-saving practices have spread to other nations, including less wealthy ones.[97]

Conclusions

Early adopters of industrialization and medical technologies had more gradual declines in birth rates and death rates than other countries whose demographic transitions occurred once antibiotics and other technologies were more abundant and available. While the population in many (especially poorer) countries is still growing, it is actually relatively stable or even decreasing in many other countries. More economic growth has raised the living standards in some countries to a level where having more children has made it difficult to increase their living standards further. We see this happening in countries that have a high GNP or income per capita. At the same time, many other countries with lower GNPs continue to grow in population as they try to improve their living standards. But blanket statements are challenging, and regional variations are substantial – such as the projected dou-bling in population on the African continent in the coming decades. Overall, we find ourselves today with a relatively few countries considered "more developed" that have stopped growing in population, while the majority of countries – most of whom are relatively less wealthy – have higher growth rates that are contributing to a planet with unprecedented population growth.

To put all nations with a certain range of GNP or national income per capita in the category of "developing" or "less developed" does not help us understand the differ-ences that exist among countries regarding population growth. It is only when you look at a country's resources, health system, education policies, economic wealth *and* the social changes that are caused by or accompany that economic growth that you can begin to understand some of the differences among countries in terms of policies to control their birth rates.

We can use a more expansive concept of development to look at the efforts many countries are making today in lowering their birth rates. First of all, we know that economic growth that benefits the majority in a country, and not just a few, is associ-ated with lower population rates. As we have seen in this chapter, if the majority are receiving a higher standard of living, they tend to reduce the number of children a family has. And other parts of our definition of development help us evaluate why some countries are more deliberate than others in enacting policies to lower birth rates. And we also need to be considering population changes in the context of social (especially including education), cultural, and economic policies, including inequality, as explored in Chapter 2.

Looking over the statements by a number of population experts, they seem to share the conclusion that the Earth faces an overwhelming challenge with its current population growth of about 1 million people every four days, increasing economic inequalities, and growing stresses on planetary boundaries. This is a problem, along with climate change and the threat of nuclear weapons, which will be discussed later in this book, that has the potential for causing untold human misery. But many of these experts also emphasize that human thinking and governmental policies are starting to change and impressive reductions in birth rates are taking place in various countries around the world. We know how to reduce birth rates, and many countries have already transitioned to a stable or even shrinking population. But there are many places where population growth continues at exponential rates. And in these places in particular, whether and how governments and society provide for those with the least means is crucial in the wake of scarce resources.

Even if population growth were to halt immediately, the consumption habits of the world's population already demand more resources than the Earth can sustain. While population growth is slowing, the world is still expected to add billions more people in the coming decades, with societies that are increasingly adopting more resource-consumptive lifestyles. What is lacking at present is the political will to do what needs to be done to address the challenges associated with ever-shifting demographics. We will do it if we take seriously the warning given in a joint statement by the US National Academy of Sciences and its British counterpart, the Royal Society of London:

If current predictions of population growth prove accurate and patterns of human activity on the planet remain unchanged, science and technology may not be able to prevent either irreversible degradation of the environment or continued poverty for much of the world.[98]

Notes

1   UN Department of Economic and Social Affairs (DESA), Population Division, World Population Prospects: The 2012 Revision, at http://esa.un.org/unpd/wpp/unpp/panel_population.htm (accessed July 2015).

2   The nine countries are India, Nigeria, the Democratic Republic of the Congo, Pakistan, Ethiopia, Tanzania, United States, Uganda, and Indonesia. See David Roberts, "I'm an Environmental Journalist, but I Never Write about Overpopulation. Here's Why," Vox (July 11, 2018) at https://www.vox.com/energy-and-environment/2017/9/26/16356524/the-population-question (accessed January 2020).

3   E. Carlsen, A. Giwercman, N. Keiding, N. E. Skakkebaek, "Evidence for Decreasing Quality of Semen during Past 50 Years," *BMJ* (1992): 305 doi: https://doi.org/10.1136/bmj.305.6854.609 (published September 12, 1992).

4   UN DESA, "Preparing the world for important population changes" UN DESA News Volume 19, No.04 (April 2015), available at http://www.un.org/en/development/desa/

newsletter/desanews/feature/2015/04/index.html: "The 1.1 billion increase in global population over the next fifteen years is expected to occur in urban areas. Africa and Asia are projected to have the largest increases in urban populations so that the number of urban areas, as well as their absolute size will continue to grow" (accessed January 2020).

5   Adrian Edwards, "Global forced displacement hits record high," UNHCR (2016), available at https://www.unhcr.org/news/latest/2016/6/5763b65a4/global-forced-displacement-hits-record-high.html (finding 1/113 people is an asylum-seeker, internally displaced or a refugee) (accessed January 2020).

6   UN DESA, Population Division, World Population Prospects: The 2012 Revision, at http://esa.un.org/unpd/wpp/unpp/panel_population.htm (accessed July 2015).

7   UN DESA, Population Division (2017). World Population Prospects: The 2017 Revision, available at https://www.un.org/development/desa/publications/world-population-prospects-the-2017-revision.html (last accessed 23 January 2020).

8   Ibid. Custom data acquired via website.

9   UN General Assembly Report A/68/190, para. 38 (July 25, 2013), at http://www.un.org/en/ga/68/resolutions.shtml Report_A_68_190.pdf (accessed November 2018).

10   UN DESA, Population Division World Population Prospects: The 2017 Revision. Custom data acquired via website.

11   "Preparing the World for Important Population Changes" *UN DESA News*, 19 (04) (April 2015) http://www.un.org/en/development/desa/newsletter/desanews/feature/2015/04/index.html; see also Roberts, "I'm an Environmental Journalist, but I Never Write about Overpopulation. Here's Why."

12   UN DESA, Population Division, World Population Prospects: The 2012 Revision, p.3 (accessed July 2015).

13   UN DESA, Population Division, World Urbanization Prospects: The 2014 Revision, Highlights (ST/ESA/SER.A/352). See also UN Habitat, State of the World's Cities 2012/2013, p. 127, at https://sustainabledevelopment.un.org/content/documents/745habitat.pdf (accessed July 2015).

14   Edward Gargan, "On Meanest of Streets, Salvaging Useful Lives," *New York Times* (January 8, 1992), p. A2.

15   2050 data based on Daniel Hoornweg and Kevin Pope Socioeconomic Pathways and Regional Distribution of the World's 101 Largest Cities, *Global Cities Institute Working Paper No. 04 2014*. Accessible here: https://sites.uoit.ca/sustainabilitytoday/urban-and-energy-systems/Worlds-largest-cities/population-projections/city-population-2050.php (accessed January 2020).

16   UN DESA, Population Division, World Urbanization Prospects: The 2014 Revision, Highlights, p. 13.

17   Ibid., p. 26 –27, at http://esa.un.org/unpd/wup/Highlights/WUP2014-Highlights.pdf (accessed July 2015).

18   UN DESA Population Division, World Urbanization Prospects: The 2014 Revision, Highlights.

19   On Shenzhen: "City Climate Leadership Awards 2014: The Winners," at http://cityclimateleadershipawards.com/2014-ccla-winners/; UN Commission on Sustainable Development, *Electric Vehicles in the Context of Sustainable Development in China* (May 2–13, 2011), p. 26, at http://www.un.org/esa/dsd/resources/res_pdfs/csd-19/Background-Paper-9-China.pdf; United Nation Environment Department. *Cities of the future: the ultimate design challenge*. November 21. 2018. https://www.unenvironment.org/news-

and-stories/story/cities-future-ultimate-design-challenge (accessed December 18, 2018). C40 Cities, "Shenzhen: New Energy Vehicle Promotion," at http://www.c40.org/ profiles/2014-shenzhen (all accessed July 2015). On Buenos Aires: C40 Cities, "Buenos Aires: Solid Urban Waste Reduction Project," at http://cityclimateleadershipawards. com/2014-project-buenosaires-plan-integral/; Buenos Aires Ciudad, "Waste Management," at http://www.turismo.buenosaires.gob.ar/en/article/waste-management (both accessed July 2015). On Curitiba: Ali Soltani and Ehsan Sharifi, "A Case Study of Sustainable Urban Planning Principles in Curitiba (Brazil) and Their Applicability in Shiraz (Iran)," *International Journal of Development and Sustainability*, 1 (2012), p. 126; Robin Wright, "The Most Innovative City in the World," *Los Angeles Times* (June 3, 1996). Curitiba's accomplishments are also described in Jonas Rabinovitch and Josef Leitman, "Urban Planning in Curitiba," *Scientific American*, 274 (March 1996), pp. 46–53; Eugene Linden, "The Exploding Cities of the Developing World," *Foreign Affairs* (January/February 1996), p. 62; Arthur Lubow, "The Road to Curitiba," *New York Times Magazine* (May 20, 2007), pp. 76–83. World Resources Institute. *Cities in Focus | Curitiba, Brazil* Video: November 10, 2010. https://www.wri.org/resources/videos/cities-focus-curitiba-brazil (accessed December 19, 2018); Buenos Aires Cuidad. *Waste Management: We aim by 2017 to treat 75% of pre-landfill waste and markedly reduce overall waste sent to landfills.* https://turismo. buenosaires.gob.ar/en/article/waste-management (accessed December 19, 2018).

20   United Nation Environment Department. *Cities of the future: the ultimate design challenge.*

21   C40, *Case Study Shenzhen carbon emission trading system*, March 20, 2018. https://www. c40.org/case_studies/shenzhen-carbon-emission-trading-system (accessed December 16, 2018.)

22   Buenos Aires Cuidad. *Waste Management: We aim by 2017 to treat 75% of pre-landfill waste and markedly reduce overall waste sent to landfills.* https://turismo.buenosaires. gob.ar/en/article/waste-management (accessed December 19, 2018).

23   World Resources Institute. *Cities in Focus | Curitiba, Brazil* Video: November 10, 2010. https://www.wri.org/resources/videos/cities-focus-curitiba-brazil (accessed December 19, 2018).

24   UN DESA, Population Division, World Urbanization Prospects: The 2018 Revision, Key Facts. P1 paragraph 1.

25   Ibid.

26   UN DESA, Population Division, World Urbanization Prospects: The 2014 Revision, Highlights, p. 1.

27   Ibid.

28   Nancy E. Riley, "Gender, Power, and Population Change," *Population Bulletin*, 52 (May 1997), pp. 14–15; Sanjay Kumar, "India: Where Are All the Girls?" *The Diplomat* (August 27, 2013) at http://thediplomat.com/2013/08/india-where-are-all-the-girls/ (accessed July 2015). UN DESA, Population Division, World Population Prospects: The 2017 Revision. Sex ratio at birth (male births per female births) data tables including filters for India and year(s) 2015–2020. http://data.un.org/Data.aspx?d=PopDiv&f=variableID%3A52 (accessed December 19, 2018); Simon Denyer and Annie Gowen, "Too Many Men, " *Washington Post* (April 18, 2018) at https://www.washingtonpost.com/graphics/2018/ world/too-many-men/ (acccessed November 19, 2018).

29   UN DESA, Population Division, World Population Prospects: The 2017 Revision. Sex ratio at birth (male births per female births) data tables including filters for India and

year(s) 2015–2020 at http://data.un.org/Data.aspx?d=PopDiv&f=variableID%3A52 (accessed December 19, 2018).

30 Denyer and Gowen, "Too Many Men"; see also Ellen Barry and Celia W. Dugger, "India to Change Its Decades-Old Reliance on Female Sterilization" *The New York Times*, (February 20, 2016) https://www.nytimes.com/2016/02/21/world/asia/india-to-change-its-decades-old-reliance-on-female-sterilization.html.

31 Rebecca Ratcliffe, "Dowries a Major Contributor to India's Gender Imbalance, Researchers Find," *The Guardian* (September 28, 2018), citing Bhalotra, Sonia & Chakravarty, Abhishek & Gulesci, Selim, "The Price of Gold: Dowry and Death in India," CEPR Discussion Papers 12712, C.E.P.R. Discussion Papers (2018).

32 UN DESA, Population Division, World Population Prospects: The 2015 Revision, Key Findings and Advance Tables. Working Paper No. ESA/P/WP.241. P4 paragraph 2.

33 UN DESA, Trends in Contraceptive Use Worldwide: 2015, at http://www.un.org/en/development/desa/population/publications/pdf/family/trendsContraceptiveUse2015Report.pdf (accessed December 2018).

34 Preparing the world for important population changes" UN DESA News Volume 19, No.04 - April 2015 http://www.un.org/en/development/desa/newsletter/desanews/feature/2015/04/index.html?fbclid=IwAR2DbxHZ_5TyCmXziVPix4Va2Gw7h40hv93gGs2qCnNzyMBjAwY_7DJIyog#14262 (accessed January 2020).

35 UN DESA, Population Division, World Population Prospects: The 2012 Revision.

36 UN DESA, Population Divisio, World Population Prospects: The 2017 Revision, Key Findings and Advance Tables. Working Paper No. ESA/P/WP/248.

37 Fred Pearce, "Japan's Ageing Population Could Actually Be Good News," *New Scientist*, 221 (2951) (January 11, 2014), at http://www.newscientist.com/article/dn24822-japansageing-population-could-actually-be-good-news.html#.VQ9YmI54qtk (accessed July 2015).

38 Ibid.

39 United Nations. *Urban and rural population by age and sex*, version 3 (2014). p. 9.

40 Percentage of the population by age for urban and rural areas of countries in three development groups, 2015. *Source:* United Nations. *Urban and rural population by age and sex*, p. 9. Paragraph 19.

41 Milena Nikolova, "Two Solutions to the Challenges of Population Aging," Brookings (May 2, 2016), available https://www.brookings.edu/blog/up-front/2016/05/02/two-solutions-to-the-challenges-of-population-aging/ (accessed December 20, 2018).

42 UN DESA, Population Division, World Population Prospects: The 2012 Revision, vol. 1, p. 7.

43 Ibid.

44 UN DESA, Population Division, World Urbanization Prospects: The 2014 Revision, Highlights, p. 66.

45 Ibid., p. 65.

46 Ibid., p 68.

47 Dynamic graphs based on United Nations data: https://www.populationpyramid.net/europe/2100/ (accessed December 20, 2018).

48 Joseph A. McFalls Jr, "Population: A Lively Introduction," *Population Bulletin*, 46 (October 1991), p. 36. See also the third edition of this publication in *Population Bulletin*, 53 (September 1998), p. 42.

49 Europe population. Dynamic graphs based on United Nations data: https://www.populationpyramid.net/europe/2100/ (accessed December 20, 2018).

50 Kevin Kinsella, and David Phillips, "Global Aging: The Challenge of Success," *Population Bulletin*, 60 (March 2005), p. 15.

51 Bryan Robey, Shea Rutstein, and Leo Morris, "The Fertility Decline in Developing Countries," *Scientific American*, 269 (December 1993), p. 63.

52 Ibid., pp. 60–7. See also Susan Kalish, "Culturally Sensitive Family Planning: Bangladesh Story Suggests It Can Reduce Family Size," *Population Today*, 22 (February 1994), p. 5; Lina Parikh, "Spotlight: Bangladesh," *Population Today*, 26 (January 1998), p. 7; and Malcolm Potts, "The Unmet Need for Family Planning," *Scientific American*, 282 (January 2000), p. 91.

53 Worldmeters website. Bangladesh; Data table at http://www.worldometers.info/world-population/bangladesh-population/ Data references - Department of Economic and Social Affairs, Population Division. *World Population Prospects: The 2017 Revision. (Medium-fertility variant)* (accessed December 20, 2018.)

54 Robey, Rutstein, and Morris, "The Fertility Decline in Developing Countries," p. 65.

55 Ibid., p. 60.

56 A discussion of the political forces that were instrumental in the Reagan and Bush administrations in developing this policy and in keeping it in force for ten years is contained in Michael S. Teitelbaum, "The Population Threat," *Foreign Affairs* (Winter 1992/1993), pp. 63–78. The policy was reversed in 1994 when the Clinton administration took office but reinstated when Bush's son became President.

57 "Transitions in World Population," *Population Bulletin*, 59 (2004), p. 25.

58 *New York Times* (August 18, 1974), p. 2.

59 UN DESA, Trends in Contraceptive Use Worldwide: 2015; John Cleland et al., "Family Planning: The Unfinished Agenda" (2006), p. 1, at http://www.who.int/reproductivehealth/publications/general/lancet 3.pdf (accessed July 2015).

60 UN DESA, Population Division, Fertility Levels and Trends as Assessed in the 2012 Revision of World Population Prospects (2012), p. vii.

61 Ibid.

62 UN DESA, Trends in Contraceptive Use Worldwide: 2015.

63 Ibid.

64 UN GA Res. 65/234 (December 22, 2010), p. 1; UN Economic and Social Council, Commission on Population and Development, Report on the 47th Session, p. 12 (2014); Programme of Action, para. 14.11 (September 1994).

65 UN Population Fund, Financing the ICPD Programme of Action: Data for 2011 Estimates for 2012/2013, Projections for 2014 (2013), p. 2, at http://www.unfpa.org/publications/financing-icpd-programme-action (accessed July 2015).

66 Population Reference Bureau, 2010 World Population Data Sheet (2010).

67 Worldmeters website. Mexico; Data table at http://www.worldometers.info/world-population/mexico-population/ reference – UN DESA, Population Division, World Population Prospects: The 2017 Revision (Medium-fertility variant) (accessed December 20, 2018).

68 UN DESA, Population Division, World Population Prospects: The 2012 Revision, vol. 1, p. 3.

69 Ellen Barry and Celia W. Dugger, "India to Change Its Decades-Old Reliance on Female Sterilization," *The New York Times* (February 20, 2016), at https://www.nytimes.com/2016/02/21/world/asia/india-to-change-its-decades-old-reliance-on-female-sterilization.html.

70 Ibid. See also UN DESA, Population Division, World Population Prospects: The 2012 Revision, vol. 1, p.3.

71 UN DESA, Population Division, World Population Prospects: The 2012 Revision.

72 Worldmeters website. China; Data table at http://www.worldometers.info/world-population/china-population/ Data references - Department of Economic and Social

Affairs, Population Division. World Population Prospects: The 2017 Revision (Medium-fertility variant).

73   Elisabeth Rosenthal, "Rural Flouting of One-Child Policy Undercuts China's Census," *New York Times* (April 14, 2000), p. A10.

74   Ibid.

75   Rosenthal, "Rural Flouting of One-Child Policy Undercuts China's Census."

76   Susan Scutti, "One-Child Policy Is One Big Problem for China," *Newsweek* (January 23, 2014) at http://www.newsweek.com/2014/01/24/one-child-policy-one-big-problem-china-245118.html (accessed July 2015).

77   Nancy E. Riley, "Gender, Power, and Population Change," *Population Bulletin*, 52 (May 1997), p. 39.

78   UN DESA, Population Division, World Contraceptive Use 2009, at http://www.un.org/esa/population/publications/contraceptive2009/contraceptive2009.htm (accessed July 2015).

79   Colin McMahon, "In Brazil, Abortion Illegal but Common," *Chicago Tribune* (November 1, 2006).

80   Mary Mederios Kent, "Shrinking Societies Favor Procreation," *Population Today*, 27 (December 1999), pp. 4–5.

81   UN DESA, Population Division (2017). World Population Prospects: The 2017 Revision, custom data acquired via website.

82   Ibid.

83   Worldmeters website. United Kingdom; Data table at http://www.worldometers.info/world-population/uk-population/. United Kingdom Population Forecast Data references - Department of Economic and Social Affairs, Population Division. World Population Prospects: The 2017 Revision (Medium-fertility variant) (accessed December 20, 2018).

84   G. Tyler Miller Jr, *Living in the Environment: Principles, Connections, and Solutions*, 8th edn (Belmont, CA: Wadsworth, 1994), p. 153.

85   E. Vernon Laux, "In a Vast Hungry Wave, Owls Are Moving South," *New York Times* (March 8, 2005), p. D2; Peter Hudson and Ottar Bjornstad, "Vole Stranglers and Lemming Cycles," *Science*, 302 (October 31, 2003), p. 797.

86   Edward J. Kormondy, *Concepts of Ecology*, 2nd edn (Englewood Cliffs, NJ: Prentice-Hall, 1976), pp. 111–12; D. Botkin, "A New Balance of Nature," *The Wilson Quarterly* (Spring, 1991), pp. 61–63.

87   Joel E. Cohen, *How Many People Can the Earth Support?* (New York: W. W. Norton, 1995).

88   Paul R. Ehrlich, Anne H. Ehrlich, and John P. Holdren, *Ecoscience: Population, Resources, Environment* (New York: W. H. Freeman, 1977), p. 716.

89   Julian L. Simon, *The Ultimate Resource* (1981), later updated as The Ultimate Resource 2 (Princeton: Princeton University Press, 1998). See also Julian L. Simon, *Population Matters: People, Resources, Environment, and Immigration* (Piscataway, NJ: Transaction, 1990).

90   Michael S. Teitelbaum, "The Population Threat," *Foreign Affairs* (Winter 1992/1993), pp. 71–72.

91   An interesting wager that Ehrlich and Simon made about whether the world's growing population was running out of natural resources (and which was won by Simon) is reported in John Tierney, "Betting the Planet," *New York Times Magazine* (December 2, 1990), pp. 52–81.

92 Joel E. Cohen, "Human Population Grows Up," *Scientific American,* 293 (September 2005), p. 55.

93 International Organization for Migration, Global Migration Indicators (2018), at https://publications.iom.int/system/files/pdf/global_migration_indicators_2018.pdf (accessed December 2018).

94 Euan McKirdy, "Climate Change Could Create 143 Million Migrants, World Bank Says," CNN (March 20, 2018) at https://www.cnn.com/2018/03/20/world/world-bank-climate-migrants-report-intl/index.html (accessed January 2020)

95 UN Water, "Water for Life Decade – Water Scarcity," at http://www.un.org/waterforlifedecade/scarcity.shtml (accessed July 2015).

96 Lorraine Chow, "1.5 Billion People Could Have Poor Access to Water by 2050, UN Warns" *EcoWatch* (March 19, 2018), https://www.ecowatch.com/global-water-access-quality-2549813548.html (accessed January 2020); Water, "Water Scarcity Fact Sheet," at ibid.; World Health Organization, "Water Fact Sheet No. 391" (June 2015), at http://www.who.int/mediacentre/factsheets/fs391/en/ (accessed July 2015).

97 Peter Gleick, "Safeguarding Our Water," *Scientific American*, 284 (February 2001), pp. 38–45.

98 "A Warning on Population," *Christian Science Monitor* (March 24, 1992), p. 20.

Further Reading

Benko, Jessica. "How a Warming Planet Drives Human Migration," *New York Times* (April 19, 2017), at https://www.nytimes.com/2017/04/19/magazine/how-a-warming-planet-drives-human-migration.html (accessed December 2018).

Cohen, Joel E., "Human Population Grows Up," *Scientific American*, 293 (September 2005), pp. 48–55. A relatively short summary of where we are at present and the challenges humanity faces as the Earth moves to a new stage of life.

Denyer, Simon and Gowen, Annie. "Too Many Men," *The Washington Post* (April 18, 2018), at https://www.washingtonpost.com/graphics/2018/world/too-many-men/ (accessed December 2018).

De Souza, Roger-Mark, John Williams, and Frederick Meyerson, "Critical Links: Population, Health, and the Environment," *Population Bulletin*, 58 (September 2003). Three critical questions about population, health, and the environment are examined. First, the relationships among the three; second, how these relationships affect human well-being; and third, what communities and policymakers can do about these situations.

Kent, Mary M., and Sandra Yin, "Controlling Infectious Diseases," *Population Bulletin*, 61 (June 2006). We know how to control most serious infectious diseases but infectious microbes continue to evolve, requiring new methods and new drugs. This article includes special short sections on diarrheal diseases, malaria, tuberculosis, and the next pandemics.

Kinsella, Kevin, and David Phillips, "Global Aging: The Challenge of Success," *Population Bulletin*, 60 (March 2005). Kinsella and Phillips examine the causes of global aging and the changes it will bring to society. They also explore various public policies related to this development.

Livi-Bacci, Massimo, *A Concise History of World Population: An Introduction to Population Processes*, 5th edn (Oxford: Blackwell, 2012). A readable history of the growth of the human population from prehistoric times to the present. The author takes a position in between that of the optimists and those predicting a catastrophe; he presents an alternative way to understand and deal with population growth.

Longman, Phillip, "The Global Baby Bust," *Foreign Affairs*, 83 (May/June 2004), pp. 64– 79. Longman does not believe that overpopulation is one of the worst dangers facing the world. Rather he argues that an aging population and falling birth rates, which we see now in many rich countries and some developing countries, should be our major concern.

McCirdy, Euan. "Climate change could create 143 million migrants, World Bank says." CNN (March 20, 2018), at https://www.cnn.com/2018/03/20/world/world-bank-climate-migrants-report-intl/index.html (accessed December 2018).

Oduh, Chika, "Report: African Population Boom + Poverty = Dangerous Mix," VOA News (August 25, 2016), at https://www.voanews.com/a/africa-population-poverty-family-planning/3480454.html (accessed December 2018).

O'Neill, Brian, and Deborah Balk, "World Population Futures," *Population Bulletin*, 56 (September 2001). This publication looks closely at population projections, how they are made, and their uncertainties. Based on these projections, the authors discuss what kind of world is likely in the future.

Peters, Adele. "Watch The Movements Of Every Refugee On Earth Since The Year 2000," Fast Company (May 31, 2017), at https://www.fastcompany.com/40423720/watch-the-movements-of-every-refugee-on-earth-since-the-year-2000 (accessed December 2018).

Picheta, Rob. "Spain to lead Japan in global life expectancy, US continues to slide." CNN (October 18, 2018), at https://edition.cnn.com/2018/10/17/health/life-expectancy-forecasts-study-intl/index.html?no-st=1543093669 (accessed December 2018).

Population Connection, World Population Video (2015), at https://vimeo.com/130468614 (accessed December 2018).

Potts, Malcolm, "The Unmet Need for Family Planning," *Scientific American*, 282 (January 2000), pp. 88–93. The author argues that falling birth rates have led some people to declare that overpopulation is no longer a threat, but it recently took just 12 years to add an additional billion people to the Earth. Many people still lack access to contraceptives. Unless they are given access to these, severe environmental and health problems will occur in large parts of the world in the twenty-first century.

Roberts, David. "I'm an environmental journalist, but I never write about overpopulation. Here's why." By David Roberts Updated, Vox July 11, 2018 https://www.vox.com/energy-and-environment/2017/9/26/16356524/the-population-question

Rogers, Peter, "Facing the Freshwater Crisis," *Scientific American*, 299 (August 2008), pp. 46–53. As world population increases, its need for fresh water as well as that of industry and agriculture soar. Yet with climate change, supplies of fresh water are becoming unpredictable. The article shows how existing technologies can be used to avert a water crisis if governments take action now.

Sanderson, Warren, and Sergei Scherbov, "Rethinking Age and Aging," *Population Bulletin*, 63 (December 2008). Demographers and policymakers have often not taken into account the fact that older people today are generally more active and healthier than in previous generations. New measures presented in this article take life expectancy differences into account.

Taylor, Adam, "The 11 countries expected to shrink dramatically this century," *The Washington Post* (August 11, 2015), at https://www.washingtonpost.com/news/worldviews/wp/2015/08/11/the-11-countries-expected-to-shrink-dramatically-this-century.

UN DESA, "Preparing the world for important population changes" UN DESA News Volume 19, No.04 (April 2015), at http://www.un.org/en/development/desa/newsletter/desanews/feature/2015/04/index.html

Wan He, Daniel Goodkind, and Paul Kowal U.S. Census Bureau, International Population Reports, P95/16-1, An Aging World: 2015, U.S. Government Publishing Office, Washington, DC,2016.

Chapter 4

Food[1]

---

1   Jason Farr contributed substantially to the research and updates reflected in this edition. Please reflect his contribution in any direct citation to this chapter.

Global Issues: An Introduction, Sixth Edition. Kristen A. Hite and John L. Seitz.
© 2021 John Wiley & Sons Ltd. Published 2021 by John Wiley & Sons Ltd.

The day that hunger is eradicated from the earth, there will be the greatest spiritual explosion the world has ever known.
                    Federico García Lorca (1898–1936), Spanish poet and dramatist

One way a civilization can be judged is by its success in reducing suffering. Development can also be judged in this way. Is it reducing the misery that exists in the world? Throughout human history, hunger has caused untold suffering. Because food is a basic necessity, when it is absent or scarce humans need to spend most of their efforts trying to obtain it; if they are not successful in finding adequate food, they suffer, and can eventually die. In this chapter we will look at hunger and also at how their levels of development affects the food people eat.

How Many Are Hungry?

According to the FAO, as of 2017, world hunger is on the rise, with nearly 821 million people estimated to be chronically undernourished, meaning they receive insufficient food on a regular basis to maintain a normal and healthy life. About 11 percent of people across the world are undernourished.[1] By region, the FAO figures show that in sub-Saharan Africa, 23.2 percent of the population is undernourished, as are about 15 percent of those in South Asia, 7 percent in Oceania (a 50% improvement in recent years), 8.9 percent in East Asia and Southeast Asia, 11.3 percent in West Asia, 6.2 percent in Central Asia, about 5.4 percent in Latin America, and 16.5 percent in the Caribbean.[2]

The World Health Organization (WHO) estimates that globally about 151 million children under 5 have stunted growth and 51 million have low weight for their height. More than one-third of the children in South Asia and East Africa have stunted growth.[3] The percentage of hungry people is decreasing in most of the major regions in the developing world but the actual number of hungry people has stayed the same or even increased in some areas. In particular, the percentage of the population who were hungry increased in West Asia from 1990 to 2016, and sub-Saharan Africa has seen some progress in terms of percentage reductions but is the only area in the world where the prevalence of hunger is over 20 percent.[4]

The world economic crises that occurred in 2008–2009 and 2020 hurt efforts to reduce global hunger. The FAO concluded that for the first time in decades, because

Food

Table 4.1 Percentage of undernourished people by region

Region	Percentage Undernourished	Number Undernourished
Sub-Saharan Africa	23.2	236,500,000
South Asia and Central Asia	14.5%	281,600,000
Oceania	7	2,800,000
East Asia and Southeast Asia	8.9	281,600,000
West Asia and North Africa	10.0	50,100,000
Latin America and Caribbean	6.1	39,300,000

Source: Food and Agriculture Organization, The State of Food Insecurity in the World: 2018.

of the crisis, both the absolute number and the proportion of malnourished people as increased."[5] In 2010, the FAO found that over 1 billion people went hungry in 2009, an increase from the previous decade which could be explained "not as a result of poor harvests but because of high food prices, lower incomes and increasing unemployment due to the economic crisis."[6]

Who are the hungry and where do they live? The answer to the first question is that, according to World Bank estimates, 80 percent are women and children.[7] Except for parts of Africa, actual starvation is uncommon in the present world. A much larger number of people die today because of malnutrition, a malnutrition that weakens them and makes them susceptible to many diseases. Children die from diarrhea in poor countries – a situation nearly unheard of in rich countries – partly because of their weakened condition.

In the year 2017, the FAO estimated about 515.1 million hungry people lived in Asia, 256.5 million lived in Africa, 39.3 million lived in Latin America and the Caribbean, and 2.8 million lived in Oceania.[8] This is due in large part to conflict, poverty, climate change, and factors related to who controls land and government policies (or lack thereof) impacting access to food. While most of the absolute numbers of people going hungry are increasing, there are indications that the number of hunger related deaths in the world has decreased during the past 30 years. In the mid-1980s, an estimated 15 million people were dying each year from hunger-related causes.[9] One estimate is that in the early 2000s about 200,000 people died yearly during famines, while about 11 million people died early from hunger-related causes.[10] Five million of these were reported to be children.[11] By 2011, an estimated 3.1 million children per year were dying of hunger – and almost half (45 percent) were under five years of age.[12]

World Food Production

How much food is produced in the world at present? Is there enough for everyone? The answer, which may surprise you, is that yes, there is enough. Food production has kept up with population growth. At the beginning of the twenty-first century, food supplies were about 25 percent higher per person than they were in the early 1960s and the real price of food (taking inflation into account) was about 40 percent lower.[13] Impressive gains were made in the poorest nations during that timeframe, where the average daily food calories available per person rose from about 1,900 to 2,700. (What was available for consumption does not indicate what individuals actually consumed.) In wealthy countries the average daily calorie supply increased from about 3,000 to 3,300 during the same period.[14] Enough food was available at the beginning of the twenty-first century to provide every person with more than 2,350 calories, the amount needed daily for a healthy and active life. But that does not mean every individual person had enough food, or could afford to eat. In the first decade of the new century, food prices rose sharply. After peaking in 2011, at just over 150 percent of 2000 prices, food prices declined gradually by February 2015 to a level that remains roughly double that of 2000.[15]

Over the past four decades, the world's output of major food crops increased significantly – the most dramatic increase happening in the production of cereals – as improved seeds, irrigation, fertilizers, and pesticides were used to increase production and new land was cultivated. Sometimes referred to as the "Green Revolution," most of this growth in production came from an increase in yield per acre rather than from an increase in the amount of cropland. In 2014, the average grain yield was just over 3.5 tons (3,657 kilograms) per hectare, almost four times what it was in 1960.[16] This impressive performance was counterbalanced, however, by the rapid growth of population also taking place in the world at this time.

Arable land

About 10 percent of the Earth's land free of ice the arable land can be cultivated. Experts estimate that about one-half of the arable land is presently being used for agriculture. The planet is facing a massive loss of arable land due to agricultural practices, urban area expansion, and climate change. This is leading to dramatic rates of loss of land from erosion, desertification, salinization, and waterlogging.

Between 1998–2013, agricultural lands lost 20% of their productivity.[17] Globally, between 1 and 6 billion hectares of land are degraded, meaning they are substantially less productive than they once were – sometimes at the brink of collapse.[18] One study found that one-third of Earth's agricultural lands have been acutely degraded.[19]

Nature makes soil very slowly – under normal agricultural conditions it takes from 200 to 1,000 years to form 2.5 centimeters of topsoil. While inputs like compost or fertilizer can provide a temporary boost to topsoil, more intense weather patterns and land use changes can quickly destroy it. Industrial agriculture can also be a part of the problem: by one estimate, about one-third of land degradation is due to industrial agriculture techniques that degrade the land.[20] An estimated 24 billion tons of topsoil is lost annually.[21] Dirt can migrate quickly: one Cornell University biologist has observed regular cases of Chinese soil migrating across the Pacific, and African soils migrating across the Atlantic during their ploughing times.[22]

Erosion is one culprit for loss of arable land, especially in areas prone to hard rains and long dry spells. Further, inadequate drainage of irrigated land can lead to waterlogging (an excessive amount of water remaining in the soil) or to salinization (toxic salts deposited on poorly drained land). It has been estimated that about 5 percent of all irrigated land seriously suffers from salinization and about 15 percent from waterlogging.[23]

Globally, about one third of agricultural land is estimated to have been acutely degraded by human activities. A situation in many countries that adversely affects their ability to produce enough food for their people is the loss of prime farmland, primarily to urban expansion and housing developments. At the beginning of the twenty-first century, the United States was losing about 2 acres of farmland every minute because of development: it was being covered over by houses, roads, shopping malls, factories, and by general urban sprawl. While the amount lost was small compared to the amount of actual and potential cropland in the US, the land lost was often prime farmland, including some of the best fruit orchards, and could be replaced only by marginal land, which was not as fertile, was more open to erosion, and was more costly to use. One-half of the lost farmland was carved into ten-acre lots, many probably for homes for the wealthy.[24]

As more people move to cities, the problem of urban sprawl devouring prime cropland is occurring across the globe. One study projects that by 2030, urban areas globally will triple in size, eating further into productive cropland. This has major implications for Africa and Asia, where 80% of the global cropland loss due to urbanization is projected to take place.[25] Although more people in wealthy nations live in urban areas than do in the rest of the world (about 75 percent compared to 40 percent), urbanization is increasing faster in the rest of the world than in the more wealthy countries.[26]

Climate

Experts are in general agreement that the Earth's climate is changing, and the global climate will continue getting warmer in the future. It is not easy to predict precisely how this will affect agriculture in specific places, but experts generally agree that climate change is increasingly compromising food security. Warming temperatures and shifting rains could make conditions worse for the growing of food in some countries and better in others, but on average the impact is both negative and significant.

While the Green Revolution dominated food development initiatives for decades, the current focus is now "Climate Smart Agriculture," a poorly defined but widely used term to reflect shifting practices in response to climate change. Climate Smart Agriculture has roughly two dimensions: first, help improve resilience of cultivations in the face of climate impacts; and second, reduce the greenhouse gas emissions from the agriculture sector. It is now understood that global temperature rise of even a half degree of warming dramatically impacts climate yields.[27] At already 1°C of warming, the Intergovernmental Panel on Climate Change has already found evidence of climate-induced migration due to impacts to agriculture.[28] And as temperatures rise from 1.5 to 2°C, the IPCC says the risk of crop failure to major commodities like corn and wheat rises from moderate to high in many regions.[29] Climate Smart Agriculture is a trend in international development that seeks to respond to this. Critics say that the term is simply repackaging some of the problematic Green Revolution approaches, while supporters cite the climate crisis as demanding increased response.

Due to climate change, there will be more variability in rainfall and extreme weather events than there has been in the recent past. The climate over the past several decades in the United States and Canada has been unusually good for agriculture, but in the coming decades yields may suffer. The US National Academy of Sciences estimates that for every 1°C (1.8°F) rise in temperature above the norm, there will be a 10 percent decrease in rice, wheat, and corn yields.[30] A greater variability of climate (higher and lower extremes of temperature and higher and lower amounts of rainfall) will probably lower agricultural production around the world, especially in light of the large amounts of marginal land now being used for agriculture. On this land – such as parts of the American West, the Canadian West, and the Russian East – a slight reduction in rainfall or a slightly shorter growing season can spell the difference between a good harvest and little or no harvest. A warmer world is apt to have less organic material in its soils as vital nutrients decompose.

The world's leading climate scientists (the Intergovernmental Panel on Climate Change) has found that climate change is already reducing wheat and maize yields globally, and further that food prices will continue to spike following extreme weather events in key producing regions.[31] While climate impacts vary across regions, overall negative impacts are predicted to outweigh any positive changes such as those associated with a longer growing season.[32] Please refer to Chapter 6 for additional discussion on climate change.

How Development Affects Food

As a nation develops, major changes start to take place in its agriculture. At present, many countries – especially those in Africa, Asia, and parts of Latin America – still subscribe to a twentieth-century development model for agriculture that embraces green revolution technologies. That said, other countries have taken different approaches, some of which we will consider in more detail below.

Industrial agriculture produces an impressive amount of food. An increasingly small number of increasingly large farms produce so much food that huge amounts of important crops such as corn, wheat, and soybeans are exported. Much of this abundance has come since World War II. At first, increased demand for farm products, along with government price supports, enabled farmers to replace old sources of power (horses and mules, then the steam engine) with new sources (gasoline engines and electric-powered machinery). Then farming began to use improved seeds, fertilizers, and chemicals to control pests – collectively known as "inputs" alongside increased mechanization and its associated energy consumption. The investments and costs of these inputs favored large-scale production over smaller scale traditional practices.

Dramatic increases in farm productivity followed in a matter of decades, and farmers were increasingly replaced by machines. Populations began shifting from rural to urban areas, and office and factory jobs become more common as fewer people farmed. Farms and agriculture businesses consolidated and became more corporate and industrial.

A key feature of industrial agriculture is in the consolidation of wealth and power associated with an increase in the size of farms and a simultaneous reduction in their number. The growth of what has become known as "agribusiness" – farms run like a big business – has meant an increased concentration of control over the production of food in the hands of larger companies instead of smaller, traditional growers. Even in industrialized countries where corporate farming dominates the market share, there are considerable subsidies as well as competition in agriculture. As a result, food in wealthy economies remains a relatively small portion of family incomes, while in poor rural areas it is often the bulk of economic activity at both a household and community level.[33]

United States: Industrial Agriculture and Farm Consolidation

The US was one of the earliest and broadest adopters of industrial agriculture. In the United States up to the 1900s, the government's policy was mainly to encourage farm production, but since the 1950s the policy has been directed mainly at managing an excess of production. The basic policy has been to prop up farm incomes by using price supports, by purchasing surpluses, and by paying farmers to grow controlled quantities. During the 1950s and 1960s, the policy of the US (and Canadian) governments was to buy up farm surpluses, a process that led to huge public reserves. Food from this reserve often was given or sold to poor nations. Food released from the public reserve during bad harvest years helped stabilize world food prices. More recently, the US government has moved away from a food reserve approach and instead encouraged and supported the export of US farm products to other nations.

Impressively, US farm output increased nearly 160 percent over a 70-year period.[34] Since World War II there has been a doubling of average US farm size but also a 60 percent decrease in the number of farms as the mechanization of American agriculture increased production and more people pursued nonfarm employment. Small, family-run farms declined dramatically in terms of market share.[35] By 1990, farmers represented only about 2 percent of the US population, down from about 30 percent in 1920. By 2000, American farmers were producing twice the output they had in 1930 with only one-third the number of farms.[36] In

Table 4.2 Number and size of US farms, 1940–2010

Year	Number of farms	Average size of farms (acres)
1940	6,400,000	170
1950	5,600,000	210
1960	4,000,000	300
1970	2,900,000	370
1980	2,400,000	430
1990	2,100,000	460
2000	2,200,000	440
2010	2,200.000	418

Source: Data from *Statistical Abstract of the United States* (Washington, DC: US Bureau of the Census, 1970, 1992, 2006, 2012), p. 582 (1970), p. 644 (1992), p. 548 (2006).

2015, large-scale family farms contributed 42% of the total value of farm production while making up only 2.9% of US farms. Conversely, small family operations made up 90 percent of US farms but only accounted for 24% of farm production value.[37] Table 4.2 shows how US farm size and numbers have changed from 1940 to 2010 as industrial agriculture increasingly displaced a more distributed array of smaller family farms.

The loss of farmland to development in the United States accelerated at the end of the twentieth century. While the population of the country grew about 15 percent from 1982 to 1997, the amount of land turned into urban areas grew nearly 50 percent. This resulted in the loss of 13 million acres of cropland, 14 million acres of pastureland, and 12 million acres of rangeland. The amount of forest land remained unchanged. Much of this loss in the United States came not only because of the sprawl of suburbs near large cities, but also because of the urban sprawl of small and medium-sized cities.[38]

Due to production-driven incentives, the United States has become the world's leading exporter of food. Many have complained that large subsidy payments by the US government and the European Union to their farmers have made it difficult for farmers in poorer nations to compete. Governments offer subsidies to exports to help stabilize the economics of industrial agriculture (which benefit most from large-scale production) and to address trade imbalances. Many nations depend on agricultural exports to boost their national incomes; far more rely on a distributed network of small farmers to feed rural households. Subsidy payments in the United States were originally designed to protect the small family farm by boosting low agricultural prices, but instead the largest farms have benefited the most. At the beginning of the twenty-first century, the top 10 percent of agricultural producers were receiving 79 percent of the subsidies. In 2016, small farmers received less than one-third of total commodity payments.[39]

As an industrial economic model began to take its toll, the United States faced serious security and environmental problems caused by its reliance on oil from the Middle East. In the first decade of the new century, it supported diverting large amounts of corn and other grains to produce ethanol for its cars, up to 30–40 percent of the US corn crop by the second decade. In 2017, 30 percent of the US corn harvests were used to make ethanol, up from 25 percent in 2009.[40] Diverting large volumes of corn for fuel has become one of the factors contributing to high food prices throughout the world.[41] Efforts to address climate change through bioenergy carbon capture and storage is likely to increase competition for arable land in the coming years.

The population of the United States comprises approximately 4 percent of the world population, yet the average American has the same ecological footprint as 8 people living in India.[42] That statement, more than any other, presents the main argument of those who maintain that there is no way the rest of the world can adopt the agricultural methods or consumer-oriented culture dominant in the United States.

Brazil: Becoming a Food Exporter by Expanding the Agricultural Frontier

Brazil followed a similar path as the United States in converting to industrial agricultural methods, and quickly became a leading major exporter of foods. With a relatively modest application of inputs, Brazil discovered that at least over the short term, it could quadruple or even quintuple yields of grains and other commodities.[43] It supported policies that deforested land for pasture and agriculture, particularly in the Amazon, where more than 60 percent of cleared land was used to grow cattle.[44] In the early 1990s there were 20–30 million cattle in the Amazon, but that number tripled in less than three decades.[45] By 2003 it was the largest exporter of beef, which fueled the high deforestation rates.

Though most notorious for its beef production, Brazil claims more than a dozen commodities for which it is one of the world's top ten producer countries.[46] Using scientific research, Brazil has created varieties of crops that can grow in the tropical and savannah soils in its vast interior that were formerly considered poor for crops. Argentina and Uruguay have also substantially increased production, and climate change may further increase their share of their agricultural exports over the coming decades as the growing season gets longer – at least before climate impacts become too destabilizing.

China: Limited Land to Grow, Many Mouths to Feed

China, with 1.4 billion people but only about 7 percent of the world's arable land, offers a case study in measures to improve grain yields, particularly rice. The size of the average farm in China is only about 2.5 acres, vastly smaller than the average of

400 acres in the United States and the large new farms in Brazil.[47] China, reluctant to become dependent on the US and other countries for its food, struggles to produce enough food for its large population.

China under Mao Zedong emphasized agriculture instead of industrialization after the "Great Leap Forward" (a crash program of economic development), which occurred at the same time as famine conditions in the late 1950s and early 1960s. Since then, China has achieved impressive increases in its agricultural production, but because of its population growth rate, the increase in food has barely kept pace with the increased population. In the late 1990s, China produced a record amount of grain and was an exporter. But rapid urbanization and industrialization led to the loss of large amounts of farmland and increased water scarcity. This, along with other factors, led to China's net import of cereal grains in 2013 reaching almost 20 million metric tons.[48]

Rice: The World's Most Popular Staple Crop

About one-half of the world's people eat rice daily. Rice is the most important food for about 3 billion of the world's people, including many of its poorest. Global rice production exceeded 500 million tons in 2018 – an all-time high.[49] China and India were the biggest producers and also some of the biggest consumers, but rice is a big crop consumed globally – accounting for roughly one-third of grain consumption in Africa.[50] China alone needs 500 million tons of grain annually and has planted nearly 30 million hectares of rice per year to feed its population of over one billion people.[51] This amounts to an average output capacity of about 6.5 tons of rice per hectare.[52]

In 2002, a team of Chinese government scientists teamed up with a private Swiss biotech company to improve nutrition and yield properties of rice by altering the genetic code of two common varieties of rice.[53] China released version two of its high-yield hybrid rice in 2006, generating 9 tons of rice per hectare, and then started work on version three to yield 13.5 tons of rice per hectare.[54]

Among the total acreage of rice fields in China, hybrid rice accounts for about 57 percent, and hybrid rice is about 20 percent more productive than traditional rice. But even more productive varieties are still subject to climate shocks, such as in the summer of 2009 when the grain output dropped to about 123 million tons due to difficult climate conditions, including strong rainfalls in the south during the harvest season, droughts in northern grain areas, and persistent low temperatures in the south.[55]

By 2014, China had identified 120 million hectares of arable land as the minimum required to ensure food security, just under the estimated 133 million hectares of arable land within the country after deducting land dedicated to forest or pasture restoration, and land deemed too polluted to be used for farming.[56] At the same time, the government shifted its focus from grain production to meat, vegetables, and fruit.[57] The government retained ownership of the land while giving farmers more of a choice in what and how to grow and sell their food.[58]

Even though the government also made efforts to protect the environment, its actions directed toward increasing agricultural production led to an increased strain on the land. For example, China's widespread use of a plastic film to help protect 20 million hectares of soil ("polyethelene mulch") has caused significant pollution to the land.[59] Significant damage to the environment came from the efforts to increase the amount of agricultural land. Forests were cut down and marginal pasture land was converted to land for crops. Significant losses of arable land continue because of the expansion of cities and industries, soil erosion, desertification, and deforestation.

As of 2018, China had lost significant amounts of arable land to industrial pollution, construction, and growing practices.[60] Hunger is certainly less of a problem in China today – but the costs have been high. Experts are divided on whether China will be able to feed itself in the future without importing large amounts of food, which would affect the world food market.[61] Some have suggested that Chinese-supported efforts to grow food in other countries as a key part of the strategy to meet rising demand.[62]

Feeding a Growing Population

Overall, food production has increased rapidly enough so that the output of food in the world has generally kept up with population growth, despite periodic food crises in certain regions. There was a decline in per capita food output in the former Soviet Union after the collapse of that country in 1991 and in sub-Saharan Africa from the mid-1970s because of low production in agriculture (which was caused in part by droughts, civil wars, and nonsupportive government policies) and because of very rapid population growth. While food production overall has kept up with population growth, the production practices popularized in the twentieth century have presented all sorts of challenges. We will now explore various dimensions of these challenges – as well as potential solutions – from the perspectives of farmers, companies, governments, and consumers.

Large industrial farms can produce massive harvests of 100 million tomatoes, but there are trade-offs to this kind of food production model, as we shall see below. What is the reason for this significant increase in production? There are many reasons, of course, but basically it is because commercial agriculture has become mechanized and scientific. Production has soared with the widespread use of specialized seeds combined with generous amounts of fertilizer, pesticides, heavy machinery, and irrigation.

The "Green" Revolution

The widespread adoption of technology supporting industrial-scale agriculture has been called the Green Revolution, which refers to enhanced food productivity as opposed to environmental benefits. This technological transition is most commonly associated with two key components: the use of new seeds, especially for wheat, rice, and corn; and the use of various "inputs," such as fertilizer, irrigation, and pesticides. The new seeds, developed over decades of cross-pollination and engineering, are highly responsive to fertilizer. If they receive sufficient fertilizer and water, and if pests are kept under control, the seeds produce high yields. The introduction of this agricultural technology in the mid-1960s brought greatly increased harvests of wheat and impressive increases in rice production in a number of Asian countries. Over a six-year period, India doubled its wheat production and Pakistan did nearly as well. Significant increases of rice production occurred in the Philippines, Sri Lanka, Indonesia, and Malaysia. Mexico's wheat and corn production tripled in only two decades. From 1960 to 2016, annual grain production around the world increased from approximately 823.5 million tons to 2.85 billion tons.[63] Not only were the harvests much larger, but multiple harvests – in some places up to three per year – became possible because of the faster maturing of the plants.

The overall economics of food are complicated and depend on diverse factors such as government subsidies, cultural practices, land tenure policies, and broader market forces.

Increased food production initially led to lower food prices globally.[64] These lower prices enabled many people – especially in less wealthy countries – to increase their calorie intake, thus leading to better health and longer life expectancy. But food prices spiked during the 2008–9 global recession and remained higher than before. This has spurred increased attention to agriculture and food price policies, particularly in Africa – including a renewed commitment to dedicate 10 percent of foreign assistance budgets to agriculture and a new kind of "Green Revolution" for the continent.

Between 1950 and 1990, grain production per acre increased about 2 percent per year, more than population growth, but then dropped to about 1 percent annually, less than population growth.[65] With its population continuing to grow, in the mid-2000s India had to import wheat for its grain stockpile in order to maintain desired stock buffers, something it had not had to do for many years.[66] Increased domestic production and enhanced stockpiles of wheat in India subsequently reversed this trend, and now economic conditions favor domestic production over imports.[67]

There are now indications that grain production is slowing down. Part of the problem the Green Revolution is now facing is that fertilizers, pesticides, and specialized seeds are expensive, and in many cases require either national or international support in order to be viable. Also, water is becoming increasingly scarce and polluted.

Ground water levels in a huge part of northern India, the most intensively irrigated region in the world, where hundreds of millions of people live, are now being depleted to unsustainable levels for the long term.[68] In China, the water table under the North China Plain, where one-half of the country's wheat and one-third of its corn are grown, is falling fast.[69] Climate is also becoming unstable, in many places hotter and dryer, reducing core grain yields.

Some negative aspects of the Green Revolution have become apparent. Specialized seeds are often more tailored to specific threats or benefits so are less resistant to over-all diseases than are some of the traditional seeds. Also, the planting of only one variety of a plant – called monoculture – is bad for soil health and nutrition, and also creates an ideal condition for the rapid spreading of disease and insects that feed on that plant. (The Irish potato blight in the mid-nineteenth century and the US corn blight of 1970 are examples of serious diseases that have attacked monocultures.) Unless specifically tailored as drought-resistant or water-tolerant varieties, these seeds can also be less tolerant of too little or too much water; traditional varieties of seeds can be more resil-ient to varied threats and better evolved to their specific environment.

Probably the most serious potential negative aspect of the Green Revolution tech-nology is the question about its sustainability. Critics have raised this question because of its tendency to increase chemical pollution, deplete aquifers, and lead to soil degradation. One other negative impact of the new technology is that some farmers and agricultural workers were hurt by it. An evaluation of 40 years of the Green Revolution states: "Those who did not receive the productivity gains of the Green Revolution (largely because they were located in less favorable agroecological zones), but who nonetheless experienced price declines, have suffered actual losses of income."[70] The African continent was one of the areas which benefited the least from the initial Green Revolution developments, and has seen renewed interest on agricultural investments this present century.

Fertilizers Synthetic fertilizers are usually needed with the specialized seeds associated with the Green Revolution. Fertilizer use has grown dramatically around the globe since 1970, especially in Asia and particularly in China. There is now evidence that the runoff of fertilizers from farmland is a significant source of pollution in rivers and lakes. Excessive nitrogen in the fertilizer and from other sources is overwhelming the natural nitrogen cycle with a variety of consequences, such as a decrease in soil fertility and toxic algae blooms. Excessive nitrogen in lakes greatly stimulates the growth of algae and other aquatic plants, which, when they die and decay, rob the water of its dissolved oxygen, suffocating many aquatic organisms.

Seas such as the Baltic Sea, the Black Sea, and even the Mediterranean in Europe are especially vulnerable to this excessive fertilization – called eutrophication. Lake Victoria in Africa, Lake Erie in North America, and Lake Taihu in China are also threatened. A large "dead zone" – about the size of the state of New Jersey – of diminished productivity has developed at the mouth of the Mississippi River in the Gulf of Mexico because of the excessive amount of nitrogen from agricultural runoff.

There are now about 500 so-called "dead zones" around the world caused by fertilizer runoff and wastewater discharges.[71] Some of these dead zones are so large they can be seen from space. A number of measures can drastically reduce this runoff. These include better timing of fertilizer applications, more exact calculation of the amount of fertilizer the crops can absorb, and more accurate delivery of the fertilizer.

Pesticides   There was a large increase in the use of pesticides (insecticides, herbicides, and fungicides) around the world in the 1970s, 1980s, and 1990s, no doubt also connected with the spreading Green Revolution. It is difficult to know how many people are being harmed by pesticides, but it is believed that the number is significant. By some estimates, as many as 200,000 deaths occur annually around the world because of pesticide poisoning and more than 1 million people are made ill.[72] Many more may become sick from indirect contact through contaminated water or through food which has not been thoroughly washed. More significantly for food purposes, pesticides may be harming beneficial insects in addition to pests. Research on neonicotinioids has found some evidence of long-term impacts on both wild and domestic bee hives.[73] Plants that depend on pollinators like bees make up 35% of global crop production. We will look further at pesticides in Chapter 8 on pollution.

Energy   Industrial agriculture basically uses large volumes of fossil fuels and water to produce large quantities of food. This type of agriculture was developed when oil was inexpensive, and water was seen as abundant. Large amounts of energy are needed to build and operate the farm machinery, to build and operate the irrigation systems, to create the pesticides, and to mine and manufacture the fertilizers. Also, huge amounts of energy are needed to process the foods, to transport them to market, to package them, and to display them in retail stores. It has been estimated that to raise the rest of the world's diet to the American level – especially one featuring its high consumption of beef – would consume nearly all the world's known reserves of oil in 15 years.[74]

The dramatic increase in energy costs in the 1970s had a profound influence on agriculture and expected rising energy costs in the future will strongly affect food production and the cost of food. As we have seen, modern, Western agriculture is energy intensive, and the spreading of that type of agriculture to the developing world via the Green Revolution also entailed a commitment to using large amounts of energy. In the past, a doubling of agricultural output required a tenfold increase in the amount of energy used.[75]

There is hope that many countries and cultures can utilize agricultural methods that do not depend on the high use of energy and energy-related inputs common on large commercial farms in richer countries. This becomes increasingly possible when adopting a diet that is lower in processed foods and meat, which would suggest rejecting the Western diet as an ideal to strive for. Various experts have confirmed that a diet primarily based on plants is better for human health as well as the environment.[76]

Irrigation   Anything that affects the availability of fresh water will seriously affect the production of food. Even more important than energy to the success of industrial agriculture is water, and agriculture consumes 70 percent of global fresh water use today.[77] Increasingly, the world's food supply is relying on irrigation. Irrigation uses more water than any other human activity.

The use of fresh water, much of it for irrigation, has increased steadily since the 1960s. In many countries, for example in many parts of Africa and the Middle East, water gets pulled from the ground faster than it can be replenished. At the height of the Green Revolution in the 1970s, irrigated land on the planet increased about 2 percent annually. Since that time irrigation has been growing about 1 percent a year. The growth has slowed partly because of the high costs of installing irrigation and the competition for fresh water. Besides the problems of waterlogging and salinization, which were mentioned earlier, increased use of irrigation can also lead to an increase in infectious diseases such as malaria and schistosomiasis. Irrigation supports some 20% of agricultural land across the globe, which amounts to about 275 million hectares – a sizeable footprint, even as it amounts to a relatively small percentage of the world's overall land area.[78]

Improvements are being made in irrigation. Irrigation technology, such as highly efficient sprinklers and drip feeding, can lessen the amount of water used substantially.[79] On the other hand, centuries-old traditional and indigenous methods are also proving to be useful and sustainable methods for water management to adapt to a changing climate.

Biotechnology

Biotechnology has been called a technology that will transform modern agriculture. Genes get edited, seeds get altered, and new crop varieties are promoted as solutions to the growing challenges facing agriculture today. Genetic engineering, the transferring of desirable genes, or traits, from one organism to another, is the best-known part of this technology. New breeds of animals and plants are being created today with this technology. Plant and animal species have changed naturally throughout the evolution of life on this planet and human beings have, for thousands of years, influenced that evolution by encouraging the growth of those plants and animals which have traits that benefit humans. But now, as one scientist has stated, "we can do all at once what evolution has taken millions of years to do."[80] By the turn of the century, genetically altered seeds were used widely in the United States, Argentina, and Canada, while other countries took more of a precautionary approach.[81] The Convention on Biological Diversity's Cartagena Protocol on Biosafety provides a global framework for the use of biotechnology that is increasingly used by many countries.

Biotechnology is still controversial. While some raise concerns related to risks that engineered organisms may compromise conventional plants with irreversible genetic impacts, its defenders point out that food crops can be developed that are resistant to insects and viruses, thus reducing the need for pesticides. Plants can be developed that can tolerate herbicides, thus allowing herbicides, which would normally harm the plant, to be used to control the weeds threatening the plant. Fruits can be developed that are resistant to spoilage. A tomato has been developed that has a natural resistance to becoming overripe, which means the tomato does not have to be picked while it is still green and relatively tasteless. However, research has shown that in countries like the United States and Canada which have widely adopted genetically modified organisms (GMOs) – manipulating the genetic code to produce certain (generally commercially valuable) traits – there is no indication that yields actually improved or fewer pesticides were used.[82]

Plants that are more nutritious are being developed, such as a new variety of rice that will contain provitamin A, an essential nutrient that is missing in present rice. In Southeast Asia particularly high proportions of the children under the age of 5 are at risk from vitamin A deficiency, which leads to vision impairment and increased susceptibility to disease.[83] Plants that can grow under harsh conditions – for example, during droughts, or in salty soils, or in temperature extremes of heat and cold – are increasingly being used to cope with climate impacts. With this technology, animals, such as pigs, can be developed to have more lean meat, and dairy cows can be developed to produce more milk – which can also reduce greenhouse gas emissions if consumption rates remain steady but meat and dairy production becomes more efficient. In the United States, about 85 percent of corn, 85–90 percent of cotton, and 90 percent of soybeans are from seeds that have been genetically modified.[84]

There is no doubt that biotechnology, the transferring of desirable genes from one organism to another, is going to have a large effect on the future of food production. One possible serious problem is that the seeds produced by using this technology generally will not reproduce themselves, so farmers must purchase seeds from a commercial producer, such as the Monsanto Corporation, every year, whereas in the past plants reproduced seeds annually which the farmers could use to plant new crops the following year. While these commercially patented seeds may yield unique and valuable varieties of crops, the practice of replacing traditional seeds is making it more difficult and expensive for farmers to grow crops, in some cases leading to higher suicide rates among struggling farmers, such as the case of 300,000 farmer suicides in India, allegedly attributed to the crushing debt associated with transitioning to GMO seeds.[85]

The critics of this new technology, who tend to be more numerous in Europe than in the United States, claim that there is a possibility that genetic engineering will alter organisms in detrimental ways that will not be fully known for years. Herbicide resistant crops might pollinate closely related plants that are now weeds, thus creating a new weed that is also resistant to herbicides. Negative publicity for bioengineering was generated in the United States in 1999 when a study showed that the pollen from corn that had been genetically altered to produce a natural pesticide can kill caterpillars of the monarch butterfly. Since most of the research today in biotechnology is being performed by private corporations that see it as a way to increase their profits, it is not surprising that most of the present genetic engineering focuses on crops and animals that can be profitably sold in the rich nations, not in the poor nations. The critics point to several large corporations that produce herbicides and other farm chemicals as being leaders in efforts to develop herbicide-resistant crops. Instead of encouraging the development of less reliance on chemicals in the growing of foods, this research will increase such reliance.

With biotech companies developing plants with either a combination of genes or with an individual gene that enables the plant to produce pharmaceutical or industrial chemicals, many have argued that stronger regulations are needed. For example, the US National Academy of Sciences has warned that genetically altered crops have the potential to pose food safety risks and environmental harm, including that it will be difficult to contain all altered genes in plants and animals or prevent any of them from having unintended environmental and public health effects.[86]

The European Union requires labels on food identifying it as genetically altered if 1 percent or more of its ingredients have been genetically altered. A crack developed in European opposition in 2004 when the European Union ended its six-year moratorium on the approval of biotech foods. In 2010, the European Commission issued guidelines for the coexistence of natural and genetically altered corps appropriate to national circumstances. These guidelines were intended to prevent the unintended presence of biotech plants in conventional and organic crops. By 2015, the European Union had implemented legislation allowing countries to "opt out" of growing GMO foods in their lands. In response, 19 European countries opted out of growing GMO crops within their territories.[87]

Because Europe imports a considerable amount of its food from Africa, many African countries have taken a more cautious approach to genetically modified organisms. Some have outright banned GMOs while others take a more regulatory approach. South Africa was the first country in Africa to put a biosafety law in place and the country has been growing GMO crops since 1996.[88] More recently, Uganda's legislature ratified a biosafety law, but the president refused to sign it. In 2018, Nigeria announced that it had reduced agribusiness "dumping" of GMO seeds in the country to a minimum, while simultaneously implementing new biosafety regulations as opposed to an outright ban.[89]

Like many technologies, biotechnology appears to have positive and negative potential. It is impossible to predict at this point which potential will dominate. Being aware of the negative possibilities and taking steps to counter them may be the best we can do at this time. Government regulations need to be regularly updated to reflect the latest research and the plants and animals need to be monitored while being grown. (The negative side of technology will be discussed further in Chapter 9.) Biotechnology could lead to major advances in agriculture in the poorer nations. Some universities, such as the University of Ghent in Belgium, private foundations, such as the Rockefeller Foundation in the United States, and governmental agencies, such as the Swiss Federal Institute of Technology and the European Community Biotech Program, are supporting research in biotechnology that is directed toward that purpose.

Fishing and aquaculture

Not too long ago many people hoped that the world food problem would be solved by harvesting fish from the oceans, but it is now generally recognized that, as one marine biologist has put it, most of the ocean is a biological desert. Nearly all the fish in the world are harvested in coastal waters and in a relatively few places further from land where there is a strong up-welling of water that brings nutrients to the surface.

Over the past 50 years there has been increasing pressure on the world's fish. A large portion of the world's major varieties of fish are now fished at or above their capacity to renew themselves, some functionally to the point of exhaustion.[90] Marine biologists estimate that in the past half-century about 90 percent of the large ocean predators such as sharks, tuna, marlin, swordfish, cod, halibut, skates, and flounder have been caught.[91]

According to the World Resources Institute ("WRI"), "substantial potential exists for increasing the ocean fish harvests with better management of fish stocks, although sound management is neither easy nor obvious."[92] WRI cites the examples of Cyprus and the Philippines where better management of fishing in their waters led to substantial increases in fish harvests in as little as 18 months. WRI also reported that Canada, the European Union, and the United States had recently adopted tougher controls over ocean fishing and reduced the size of their fishing fleets.

One type of fishing that does hold promise for an increase in catch is aquaculture, the farming of fish and seafood inland and in coastal waters. By 2005 about 30 percent of the fish eaten in the world came from fish farms.[93] Nearly nonexistent commercially a generation ago, aquaculture has become an over $45 billion industry. More than half of the salmon eaten in the United States, about one-third of the shrimp, most of the clams and oysters, and nearly all the trout and catfish came from fish farms by the end of the twentieth century.

Here is the way one newspaper described techniques being used in aquaculture, already common in the 1980s:

> Scientists are growing fish twice as fast as they grow naturally, cutting their feed requirement by nearly half, and raising them on a diet of ground chicken feathers and soybeans. Fish are now vaccinated against disease, sterilized so that their energy is spent growing not reproducing, and given hormones to turn females into males and males into females, changes that can be used to improve growth, taste and control of selective breeding.[94]

Fish farming is popular in many countries, especially in Asia, which is the home for about 89 percent of the industry. China has about 60 percent of worldwide production.[95] Aquaculture was developed in China several thousand years ago. It is now becoming more popular again, particularly to sate the appetites of people in wealthier consumers, who – partly for health reasons (because fish are low in fat, and fish oil is reported to have beneficial properties) – are consuming more fish. In addition to fish farming in cultivated ponds, farmers are also increasingly turning to "aquaponics," the practice of farming crops with the waste from aquaculture.[96] Genetic engineering is also being used to create new species of fish.

There are environmental concerns with this rapidly growing industry. Thailand has cleared a large part of its mangrove swamps to make way for shrimp ponds, thus losing a critical habitat for many aquatic species and opening its coasts to erosion and flooding. A 20-acre salmon operation can produce as much organic waste as a city of 10,000 people. There is also a fear that fish that escape from the farms can mate with their wild relatives and harm the natural gene pool. It has been estimated that in 2007 about 700,000 salmon escaped from fish farms in Norway, the largest salmon fish farm producer in the world.[97] On the east and west coasts of the United States from the mid-1980s to 2000, over 500,000 salmon were estimated to have escaped from their pens.[98]

Traditional/sustainable/organic agriculture

One way to produce food with less contamination of the water and air and some-times help preserve the natural fertility of the soil is through traditional, sustainable, or organic agriculture. This resource-conserving and lower impact agriculture utilizes a number of old, proven techniques and a sophisticated understanding of natural nutrient cycles and ecological relationships. According to the World Resources Institute, it includes various practices like "crop rotation, reduced tillage or no-till, mechanical/biological weed control, integration of livestock with crops, reduced use or no use of chemical fertilizers and pesticides, integrated pest management, and provision of nutrients from various organic sources (animal manures, legumes)."[99] A demand by consumers for foods free of possible contamination by chemicals led to a large increase in organic farming in the United States beginning in the 1990s. In 2002, for the first time, the US government developed organic certification standards.[100] Organic farming is supported with governmental subsidies in Europe, but the United States only partially supports the cost of certification.[101] In 2012, organic food sales reached $28.1 billion, over 4 percent of total food sales.[102] By 2016, total sales reached approximately $43 billion, a 20 percent increase over just three years prior.[103]

Whether organic farming will ever become widespread in the $500 billion food industry in the United States is unknown, but the trend is that organic food production and consumption are increasing. The main criticism of organic farming is that it is less productive than conventional farming, and thus the prices of its foods are relatively high. There is still some debate on this question, and the findings are inconclusive.[104] A Swiss study published in 2002 comparing organic and conventional farms – the most comprehensive study of its time – found that organic farming leaves the soils healthier and is more energy efficient, but average crop yields are about 20 percent lower.[105] A long-term US study found opposite results, with yields about equal in corn and soybean production using organic and conventional methods, and in drought years organic corn yields were significantly higher than conventional farm yields.[106]

Impressive evidence of the worth of alternative agriculture techniques came in China in the summer of 2000. At that time the results of one of the largest agricultural experiments ever undertaken were announced. Under the direction of an international team of scientists, tens of thousands of rice farmers in one province participated in a simple experiment that didn't cost them any money, didn't involve the use of any chemicals, and resulted in them gaining a nearly 20 percent increase in their yields of rice. What the farmers did was plant two varieties of rice in their fields rather than just one. The result of changing from a monoculture to using diversity was to nearly wipe out the most devastating disease that affects rice, one that destroys millions of tons each year, causing farmers losses of several billion dollars. Scientists involved in the study believe the startling results can apply beyond rice. An ecologist at the University of Washington stated that "what's really neat about this paper [which announced the results of the experiment] is that it shows how we've lost sight of the fact that there are some really simple things we can do in the field to manage crops."[107]

Although modern, mechanized agriculture generally – but not always – produces a higher volume of food than the traditional agricultural systems (especially over the short term), modern agriculture is not necessarily the most sustainable option for rural economies. Traditional agricultural practices tend to occupy a higher share of a country's economy than they do in those countries where industrial agricultural practices are more widespread (see Figure 4.1 for the contribution of agriculture to countries' economies). Traditional agriculture generally uses much less fossil fuel energy than industrial agriculture. Moreover, in traditional agriculture the amount of energy used in the form of farm labor and materials is typically small compared with the yield in calories. Returns up to 50 to 1 are possible, although more common are returns of 3:1 up to 15:1, whereas in industrial agriculture more energy is often expended than produced.[108] To produce and deliver to a US consumer one can of corn which has 270 calories in it, a total of about 2,800 calories of energy must be used. To produce about 4 ounces of beefsteak, which also provides about 270 calories, an astounding 22,000 calories of energy must be expended.[109] A specialist on water use estimates it takes between 16,000 and 70,000 kilograms of water to produce one kilogram of beef.[110] Anthropologists Peter Farb and George Armelagos give us one perspective we need in order to judge the effects of industrial agriculture:

> In short, present-day agriculture is much less efficient than traditional irrigation methods that have been used by Asians, among others, in this century and by Mayans, Mesopotamians, Egyptians, and Chinese in antiquity. The primary advantage of a mechanized agriculture is that it requires the participation of fewer farmers, but for that the price paid in machines, fossil fuels, and other expenditures of energy is enormous.[111]

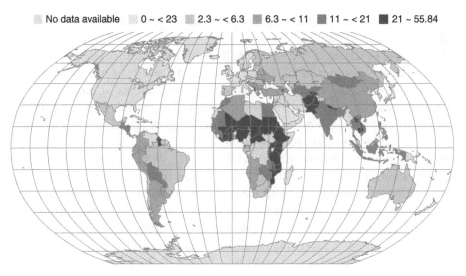

No data available   0 ~ < 23   2.3 ~ < 6.3   6.3 ~ < 11   11 ~ < 21   21 ~ 55.84

Figure 4.1   Contribution of agriculture as share of Gross Domestic Product, 2012 (percent)
Source: FAO, *Food and Nutrition in Numbers 2014*, p. 5, Figure 1.

Causes of World Hunger

Unprecedented amounts of food in the world do not mean, unfortunately, that everyone is getting enough food. If there is more than enough food being grown at present for the world's population, but about 11 percent of the Earth's people are undernourished, what is causing hunger in the world?[112] Food authorities generally agree that poverty is the main cause of world hunger, but this does not tell the full story, because as we have already seen, underlying social and political tensions as well as overall development pathways can influence the inequality and economic conditions that lead to poverty. This is the reason one food expert has written that "Malnutrition and starvation continue more or less unchanged through periods of world food glut and food shortage."[113]

In 2007–2008 the global recession caused a massive food crisis. The recession dramatically reduced incomes and this along with persistently high food prices led to reduced access to food for many low income groups, especially those who spend a large portion of their incomes on food in both the urban and rural poor. By 2010, the food crisis had lessened, but the FAO still identified 30 countries in need of external assistance because of "crop failures, conflict or insecurity, natural disasters, and high domestic food prices."[114] In September of 2018, the United Nations Food and Agricultural Organization (FAO) reported that 39 countries were in need of external food assistance due to "crises related to lack of food availability, widespread lack of access to food, or severe but localized problems."[115] In 2020, hunger rates further spiked due to Covid-19.

A respected Canadian geographer, Vaclav Smil, has expressed concern that even if the total amount of arable land is sufficient to sustain the Earth's population for at least decades to come, many of the world's poorest may suffer. He sees the near future as follows:

> Undoubtedly, the total area of potential farmland is quite large, but its ... distribution is highly uneven and its initial quality will be generally inferior to the existing cropland. ... [T]he affluent countries should not experience any weakening of their food production capacity because of the declining availability of farmland [but] ... low income societies tell a different story. Combination of continuing population growth and uneven ... distribution of potentially available farmland will only increase substantial differences in per capita availability of arable land in those countries. ... [P]er capita land availability remains high in Latin America, and more than adequate in sub-Saharan Africa. The greatest concerns exist, and will intensify, in the Middle East and in South and East Asia.[116]

Yet regardless of the cause, the sad truth is that hundreds of millions of people lack the resources to get adequate and nutritious food on a regular basis. The world's poorest cannot afford to purchase the food they need, whatever its price. In tropical Africa and remote parts of Latin America and Asia, low agricultural productivity tends to be the main reason for hunger, with not enough food being grown.[117]

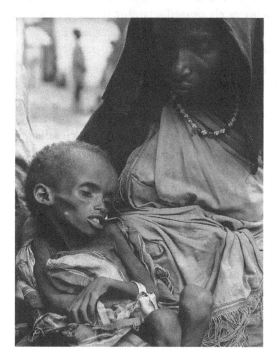

Plate 4.1 Starvation in Somalia

Source: CARE: Zed Nelson

Other low income people suffer during food shortages when the price of food increases dramatically, as it did during the early 1970s when world prices of rice, wheat, and corn doubled in just two years. A 2007 study of 13 countries found that food represented between 56 and 78 percent of consumption in poor households (with slight variation depending on whether the household was rural or urban), consistent with historic trends.[118] If world demand is high for certain foods, such as beef for the US fast food market, then the large landowners in developing countries grow food or raise cattle for export rather than for domestic consumption. This tends to cause domestic food prices to increase since the supply of local foods is reduced. A more recent example was the world recession of 2008–9, which combined with high food prices to disproportionately impact the world's poor.

Malnutrition in infants has been caused in part from a failure by families to fully embrace exclusive breastfeeding of their babies for six months, a lack of safe drinking water for preparing non-breastfed food (which can cause diarrhea), and in some cases aggressive advertising by formula milk manufacturers. Malnutrition during an infant's first two years of life can lead to permanent damage to their mental capabilities in addition to stunted growth.[119] The World Health Organization believes optimal rates of breastfeeding could save globally the lives of about 820,000 children.[120]

With spreading economic development, famines are becoming rarer than they were in the past. But a number of major famines occurred in the twentieth century. In the Soviet Union in the early 1930s, Stalin forcibly collectivized agriculture and deliberately caused a famine in the area where most of the grain was grown – the Ukraine and Northern Caucasus – in order to break the resistance of the peasants. An estimated 7 million people – 3 million of them children – died in that famine.[121] Another country with a communist government experienced the worst famine in the twentieth century. Although it was kept secret from the outside world while it was occurring, China had a famine in the late 1950s and early 1960s that led to an estimated 30 million deaths. The famine was caused mainly by misguided governmental policies during the period known as The Great Leap Forward.[122]

Much land was being used to grow export crops such as cotton and peanuts in the Sahel, a huge area in Africa just south of the Sahara desert, when a famine hit that area in the early 1970s. Six years of drought, rapid population growth, and misuse of the land led to widespread crop failures and livestock deaths. It is estimated that between 200,000 and 300,000 people starved to death in the Sahel and in Ethiopia before international aid reached them.[123] While food insecurity and the threat of famine improved, they never disappeared, and conditions have worsened in recent years. A poor rainy season in 2017 led to water deficits affecting the conditions and availability of livestock. This impact on the livelihoods of pastoralists and agro-pastoralists, combined with already high levels of food insecurity, contributed to an increase in the number of people in need of immediate food assistance from 5.2 million in December 2017 to 7.1 million by March of 2018.[124] Climate impacts and conflicts exacerbated the food crisis.[125]

Famine also hit Cambodia in the 1970s. Years of international and civil war, coupled with the genocidal policies under the leadership of Pol Pot, led to an estimated 10,000 to 15,000 people dying every day during the worst of the famine in 1979. A highly successful international aid effort, first organized by private organizations and then joined by governmental agencies, saved the Cambodian people from being destroyed.

Famine hit again in Africa in the mid-1980s, and early and late 1990s. Television pictures of starving people in Ethiopia led to a large international effort by private organizations and by governments to provide food aid. The famines in Ethiopia, Somalia, and the Sudan, and in other sub-Saharan African countries, were not caused only by the return of a serious drought to the region. The causes of these famines were much the same as those that brought on the famine in Africa in the early 1970s: rapid population growth and poor land management. In addition, the extensive poverty in the region, a worldwide recession which seriously hurt the export-oriented economies of the African countries, civil wars, and governmental development policies that placed a low priority on agriculture have been identified as likely causes.[126]

North Korea experienced a famine for about four years in the mid- and late 1990s. An estimated 2 to 3 million people died – about 10 percent of its population. The famine led to stunted growth in about two-thirds of the children under 5. This made it, relatively, one of the worst famines in the twentieth century, comparable to the famines in the other two totalitarian regimes. Like the Soviet Union and China, North Korea was a closed society at the time of the famine and evidence of the famine was kept secret. Although a flood and drought were partly to blame, the main causes appear to be the inflexible political and economic systems and the downfall of the country's long-term patron – the Soviet Union. Serious food shortages continue to the present. Food donors have become increasingly reluctant to continue to help the country as the food shortage drags on, and North Korea has admitted making costly efforts to develop nuclear weapons at the same time that its people were starving.[127]

Famine continues to afflict parts of the world in the 21st century, primarily in areas known for the 'Four Famines,' in Yemen, South Sudan, Nigeria, and Somalia. In February 2017, the UN declared famine in parts of South Sudan and issued a call to action to the international community, stating that 20 million people across the four countries, including 1.4 million severely malnourished children, were at risk of famine (6 million people in South Sudan alone required urgent food assistance).[128] In late 2018, the UN declared famine in Yemen, reporting that 73,000 Yemeni civilians were enduring famine conditions.[129] The famine in Yemen is largely the result of a conflict between Houthi rebels and Saudi Arabia, which has imposed sanctions and blockades severely limiting food access, and which may have resulted in the deaths of 85,000 children from starvation between 2015 and 2018.[130] The crises in South Sudan, Nigeria, and Somalia are the result of a combination of conflicts and adverse climate conditions impacting food production.[131]

The Secretary-General of the United Nations appointed a Hunger Task Force in 2002 to pursue the Millennium Development Goal to reduce the number of hungry people in the world by one-half by 2015. The Task Force's message to political leaders of both rich and poor nations was that "halving hunger is within our means; what has been lacking is action to implement and scale up known solutions."[132] While the goal of halving hunger by 2015 was not met, global efforts to reduce the number of hungry people successfully reduced the proportion of undernourished people in developing regions from 23 percent in 1990–2 to 12.9 percent in 2014–16, very near the MDG target.[133] Now, nations have adopted a new goal of ending hunger by 2030 as one of the UN's Sustainable Development Goals. It is an ambitious goal, especially in the wake of climate challenges, but recall that there is enough food available to feed the planet and the MDG hunger taskforce message still stands: we have the ability to address hunger, the issue is one of political will to scale up solutions and address the underlying inequality and geopolitical challenges that drive hunger crises in the first place.

How Food Affects Development

The availability of food has a direct effect on a country's development. Possibly the most destructive and long-lasting development impact is the absence of food – or, more often, of the right kinds of food – for the children of the less developed nations. (As mentioned in Chapter 3, the death of many children in poor nations at birth or in their first few years is one of the causes of high birth rates.) From 2003 to 2008, about 30 percent of children under 5 in rural areas were undernourished, while about 20 percent of a comparable group in urban areas were hungry.[134] In a positive trend, between 2000 and 2017, the number of stunted children under 5 worldwide declined from 198 million to 151 million, although numbers have increased roughly 3 percent in West and Central Africa.[135] According to UNICEF, for children under 5, nearly half of all deaths can be attributed to hunger, accounting for about three million lives lost each year.[136] Pneumonia and diarrhea appear to be the main immediate causes of children's deaths.

A deficiency of vitamin A leads to blindness in about 250,000 to 500,000 children a year in developing countries. About one-half of the children die during the first year after losing their sight.[137] More common than blindness are the harmful effects malnutrition has on the mental development of children. Eighty percent of the development of the human brain occurs before birth and during the first two years after birth. Malnutrition of the pregnant mother or of the child after birth can adversely affect the child's brain development and, along with limited mental stimulation, which is common in poor homes, can lead to a reduced capacity for learning.

Malnutrition also reduces a person's ability to ward off diseases since it reduces the body's natural resistance to infection. Measles and diarrhea, which are not generally serious illnesses in wealthy nations, often lead to the death of children

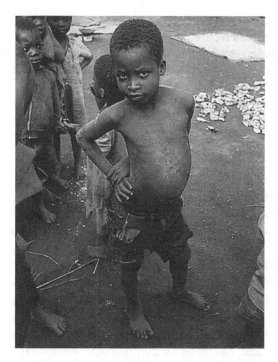

Plate 4.2   The bloated belly is a sign of malnutrition, a major cause of stunting and death in children worldwide

Source: CARE: Joel Chiziane.

in poor nations; in fact, diarrhea is the second greatest cause of death of children for the global poor. When a child has been weakened by malnutrition, sickness is likely to come more frequently and to be more serious than that experienced by a well-nourished child.

Malnutrition can play a role in productivity levels, particularly for people who are chronically obese or undernourished (and may also suffer from parasitism and disease). The World Health Organization believes that iron deficiencies among the hungry play a large role in their lack of productivity. According to the UN World Food Programme, iron deficiency is the most prevalent form of malnutrition worldwide, affecting productivity by impeding cognitive development and leading to lethargy.[138] A poor nation that must spend limited funds to buy imported food cannot use those funds to support its development plans. And, more importantly, a nation whose main and most important resource – its people – is weakened by malnutrition is unlikely to generate the kind of economic development that actually does lead to an improved life for the majority of its people. James Grant, former head of the United Nations Children's Fund (UNICEF), has described well the interrelatedness of all key elements of development:

A cat's cradle of … synergisms links almost every aspect of development: female literacy catalyzes family planning programmes; less frequent pregnancies improves maternal and child health; improved health makes the most of pre-school or primary education; education can increase incomes and agricultural productivity; better incomes or better food reduces infant mortality; fewer child deaths tend to lead to fewer births; smaller families improve maternal health; healthy mothers have healthier babies; healthier babies demand more attention; stimulation helps mental growth; more alert children do better at school ... and so it continues in an endless pattern of either mutually reinforcing or mutually retarding relations which can minimize or multiply the benefits of any given input.[139]

The type of food

As a nation develops, its diet also changes. The wealthier a nation becomes, the more calories and protein its citizens consume. The average citizen of a Western industrialized nation consumes many more calories and much more protein than he or she needs for good health. Excess calories are associated with processed foods; much of the excess in protein comes from a large increase in meat consumption. As a country's consumer class expands, diets typically shift in tandem with a changing income base.

Demand for processed foods increases while at the same time work becomes more sedentary. With increased income, calories and protein become more abundant but nutritional value of food becomes less reliable. Processed grains lose nutritional value and roughage as they become refined; fewer vegetables get consumed and fiber intake plummets. This shifting diet, combined with a more sedentary lifestyle, is associated with obesity, diabetes, heart disease, and other medical problems.

People in wealthier countries consume a higher amount of meat per person – about 150 pounds annually (69 kilograms) for the EU and OECD countries generally; some countries like Brazil consume even more – about 175 pounds (79 kilograms) annually per person. During the last 40 years of the twentieth century, per capita meat consumption in Europe went up about 100 percent and then down about 25%, while it increased in Brazil about 150 percent and remained that way.[140] Excessive calories and excessive meat consumption have been associated with serious health problems in addition to environmental impacts of deforestation, water pollution, and climate change. As supermarkets and corporate farming become more common and people grow less of their own food, fresh vegetables – which also give necessary fiber – can become replaced by processed, defibered products which are less nutritious.

Figure 4.2 shows the per capita consumption of animal products in developing countries. Note the increase in the consumption as incomes rise. Often the consuming of meat instead of grains in order to get protein, which is needed for human growth and development, is a very inefficient use of food.[141] For every 16 pounds of grain and soybeans fed to beef cattle in the United States, about 1 pound of meat for human consumption is obtained. About three-quarters of the food energy in the diet of people in Asia comes directly from grain (about 300–400 pounds a year), whereas someone in the United States consumes nearly 1 ton of grain per year, but 80 percent of it is first fed to animals.[142] Livestock consumed over one-third of the total calories produced by crop harvests across the globe, but only about 10% of these calories contributed to human diets.[143]

Plate 4.3 Obesity is an increasing health and nutrition challenge globally, particularly in some wealthier countries like the United States

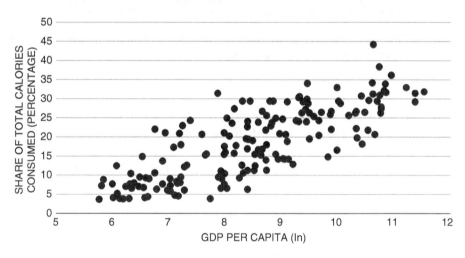

Figure 4.2 Correlation between consumption of animal products and GDP per capita in developing countries

Source: FAO, *The State of Food and Agriculture, 2007*, p.31.

This shifting diet, combined with a more sedentary lifestyle, is associated with obesity, diabetes, heart disease, and other medical problems. A full 30 percent of the planet is now obese or overweight, even as malnutrition and hunger continue to plague nearly 10 percent of the population.[144] Processed foods and fast food restaurant proliferation have contributed to this trend through their extensive advertising, vast expansion of outlets, and the increasing size of the portions of food and beverages served. Table 4.3 gives the percentage of overweight and obese males and females in a select group of countries.

Plate 4.4 Tropical rainforests are being cut down to clear land to raise beef cattle for the US fast-food market – the so-called "hamburger connection"

Source: United Nations.

We end this section with a short explanation of how development has affected the first food babies receive after birth. In the second half of the twentieth century, a rapid decline in breastfeeding took place across the globe, although by the end the trend had reversed: from 1990 to 2000, there was a 15 percent increase in breast-feeding. In 2018, according to UNICEF, in the vast majority of countries, about 40 percent of infants 0–5 months of age were being exclusively breastfed.[145] A 2018 UNICEF analysis of 123 countries showed that 95 percent of babies are breastfed at some point, but there is wide variation between high income countries and low and middle income countries. In high income countries, 1 in 5 babies are never breast-fed, while in low and middle income countries, only 1 in 25 babies are never breast-fed.[146] Low income countries have higher rates of breastfeeding after one year as well, with most babies still being breastfed compared to fewer than 20 percent in many high income countries.[147]

This overall low global rate for consistent breastfeeding is partly due to urbaniza-tion, the increasing number of women in the workforce, cultural attitudes, and the promotional efforts of formula-making companies (the latter more of a factor in the past than at present). But is formula better for a child than breast milk? Nutritionists agree that human milk is the best food for babies. According to UNICEF, breastfed children have a chance of survival in the early months that is at least six times greater than non-breastfed children.[148] Breastfeeding is also the safest, cheapest, and easiest way to feed babies. Breastfeeding probably improves bonding – a special

Table 4.3 Percentage of adults overweight and obese (various countries)

Country	Male	Female
Greece (2003)	79	55
Saudi Arabia (2013)	58	62
Germany (2008–11)	67	53
USA (2015/16)	75	70
Mexico (2012)	69	73
England (2016)	66	57
Spain (2014/15)	69	53
Canada (2007/9)	70	47
Russia (2000)	41	49
Netherlands (1998–2002)	54	39
Italy (2008–12)	72	57
Brazil (2008/9)	50	48
China[a] (2011 obesity only)	12	11
Japan (2012)	30	19

"Overweight" and "obese" are labels for ranges of weight that are greater than what is considered healthy for a given height.
[a] China data on obesity only.
Source: International Obesity Task Force (IOTF), "Global Prevalence of Adult Obesity," updated November 2018, athttp://www.worldobesity.org/ (accessed December 2018).

feeling of closeness – between the mother and the baby, and it gives the baby antibodies which enable it to fight off infection; this is especially important since an infant's own immune system is not fully developed during the first year. Many of the harmful effects of bottle-feeding include diarrhea or other sickness resulting from dirty water, a lack of refrigeration, and/or sterilization challenges.

Many working mothers have found bottle-feeding more convenient, and some cultures are unsettled by the sight of a woman breastfeeding in public. Due in part to shifting cultural attitudes where many of the previous generation did not acquire knowledge on breastfeeding to pass along to the next generation, a special organization – La Leche League – was formed by some women to help others learn about breastfeeding and to aid them with any difficulties they experience. What we find in this case is a modern society turning away from one of the most basic human functions and then having to relearn the advantages of this bodily function and how to practice it.

The general recognition of the harmful effects that were generated by the adoption of bottle-feeding by less developed nations led the World Health Organization in 1981 to adopt, by a vote of 118 to 1 (only the United States voted "no"), a nonbinding code restricting the promotion of infant formula.[149] In 2018, the WHO passed another resolution to promote breastfeeding, although its introduction for passage was nearly thwarted by the United States, which was criticized by many as a demonstration of the lobbying power of the $70 billion baby food industry, which consists largely of companies based in the United States and Europe.[150]

The Mediterranean diet[151]

Would you like to lower your risk of high blood pressure, stroke, heart disease, and cancer? Decrease your chance of getting Parkinson's or Alzheimer's diseases? Many in the medical profession now believe the closer a person follows the diet of people in countries bordering the Mediterranean Sea, the more likely they will achieve these benefits. Here are the main ingredients of the Mediterranean diet:

1   Eat a generous amount of fruits and vegetables, including whole grains and legumes (such as beans and peas).
2   Use olive oil or canola oil.
3   Eat daily low to moderate amounts of cheese and yogurt.
4   Use herbs and spices instead of salt to flavor foods.
5   Drink red wine in moderation during meals.
6   Eat fish or shellfish at least twice a week.
7   Eat nuts in moderation.
8   Consume very little red meat.

Map 4.1   The Mediterranean

What's your Footprint?

Your food choices have a big impact on the Earth. In 2017, the global population was already using approximately 1.7 times more of the Earth's resources than could be replenished, and if current trends continue the world will demand the resources of three Earths by 2050 (Figure 4.3).[152] Most people in wealthy nations use much more

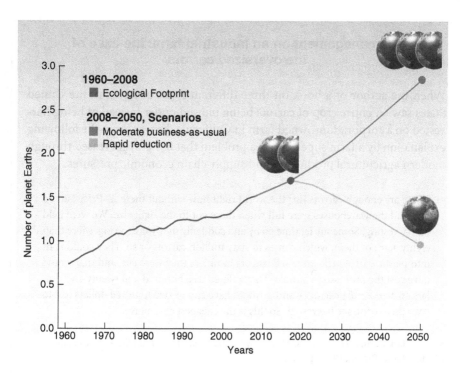

Figure 4.3 Number of Earths required to sustain global population, 1960–2050 (scenarios)

Source: Footprint Network, at http://www.footprintnetwork.org/en/index.php/GFN/page/ world footprint/

than their share, while the world's poor tend to tread very lightly. The world has a limited amount of arable land, and there is simply not enough land on the planet to support a global population following a diet high in processed foods, saturated fat, and large amounts of animal meat. Calculate your footprint at https://www.footprintnetwork.org/resources/footprin-calculator/.

Food Waste and Food Loss

It is difficult to estimate how much food is grown but not consumed in the world. This includes food loss (i.e. lost during production and thus unavailable for consumption) and food waste (i.e. food produced and available for consumption but not actually consumed).[153] A 2011 study commissioned by the FAO concluded that, at the global level, approximately one-third of food produced for human consumption is lost or wasted, amounting to roughly 1.3 billion tons per year.[154] It is assumed that as national incomes increase, the amount of food wasted also increases. But food loss is also a problem in less wealthy countries, where up to 40% of food never makes it to market and compromises small scale farmers' incomes by some 15 percent.[155] In light of planetary boundaries and projected increases in global food demand, globally recognized scientists and policy makers have recommended cutting food waste and food loss in half, in line with Sustainable Development Goals 12 and 13.[156]

Mismanagement on an industrial farm: the case of the oversized carrots

When the author of a book on three different types of farms in the United States saw an entire crop of carrots being plowed under instead of being harvested on a corporation-owned farm in California, he was given the following explanation by a farm supervisor – a problem that has only increased through modern agricultural production and supply chain economic pressures:

> There are enough carrots [in] the world right now without these ... Price isn't so hot, and the warehouses were full when these got to the right size. We were held off harvesting. Someone let time go by and suddenly they were too big. More than eighty acres of them, which comes to sixty million carrots or so. They couldn't fit into plastic carrot sacks they sell carrots in unless they were cut, and that would have cost the processor a bundle. They offered us a hundred and twenty-five dollars an acre for the carrots – and it would have run us two hundred dollars just to have them contract-harvested. So this is the cheapest alternative.

Source: Mark Karma, *Three Farms: Making Milk, Meat and Money from the American Soil* (Boston: Little, Brown, 1980), p. 248.

The US supermarket, better than any other institution, illustrates the abundance that modern agriculture can produce. In many developed countries, consumers demand that the produce they buy look cosmetically perfect. This leads to the wasting of much of the food successfully harvested. One study in 2009 of fresh fruit and vegetables in the United Kingdom found that about 25 to 40 percent of this food was "rejected" by the supermarkets.[157] Studies in the US and the UK have found that household food waste is also significant. The US Environmental Protection Agency in 2008 estimated about 15 percent of the solid waste collected in the country was food waste. And in the UK studies in 2008–9 estimated households wasted 25 percent of their food per year.[158] The agriculture ministry in Japan estimated 23 million tons of food was thrown away in 2007. About 30 percent of the food Japanese restaurants prepared was discarded.[159] In total, 2011 estimates of per capita food waste by consumers in Europe and North America were at 95–115 kilograms per year, while sub-Saharan Africa and South/Southeast Asia were 6–11 kilograms per year.[160]

The Future

Foreign assistance and government policies play a significant role in agricultural production outcomes. For example, in the late 1900s, within 10 years of experiencing a major famine, Ethiopia was able to double grain production within two years and then become a net exporter of grains. This was due in part to US foreign

Plate 4.5   Street vendors sell food to many urban dwellers

Source: Ab Abercrombie.

assistance and in part to favorable financing from the national government that encouraged farmers to purchase fertilizer and specialized seeds.[161]

Certainly, without the increased production that came with the Green Revolution many countries would have already lost the battle to have enough food available for their rapidly growing populations. The late Dr Norman Borlaug – a US scientist who received the Nobel Peace Prize for his work in developing high-yield wheat, and the person considered to be the "father" of the Green Revolution – has stated the Green Revolution was not meant to be the final solution for the world's food problem: it was designed to give nations a breathing space of 20 or 30 years during which time they could work to bring their population growth under control. Borlaug was disappointed that many nations did not increases their food supplies in proportion to their populations. Figure 4.4 indicates some of the key drivers of changes in food systems, many of which are affected by government policies.

Governmental Food Policies

The availability of food is such a basic need that no government that we know of adopts a "hands off" policy regarding its production, price, and distribution. Most nations have scarce public funds, so decisions must be made judiciously about where to apply them. It should not be surprising to students of government that public

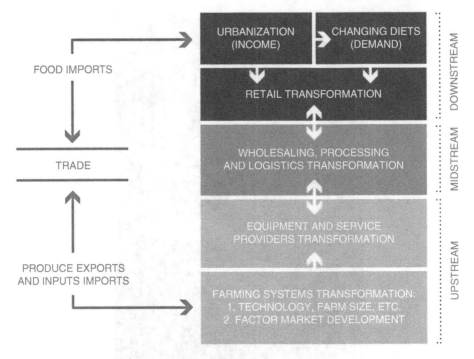

Figure 4.4 Main drivers of food system transformation.

Source: Food and Agriculture Organization, State of Food and Agriculture 2017, p. 27.

funds usually go to benefit groups with political visibility and power. Political leaders want to stay in power, and it is often the traditional political and economic elites who will influence the leaders' length of stay rather than the more politically marginalized groups, which often include small farmers and the rural poor. In many nations, increasingly urban populations are demanding plentiful and inexpensive food – sometimes to the point of riots – which can influence leaders' priorities and policies. Of those nations who have chosen to prioritize agricultural development, governments have taken a variety of approaches, some centralized and some decentralized, with varying results.

While not every government has chosen to prioritize the livelihoods of its rural farmers, there have been a few Asian countries – notably Japan, South Korea, and Taiwan – that brought significant prosperity to their rural areas through carefully designed decentralized policies. First, they enacted land reform measures – in Japan's case under the US occupation force's direction after World War II – which ended absentee landlordism and exploitative tenancy arrangements. The land was basically turned over to those who farmed it. Second, cooperatives were established to help small farmers purchase inputs to increase production, such as seeds and fertilizers, and market their harvests. The governments also provided information and aid to the farmers through an active agricultural extension service and by supporting agricultural research. Japanese small farmers generated some of the highest yields per acre in the world, and the mechanization they used on their farms – mainly small machines – tended to increase rural employment, not decrease it. Double and even triple harvests per year on the same piece of land became possible, and more laborers were required to handle these harvests.

Another historically significant set of centralized policies came from the Soviet Union, which pursued a radically different plan from China. Under Stalin's long rule, the country placed industrialization first, and agriculture was used to support that industrialization. Also, the desire to remove the political opponents of the ruling communists – the prosperous small farmers known as "kulaks" – and the desire to substitute state-owned and collective farms for privately owned farms, led to what is commonly recognized as the destruction of efficient agriculture in that country. The Soviet Union's inability to grow enough food to feed its people caused it to import large amounts of wheat from the United States and other capitalist countries.

Future Food Supplies

How much food can be grown in the world? How many can be fed? Like most of the questions raised in this book, there are no simple answers. Also, it is not hard to find experts who give very different answers to these questions. Consider all the topics

Plate 4.6 Women fishing in the Zambezi river

Source: Clarence Abercrombie.

discussed in this chapter which are directly related to these important questions: climate change, energy costs, alternative/sustainable agriculture, biotechnology, fishing and aquaculture, and, finally, expected future food production.

Will the world be able to produce enough food for its rapidly expanding population? Where should food be grown, and by whom? These are hard questions to answer. Many experts failed to predict the progress that has been made in food production in the past few decades, so it would be easy to discount the warnings by some of them now. Yet some very disturbing signs exist.

Most of the good farmland in the world is already being used, and efforts to address climate change mean that agricultural land should not expand at the expense of tree cover.[162] Even if governments decide that growing food is more important than avoiding deforestation, considering the social and political obstacles that must be overcome to develop such areas, it is difficult to estimate the potential for increasing the amount of farmland. Large amounts of potential farmland exist in Latin America and Africa. The Brazilian *cerrado* and the grasslands of sub-Saharan Africa have the largest reserves of arable land. Much of the remaining potential arable land is far from dense population centers and a lot of it is marginal land, which is costly to bring into production and to maintain. Beyond the land governance and tenure challenges of working with rural and pastoralist households, Large investments would be needed to develop it – to build roads to it and to transport its products to market, to irrigate it, and to fertilize it.

These estimates also must take into consideration the large amount of present farmland being lost to agriculture through urbanization, through erosion caused by the cutting down of forests and overcropping, through the spreading of desert-like conditions (desertification) because of overgrazing and farming on the edge of deserts, and through the loss of irrigated lands (salinization and waterlogging) because of poor drainage. The Earth's growing population and the type of diet its people choose will also greatly affect the amount of land needed to feed everyone. Regardless, it is clear that with many more mouths to feed and shifting preferences as people get more wealth there is a growing demand for food but also increasing competition and pressures on arable land. This has led to various approaches of varying degrees of success to address the challenge of feeding billions on a finite amount of land.

Lester R. Brown, the founder of both the Worldwatch Institute and the Earth Policy Institute, cites four crucial factors affecting the availability of food in the future: rapid population growth, loss of topsoil, spreading water shortages, and climate change. Unless drastic action is taken to reduce these threats, he has warned that the food production could collapse in the future.[163]

The World Resources Institute considered the threats from climate change, population and consumer changes affecting food demand, and the amount of land available to grow food across the world and concluded that major transformations are needed in food systems.[164] In the 2018 report Creating a Sustainable Food Future, they identify three key gaps: first, the gap between the amount of food produced in 2010 and the amount of food that will be needed by 2050 amounts to 7,400 trillion calories, or 54% more crop calories than currently produced.[165] Second, there is a

593 million hectare gap in the amount of land needed to grow that amount of food required for agriculture in 2050. Third, they cite a climate gap where greenhouse gas emissions from agriculture and associated deforestation and land use changes must be addressed in order to avoid additional impacts to yields.[166]

To address these gaps, the report offers a "menu" of key solutions:[167]

- Reduce demand by addressing food loss and waste and reverse the trend of increases in global meat and dairy consumption.
- Increase productivity through improved efficiency of natural resource use and support intensification with agroecology systems.
- Support increased reforestation and pasture restoration, including by recognizing the tenure rights of traditional communities with a proven track record of managing the land sustainably.
- Increase fish supply as a means to support increased demand for protein with less impact on the land.
- And reduce greenhouse gas emissions from agricultural production, including by stopping deforestation and avoiding high-emitting growing techniques.

Reading these solutions, what recommendations do you think would create the changes needed to see more sustainable food systems? Would you target overconsumption in wealthy economies or the corporate consolidation of production? Would you target companies marketing junk food to children? Would you prioritize support to small-scale farmers, especially women? Would you work to improve government policies on food access or regulate trade in commodities? Would you try to shift cultural norms about eating meat? There is no shortage of proposed solutions to help address global food challenges, but the political and behavioral mechanisms for change are challenging. While the politics of food can be quite intractable, it is clear that many are seriously questioning the food production practices popularized in the twentieth century and exploring the ways and means to chart a different path for food going forward.

Conclusions

One of the most fundamental problems many nations face is how to end hunger. The rapid growth of their populations and the past neglect of agricultural development have resulted in increased suffering in rural areas. Although this may be changing, advances in technology have helped to keep the overall production of food in many poor countries ahead of their increased needs, although it is unclear how technological innovations have impacted traditional household incomes. Widespread poverty in the rural districts as well as in some urban areas has meant that many people cannot afford to purchase the food that is available in the market. An emphasis on agricultural development and on increasing employment in both rural and urban areas is needed in order to provide increased income to larger numbers of the poor.

Rich nations face major food problems also. Here the problems are quite different from those faced by poorer nations. The rich nations need to learn how to produce nutritious food and retain a prosperous agricultural sector, as well as to help make sure their poorest residents are able to obtain affordable and healthy food. Obesity is an increasing problem in some economies where foods high in calories are regularly available.

There are indications some people have increasing concerns about the types of food in the modern diet. Whether this desire for more healthful foods and the awareness of the connection between food and health will spread from a minority to the majority of people is not yet clear. Yet in economic systems where consumers can freely exercise their preferences, the potential exists for important changes to occur fairly rapidly. For example, in the United States the relatively recent awareness of the connection between fatty foods and heart attacks has led to the production of many types of lower fat foods.

The picture regarding the health of the farm economy in some developed countries does not look bright. The United States has not yet learned how to maintain a sustainable, prosperous agricultural sector. Its productive capabilities are impressive but, as this chapter has pointed out, its high dependency on uncertain, polluting, and potentially very costly energy supplies, and its tendency to undermine the land upon which it rests make its future uncertain.

The main factor that makes any conclusions about food so hard to make is the changing climate. A large amount of uncertainty still exists regarding this subject and agriculture, but we know climate and agriculture go together about as closely as any two subjects can. Temperature, rainfall, length and dates of growing seasons, and extreme weather events all directly affect harvests. We must study the scientific facts and predictions of climate change if we are to understand the possibilities for food in our future. We will have an opportunity to do this in Chapter 6 on climate change.

Notes

1   The Guardian, World hunger rising for the first time this century (September 15, 2017), athttps://amp.theguardian.com/global-development/2017/sep/15/alarm-bells-we-cannot-ignore-world-hunger-rising-for-first-time-this-century (accessed January 2020).

2   Food and Agriculture Organization (FAO), *The State of Food Insecurity in the World 2018*, at http://www.fao.org/3/I9553EN/i9553en.pdf, p. 3, 4 (accessed October 2018); see also FAO, *The State of Food and Agriculture*, 2009, Foreword, at http://www.fao.org/docrep/012/i0680e/i0680e.pdf (accessed July 2015). In this chapter, "hunger" and "undernourishment" refer to the consumption of insufficient calories, whereas "malnutrition" refers to the lack of some necessary nutrients, usually protein. For the sake of simplicity, this chapter equates hunger with undernourishment and malnutrition.

3   World Health Organization (WHO), "Levels and Trends in Child Malnutrition," http://www.who.int/nutgrowthdb/2018-jme-brochure.pdf?ua=1 (accessed October 2018)

4   FAO, *The State of Food Insecurity in the World, 2018*, p. 4.

5   Ibid., p. 104.

6   FAO, "FAO and the Eight Millennium Development Goals: Goal 1: Eradicate Extreme Poverty and Hunger," Factsheet, 2010.

7   See generally https://www.thp.org/knowledge-center/know-your-world-facts-about-hunger-poverty/ (January 2020).

8   FAO, *The State of Food Insecurity in the World 2018*, p. 6.

9   Roy L. Prosterman, "The Decline in Hunger-Related Deaths," *Hunger Project Papers*, No. 1 (San Francisco: Hunger Project, 1984), p. ii.

10 Marc Cohen, "Crop Circles," *Natural History*, 112 (October 2003), p. 64.

11 Brian Halweil, "Grain Harvest and Hunger Both Grow," in Worldwatch Institute, *Vital Signs 2005* (New York: Worldwatch Institute, 2005), p. 22.

12 World Food Program, "Hunger Statistics," at http://www.wfp.org/hunger/stats (accessed July 2015).

13 United Nations Development Programme (UNDP), United Nations Environment Programme (UNEP), World Bank, and World Resources Institute (WRI), *A Guide to World Resources 2000–2001* (Washington, DC: WRI, 2000), p. 10.

14 UNDP, UNEP, World Bank, and WRI, *World Resources 2008* (Washington, DC: WRI, 2008), pp. 210–11.

15 UN Food and Agriculture Organization (FAO), "Food Price Index," at http://www. fao.org/worldfoodsituation/foodpricesindex/en (accessed July 2015).

16 World Bank, World Development Indicators, "Cereal Yield," at http://data. worldbank.org/indicator/AG.YLD.CREL.KG (accessed July 2015).

17 Jonathan Watts, "Third of Earth's Soil is Acutely Degraded Due to Agriculture," *The Guardian* (September 12, 2017), at https://www.theguardian.com/environment/2017/sep/12/third-of-earths-soil-acutely-degraded-due-to-agriculture-study (accessed December 2018)

18 UN Global Land Outlook report (2018), at https://knowledge.unccd.int/sites/default/files/2018-06/GLO%20English_Full_Report_rev1.pdf (accessed December 2018).

19 Jonathan Watts, "Third of Earth's Soil is Acutely Degraded Due to Agriculture," *The Guardian* (September 12, 2017), at https://www.theguardian.com/environment/2017/sep/12/third-of-earths-soil-acutely-degraded-due-to-agriculture-study (accessed December 2018)

20 Ibid.

21 FAO, Terrastat database, "World Human-Induced Land Degradation Due to Agricultural Activities."

22 Bill McKibben, "A Special Moment in History," *Atlantic Monthly*, 281 (May 1998), p. 60.

23 Ibid.

24 Elizabeth Becker, "Two Acres of Farm Lost to Sprawl Each Minute, New Study Says," *New York Times*, October 4, 2002, p. A19.

25 Emma Bruce, "Growing Mega-cities will Displace Vast Tracts of Farmland by 2030, Study Says," *The Guardian* (December 27, 2016), retrieved from https://www.theguardian.com/environment/world-on-a-plate/2016/dec/28/growing-mega-cities-will-displace-vast-tracts-of-farmland-by-2030-study-says (accessed December 2018).

26 FAO, *The State of Food and Agriculture, 2009*, p. 11.

27 Intergovernmental Panel on Climate Change (IPCC). Global Warming of 1.5°C. An IPCC Special Report (Geneva: IPCC 2018).

28 Ibid.

29 Ibid.

30 Lester Brown, "Could Food Shortages Bring Down Civilization?" *Scientific American*, 300 (May 2009), p. 55.

31 IPCC, Global Warming of 1.5°C. An IPCC Special Report.

32 Ibid., p. 4.

33 World Economic Forum, "Which countries spend the most on food? This map will show you" at https://www.weforum.org/agenda/2016/12/this-map-shows-how-much-each-country-spends-on-food/ (accessed January 2020).

34 National Research Council, *Toward Sustainable Agricultural Systems in the 21st Century* (Washington, DC: National Academies Press, 2010), pp. 43–4.

35 Ibid., pp. 45–8.

36 C. Peter Timmer, "Unbalanced Bounty from America's Farms," *Science*, 298 (November 15, 2002), p. 1339.

37 Jason MacDonald, "Large Family Farms Continue To Dominate U.S. Agricultural Production", Amber Waves Blog, UDSA, March 6, 2017, at https://www.ers.usda.gov/amber-waves/2017/march/large-family-farms-continue-to-dominate-us-agricultural-production/ (accessed December 1, 2018).

38 William Stevens, "Sprawl Quickens Its Attack on Forests," *New York Times*, national edn (December 7, 1999).

39 USDA Economic Research Service, "America's Diverse Family Farms 2017 Edition," *Economic Information Bulletin 185,* December 2017, retrieved from https://www.ers.usda.gov/webdocs/publications/86198/eib-185.pdf (accessed January 2020).

40 US National Corn Growers Association, Corn Usage by Segment 2018 (citing United States Department of Agriculture, ERS Feed Outlook February 2019; Pro Exporter Network, Crop Year Ending 2019), at http://www.worldofcorn.com/#corn-usage-by-segment (accessed 26 January 2020).

41 Brown, "Could Food Shortages Bring Down Civilization?" p. 53.

42 Global Footprint Network. (2018). [Interactive map showing the ecological footprint for countries in 2014], retrieved from http://data.footprintnetwork.org/#/ (accessed December 2018).

43 Larry Rohter, "South America Seeks to Fill the World's Table," *New York Times* (December 12, 2004), p. 1.

44 Council on Foreign Relations, Info-Guide on Amazon Deforestation, at https://www.cfr.org/interactives/amazon-deforestation (accessed December 2018).

45 Council on Foreign Relations, Info-Guide on Amazon Deforestation, at https://www.cfr.org/interactives/amazon-deforestation (accessed December 2018).

46 FAOSTAT, "Food and Agricultural Commodities Production," at http://faostat.fao. org/site/339/default.aspx (accessed July 2015).

47 Tracie McMillan, "How China Plans to Feed 1.4 Billion Growing Appetites, " *National Geographic Magazine* (February 2018), at https://www.nationalgeographic.com/magazine/2018/02/feeding-china-growing-appetite-food-industry-agriculture/ (accessed December 2018).

48 James Hansen and Fred Gale, "China in the Next Decade: Rising Meat Demand and Growing Imports of Feed," (April 7, 2014) at https://www.ers.usda.gov/amber-waves/2014/april/china-in-the-next-decade-rising-meat-demand-and-growing-imports-of-feed/ (accessed December 2018) (accessed December 2018)

49 FAO, Crop Prospects and Food Situation Quarterly Global Report (March 2019), available athttp://www.fao.org/3/ca3696en/ca3696en.pdf (accessed January 2020).

50 Ibid.

51 International Rice Research Institute, "China," at http://irri.org/ourwork/locations/china (citing China's ministry of agriculture; last accessed July 2015).

52 Ibid.

53 Nicholas Wade, "Experts Say They Have Key to Rice Genes," *New York Times* (April 5, 2002), p. A19. For more on the scientific significance of this event, see Ronald Cantrell and Timothy Reeves, "The Cereal of the World's Poor Takes Center Stage," and Dennis Normile and Elizabeth Pennisi, "Rice: Boiled Down to Bare Essentials," both *Science*, 296 (April 5, 2002), pp. 53, 32–6.

54 Jimin Li, Yeyun Xin, and Longping Yuan, "Hybrid Rice Technology Development: Ensuring China's Food Security", IFPRI Discussion Paper 00918, International Food Policy Research Institute, November 2009, at http://www.ifpri.org/sites/ default/files/ publications/ifpridp00918.pdf (accessed July 2015).

55 Xinhua, "China to Finish Work on New Hybrid Rice in 2012," *China Daily* (October 26, 2010).

56 Dexter Roberts, "China Aims for Food Security as Pollution Destroys Crop Land," Bloomberg Business, January 21, 2014, at: http://www.bloomberg.com/ bw/articles/2014-01-21/china-aims-for-food-security-as-pollution-destroys-cropland; Ministry of Agriculture of the People's Republic of China, "No. 1 Central Document Targets Rural Reform", January 20, 2014, at http://english.agri.gov.cn/ news/dqnf/201401/ t20140120 21064.htm (both accessed July 2015).

57 Lucy Hornby, "China Scythes Self Sufficiency Policy," *Financial Times* (February 11, 2015).

58 Philip P. Pan, "The Land that Failed to Fail," *The New York Times* (November 18, 2018), retrieved from https://www.nytimes.com/interactive/2018/11/18/world/asia/china-rules.html (last visited November 24, 2018).

59 Bloomberg News, "Plastic Film Covering 12% of China's Farmland Pollutes Soil," *Bloomberg News* (September 5, 2017), at https://www.bloomberg.com/news/articles/2017-09-05/plastic-film-covering-12-of-china-s-farmland-contaminates-soil (accessed December 2018).

60 David Stanway, "China's Total Arable Land Falls for Fourth Year in 2017: Resources Ministry," *Reuters* (May 19, 2018), retrieved from https://www.reuters.com/article/us-china-agriculture-land-idUSKCN1IK059 (accessed December 2018).

61 Compare Peng Gong, "China Needs No Foreign Help to Feed Itself," *Nature* 474, 7 (June 1, 2011), at https://www.nature.com/news/2011/110601/full/474007a.html (accessed December 2018) with Hansen and Gale, "China in the Next Decade: Rising Meat Demand and Growing Imports of Feed."

62 "Farming the World: China's Epic Race to Avoid a Food Crisis," *Bloomberg News* (May 22, 2017), at https://www.bloomberg.com/graphics/2017-feeding-china/ (accessed December 2018).

63 Calculated using data from the USDA Foreign Agricultural Service: Production, Supply, and Distribution online database, at http://apps.fas.usda.gov/psdonline/psdQuery.aspx (accessed July 2015); see also World Bank Data, "Cereal Production (metric tons)," at https://data.worldbank.org/indicator/AG.PRD.CREL.MT?view=chart (accessed December 2, 2018).

64 R.E. Evenson and D. Gollin, "Assessing the Impact of the Green Revolution, 1960 to 2000," *Science*, 300 (May 2, 2003), p. 761.

65 Lester Brown, "Could Food Shortages Bring Down Civilization?" p. 55. See also Keith Bradsher and Andrew Martin, "Crop Research Is Neglected, and Third World Pays Price," *New York Times* (May 18, 2008), p. 12; Mark Welch, "World Grain Production:

Keeping up with Demand," *Abilene Reporter-News* (January 18, 2015), at http://www.reporternews.com/business/agriculture/world-grainproduction-keeping-up-with-demand 60766794 (accessed July 2015).

66 Somini Sengupta, "India's Growth Outstrips Crops," *New York Times* (June 22, 2008), p. 10.

67 USDA Foreign Agricultural Service, Global Agricultural Information Network (GAIN) Report: *India: Grain and Feed Annual, 2014*, at http://gain.fas.usda.gov/Recent%20GAIN%20Publications/Grain%20and%20Feed%20Annual New%20Delhi India 214-2014.pdf (accessed July 2015).

68 Richard Kerr, "Northern India's Ground Water Is Going, Going, Going ..." *Science*, 325 (August 14, 2009), p. 798.

69 Bloomberg News Brown, "Could Food Shortages Bring Down Civilization?" p. 54.

70 Evenson and Gollin, "Assessing the Impact of the Green Revolution, 1960 to 2000," p. 762.

71 Damian Carrington, "Oceans Suffocating as Huge Dead Zones Quadruple since 1950, Scientists Warn" *The Guardian* (January 4, 2018), retrieved from https://www.theguardian.com/environment/2018/jan/04/oceans-suffocating-dead-zones-oxygen-starved (accessed December 2, 2018).

72 United Nations Special Rapporteur on the Right to Food, "Report of the Special Rapporteur on the right to food," A/HRC/34/48, February 24, 2017, retrieved from https://documents-dds-ny.un.org/doc/UNDOC/GEN/G17/017/85/PDF/G1701785.pdf?OpenElement (accessed December 2, 2018).

73 John Schwartz, "Decline of Pollinators Poses Threat to World Food Supply," *New York Times* (February 26, 2016), at https://www.nytimes.com/2016/02/27/science/decline-of-species-that-pollinate-poses-a-threat-to-global-food-supply-report-warns.html (accessed December 2018).

74 Raymond Hopkins, Robert Paarlberg, and Mitchel Wallerstein, *Food in the Global Arena* (New York: Holt, Rinehart & Winston, 1982), p. 102.

75 William Ophuls, *Ecology and the Politics of Scarcity* (San Francisco: W. H. Freeman, 1977), p. 54.

76 See, e.g. EAT-Lancet Commission, Food Planet Health: Healthy Diets From Sustainable Food Systems (2018), summary at https://eatforum.org/content/uploads/2019/01/EAT-Lancet_Commission_Summary_Report.pdf (accessed January 2020).

77 Tariq Khokhar, "Chart: Globally, 70% of Freshwater is Used for Agriculture," *The Data Blog*, World Bank, March 22, 2017, retrieved from https://blogs.worldbank.org/opendata/chart-globally-70-freshwater-used-agriculture (accessed December 1, 2018).

78 FAO, "Did you know...?" *Aquastat*, December 2014, retrieved from http://www.fao.org/nr/water/aquastat/didyouknow/index3.stm (accessed December 2, 2018); see also World Development Indicators, "Agricultural Irrigated Land (Percent of Total Agricultural Land)," at http://data.worldbank.org/indicator/AG.LND.IRIG.AG.ZS/countries (accessed July 2015).

79 For example, by these methods, Israel reduced its water consumption for irrigation by about 35 percent between 1951 and 1990 with no loss of productivity. See William Bender and Margaret Smith, "Population, Food, and Nutrition," *Population Bulletin,* 51 (February 1997), p. 33.

80 Harold M. Schmeck, "Jr. Gene-Altered Animals Enter a Commercial Era," *New York Times* (December 27, 1988), p. C1.

81 David Barboza, "Development of Biotech Crops Is Booming in Asia," *New York Times* (February 21, 2003), p. A3.

82 Danny Hakim, Doubts About the Promised Bounty of Genetically Modified Crops. *New York Times* (October 29, 2016), at https://www.nytimes.com/2016/10/30/business/gmo-promise-falls-short.html (accessed December 2018).

83 Mary Lou Guerinot, "The Green Revolution Strikes Gold," *Science*, 287 (January 14, 2000), pp. 241–3.

84 "Adoption of Genetically Engineered Crops in the U.S.," USDA data set, at http://www.ers.usda.gov/Data/BiotechCrops (accessed July 2015).

85 See, e.g. "How Monsanto Seeds Changed Cotton Farming In India," *The Logical Indian* (April 9, 2016), available at https://thelogicalindian.com/environment/how-monsanto-seeds-changed-cotton-farming-in-india/ (accessed January 2020)

86 See Carol K. Yoon and Melody Peterson, "Cautious Support on Biotech Foods by Science Panel," *New York Times* (April 6, 2000), p. A1; Andrew Revkin, "Panel Urges US to Tighten Approval of Gene-Altered Crops," *New York Times* (February 22, 2002), p. A18; and Andrew Pollack, "No Foolproof Way Is Seen to Contain Altered Genes," *New York Times* (January 21, 2004), p. A10.

87 Lorraine Chow, "It's Official: 19 European Countries Say 'No' to GMOs," *Ecowatch* (October 5, 2015).

88 Lominda Afedraru," New Biotech Crop-breeding Technologies Struggle for Traction across much of Africa," *Genetic Literacy Project* (December 17, 2018), at https://geneticliteracyproject.org/2018/12/17/new-biotech-crop-breeding-technologies-struggle-for-traction-across-much-of-africa/ (accessed January 2020)

89 Michael Eboh and Tochukwu Maxwell, "Nigeria no Longer Dumping Ground for GMO Production," *Vanguard* (December 26, 2018), at https://www.vanguardngr.com/2018/12/nigeria-no-longer-dumping-ground-for-gmo-products-fg/ (accessed January 2020)

90 FAO, *The State of World Fisheries and Aquaculture 2018*, (Rome: FAO, 2018), retrieved from http://www.fao.org/3/i9540en/I9540EN.pdf, p. 6.

91 Worldwatch Institute, *Vital Signs 2005*, p. 26.

92 WRI, UNEP, UNDP, and World Bank, *World Resources 1998–99*, p. 196.

93 FAO, *The State of Food and Agriculture, 2005* (Rome: FAO, 2005), p. 134.

94 William Greer, "Public Taste and US Aid Spur Fish Farming," *New York Times* (October 29, 1986), p. 1.

95 FAO, *The State of World Fisheries and Aquaculture 2018*, (Rome: FAO, 2018), retrieved from http://www.fao.org/3/i9540en/I9540EN.pdf, p 27 (accessed January 2020).

96 See, e.g., Jessica Schremmer, "Aquaponic venture described as 'growing two crops on one drop of water," ABC News (April 24, 2019), at https://www.msn.com/en-au/news/other/aquaponic-venture-described-as-growing-two-crops-on-one-drop-of-water/ar-BBWdLKR (accessed January 2020).

97 Wilfred Vuillaume, "Escapes from Norway's Fish Farms Threaten Wild Salmon," Agence France-Presse (January 19, 2007), at http://www.spacedaily.com/reports/Escapes From Norways Fish Farms Threaten Wild Salmon 999.html (accessed July 2015).

98 Erik Stokstad, "Engineered Fish: Friend or Foe of the Environment?" *Science*, 297 (September 13, 2002), p. 1797.

99   WRI, *World Resources 1992–1993*, p. 100. See also John P. Reganold, Robert I. Papendick, and James F. Parr, "Sustainable Agriculture," *Scientific American*, 262 (June 1990), p. 112. A fuller description of alternative agriculture is contained in National Resource Council, *Alternative Agriculture* (Washington, DC: National Academy Press, 1989).

100   UDSA, National Organic Program website, at http://www.ams.usda.gov/AMSv1.0/nop (accessed July 2015).

101   USDA, National Organic Program: Organic Certification Cost Share Programs, at http://www.ams.usda.gov/AMSv1.0/NOPCostSharing (accessed July 2015).

102   Catherine Greene, "Growth Patterns in the US Organic Industry," *Amber Waves* (October 24, 2013), at http://www.ers.usda.gov/amber-waves/2013-october/growthpatterns-in-the-us-organic-industry.aspx#.VQIsW9LF HU// (accessed July 2015).

103   Zlati Meyer, "Organic Food is Pricier, but Shoppers Crave It," *USA Today* (July 27, 2017), retrieved from https://www.usatoday.com/story/money/2017/07/27/organics-popularity-higher-than-ever-43-billion-2016/500129001/ (accessed December 2, 2018).

104   Johnson, Nathaniel, "Do Industrial Agricultural Methods actually Generate more Food per Acre than Organic Ones?" *Grist* (October 14, 2015), available at https://grist.org/food/do-industrial-agricultural-methods-actually-yield-more-food-per-acre-than-organic-ones/ (accessed November 25, 2018).

105   Erik Stokstad, "Organic Farms Reap Many Benefits," *Science*, 296 (May 31, 2002), p. 1589; see also James Conca, "It's Final – Corn Ethanol Is of No Use," *Forbes* (April 20, 2014), at http://www.forbes.com/sites/jamesconca/2014/04/20/its-final-cornethanol-is-of-no-use/ (accessed July 2015).

106   David Pimentel, "Changing Genes to Feed the World," *Science*, 306 (October 29, 2004), p. 815.

107   Carol Kaesuk Yoon, "Simple Method Found to Increase Crop Yields Vastly," *New York Times* (August 22, 2000), p. D1. See also Dennis Normile, "Variety Spices up Chinese Rice Yields," *Science*, 289 (August 18, 2000), pp. 1122–3.

108   Brian DeVore, Land Stewardship Project, "Counting Calories in Agriculture (2006)," at https://www.mepartnership.org/counting-calories-in-agriculture/ (accessed December 2018); see also William Ophuls, *Ecology and the Politics of Scarcity* (San Francisco: W. H. Freeman, 1977), pp. 42–3. The energy expended in modern agriculture is mainly nonhuman energy, of course, and most people consider that to be one of modern agriculture's most attractive features.

109   Peter Farb and George Armelagos, *Consuming Passions: The Anthropology of Eating* (Boston: Houghton Mifflin, 1980), p. 69.

110   Peter Gleick, "The Water to Grow Beef," blog post, May 5, 2009, at http://blog. sfgate. com/gleick/2009/05/05/the-water-to-grow-beef/ (accessed July 2015).

111   Farb and Armelagos, *Consuming Passions*, pp. 69–70.

112   FAO, *The State of Food Insecurity in the World, 2018*, p. 3

113   John R. Tarrant, *Food Policies* (New York: John Wiley, 1980), p. 12.

114   FAO, *Crop Prospects and Food Situation*, No. 3 (September 2010), p. 1, at http://www.fao.org/docrep/012/ak354e/ak354e00.pdf (accessed July 2015).

115   FAO, "Countries Requiring External Assistance for Food," at http://www.fao.org/giews/country-analysis/external-assistance/en/ (accessed July October 2018).

116   Vaclav Smil, *Feeding the World: A Challenge for the Twenty-First Century* (Cambridge, MA: MIT Press, 2000), pp. 36–9.

117 Pedro Sanchez and M. S. Swaminathan, "Cutting World Hunger in Half," *Science*, 307 (January 21, 2005), p. 357.

118 Felicity Lawrence, "The World's Poorest People, who Spend up to 80% of their Income on Food, will be Hit Hardest According to Oxfam," *The Guardian* (May 31, 2011), at https://www.theguardian.com/environment/2011/may/31/oxfam-food-prices-double-2030 (accessed January 2020); see also Abhijit V. Banergee and Esther Duflo, "The Economic Lives of the Poor," *Journal of Economic Perspectives*, 21 (1) (2007), pp. 141, 167.

119 World Health Organization, "10 Facts on Breastfeeding," at https://www.who.int/features/factfiles/breastfeeding/en/ (accessed December 1, 2018).

120 WHO, "Infant and Young Child Feeding: Model Chapter for Textbooks for Medical Students and Allied Health Professionals," 2009, Section 1.3, at http://www.who.int/maternal child adolescent/documents/9789241597494/en/ (accessed July 2015).

121 Robert Conquest, *The Harvest of Sorrow: Soviet Collectivization and the TerrorFamine* (New York: Oxford University Press, 1986).

122 Jasper Becker, *Hungry Ghosts: Mao's Secret Famine* (New York: Free Press, 1997); and Penny Kane, *Famine in China, 1959–1961: Demographic and Social Implications* (New York: St Martin's Press, 1988).

123 *New York Times* (June 7, 1983), p. 1; John Mellor and Sarah Gavian, "Famine: Causes, Prevention, and Relief," *Science*, 235 (January 1987), p. 539.

124 FAO, "West Africa – Sahel," *GIEWS Update,* July 3, 2018, retrieved from https://reliefweb.int/sites/reliefweb.int/files/resources/ca0323en.pdf (accessed January 2020).

125 Nellie Peyton, "U.N. calls for urgent aid to Sahel as hunger crisis looms," *Reuters* (May 3, 2018), retrieved from https://www.reuters.com/article/us-sahel-hunger-un/u-n-calls-for-urgent-aid-to-sahel-as-hunger-crisis-looms-idUSKBN1I42CL (accessed December 2018).

126 For a fuller discussion of the causes of the African famines, see Carl K. Eicher, "Facing up to Africa's Food Crisis," *Foreign Affairs*, 61 (Fall 1982), pp. 151–74; a series of articles on Africa in the *Bulletin of the Atomic Scientists*, 41 (September 1985), pp. 21–52; and Michael H. Glantz, "Drought in Africa," *Scientific American*, 256 (June 1987), pp. 34–40.

127 Kavita Pillay, "The Politics of Famine in North Korea," in *Ninth Annual Report on the State of World Hunger 1999* (Silver Spring, MD: Bread for the World Institute, 1998), p. 24; James Brooke, "Food Emergency in North Korea Worsens as Donations Dwindle," *New York Times* (December 5, 2002), p. A16; "North Korea, Facing Food Shortages, Mobilizes Millions from the Cities to Help Rice Farmers," *New York Times* (June 1, 2005), p. A6; Jonathan Cheng, "United Nations' Food Aid Program for North Korea Lacks Donors," *Wall Street Journal* (August 26, 2014), at http://www. wsj.com/articles/united-nations-food-aid-program-for-north-korea-lacks-donors1409047712 (accessed July 2015).

128 UN Office for the Coordination of Humanitarian Affairs, "Address and Prevent Famine in Four Countries," April 2017, retrieved from http://interactive.unocha.org/emergency/2017_famine/ (accessed December 2018).

129 Robbie Gramer and Colum Lynch, "U.N. Body Declares Famine Conditions in Parts of Yemen," *Foreign Policy* (December 5, 2018), retrieved from https://foreignpolicy.

com/2018/12/05/united-nations-world-food-program-body-declares-famine-conditions-in-parts-of-yemen-conflict-humanitarian-crisis-middle-east-congress-trump-saudi-arabia-mohammed-bin-salman-jamal-khashoggi-pressure-en/ (accessed December 2018).

130   Palko Karasz, "85,000 Children in Yemen May Have Died of Starvation," *New York Times* (November 21, 2018), retrieved from https://www.nytimes.com/2018/11/21/world/middleeast/yemen-famine-children.html (accessed December 2018).

131   Kimberly Curtis, "The 'Four Famines,' Explained," *UN Dispatch* (March 17, 2017), retrieved from https://www.undispatch.com/four-famines-explained/ (accessed December 2018).

132   Sanchez and Swaminathan, "Cutting World Hunger in Half," p. 357.

133   UNDP, *The Millennium Development Goals Report 2015*, at http://www.un.org/millenniumgoals/2015_MDG_Report/pdf/MDG%202015%20rev%20(July%201).pdf (accessed December 2018).

134   WHO and UNICEF, *Global Strategy for Infant and Young Child Feeding* (2003), p. 5, at http://www.who.int/nutrition/publications/infantfeeding/9241562218/en/ (accessed July 2005).

135   UNICEF, "Malnutrition in Children – UNICEF Data," at https://data.unicef.org/topic/nutrition/malnutrition/# (accessed December 1, 2018).

136   Ibid.

137   WHO "Micronutrient Deficiencies: Vitamin A Deficiency," at http://www.who. int/nutrition/topics/vad/en/ (accessed July 2015).

138   As reported by the UN World Food Programme in "Types of Malnutrition," at http://www.wfp.org/hunger/malnutrition/types (accessed July 2015).

139   As quoted in James Grant, *A Shift in the Wind*, Hunger Project Papers, No. 15 (San Francisco), p. 4.

140   OECD, "Meat consumption (indicator)," 2018, doi: 10.1787/fa290fd0-en, at https://data.oecd.org/agroutput/meat-consumption.htm (accessed December 2, 2018).

141   The consumption of meat (and, also, milk from cows and goats) can make nutritional sense. Cows and sheep, for example, can consume grasses, which people are unable to digest, in places where the climate or the condition of the land makes the growing of crops impossible.

142   A Well Fed World, "Feed:Meat Ratios," October 26, 2015, at https://awfw.org/feed-ratios/ (accessed December 2018).

143   Emily S Cassidy et al, "Redefining agricultural yields: from tonnes to people nourished per hectare." *Environmental Research Letters*, 8, (August 2013), http://iopscience.iop.org/article/10.1088/1748-9326/8/3/034015/pdf; see also FAO, *The State of Food and Agriculture, 2009*, p. 29.

144   Jamie Oliver, Ertharin Cousin, and Gunhild Stordalen, Rebooting the Food System (September 21, 2017), *Huffington Post,* at https://www.huffingtonpost.com/entry/rebooting-the-food-system_b_12102440 (all accessed December 2018).

145   UNICEF, "Infant and young child feeding," July 2018, retrieved from https://data.unicef.org/topic/nutrition/infant-and-young-child-feeding/ (accessed December 2018).

146   UNICEF, *Breastfeeding: A Mother's Gift, for Every Child*, 2018, retrieved from https://www.unicef.org/publications/files/UNICEF_Breastfeeding_A_Mothers_Gift_for_Every_Child.pdf (accessed January 2020).

147 "Breastfeeding: Achieving the New Normal," Editorial, *The Lancet* (January 30, 2016), retrieved from https://www.thelancet.com/action/showPdf?pii=S0140-6736%2816%2900210-5 (accessed January 2020).

148 UNICEF, *Breastfeeding: A Mother's Gift, for Every Child*.
A Well Fed World, "Feed:Meat Ratios."
Emily S. Cassidy et al., "Redefining Agricultural Yields: From Tonnes to People Nourished per Hectare," *Environmental Research Letters*, 8 (August 2013), http://iopscience.iop.org/article/10.1088/1748-9326/8/3/034015/pdf; see also FAO, *The State of Food and Agriculture, 2009*, p. 29.
UNICEF, "Breastfeeding," at http://www.unicef.org/nutrition/index 24824.html (accessed July 2015), citing *The Lancet*, 2008.

149 According to the World Bank as reported in Celia Dugger, "Report Warns Malnutrition Begins in Cradle," *New York Times* (March 3, 2006), p. A6. Caryn Finkle, "Nestle, Infant Formula, and Excuses: The Regulation of Commercial Advertising in Developing Nations," *Northwestern Journal of International Law and Interests*, 14 (3) (1994), p. 602.

150 Andrew Jacobs, "Opposition to Breast-Feeding Resolution by U.S. Stuns World Health Officials," *New York Times* (July 8, 2018), retrieved from https://www.nytimes.com/2018/07/08/health/world-health-breastfeeding-ecuador-trump.html (accessed December 2018).

151 Mayo Clinic, "Mediterranean Diet: A Heart-healthy Eating Plan," November 3, 2017, retrieved from https://www.mayoclinic.org/healthy-lifestyle/nutrition-and-healthy-eating/in-depth/mediterranean-diet/art-20047801 (accessed December 2018).

152 Footprint Network, "Earth Overshoot Day 2017 is Aug. 2, the Earliest Date since Ecological Overshoot Began in the Early 1970s," at https://www.footprintnetwork.org/2017/06/27/earth-overshoot-day-2017-2/ (accessed December 2, 2018).

153 See generally FAO, "What is food loss and food waste?" at http://www.fao.org/food-loss-and-food-waste/en/ (last visited April 2019).

154 FAO, *Global Food Losses and Food Waste: Extent, Causes and Prevention* (Rome: FAO, 2011), Executive Summary.

155 Rockefeller Foundation, "YieldWise Food Loss: Reducing loss from what we grow and harvest," at https://www.rockefellerfoundation.org/our-work/initiatives/yieldwise/ (accessed April 2019); see also Julian Parfitt, Mark Barthel, and Sarah Macnaughton, "Food Waste within Food Supply Chains: Quantification and Potential for Change to 2050," *Philosophical Transactions of the Royal Society: Biological Science*, 365 (September 2010), pp. 3065–81, Table 6.

156 See, e.g. EAT-Lancet Commission, Food Planet Health: Healthy Diets From Sustainable Food Systems.

157 Julian Parfitt et al., "Food Waste within Food Supply Chains," Table 6.

158 Ibid.

159 Phillip Brasor, "Japan Loves Wasting Food," *Japan Times* (March 1, 2009).

160 FAO, *Global Food Losses and Food Waste*, Executive Summary.

161 Charles Mann, "Reseeding the Green Revolution," *Science*, 277 (August 22, 1997), p. 1041.

162 Tim Searchinger, Richard Waite, Craig Hanson, Janet Ranganathan, Patrice Dumas and Emily Matthews, "Creating a Sustainable Food Future: A Menu of Solutions to Feed Nearly 10 Billion People by 2050," World Resources Institute (December 2018).

163   See Brown, "Could Food Shortages Bring Down Civilization?", p. 50. Here are some of
       the reasons Brown expressed concern. First, he cites the fact that during six of the years
       between 2000 and 2009, world grain production was less than consumption, necessi-
       tating the use of food reserves. Second, Brown cites the study previously mentioned in
       this chapter by the National Academy of Sciences, the top science body in the United
       States, that as temperature increases there will be a significant decrease in rice, wheat,
       and corn production. Third, Brown notes the falling water tables in China, India, the
       United States, and other places that feed the irrigation systems of many major grain
       producing regions.
164   Searchinger et al., "Creating a Sustainable Food Future."
165   Ibid, p.1.
166   Ibid.
167   Ibid.

Further Reading

Brown, Lester R., *Full Planet, Empty Plates: The New Geopolitics of Food Scarcity* (New
    York: W. W. Norton & Co., 2012). Brown believes that present policies and human
    demands are undermining the Earth's capacity to provide enough food for an expand-
    ing population. He recommends a number of steps that could be taken to change this
    situation.
Gardner, Bruce L., *American Agriculture in the Twentieth Century: How It Flourished and
    What It Cost* (Cambridge, MA: Harvard University Press, 2002). This book has been
    called a definitive history. There is a tension in the book between the story of the amaz-
    ing growth of productivity in American farms and the story of how that growth came
    about and who benefits from it.
Jacobson, Michael E., and the Staff of the Center for Science in the Public Interest, *Six
    Arguments for a Greener Diet: How a More Plant-Based Diet Could Save Your Health and
    the Environment* (Washington, DC: Center for Science in the Public Interest, 2006). This
    book argues a diet with less meat would reduce chronic diseases, reduce foodborne ill-
    nesses, benefit the soil, water, and air, and reduce animal suffering.
Nestle, Marion, *Food Politics: How the Food Industry Influences Nutrition and Health*, re. edn
    (Berkeley: University of California Press, 2013). Nestle, a professor in the Department
    of Nutrition and Food Science at New York University, seeks to show how the food
    industry, in order to increase its profits, works to encourage people to eat more, thus
    contributing to the obesity epidemic.
Pollan, Michael, *The Omnivore's Dilemma: A Natural History of Four Meals* (New York:
    Penguin Press, 2006). Written like a novel, this is a very interesting book. But it's not
    written by a novelist. Rather the author is a professor of environmental and science
    journalism at the University of California, Berkeley, one of the top universities in the
    United States. Pollan traces three very different diets from Earth to the plate: the industrial
    (the diet of most Americans), the organic, and the hunter-gatherer.
Postel, Sandra, "Growing More Food with Less Water," *Scientific American*, 284 (February
    2001), pp. 46–51. With the population expanding and the climate getting warmer we
    will need to grow more food with less water. Postel shows how it can be done.

Pringle, Peter, *Food, Inc.: Mendel to Monsanto – the Promises and Perils of the Biotech Harvest* (New York: Simon & Schuster, 2003). A balanced account of a controversial subject, Pringle criticizes the extreme claims of both the biotech companies and the environmental critics.

Roberts, Paul, *The End of Food* (New York: Houghton-Mifflin/Bloomsbury, 2008). Roberts, the author of the best-selling book *The End of Oil*, argues that the globalization of our food supply and the increasing popularity of the Western-style diet has driven our food system out of balance. Roberts believes system-wide collapse is possible and recommends ways it might be prevented.

Ronald, Pamela C., and Raoul W. Adamchak, *Tomorrow's Table: Organic Farming, Genetics, and the Future of Food* (New York: Oxford University Press, 2008). This unique book presents the positive aspects of both organic agriculture and genetic engineering. The authors show how the two approaches can be used together to help solve our present food crisis.

Runge, C. Ford, Benjamin Senauer, Philip Pardey, and Mark Rosegrant, *Ending Hunger in Our Lifetime: Food Security and Globalization* (Baltimore: Johns Hopkins Press, 2003). In the first part of the book the authors discuss the difficulties we will face in the effort to end hunger during our lives. In the second part the authors give their solutions.

Chapter 5

Energy[1]

1   Carlos Saavedra contributed to the research and updates reflected in this edition.

Global Issues: An Introduction, Sixth Edition. Kristen A. Hite and John L. Seitz.
© 2021 John Wiley & Sons Ltd. Published 2021 by John Wiley & Sons Ltd.

> *A human being, a skyscraper, an automobile, and a blade of grass all represent energy that has been transformed from one state to another.*
>
> Jeremy Rifkin, *Entropy* (1980)

The Relationship between Energy Use and Development

What do you use energy for? One way to study the progress of the human race is to focus on the way humans have used energy to help them produce goods and services. People have constantly sought ways to lighten the physical work they must do to get the things they need – or feel they need – to live decently.

Think about it: we use energy every day. Going from one place to another takes energy, whether it is on foot, on bicycle, or in a vehicle. Cooking food requires energy, regardless of the type of oven or cooker. Reading at night uses light, either from burning a candle or from a light – both of which produce energy. Nearly everything in your house required energy in its creation, and many of these things may have required a great deal in their manufacturing and distribution to reach your home. This book alone required energy to write, to print, to distribute, and you require energy to read it. Put simply, energy comes in many different forms, and whatever the form, it is absolutely key to daily functioning.

Where does all of this energy come from? It depends very much on the kind of energy used. The harnessing of fire was a crucial step in human evolution, as it provided early humans with heat, enabled them to cook their foods, and helped them to protect themselves against carnivorous animals. Next came the domestication of animals. Animal power was an important supplement to human muscles, enabling people to grow food on a larger scale than ever before. Wood was an important energy source for much of human history, as it still is for a large part of the world's population. The replacement of wood by coal to make steam in Britain in the eighteenth century enabled the Industrial Revolution to begin.

It is coal that has fueled much of the world's economic booms (including China's) by abundantly burning cheap energy for increased industrial production. The relatively low price of coal is deceptive and does not factor in climate and other

Plate 5.1   In some areas, human-powered vehicles are more common than oil-fueled
vehicles

environmental costs such as mercury pollution and particulate matter (see the
Chapter 8 discussion about pollution).

The use of energy in the world has increased dramatically in the years since
the end of World War II in 1945, a period of rapid development in the industrialized countries and one marking the beginning of industrialization in a number
of developing countries. Figure 5.1 shows this well. By 1970, oil had overtaken
coal as the principal commercial energy source in the world. In the 1970s,
nuclear power was introduced, but following a number of disasters has not been
widely adopted.

Up through the end of the twentieth century, most of the increased energy use
took place in nations who industrialized early with coal, then used oil, and built up
a consumer culture of ever-increasing production and consumption as the backbone
of the economy; however, by the twenty-first century, big changes were emerging.
Figure 5.1 shows energy use in the twentieth century, while Figure 5.2 shows the
world's supply by energy type in more recent decades.

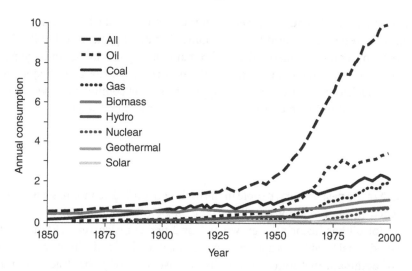

Figure 5.1 Global energy consumption, 1850–2000 (twentieth-century development model)

Source: Robert Service, "Is It Time to Shoot for the Sun?" *Science*, 309 (July 22, 2005), p. 550.

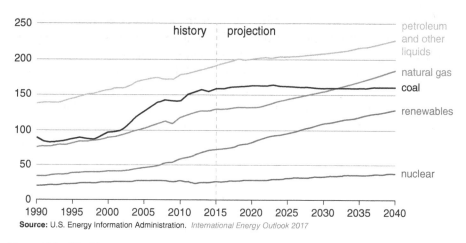

Figure 5.2 World energy consumption by source, 1990–2040 (in quadrillion BTUs)

Nonrenewable Energy Sources

Oil, natural gas, coal, and uranium are the main sources of nonrenewable energy. Many countries have followed the twentieth-century development model, which is predicated on the cheap and abundant combustion of energy, which in the twentieth century came almost entirely from nonrenewable supplies. Please refer to Figure 5.1 for an illustration of how fast oil, gas, coal, and nuclear consumption accelerated after World War II. According to many analysts the world is not about to run out of fossil fuel reserves. However, many of the world's leading scientists have said that burning even a significant amount of what we know is available in these reserves can lead to catastrophic climate impacts. But despite climate concerns, nonrenewable energy demand remains strong, attributed in large part to the fact that development planning over the past century prioritized major investments that locked in infrastructure to support fossil fuel combustion – which raises the cost of transitioning to climate-friendly development pathways.

Oil

For much of the past century, people in the high-consuming economies have become entrenched in an economy heavily reliant on petroleum products.[1] The world's demand for oil has historically grown at 1 or 2 percent each year, although prices have varied considerably.[2] Despite our increasing knowledge of climate change, oil is the most dominant fuel source, primarily because most of global trade and transit depend on it. While electricity has low carbon substitutes, unless and until electric vehicles dominate the transport sector, oil has few substitutes. As such, oil being consumed globally at prodigious rates – about 95 million barrels a day were produced in 2017.[3]

The Middle East, which supplies much of the oil imported into the United States and Western Europe, is a politically complex area. It is torn by regional conflicts, religious conflicts, social and ideological conflicts, and, in the past, by East–West competition. A large amount of the oil involved in international trade is carried on ships that must pass through a single strait in the Persian Gulf – the Strait of Hormuz. This is an example of how over-dependence on 20th century technologies has resulted in complex geopolitical dynamics.

Many experts predict that the largest increase in demand for oil in the coming years will come from increasingly industrialized economies with large populations – such as China and India – and not from nations who were early adopters of industrialization, which have mostly stabilized their energy use and are becoming more energy efficient.

Future demand is expected to be met in notable part by new US and Canadian shale extraction plus new reserves in countries like Brazil and Bahrain.[4] Canada has large deposits of tar sands, which hold as much as 175 billion barrels of oil, but it is relatively expensive and environmentally destructive to extract. Since the mid-2000s, about 1 million barrels of oil a day have been extracted from the oil sands.

Now, due to climate change, experts are predicting that unless there is a revolutionary technological breakthrough for fossil fuels to be burned with dramatically lower carbon emissions, much of the existing oil reserves will need to remain untapped if the world is going to avoid catastrophic climate change. So not only does the price of oil impact energy-intensive economies, but climate concerns combined with the availability and price of electric vehicles may mean that continued reliance on oil is no longer inevitable.

Global Oil Supplies and Price Shocks

Given how essential global transport and trade are for economic development, it is perhaps not surprising that the global economy is also very closely bound to oil supplies. For oil-dependent economies, oil price shocks reverberate far and wide. Consider, for example, Figure 5.3, which shows clearly how oil prices spiked prior to the global economic recession of 2008–9, and then fell sharply as the economy contracted.

The first oil shock took place in 1973 and 1974. The 1973 Arab–Israeli war led a number of Arab oil-producing countries to stop shipping oil to the United States and other countries allied with Israel. American motorists lined up at gas stations, vying for limited supplies. The Organization of Petroleum Exporting Countries (OPEC), of which most oil-exporting nations are members, seized the opportunity to raise oil prices significantly, and prices quadrupled.

The second oil shock came in 1979–80, prompted by the Iranian Revolution and the ousting of the Shah as the head of the Iranian government. Iranian oil shipments to the United States stopped, but the real shock came when OPEC doubled its prices. Many consumers in places like North America had refused to believe there was a real energy crisis after the first oil shock and had returned to their normal high consumption of petroleum products after the Arab embargo was lifted; but the second oil shock convinced most people that there was indeed an energy crisis. While many had blamed either US oil companies or the US government for creating the first oil crisis, the second shock clearly demonstrated that something had fundamentally changed in the world. What became apparent to many was that the United States, and most other developed nations, were dependent on one section of the world for

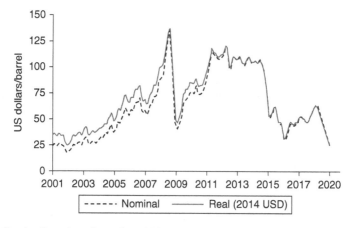

Figure 5.3 Crude oil spot market prices 2000–2020

Source: International Energy Association, Oil Information: Overview (2018 edn), p.12.

a significant part of their energy, and that they could no longer control events in that part of the world.

The huge increase in oil prices in the 1970s cast a cloud over the development plans of many nations. Most of these plans were based upon an assumption that reasonably cheap oil would be available, as it had been for the West, to support their industrialization. Most of the developing countries have little or no coal or oil themselves. The development plans called for these countries to export natural commodities, nonfuel resources, and light manufactured goods; it was assumed that the earnings from these exports would be sufficient to pay for the fuel they would need to import. The success of the development plans also depended upon countries being able to attract enough capital for investment in businesses.

The large increases in the price of oil made by OPEC in the 1970s led to a massive transfer of wealth from the developed nations to part of the developing world – arguably "the quickest massive transfer of wealth among societies since the Spanish Conquistadores seized the Incan gold stores some four centuries ago."[5] Higher oil prices led to low economic growth, higher inflation, big trade deficits, and increased unemployment in the United States and other high-consuming nations. For poorer oil-importing countries alike, the cost of their imported oil also went up and caused some of them to acquire huge debts to pay for the oil they needed. Daniel Yergin, the coeditor of an important report on energy from Harvard Business School, assessed the potential consequences of the oil shocks in the following terms:

> The unhappy set of economic circumstances set in motion by the oil shocks contains the potential for far-reaching crises. In the industrial nations, high inflation, low growth, and high unemployment can erode the national consensus and undermine the stability and legitimacy of the political system. In the developing world, zero growth leads to misery and upheavals. Protectionism and accumulation of debt threaten the international trade and payments system. And, of course, there is the tinder of international politics, particularly involving the Middle East, where political and social upheavals can cause major oil disruptions and where fears about and threats to energy supplies can lead to war.[6]

When OPEC increased fuel prices, no exceptions were made for the poorer countries; they were required to pay the same high prices for their oil imports as the rich nations had to pay. Added to that burden was the one created by the global recession, which the higher oil prices had helped to create. As the recession deepened in the West, the industrialized countries cut back on their imports from the developing nations. Many of these countries borrowed heavily from commercial banks to pay for their higher oil bills and accumulated staggering debt. The foreign debt of the less developed countries in the mid-1990s rose to about $1.9 trillion USD. Brazil incurred the largest foreign debt of all the developing nations, over $150 billion USD, in the mid-1990s.

The third oil shock came in 1990–1. Iraq invaded Kuwait and threatened Saudi Arabia. In order to prevent Iraq from becoming the dominant power in the Middle East and having significant influence on the production and pricing of oil from that region, the United States led a coalition of forces in driving Iraq out of Kuwait. The war, which lasted just six weeks, involved half a million US soldiers and token troops from other nations.[7] The allied forces had few casualties, but the retreating Iraqi forces, which suffered large casualties, sabotaged more than 700 oil wells in Kuwait, setting about 600 on fire.[8] In 1990, the price of oil increased dramatically right after the Iraqi invasion of Kuwait, but by the end of the war the price had dropped back to the prewar level. That price did not reflect the real cost of oil, which arguably should have included the cost of the war. (It has been estimated that by the mid-1980s the United States was spending seven times as much keeping the shipping lanes open to the Middle East oil fields as it was for the oil itself.[9]) In 2003, the United States invaded Iraq, an action with relatively few allies which was opposed by much of the world, who alleged the US invaded to secure oil supplies.

In 2020, the global Covid-19 pandemic hit a "reverse" shock, where oil futures actually dropped below zero due to a precipitous decline in oil consumption due to the economic slowdown associated with lockdown measures in place in many of the world's biggest economies.

Coal

Coal energy expectations are shifting rapidly. Although coal is a much more abundant resource than oil or natural gas, the unsustainability of coal (both economically and environmentally) has resulted in many efforts to transition to alternative energy sources. It is estimated that the Earth has 1 trillion tons of recoverable coal, with one-quarter of it in the United States.

Among the many serious pollutants emitted when coal is burned, mercury, sulfur dioxide, and carbon dioxide are all significant. Historically, about 40 percent of carbon dioxide emissions around the world have come from the burning of coal. Coal has proven so damaging to climate and human health that there are now efforts underway to dramatically decrease the amount of coal used for energy.[10]

The Intergovernmental Panel on Climate Change has said that phasing out coal production by around 2040 is a key priority for keeping global temperature increases to around 1.5 degrees.[11] In response to climate concerns combined with shifting economics, Scotland has led the way in the United Kingdom to stop burning coal, India has announced a moratorium on new coal plant construction, and Beijing has shut all major coal-fired powerplants due to pollution problems.[12]

China: Coal Titan

At the end of the first decade in the twenty-first century, China was burning more coal than the United States, Europe, and Japan combined. By 2017, coal supplied approximately two-thirds of China's energy demand.[13] By 2013, China was burning over 4 billion tons of coal annually, amounting to half of global coal use.[14] Despite a considerable commitment to increase renewable energy use, China's use of coal – the most polluting fossil fuel – has claimed a significant toll on the environment. Owing to a combination of economic, climate, pollution, and production challenges, China claimed its coal use has already peaked and was on the decline from 2013–16.[15] But is this a temporary decline or permanent shift? Various researchers found China's coal consumption in 2017 rebounded to a 1–3 percent increase, leaving experts to debate whether coal use really is on the long-term decline.[16] Given the economics of natural gas and renewable energy compared to coal, the overall view is that this increase is temporary and that, most likely, coal use in China may continue to decline, at least as a relative percentage of the energy mix.[17] But China's coal mining production tells a potentially different story.

In addition to massive increases in energy consumption, China is also a major energy producer, commanding a full 45 percent of the world's coal supplies (the United States is the second biggest producer at about one quarter of China's yield), and its appetite for coal is so high that it also is the world's biggest importer of coal.[31] Most of China's coal is situated in the northern part of the country, removed from the eastern coastal provinces that have seen considerable economic growth. In 2018, China increased its coal mining capacity target to over 400 million tons, a 10 percent increase from recent years.[18]

Let's look again at Figures 5.1 and Figure 5.2. If we compare them, we begin to see the story of what has happened since the turn of the century: do you see the shift in energy supply towards more natural gas and renewables, and less coal?

Natural Gas

Natural gas consumption is on the rise, owing to a combination of economic, political, and environmental reasons. Natural gas is often touted as the lowest carbon emitting fossil fuel, emitting substantially less carbon dioxide than that emitted by coal, but this can be offset by leakage during production of the much more potent methane gas. By 2016, global gas use had spiked to 2–3 percent a year, spurred in notable part by a surge in demand from China (Asia accounts for half of the global increase in natural gas demand).[19]

Proven reserves of natural gas are estimated to be larger than those of oil. Some of the largest reserves are in Bahrain, Russia, Iran, Qatar, and Saudi Arabia, as well as shale gas reserves in the United States. These gas producers are finding new markets for their exports, with liquid natural gas importing countries growing in number: from 15 in 2005 to roughly 40 in 2017.[20] Europe now uses natural gas for 20 percent of its energy, much of it coming from Russia. More than a third of the energy in the United States now comes from natural gas, which has displaced coal since about 2016 as the biggest source of energy – a trend which is increasing throughout the world.[21]

The Energy Transition

Are we running out of energy? Of course not. Everything is made out of energy, and, as students learn when studying the laws of thermodynamics, energy cannot be destroyed. These laws also state that energy cannot be created: all we can do is to transform it from one state to another. And when energy is transformed, or in other words, when it is converted from a stored to kinetic state to be used for some work (i.e. energy gets "generated," such as by machines at a power plant), the energy is changed from a more useful to a less useful form. All types of energy eventually end up as low-grade heat.

So, if everything is energy and energy cannot be destroyed, why is there an energy and climate crisis? Countries are facing an energy crisis because they can no longer depend on abundant supplies of cheap energy from traditional sources, which generate massive emissions of carbon dioxide (CO_2) and other pollutants. The world is entering a period of transition from one main energy source – oil – to a variety of sources. This is the third energy transition the world has passed through: the first was from wood to coal, and the second from coal to oil (Figure 5.4).

By the second decade of the twenty-first century, renewable energy had taken off, and natural gas began displacing coal in a number of countries. In 2016, fossil fuels made up about 81 percent of the energy used, with oil about 31.9 percent, coal about 27 percent, and natural gas about 22 percent. Nonfossil fuels – mainly hydroelectric, nuclear, geothermal, biomass, wind, and solar – accounted for about 18.9 percent of energy production in 2016, a dramatic increase from decades prior.[22]

More and more, people now recognize that the world must shift from its reliance on nonrenewable and dangerously polluting fossil fuels to energy sources that are renewable and less polluting. Many are starting to reduce their dependence on imported oil, which must end since this unclean fuel is neither cheap nor secure. Costa Rica, for example, hardly used any fossil fuels in 2016 and has decided to ban fossil fuels and become the world's first decarbonized

World total primary energy supply (TPES) by fuel

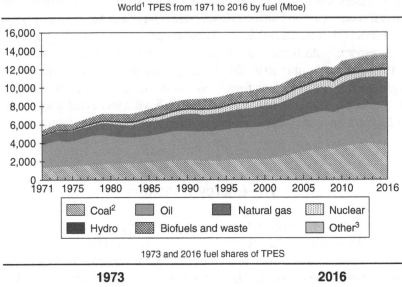

World[1] TPES from 1971 to 2016 by fuel (Mtoe)

Legend: Coal[2], Oil, Natural gas, Nuclear, Hydro, Biofuels and waste, Other[3]

1973 and 2016 fuel shares of TPES

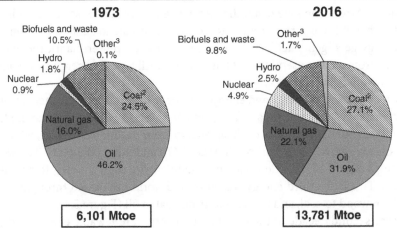

1973

Biofuels and waste 10.5%
Other[3] 0.1%
Hydro 1.8%
Nuclear 0.9%
Coal[2] 24.5%
Natural gas 16.0%
Oil 46.2%

6,101 Mtoe

2016

Other[3] 1.7%
Biofuels and waste 9.8%
Hydro 2.5%
Nuclear 4.9%
Coal[2] 27.1%
Natural gas 22.1%
Oil 31.9%

13,781 Mtoe

Figure 5.4   Global energy supply

Note: Mtoe is million tons of oil equivalent, the energy required to burn one ton of oil; TPES is total primary energy supply; "Coal" includes peat and oil shale; "Other" includes geothermal, solar, wind, heat, etc.

Source: International Energy Agency, *Key World Energy Statistics 2018*.

society.[23] If other countries follow Costa Rica's example, what will be the new principal energy source(s) for industries across the globe? As in many transitions, the end to be reached is yet to be determined. The only clear thing now is that the present state of affairs is no longer viable. We are in the beginning years of the energy transition.

For the rest of this section, we will examine the growing role of renewable and other nonfossil fuel sources of energy.

Renewable Energy Sources

Governments are increasingly supporting renewable energy to meet energy production needs. Costa Rica, for example, ran entirely on renewable energy for the first 300 days in 2017.[24] Germany used renewable energy to fuel more than a third of the country's power supply in 2017.[25] All the countries in North America have pledged to get half their electricity from "clean" power by 2025 – much of which is from renewable sources.[26] Indeed, the economics of renewable sources are shifting significantly – to the point that solar power outcompetes coal in many places.[27] Renewable energy can be obtained in a variety of ways: from wood, falling water, wind, wastes, hydrogen, and, of course, from direct sunlight. We will briefly examine each of these.

Solar Power

The sun produces a great deal of energy and is expected to continue to shine at its present brightness for at least one billion years more. Each year the Earth receives from the sun about ten times the energy that is stored in all of its fossil fuel and uranium reserves. Direct sunlight can be used to generate heat and to produce electricity, either indirectly in solar thermal systems or directly by using photovoltaic or solar cells. Solar thermal systems collect sunlight through mirrors or lenses and use it to heat a fluid to extremely high temperatures. The fluid heats water to produce steam, which is then used to drive turbines to generate electricity.

Plate 5.2   Solar thermal power plant, California
Source: US Department of Energy.

In 2005, the main use for solar power in the United States was for heating swimming pools. That is no longer the case: in roughly a decade, solar power became one of the most rapid expanding energy generation sources on the market. This trend is a broad one – certainly not limited to the US or even to wealthy countries. Indeed, the world market for solar energy generation has skyrocketed. Some regions, such as parts of South Asia, the Middle East, and North Africa, are particularly well suited for large-scale solar thermal plants, and these plants are becoming cost competitive. Solar energy can be used well in moderately or intensely sunny places. Much of the world fits this criterion – especially in India and parts of sub-Saharan Africa which are home to a disproportionate number of households without even basic access to electricity. Solar energy is collected nearly as efficiently by small, decentralized collectors as it is by larger, centralized units – and is more competitive than the cost of coal in many of these areas.

Over the past decade, solar use has virtually exploded across the globe, and now out-competes coal in many places, especially those without an electric grid already built. The cost of solar energy from solar thermal plants has been dropping rapidly. For example, from 2010–16, the cost of utility-scale photovoltaic systems decreased roughly 10–15% *each year*.[28] If one includes the hidden costs of fossil fuels – that is, the costs society bears now and will bear in the future because of the pollution produced and the costs of military forces to ensure access to them – solar energy is clearly less expensive than fossil fuels right now; even without these costs, it is still cheaper in many areas – especially rural ones.

Plate 5.3 Solar energy provides power for a water pump in Morocco

Source: USAID Photo Agency for International Development.

China produces the most solar cells in the world. In 2012, China's solar capacity was "only" 3.4 gigawatt (GW) but by 2017 that had spiked to 130 GW.[29] In countries like Kenya, rural solar photovoltaic installations have risen exponentially. Germany was a relatively early adopter, with solar reaching 14 percent of its electricity supply as early as 2008.[30] In the US, solar photovoltaic installations were doubling by 2009.[31]

Wind

Wind is an energy source that has been commonly used in the past for power as well as for the cooling of houses. It is still used for these purposes in many countries and has seen a resurgence around the world, scaled up dramatically from the windmills of the past. Wind turbines are much bigger and much more efficient than traditional windmills, and can be located anywhere wind is found: on top of a mountain, across the plains, and even offshore across the ocean.

In the United States, the state of California constructed 16,000 wind turbines in just three mountain passes in areas that have fairly steady wind. The early dominance of California in producing wind power probably had more to do with the tax incentives that the state gave in order to promote this form of energy than with wind conditions. The California wind farms began going up in 1981 after the federal government passed a law that encouraged small energy producers, and after both the federal government and the State of California gave tax credits to wind producers. Texas has surpassed California as the top producer of wind power in the US.[32] In 2010, Iowa, a state in the Midwest of the United States, was getting a US record of 14 percent of its electricity from wind.[33] According to the American Wind Energy Association, the total wind power operating in the United States in 2017 avoided an estimated 189 million metric tons of CO_2 – a tripling from less than a decade prior, owing to massively increased installations of wind turbines located both onshore and offshore.[34] Other countries have seen similarly rapid rates of adoption.

In 2010, Europe was getting about 5 percent of its electricity from wind, and this has been increasing substantially each year. Attracted by the success of wind farms in California and elsewhere, a number of European countries such as Germany, Denmark, Spain, Italy, Britain, and the Netherlands have greatly increased their wind power. The European Union has set a goal of getting about 20 percent of its electricity from wind and other renewable sources by 2020. By 2015, some 40 percent of Denmark's electricity came from wind power, and on one particularly windy day the country's wind generation exceeded its entire national demand by 140 percent.[35] In 2017 Spain got about 19 percent of its electricity from wind (and one-third total from renewables); Germany got about 16 percent.[36] These are more than double the amounts from just a decade ago.[37]

China has begun installing wind turbines from Inner Mongolia to offshore from its eastern coasts as part of its goal to secure more of its energy from renewable sources. China has surpassed the United States as the world's largest market for wind turbines. In 2017, China's wind capacity was 169 GW, skyrocketing up from 61 GW in 2012.[38]

Plate 5.4   Wind turbines in Altamont Pass, California

Source: US Department of Energy.

The main challenges with relying entirely on wind and solar for national energy needs is that energy is not usually generated around the clock, and thus must be stored in some way so it can be used when the wind stops or the sun goes down. Innovations in storage batteries continue, but remain relatively expensive for wide-spread generation – and can have significant environmental impacts during their manufacturing and production. Another problem with wind is that the choices of windy places in the world are relatively few and unevenly distributed. They are also often in remote locations, far from population centers, and in areas of great natural beauty, which some feel the windmills spoil. Past problems such as the noise the wind turbines make as the blades whirl (some blades are as large as the wingspan of a 747 aircraft) and the killing of birds have been partly solved by improvements in turbine design and more care given to their location. However, other challenges persist, such as "shadow flicker" effects for turbines located near population settlements.[39]

In other cases, such as in coastal areas with strong and steady winds, many wind farms have been located offshore in places like the United States, Europe and China.

Hydroelectric Power

Hydroelectric power is generated from falling water and is a potentially clean source of energy, causing little pollution. A large potential for developing this type of energy still exists in Africa, Latin America, and Asia. Large dams, which often need to store the water for the electric generators, usually seriously disturb the local environment, sometimes require the displacement of large numbers of people, and cause silting behind the dam, which limits its life.

While most of the best sites for large dams in the industrialized countries have already been developed, a potential exists for constructing some small dams and for installing electric generators at existing dams that do not have them. There are also several very large dams being constructed in Africa and Asia which have major social and environmental costs as well as substantial infrastructure and transmission costs, and sometimes have the added problem of either flooding out local communities or bypassing others located under power lines installed to export energy to more densely populated areas.

China has built the world's largest dam, the Three Gorges Dam, which is designed to produce annually an amount of electricity equal to that produced by 50 million tons of coal. More ambitious than the United States' Tennessee Valley Authority initiative to massively scale up hydropower to electrify rural households in the southeast US last century – or the Congo's Grand Inga Dam this present one – the Three Gorges Dam has been controversial in terms of environmental impact, people displaced, and land flooded for its construction, although there is no question that it is generating very large amounts of electricity. The dam has its critics who, among many other complaints, point to the millions of people who had to be relocated to make room for its huge reservoir, and the possible large amounts of methane that will rise from the reservoir as the submerged vegetation rots. Methane (CH_4) is many times more powerful as a greenhouse gas than is carbon dioxide (CO_2), which makes it more difficult to use climate change to justify an energy transition to large hydropower where large methane-emitting dams are proposed.[40]

Beyond large and small dams, there are other innovative technologies to harness power from running water. For example, Portland, Oregon – a city in the United States – started generating electricity from turbines installed inside the city's water pipes.[41]

Wood, Agricultural/Forestry Residues, and Animal Dung

These are still the principal fuels in many countries. Bioenergy comprised 14 percent of the world's supply in 2013.[42] Rural communities in sub-Saharan Africa, as in the South Asian countries of India, Pakistan, and Bangladesh, use these traditional fuels to cook their food and to provide heat and light. In fact, except for their own muscle power and the aid of a few domestic animals, the majority of villagers in many rural areas have no other source of energy. Rapidly expanding populations in areas without access to electricity are placing high demands on the use of wood; at the same time, modern agricultural requirements and development in general are leading to the clearing of vast acres of forests. Acute shortages of firewood already exist in wide areas of Africa, Asia, and Latin America. Meanwhile, wealthier places like the UK have rapidly scaled up wood-fired furnaces as a substitute to the burning of coal, outsourcing natural resource extraction to forests abroad.[43]

Biomass is the name given to the production of liquid and gaseous fuel from crop, animal, and human wastes; from garbage from cities; and from crops especially grown for energy production. Millions of generators that create methane gas from animal and human wastes are producing fuel for villages in India and China. Brazil uses a considerable amount of biofuels for energy (9 percent of its total energy supply), specializing in sugar-cane production to produce low-pollution alcohol for fuel for automobiles.[44] In 2017, biomass supplied about 5 percent of total energy use in the United States, including biofuels (mainly ethanol), wood fuels, and municipal waste.[45] An important part of Brazil's success came when the automobile industry in Brazil developed new technology that permitted it to produce an engine that can use either gasoline, alcohol, or a combination of both. This allows drivers to select the cheapest fuel, which at present is alcohol.

Some cities are burning their garbage mixed with coal and/or natural gas to produce electricity. It is difficult to estimate how widespread this form of energy generation will become in the future. Some see good potential while others mention its negative aspects, such as the emission of harmful gases and foul odors from burning garbage.

In order to reduce its dependence on oil from the Middle East and other insecure areas, the United States granted large subsidies to farmers to encourage them to grow corn for processing into ethanol. By 2009, about 30 percent of the US corn crop was being grown to produce ethanol for automobiles. A debate has occurred over how much this move contributed to higher food prices around the world.

Research into nonfood crops that can be used to make biofuels, such as wood waste, weed-like energy crops, agricultural residues, and cornstalks, is being conducted. These are often called "second generation biofuels," and they attempt to generate energy with less direct competition for arable land than fuels like ethanol. A recent report has concluded: "Cellulosic biofuels – liquid fuels – made from inedible parts of plants – offer the most environmentally attractive and technologically feasible near-term alternative to oil."[66] Considerable research is now underway to find cost effective technologies to capture carbon emissions from biofuels. Known as "BECCS," for bioenergy carbon capture and sequestration, this technology carries the potential to pull more carbon dioxide out of the air as the plants grow than is emitted back into the atmosphere from energy generation. Despite the promise that BECCS offers for negative CO_2 emissions, concerns persist as they do with conventional biofuels that there is only so much land available in the world, and dedicating land for carbon farming can compete with efforts to grow and provide food.

Geothermal Energy

Heat that is produced within the Earth's interior is not a form of solar energy but is a renewable form of energy. Geothermal energy is stored often in pools of water or in rock, or as steam under the Earth's cool crust. Because it involves drilling deep wells and installing fairly elaborate piping systems, geothermal energy is typically used in geographically strategic places as opposed to adopted at the individual household level (like solar). Still, geothermal energy accounted for about 14,000 megawatts of energy in 2017.

The United States is the biggest generator of geothermal energy, followed by the Philippines, Indonesia, and Turkey. Iceland uses this form of energy to heat many of its homes, and Russia and Hungary heat extensive greenhouses with it. In 2009, geothermal energy provided Iceland and El Salvador with about 25 percent of their electricity, and the Philippines, Kenya, and Costa Rica with about 15 percent of their electricity. New Zealand, Mexico, Italy, and Japan round out the list of the biggest geothermal producers.[46]

Plate 5.5   Geothermal power plant, California

Source: US Department of Energy.

Hydrogen-Powered Fuel Cells

Hydrogen-powered fuel cells have the potential to become a major nonpolluting and efficient source of energy for vehicles. In fuel cells, hydrogen is combined at low temperatures with oxygen supplied from the air to produce electricity, which is used to run an electric motor. Vehicles powered by the electric motor would be clean, quiet, highly efficient, and relatively easy to maintain. No battery is required, and basically the only substance coming from the exhaust is water. Hydrogen can be obtained from water by a process that itself uses electricity. If the electricity used to make hydrogen comes from renewable and nonpolluting sources, such as solar power, wind power, or hydroelectric power, hydrogen fuel cells are a renewable and clean source of energy. If a polluting fuel such as coal is used to make hydrogen, the fuel cell would be neither clean nor renewable.

By 2000, nearly all automobile companies were putting a major effort into developing cars using fuel cells, even though at the time hydrogen fuel cells cost about a hundred times as much per unit of power as the internal combustion engine powered by gasoline.[47] The US National Academy of Sciences in 2004 estimated that the transition to a hydrogen economy would take decades because of the serious challenges involved, and this is proving true.[48] One major problem is the need to create thousands of hydrogen fueling stations, a challenge similar to cars that plug into an electrical source to recharge. One industrialist in the United States put it this way: "It's the classic chicken-and-egg dilemma. There's no demand for cars and trucks with limited fueling options, but no one wants to make the huge investment to create a fueling infrastructure unless there are fleets of vehicles on the road. So, the question is: How do we create demand?"[73] Notwithstanding the infrastructure and cost challenges, in 2015 Toyota began piloting hydrogen cars for consumers.

Nuclear energy is the last source of energy we will examine. Please see the final section of this chapter for this examination. We have decided to give it its own section because of its controversy, importance, and complexity.

Energy and Development: Critical Challenges and Opportunities

The necessity of modern energy for economic and social needs, especially considering the relatively high cost of energy compared to incomes for the poorest people, has increased focus on the energy needs of the world's poorest people. Consider that approximately 1 billion people lack access to any form of electricity or modern energy.

The early stages of industrialization are energy intensive. Modern transportation and manufacturing systems, upon which industrialization rests, utilize large amounts of energy, as does the construction industry. When energy is cheap and abundant, it enables machines to process resources much faster and in much bigger volumes than by manual labor. Wealth gets created as natural resources are processed and sold.

Lower income countries have relatively few fuel reserves and limited ability to purchase expensive oil or other supplies to fuel the scale of energy demanded by large-scale industrialization. This places constraints on following the nineteenth- and twentieth-century economic development pathways that enabled most of the currently wealthy countries to industrialize and grow their economies, which are further exacerbated by the negative impacts of fossil fuels on the Earth's climate. Nations are increasingly facing challenges in pursuing a development path radically different from the one followed by historically wealthy nations that developed their economies through cheap and abundant combustion of fossil fuels.

Notwithstanding a growing push for clean and affordable energy, conventional sources have dominated the first two decades of the twenty-first century. Billions of people use very few fossil fuels at all, relying mainly on wood, charcoal, cow dung, and crop residues for cooking fuel and for heat. According to one study, a 1 percent increase in urbanization led to 14 percent greater consumption of charcoal.[49] Population pressures and the lack of affordable modern energy supplies are increasing the demand for traditional fuels in the Global South. This has its own economic and environmental consequences in the form of air pollution from particulate matter and deforestation. Further, the shortage of firewood in the south of the African continent has been increasing as population growth has caused consumption of wood to exceed the growth of new supplies in many areas. Moreover, as firewood becomes expensive or unavailable in rural areas, people switch to burning dried cow dung and crop residues, thus preventing important nutrients and organic material from returning to the soil.

Across the globe, more than 1 billion people lack access to electricity – with over 600 million people in sub-Saharan Africa alone.[50] In 2015, the United Nations launched Sustainable Development Goal 7, with a target of universal and sustainable energy access for all. To help reach this goal, the UN launched a program called Sustainable Energy for All, focused primarily on electrifying the parts of India and sub-Saharan Africa who claim the overwhelming majority of households that lack access to electricity. Governments are also stepping up to the challenge. For example, more than a dozen government agencies in the United States have supported an initiative called "Power Africa," as well as providing US$1 billion USD of finance for renewable energy in India.

Provided sunlight is adequate and storage is not cost-prohibitive, renewable solar energy is now seen as a leading solution for powering rural households. Unlike fossil fuels which depend on large, centralized generation stations and extensive grid structures, renewable energy like solar is modular, scalable, and can be installed in individual households and also connected as "mini-grids" at the community level. The economics of this kind of renewable energy are outcompeting fossil fuel supplies, and "King coal" no longer reigns as the desired energy supply in many rural áreas. This is a hopeful message that not only provides opportunities for sustainable energy access but also can help fight climate change by accelerating the transition from fossil fuels to low carbon supplies in shifting development pathways.

National Approaches to Energy and Development

Governmental support of the use of fossil fuels through subsidies helped keep the price of fossil fuels low and is one of the crucial factors we need to know when we examine climate change – perhaps the most important energy and environmental issue the world faces today. Even in the first two decades of the twenty-first century, governments continued supporting the burning of fossil fuels with huge government subsidies. Throughout the early 2000s, payments to the fossil fuel industries fluctuated annually according to the price of energy supplies, demand, domestic energy policies, and exchange rates. In 2008, when international energy prices were very high, subsidies were about $560 billion USD.[51] By 2009, subsidies totaled about $310 billion, including about $125 billion for oil products and $85 billion for natural gas.[52] But by 2015, subsidies had started to subside, in tandem with a pledge by wealthy countries to eliminate fossil fuel subsidies by 2025.[53]

Let us look now at a few key countries and regions to see their energy and development pathways (Figure 5.5).

Plate 5.6 Shortage of wood is a part of the energy crisis, since many urban dwellers in developing nations rely on wood as their major source of fuel

Source: Ab Abercrombie.

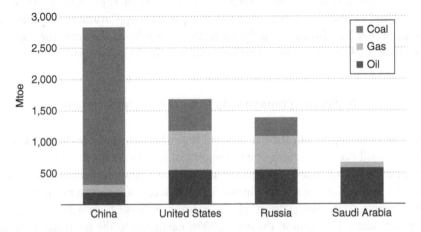

Figure 5.5 Global fossil fuel production in select countries (2016)

Source: IEA. World Energy Outlook 2017, p.485.

China Although China's energy situation is not typical because of its vast reserves of coal, it does have a typical problem: how to provide a growing population with enough fuel in a manner that does not seriously harm the environment. China's population is so large, and its economy is transitioning at such a rapid pace, that its demand for energy is huge – and its energy production and consumption from nearly every source dwarfs the rest of the world.

China, the largest user of energy in the world, has been in a very energy-intensive period of its development as it focuses on manufacturing and exporting material goods. The vast majority of China's electricity use is for industry, not households.[54] As China continues to increase industrial production and its consumer class continues to increase in demand, there is concern that the sheer size of its energy demand yields major health, climate, and political impacts. Here are some of the measures China has taken increase its energy supply:

- Implementing the world's largest program to use methane gas as fuel in rural areas. The gas is produced by fermenting animal and human wastes in simple generators; after the gas is produced, the remains are used as fertilizer for crops.
- Increasing oil imports. China was self-sufficient in oil until the mid-1990s, but a massive increase in consumer car purchases has exploded demand – with a 13 percent increase in oil imports from 2016–17.[55] China has made large investments in foreign oil-producing nations across the globe. The Chinese market for new cars is the largest in the world, with more car sales year than the US, Germany, and Japan combined.[56] This rapid growth in demand for cars has led the government to not only increase its supply of oil but also to address health and environmental consequences through aggressive expansion of electric vehicles and improved efficiency and emissions standards, and alternative fuel sources.[57]
- Increasing nuclear power production – it is poised to become the world's top nuclear energy producer before 2030. In the first two decades of the twenty-first century, China expanded its nuclear capacity tenfold and added dozens of new nuclear power plants – a major portion of the world's new nuclear power construction.[58] Since many of these plants are located near large cities, safety concerns have been raised over this rapid expansion.[59]
- Expanding renewable energy sources, such as solar and wind power, small hydroelectric dams, and biomass. Wind power alone accounts for roughly 10 percent of China's energy mix, and hydropower generates even more energy than wind due to large and controversial hydropower. China also represents more than 70 percent of the solar thermal market and leads the world in solar production, with solar PV production increasing by more than 75 GW from 2010–16.[60]

China is the world's largest producer of fossil fuel energy as well as the top coal importer and also one of the biggest coal producers – and consequently the world's biggest greenhouse gas emitter, despite being 25 percent more efficient than most other countries who amassed wealth through high-emitting industrialization

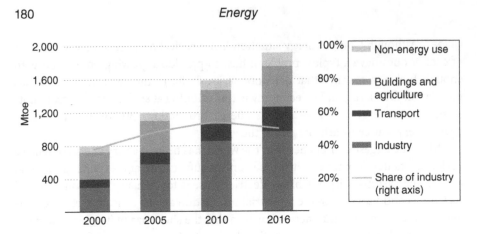

Figure 5.6 China's primary energy consumption

Source: IEA. World Energy Outlook 2017, p. 476.

development pathways.[61] In the first two decades of the twenty-first century, China's electricity consumption quadrupled.[62] By 2009 it had overtaken the United States as the largest total user of energy as well as greenhouse gas emissions. Beyond electricity use, the transportation sector accounts for much of China's continued growth in energy consumption. Other parts of Asia are expected to follow suit.

China is not only the world's biggest greenhouse gas emitter, but other pollution–especially from massive industrial production – is causing serious health and environmental problems. The country's air and water pollution levels are so extensive that by 2019, China was home to more than half of the 100 most polluted cities in the world.[63] But this is starting to change: under China's 13th Five-Year Plan, the country is taking measures to control emissions and address air pollution, as well as prioritizing low-emitting fuels as it diversifies its energy mix (Figure 5.6).[64]

The United States   The United States has historically been the largest buyer of oil in the world. In the past, much of it came from a single country: Saudi Arabia. Over the past two decades, China became the fastest growing oil market in the world, buying more oil from Saudi Arabia than the United States. But that growth seems to have slowed in tandem with overall economic growth.[65]

The US energy sector remains overwhelmingly dependent on oil and coal, but that is starting to change, with natural gas overtaking coal in 2016 for total electricity production.[66] Increasingly, the US is exporting fossil fuel energy as its domestic energy mix becomes less oil- and coal-intensive. Natural gas (particularly due to fracking, see Chapter 8) and renewable energy take up an increasing percentage of the market share, in part due to efforts to limit carbon dioxide emissions associated with climate change.

In 2017, 37 percent of US energy came from oil, 29 percent from natural gas, 14 percent from coal (down 10 percent since 2008), 11 percent from renewable sources, and 9 percent from nuclear electric power.[67] By 2016, more power was being

Table 5.1 Top world oil producers, 2017

	Country	*Production (million barrels per day)*
1	United States	15.65
2	Saudi Arabia	12.09
3	Russia	11.21
4	Canada	4.96
5	China	4.78
6	Iran	4.69
7	Iraq	4.45
8	United Arab Emirates	3.72
9	Brazil	3.36
10	Kuwait	2.82

Source: EIA, "What countries are the top producers and consumers of oil?", at https://www.eia.gov/tools/faqs/faq.php?id=709&t=6 (accessed December 26, 2018).

produced from natural gas than from coal. Meanwhile, crude oil imports to the United States fell by more than 1.3 mb/d between 2010 and 2016 (to 7.9 mb/d) while exports surged to 0.9 mb/d.[68] Even as the US remains a net oil importer, the combined changes of reduced imports and increased exports alongside a rapid increase in shale-based production are dramatically impacting the economic and political dynamics of oil flows at the global level.[69]

Historically, the United States has lacked a coherent energy policy, typically taking a decentralized approach to electricity production and a politically variable approach to oil and transportation. By 2013, the United States was the world's biggest producer of oil (see Table 5.1), although about 40 percent of the oil consumed in the United States was still imported.[70] In 2017, the United States imported most of its oil from Canada, followed by Saudi Arabia, Mexico, Venezuela, and Iraq – in that order.[71] Meanwhile, government agencies at the state levels are increasingly implementing policies to increase energy efficiency, reduce carbon emissions, and promote lower-carbon fuels, even as national-level policies have been inconsistent.

Why has it been so difficult for the United States to enact an effective energy policy? Part of the reason is that the inertia of an oil- and coal-intensive infrastructure is hard to overcome. The national infrastructure was built for an economy of ever-increasing production and consumption, in energy as well as in material goods, and the transition to a more sustainable economic development pathway is not easy. Also, very large economic interests, such as those of the oil companies, benefit from the status quo and use their huge financial resources to influence government policy on energy. They spend large amounts in elections supporting favored candidates, benefiting from not only political allies but also a 2010 US Supreme Court decision removing certain limits on campaign funding by corporations, unions, and others.

In 2017, vehicles in the United States took about 47 percent of its oil consumption.[72] The cost of oil in the United States, in one sense, remains very low. Gasoline, for example, is about half the price in the United States as in Europe. Table 5.2 shows

Table 5.2 US gasoline prices, 1950–2017[76]

Year	Retail price per gallon of regular gas ($)
1950	0.27
1960	0.31
1970	0.36
1980	1.21
1990	1.16
2000	1.69
2010	2.78
2012	3.64
2014	3.36
2016	2.14
2017	2.40

Sources: Data from "Dollars and : Sense, July–August 1980," in Kenneth Dolbeare, *American Public Policy* (New York: McGraw-Hill, 1982), p. 113; *The World Almanac and Book of Facts 2006* (New York: World Almanac Books, 2006), p. 138; US Energy Administration, *Monthly Energy Review* (October 2010), p. 122; US Energy Administration, *Monthly Energy Review* (October 2018), p. 154.

Table 5.3 Per capita and total electricity consumption by region of the world, 2016

	Per capita electricity use (kWh/person)	Total electricity use (TWh)
World	3,110	23,107
OECD	8,048	10,338
United States	12,825.04	4,147.5
Canada	14,844	538.3
France	7,148	477.9
Australia	9,911	243
Japan	7,974	1,012.3
Middle East	4,070	948
Saudi Arabia	9,818	316.9
Qatar	15,477	39.8
Non-OECD Asia	1,040	2,568
China	4,279	5,898.9
India	918	1,216.1
Non-OECD Americas	2,106	1,031
Bolivia	757	8.2
Brazil	2,504	520
Africa	576	705
Kenya	165	8
South Africa	4,031	225.4

TWh refers to terawatt hours. A terawatt is equal to 1 trillion watts.
Source: International Energy Agency, *Key World Energy Statistics 2018*, pp. 29–34.

this fact as well as any set of figures can, as it focuses on the changes in the price of gasoline in the United States from 1950 to 2009. The table also helps us understand another important feature of the energy crisis, especially as it has affected the United States: the period of cheap gasoline was a relatively long one.

What this means is that the "real," or true, cost of oil is not indicated by its price and thus consumers in the United States feel no urgency in demanding – or the government in producing – an energy policy that would break the dominance of oil in their society. As some energy analysts have suggested, the complete "social" cost of oil would include not only military and climate costs, but also the increased healthcare costs associated with the burning of petroleum, and the subsidies by the government to the oil industry.

The International Center for Technology Assessment once estimated that if the price of gasoline reflected all the environmental, military, and health costs of using it and subsidies to the oil industry, its price would be at least $14 USD a gallon.[73] Gasoline sales taxes can be used to cover some of these hidden costs – which otherwise are borne by the whole society in their general taxes and in healthcare costs – but the tax on gasoline in the United States has historically been much lower than that in other major industrialized nations.[74] In October of 2018, the typical price of a gallon of gasoline in the United States was $3.15, reflecting approximately 2 percent of average income and approximately half of the price in many European countries.[75]

Western Europe   Due in large part to climate concerns, many countries in Europe are increasingly transitioning away from fossil fuels. In 2017, the United Kingdom – the country that iconically pioneered coal-fired industrial development – announced it would stop producing coal-powered energy.[77] Norway began excluding dozens of coal companies from its sovereign asset investments, up to 69 by 2017 with another 13 under observation.[78]

Despite concerted efforts to address climate change, most Western European countries are more dependent on imported oil than is the United States, although oil and liquid fuel consumption is projected to decline slightly in the coming decades.[79] Traditionally, European governments have let the prices for imported fuel go up as determined by the world market and have tried to encourage energy conservation through the use of high taxes. France has emphasized nuclear power as its response to the energy crisis, and by 2016 it was producing about 80 percent of its electricity from that source – one of the highest rates in the world.[80]

The discovery of oil and natural gas under the North Sea aided mainly Norway and Britain. This large deposit allowed Britain to be self-sufficient in oil for several decades, but production peaked in 1999 and has been declining since then. By 2004 Britain was importing more oil than it exported.[81] In 2016, 38 percent of Britain's energy came from natural gas, 38 percent from petroleum, 6 percent from coal, and 17 percent from nuclear and renewable sources, which accounted for just 1 percent in 2000.[82] Norway, which is a major oil producer at the global level, nevertheless generates nearly all of its electricity from lower-emitting hydropower.[83] Further, Norway is in the process of reducing coal assets from nearly a trillion dollars of state-owned investments.[84]

Japan   Japan has no significant oil, natural gas, or coal deposits and is particularly dependent on imported oil. A consensus quickly developed, after the first oil shock in 1973, that Japan's dependency on oil must be reduced. The government encouraged conservation and increased efficiency in using energy and the people responded. This is in no small part due to the fact that Japan is a relatively wealthy country but culturally it is not as high consuming as some other wealthy countries.

The consensus that developed in Japan after 1973 emphasized a shift from consumption to restraint. It included a belief that the economy had to shift to "knowledge intensive" industries that use relatively little energy, and that energy efficiency was the key element in the adjustment the country needed to make to this new situation. It moved quickly into knowledge-based and electronic and computer-based industries. By the end of the first decade of the twenty-first century, Japan had reduced its dependency on oil from about three-quarters of its energy consumed in the mid-1970s to less than one-half.[85] In 2017, the mix of Japan's energy sources was as follows: 42 percent oil, 27 percent coal, 23 percent natural gas, less than 1 percent nuclear, and 8 percent hydroelectric and other renewables.[86]

It is interesting to note some of the differences between Japanese and US societies that have undoubtedly affected their different responses to the energy crisis. Because of their history and their limited land and resources, the Japanese have always assumed scarcity and insecurity of resources such as fuel, whereas the Americans have relied on an economy of presumed abundance and have assumed it will continue. Japanese industries have been traditionally more willing than their US counterparts to make long-term investments, the American companies often being more concerned with making short-term profits. The Japanese know that their goods must compete well in international trade if they are to maintain their high living standards. Japan is used to change and adaptation.

Japan made significant progress in the period between the oil shocks in the 1970s and the third one in 1990 and 1991. By 1990, the energy efficiency of the Japanese economy had improved to such an extent that the production of goods and services took only one-half the energy it took in the late 1970s.[87] The increased efficiency in the automobile and steel industries came after the government set ambitious goals for them to reach.

Another action taken by the government after the early crises was to build large oil storage facilities. By the early twenty-first century, Japan had nearly six months' supply of oil in storage tanks, more than any other nation. The country also sought to diversify its sources of oil, and was successful for a while, but it has consistently relied on imported oil to supply much of its energy demands, with the vast majority (over 80 percent) supplied from the Middle East.[88] The Japanese government made nuclear power one of the key parts of its plans to reduce its dependency on imported oil. In 2007, Japan had 55 operating nuclear power plants. Japan also planned to build a number of fast-breeder reactors to reduce its dependency on imported uranium, and in the early 1990s it began importing plutonium from France (recycled from spent uranium fuel from Japanese power plants) for those reactors. By the early 2000s, Japan had spent tens of billions on developing fast-breeder reactors that use plutonium as a fuel and, in theory, produce more nuclear fuel than they burn.

In 2011, a tsunami (tidal wave) caused the cooling systems of a group of nuclear reactors in northeast Japan to fail. This led to the release of large amounts of radiation into the air and sea and to the evacuation of nearby residents. As a result of the Fukushima disaster, Japan's energy mix has changed substantially. After the disaster, Japan's use of liquid fuels – such as petroleum – for energy generation increased by 22 percent in one year alone.[89] By 2017, nuclear had declined to only 1 percent of Japan's total energy supply, a 90 percent decrease below pre-tsunami levels.[90]

The Decoupling of Energy Consumption and Economic Growth

Historically, there appeared to be a one-to-one relationship between economic growth and energy growth. For example, a 10 percent increase in the amount of goods and services produced in the country was accompanied by an approximately 10 percent increase in the amount of energy consumed. But the oil shock of 1973 seemed to have challenged this relationship, and more recent climate concerns seem to have further severed it. Between 1977 and 1985 the US economy grew about 30 percent but the amount of oil used dropped nearly 20 percent.[91] During that time the United States began to use energy much more efficiently than it had before 1977, no doubt in response to higher oil prices. Then, in the mid-1980s, the price of oil fell dramatically and remained relatively low for over a decade. Probably in large part because of that sustained price drop, the efforts to further conserve energy in many countries slowed down.

However, in the second decade of the new millennium, a clear trend began to emerge. In tandem with the adoption of the Paris Agreement on climate change, carbon emissions remained flat while economic growth surged. The International Energy Association attributes this decoupling to changes in China's energy mix: coal's share declined by 10 percent in four years, while low-emitting sources like wind and hydropower increased from 19 to 28 percent.[92]

This decoupling of energy use, greenhouse gas emissions, and economic growth is not surprising once one realizes that there are a number of countries with high levels of economic prosperity that have traditionally used much less energy than does the United States. In 2012, the United Kingdom, Germany, and Japan – countries with high living standards – used about one-half of the energy per person that people living in Canada and the United States used. But the United States improved, and by the mid-2000s it was using nearly 50 percent less energy per dollar of economic output than it had 30 years before, because the economy transitioned in part from energy-intensive heavy industries towards more service industries, which are less energy intensive.[93]

Energy conservation and energy efficiency is a smart investment: the cost of saving energy (through such measures as improving the fuel efficiency of cars, improving the efficiency of industrial processes, insulating houses, and so on) is lower than the cost of most energy today.

Table 5.3 shows per capita and total electricity consumption by region of the world. Consumption per capita and as a total tell different sides of the story. For example, per capita, the Chinese burn less coal (the most polluting fossil fuel) than North Americans do, but the total amount of coal used in China is more than four times that used in the United States.[94]

Part of the reason many European countries use much less energy per person than does the United States is that they are smaller countries with populations that are not nearly as dispersed. US homes also tend to be larger and spaced further apart, while vehicles tend to be larger and less fuel efficient – perhaps due in part to gasoline prices that are half that of many European countries due to lower fuel taxes.

The United States cannot do anything about its size, but there are things that can be done to improve the energy efficiency of its transportation equipment. The federal government passed a law in 1975, over the strong opposition of the automobile industry, requiring the fuel efficiency of American automobiles to be gradually improved, doubling in efficiency by 1985.[95] During the 1990s no improvement was made in auto fuel efficiency in the United States. With relatively low gasoline prices, and fading memories of the energy crisis, US auto makers and consumers prioritized fashion and performance over fuel economy.[96]

Most of the long-distance hauling of freight in the United States is by truck, and a truck uses much more energy to move a ton of freight than does a freight train. The US government, by its vast expenditure of funds on the interstate highway system, its much lower tax on gasoline than in Europe and Japan, and its relatively small amount of expenditures that benefit the railroads, has done much to promote the use of trucks over trains in the country.

From the early 1980s to the early 2000s, the US automobile industry used its improved technology to produce vehicles that had faster acceleration, were larger and heavier, and had slightly lower fuel economy. The average vehicle in 2002 had nearly 100 percent more horsepower, accelerated nearly 30 percent faster, and was also about 25 percent heavier.[97] Finally, in 2007, the government instructed the auto industry to improve the fuel efficiency standards of its new cars to 35 miles per gallon by 2020, a significant improvement but still lower than many European, Japanese, and Chinese autos. And the United States had plans to improve fuel efficiency standards to 55 miles per gallon by 2025.[98]

In 1999, Japanese-made hybrid automobiles that used a gasoline engine and an electric motor appeared on the market. These hybrid vehicles were highly energy efficient and had low emissions. US companies followed suit in producing such cars, and their market share has increased despite them being more expensive than conventional cars. The biggest limitation to switching to an all-electric car is the charging infrastructure required to re-fuel over longer distance trips. Even so, there is growing demand for electric cars in countries like the US and China and an expanding infrastructure to support them. Germany, for example, has decided to phase out the sale of gasoline-combustion engines by 2030.[99]

Conservation/Energy Efficiency

Conservation is not commonly thought of as an energy source, but given the energy it frees up to be used elsewhere ("energy savings"), it should properly be regarded as a major untapped strategy in a smart energy mix. There are three ways to save energy: by performing some activity in a more energy-efficient manner (e.g. designing a more efficient motor); by not wasting energy (turning off lights in empty rooms); and by changing behavior (walking to work or to school).[100]

To many people, the term "conservation" means deprivation, or doing without something; but a Harvard study, and many others since, have shown that much energy conservation can take place without causing any real hardship. In fact, efficient appliances often save money and pay for themselves within a few years – and generate cost savings after that!

Many businesses now recognize that making their operations more energy efficient is a good way to increase profits. The investments the companies make to redesign their business operations, so they reduce their energy usage, are soon repaid by lower energy bills. It is encouraging to know that one key measure to address climate change can be quite profitable!

One conservation method that even fossil fuel generation can apply is called "cogeneration," which is the combined production of both electricity and heat in the same installation. Electricity is produced by burning fuel, and unless it is captured, the heat from the generation of the electricity gets passed off into the air or into lakes and rivers as waste. In cogeneration plants, the heat from the production of electricity – often in the form of steam – can be used for industrial processes, to power turbines, or for heating homes and offices. The production of electricity and steam together uses about one-half the amount of fuel as does their production separately. Cogeneration is more common in Europe than the United States, where electric utilities often give cheaper rates to their big industrial customers, thus reducing the incentive to adopt the process.

If the United States ever does reach the goal of energy savings that the Harvard report believes is possible, it will be because of a combination of governmental policies encouraging conservation and action by millions of individuals. The United States is a country where people respond well to incentives to promote conservation practices, but such governmental incentives have so far been rather weak. In contrast to weak efforts by the federal government, some of the US states have done more to encourage conservation and the use of renewable energy. For example, the state of California allowed homeowners to deduct 55 percent of the cost of solar devices from their state taxes. (This law no doubt partly explains why California leads the nation in the number of solar devices installed in homes.) The city of Davis, California changed its building code so that all new homes in the city must meet certain energy performance standards.

Many homes are not designed to use energy efficiently. For example, if houses with large window surfaces in northern latitudes are positioned to face the south, they can gain more heat from the low winter sun, and these windows could be shaded by deciduous trees or an overhang to keep out the high summer sun. Simple measures like planting trees to obtain shade can have a significant cooling effect on a house, a city street, or a parking lot, reducing temperatures by as much as 10 to 20 degrees over unshaded areas. In many cities, houses are becoming more energy efficient.

Saving energy often takes an initial investment. Knowing this fact helps us understand why eliminating subsidies for oil and natural gas, which will lead to higher prices of those fuels, is not always enough for people to adopt energy-saving technologies. The better informed and more affluent might recognize that an investment in insulation or a more expensive water heater makes good sense and will save money over the long run, but those with lower incomes may not have the extra money to make the initial investment. Those with lower incomes often spend far more of their income on energy than do those on higher incomes, and could benefit from the better insulated house or the more fuel-efficient car, but the initial investment may be cost-prohibitive. Higher prices for fuel can help to reduce energy consumption, but income-sensitive governmental incentives (e.g. tax rebates) and regulations (e.g. fuel efficiency standards) can assist a more inclusive transition toward energy conservation.

Some real progress is being made in conservation/energy efficiency efforts around the world, but much more can be done. As we will mention in the next chapter on climate change, China is relying heavily on conservation and energy efficiency improvements to achieve its stated goal of reducing the amount of carbon dioxide (its so-called "carbon intensity") it emits to produce economic growth. This has been difficult to do with high-carbon sources like coal. Still, while China has become the world's chief producer of greenhouse gases, it has also become a leader in reducing the carbon intensity of its emissions.

Nuclear Power: A Case Study

In this final section we will look closely at nuclear power, which historically has been surrounded by political controversy. An expansion of nuclear power is now taking place because of the increasing need for energy in rapidly growing economies, such as China, and as one of the ways to decrease the world's dependency on oil and coal, such as in the United States, which sees nuclear power as a way to deal with security and environmental concerns. There are strong arguments for and against this energy source, illustrating the complexity of many important issues today, with no easy right or wrong answers. Decision-makers should consider both the pros and cons of the issue. We have decided to present this subject to the reader as a case study instead of trying to give the "correct" decision, highlighting the need for decision-makers to set priorities.

The potential and the peril

Nuclear power was seen by many in its early years as the answer to the world's energy needs. Its promoters claimed it would be a nonpolluting and safe form of energy that could produce electricity "too cheap to meter." After the destructive power of the atom was demonstrated with the bombing of Hiroshima and Nagasaki, people welcomed the thought that atomic research could also be used for peaceful purposes. The first prototype of a commercial nuclear power plant began operation in the United States in 1957.

The first generation of nuclear power reactors took the form of fission, light-water reactors. These reactors operate with the same process that was used to explode the early atomic bombs – the splitting of the core (the nucleus) of the atoms of heavy elements, which releases tremendous energy. Uranium-235 (^{235}U) is the fuel used in these reactors. The chain reaction that comes with the splitting of the uranium nucleus is controlled through the use of fuel rods affecting the reactor core to manage a chain reaction that produces sustained heat, which is then used, as it is in coal- and oil-fed power plants, to produce steam. The steam drives the turbines that generate electricity.

The uranium used in the common light-water reactors must be enriched so that it contains a higher percentage of Uranium -235 than found in nature. This is done in very large, very expensive enrichment plants that utilize huge amounts of electricity themselves. Because of the difficulty of obtaining the required Uranium -235, it was originally planned to reprocess the spent fuel rods from the power reactors to extract unused uranium, thus making uranium supplies last longer. Controversy has surrounded these reprocessing plants, partly because plutonium, one of the deadliest known substances and the fuel for the Nagasaki bomb (the bomb dropped on Hiroshima utilized uranium), is produced during the reprocessing. Three commercial reprocessing plants were built in the United States – one in Illinois, one in New York, and one in South Carolina – but none are operating at present. The shutdowns occurred because of technical difficulties, safety concerns, and the fear that such plants made plutonium too accessible.

Another way to handle the relative scarcity of fuel for the light-water reactors would be by building a second generation of power reactor. These reactors, known as the fast-breeder reactors, use plutonium as their fuel and will actually produce more fuel than they consume. The attractiveness of this feature was countered by the great complexity of the plants and the increased danger that would come from an accident, since plutonium was being used instead of the less radioactive uranium. Plutonium is extremely harmful if inhaled or digested and has a half-life (the amount of time for one-half of the substance to disintegrate or be transformed into something else) of over 24,000 years. Between the 1970s and the 1990s, the United Kingdom, Germany, the United States, France, Russia, and Japan built experimental fast-breeder reactors. By 2009 all, except the one in Japan, had been shut down because of technical difficulties, spiraling costs, and a concern for safeguarding the plutonium. But in that year China, India, and Russia were still planning or building a new generation of experimental fast-breeder reactors.

Fusion nuclear power, which is still in the experimental stage, might be called a third generation of nuclear energy. Fusion energy is created by the same process that creates the energy in the sun and is the process used in the hydrogen bomb, which is vastly more powerful than the fission atomic bombs. Instead of splitting atoms, as happens in fission, in fusion atoms are fused together. The process is highly complicated and demands temperatures (millions of degrees) and pressures with which scientists have little experience. The attractiveness of the fusion process is that it is an inherently safer process than fission and generates much less radioactive waste. Much of its fuel is deuterium, a nonradioactive material from seawater that is the second most common form of elemental hydrogen, while the other main component of its fuel is tritium, which is radioactive and derived from lithium – a fairly abundant (and not naturally radioactive) element.

In 1991, after nearly a half-century of research and many billions of dollars, a breakthrough in fusion research occurred as a European team for the first time produced a significant amount of energy from controlled nuclear fusion. Thirty-five nations (European Union, Japan, Russia, China, South Korea, India, and the United States) have agreed to cooperate in building a large experimental fusion reactor in France, which was halfway complete in 2017 with the first plasma experiments slated for 2025.[101] Its cost is estimated to be 17 billion euros to operate, and over 800 million euro to close it down.[102] The cost will be shared by the seven nations building it. One fact alone indicates the huge scientific challenge of this project. To be successful, the temperature within the reactor must reach 150 million degrees Celsius, or ten times the temperature at the core of our sun. The goal of the project is to deliver ten times the power it consumes.

In 2014, the United States began supporting new nuclear reactors for the first time since 1977 (about 100 orders for plants were canceled during the 1970s).[103] The slowdown occurred because of the reduced demand for electricity (caused by the rapidly increasing cost of power, conservation measures, and an economic recession), the skyrocketing cost of building the plants (plants that were originally estimated to cost from $200 to $300 million wound up costing from $1 to $2 billion), and increasing concern about the safety of the plants.

In 1979, the partial meltdown of the core of a nuclear reactor located at the power plant at Three Mile Island, Pennsylvania, United States, led to a release of some radioactive steam and gas from the plant and the consequent official recommendation that nearby pregnant women as well as young children be evacuated. Although no one was killed, and the release of the radioactive substances was later judged by a presidential investigation committee to have caused no danger to public health, the cleanup from the accident cost about $1 billion, and the accident increased public fears about nuclear power. It has been estimated that new safety requirements for nuclear power plants which were issued by the federal government after the Three Mile Island accident, as well as delays in the construction of new plants and more temporary shutdowns of existing plants caused by the concerns raised by that accident, added $130 billion to the cost of nuclear electricity in the United States between 1979 and 1992. Two lessons learned from the accident were that it was easier to destroy a reactor core than many experts had thought possible, but also it was harder to rupture the reactor vessel (the steel pot 5 inches thick that holds the core) than many had thought possible. On one hand, this confirmed concerns about the possibility of nuclear accidents and reactor meltdown; on the other, it demonstrated that not all accidents lead to catastrophic disaster.

In 1986, when the nuclear power plant at Chernobyl in the Soviet Union exploded, about 50 tons of radioactive particles – ten times the fallout at Hiroshima – fell across parts of the Soviet Union. The accident also spread radiation around the world, with significant amounts falling on some European countries. More than 100,000 people were evacuated from an area of about 300 square miles (78,000 hectares) around the plant. About 30 people died from the catastrophe during the following few months, while many more were impacted by cancers, birth defects, and other health problems. It is believed that both flaws in the design of the reactor and mistakes by the operators of the plant were responsible for the disaster.

While the Soviet Union was much more candid about the accident than it had been about previous nuclear disasters (such as the explosion in 1957, which was kept secret, of a tank that contained high-level nuclear waste and that contaminated thousands of square miles in the area of the Ural Mountains), it is now known that secret government decrees were issued one and two years after the accident, designed to cover up the full extent of the damage. Four years after the accident, the Soviet Union acknowledged that 4 million people were still living on ground contaminated by the explosion and the government voted to spend $26 billion on further Chernobyl related expenses, including the resettlement of 200,000 people living in the most contaminated areas. A United Nations report released in 2005 estimated that 4,000 people were expected to die from cancer from the explosion's fallout. Some experts disagree with the United Nations estimate and believe the final cancer toll from the fallout could be in the tens of thousands.

After a three-decade withdrawal of interest in nuclear power in many countries, except a few such as France and Japan, more than 40 countries (including the United States), showed a new interest in nuclear power in late 2010. This interest came because of a serious shortage of electricity in countries such as China and India that were having major economic growth, rising prices of oil, insecure sources of imported energy, and global warming concerns. By mid-2010 there were about 440 nuclear power reactors operating in the world. Nearly 60 reactors were under construction at that time. (Figure 5.7 shows global nuclear production from 1971 to 2012.)

As mentioned before, in March 2011 a massive earthquake near the northeastern coast of Japan was followed by a tsunami (tidal wave) that inflicted huge damage to the coastal region where the Fukushima nuclear facility was located. Tens of thousands of people in nearby towns were evacuated as the reactors were seriously damaged.[104] They released a large amount of radiation into the air and sea. This became the biggest nuclear accident since Chernobyl. Five years after the meltdown, the reactor continued releasing radiation-contaminated water into the sea; cleanup was still a distant prospect.[105] As of 2017, most of the nearby towns remain empty and Japan's energy mix no longer envisions nuclear as a source. Since that time, nuclear power has significantly decreased.

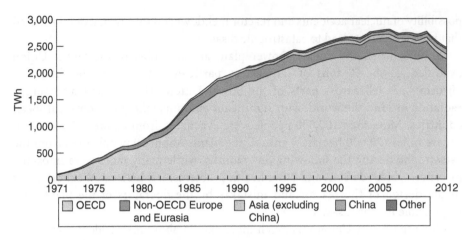

Figure 5.7 Global nuclear production from 1971 to 2012

Source: International Energy Agency, *Key World Energy Statistics 2014*, p. 16.

The choice

Two basic political alternatives exist regarding nuclear power: the government can withdraw its support for the nuclear power industry, or it can continue to promote nuclear power and encourage its development. We will examine the main arguments being presented on both sides in this debate.

Withdraw support for nuclear power As the accidents at Chernobyl and Fukushima show, nuclear power plants run the risk of catastrophic accidents. Society should not have to accept such a risk. The Three Mile Island accident proved that the interaction of human error and failure of equipment can lead to events that no one had ever guessed could happen. One hundred alarms went off in the first few minutes at Three Mile Island, making it impossible for the operators to control the situation. And at Chernobyl a series of errors by the operators of a reactor which was inherently difficult to run generated forces and effects that up to then had never been experienced. Nuclear technology assumes better human performance and understanding than history shows can be achieved.

Nuclear power also increases the danger of the proliferation, or the spread, of nuclear weapons to additional nations currently without nuclear capabilities or resources. The knowledge and installations that a nation acquires when it develops nuclear power can be utilized to develop nuclear bombs. While it is true that most nuclear power plants do not use fuel that can readily be used to build bombs, the reprocessing of the spent fuel from the plants can produce fuel for weapons. Reprocessing technology is spreading around the world. For example, in 1975 West Germany sold Brazil reprocessing technology even though Brazil had never signed the Non-Proliferation Treaty, which would commit it not to use it to develop nuclear weapons. As more nations gain expertise in nuclear energy and acquire nuclear weapons, the chances that the weapons will be used will greatly increase.

The danger of terrorists stealing plutonium to make a bomb or to use as a poison to be spread in the atmosphere over a city or in its drinking water is real. The knowledge of how to make nuclear weapons is widespread, and only about 20 pounds of fissionable material is required to make a crude bomb. If, or probably more realistically when, terrorists do acquire a nuclear capability, threatened nations will probably respond by giving their police and governments increased power. The United States could become more authoritarian because of such a threat, with consequent restrictions on personal freedom and privacy.

Another disturbing consequence of nuclear energy is that large amounts of radioactive wastes from nuclear facilities are accumulating in the United States because no permanent way to store this material has yet been created. After spending $9 billion over 22 years to build a nuclear waste storage facility in Yucca Mountain, Nevada, concern over its ability to keep the wastes isolated led the United States to eventually abandon the effort. Some of the nuclear waste must be stored for a minimum of 100,000 to 200,000 years in such a way that it does not come into contact with humans or with any part of the environment. We show an overwhelming arrogance and unconcern for future generations when we say we can do this; this is made apparent when we remember that the United States is only 200 years old and human civilization about 5,000 years old. Several hundred thousand gallons of nuclear wastes have already leaked out of steel tanks at sites in Hanford, Washington and near Aiken, South Carolina, where military wastes are stored.

The high cost of nuclear power makes it difficult to justify in economic terms, especially when taking into account the entire lifecycle of nuclear material and waste. If one includes the cost of its development and the costs of the attempts to find a safe way to store wastes – both of which have been financed by public funds – nuclear power would not be competitive with other forms of energy. And the cost of decommissioning and possibly hauling away for storage worn out and highly radioactive nuclear power plants, which have a life expectancy of 30 to 40 years, will further add to the costs of nuclear power.

Nuclear power plants create thermal pollution, raising the temperature of the atmosphere and of the water in lakes, bays, and rivers often used to cool the reactors. The warmer water can be deadly to many kinds of fish and other forms of life in the lakes and rivers. The present light-water reactors convert only about 30 percent of their fuel into electricity; the rest is turned into waste heat.

Nuclear power cannot replace imported oil. Only about 10 percent of the world's oil is used to generate electricity; most of it is used to run vehicles, provide heat for homes and industry, and make chemicals. Nuclear power, for the foreseeable future, can be used only to make electricity, and, besides being of relatively limited use, electricity is a very expensive form of energy. The huge public investments which continue to go into nuclear energy (mainly through government subsidies) prevent public funds from being used to develop alternative sources of energy which would be more useful, safer, and cleaner.

Continue to support nuclear power   We accept chemical plants despite accidents associated with them, such as that at Bhopal in India in 1984 which killed more than 3,000 people, and we accept dams despite accidents associated with them, such as at the Vajont Dam in Italy in 1963, which killed about 2,000 people. So why should the accidents at Chernobyl, Fukushima, and Three Mile Island make us reject nuclear power? Nuclear power plants in the United States have become much safer because of new procedures and safety devices adopted since the Three Mile Island accident. And a number of highly respected scientists now believe that it is possible to build a nuclear power plant which is inherently safe, one which would be so designed that if anything unusual happened it would automatically cease functioning without any action needed by human beings or by machines. Nuclear power has enjoyed relative success in France, which boasts a relatively strong safety and anti-proliferation record.

A person gets more exposure to radiation in a year by taking a single round-trip coast-to-coast jet flight, by watching color television, or by working in a building made of granite than anyone would by living next to a nuclear power plant. Humans have evolved over millions of years living on a mildly radioactive planet and have prospered. Few things in life are risk-free, and the risks associated with nuclear power are relatively benign compared with the risks people take every day in their lives.

The accusation that nuclear power will contribute to the proliferation of nuclear weapons is exaggerated. A nation that wants to build a nuclear weapon can get sufficient plutonium from its nuclear research facilities. This is exactly how India got plutonium for the nuclear device it exploded in 1974. All of the major powers that have acquired nuclear weapons built these weapons before they acquired nuclear power.

It would be very difficult for a terrorist to steal plutonium in the United States. The US military has been shipping plutonium by convoy for many years and very effective means have been devised to protect the shipments from hijacking. Good security measures are also in effect in plants that produce plutonium. Although the knowledge of how to construct nuclear bombs is no longer secret, the actual construction of such a device is very difficult. If the construction of nuclear weapons were easy, more nations would have them than the handful that do at present.

A way to store nuclear wastes permanently has been devised and is actually being used in Europe. The wastes can be solidified, usually in glass, and then stored in geologically stable underground facilities. Sweden and Finland have chosen underground repositories in stable granite rock and France, Switzerland, and Belgium are investigating potential repositories in clay. Most of the nuclear wastes in the United States are being created in its military program, and these wastes will continue to build up even if every nuclear power plant was closed.

A great danger to the world is caused by the shortage of oil. Without secure sources of energy, such as nuclear power – especially in regions with relatively weak potential for solar, wind, and hydropwer – it is likely that more wars will occur as nations fight to keep their sources of oil secure. The development of nuclear power can help to reduce this dangerous dependency on foreign sources of energy.

Nuclear power is much less polluting than the main alternative energy source – coal – that will be greatly expanded if nuclear power does not continue to be produced. Except for the construction of the reactor, nuclear power produces no carbon dioxide that causes climate change, no waste gases that produce acid rain, as coal burning does, and no smog or any of the other harmful effects commonly associated with coal. Nuclear power is generally much easier on the landscape than is coal; the average nuclear power reactor uses only about 30 tons of fuel a year while the average coal-burning electric plant uses about 3,000 tons of fuel per *day*. By slowing down the approval of new nuclear plants, the critics of nuclear power are causing nations to burn more coal. This causes many more people to die and more environmental damage from pollution than would have been the case if new nuclear plants had made the increased coal-burning unnecessary.

No energy option should be rejected during this period of transition. Nuclear power is one of the few alternatives we have to produce large amounts of energy during the rest of this century while the search for a sustainable fuel to take the place of oil and coal continues.

Conclusions

The energy transition the Earth is passing through is possibly the most important one human beings have encountered during their long evolution on the planet. The very suitability of the planet for high civilization is threatened by the fossil fuels they rely on to power the machinery that makes their products, runs their transportation systems, fuels their high-tech agricultural systems, and heats and cools their homes. The burning of these fossil fuels has led to wars as nations have fought over the control of oil, the main fossil fuel the people of the Earth depend on at present. As long as that dependency remains, more conflicts seem likely.

But more wars are not the main problem our use of energy might bring. The effect our reliance on fossil fuels is having on our climate at present and its possible effects in the future are why a transition to new energy sources is crucial. Time is limited. If too much time is taken for this energy transition to occur, the population of the Earth is large enough and its industrialization great enough – with both still growing – that the changing climate could bring widespread suffering and destruction to many, but especially to the poorest nations.

Other energy sources are available that don't cause conflicts among nations or threaten our climate, but it will take major efforts by governments and individuals to make them prominent. The careful reader of this book is learning about these renewable and nonpolluting sources of energy and of some of the difficulties standing in the way of their wider use.

The efforts of the leading industrial nation, the country that produces more goods and services than any other and, in the past, has released more pollutants that affect the climate than any other – the United States – have been very disappointing. American scientists have been leaders in gathering the evidence that our climate is

changing because of human actions, but so far the US Congress has been unrespon-
sive, and the executive branch under President Donald Trump rolled back laws and
policies put in place under the previous administration to help address climate
change. Has this lack of action in the US to address the climate threat been because of
the political power of the fossil fuel and automotive industries which have opposed
taking action, or is it because the American public lacks an understanding – or concern – that new energy initiatives are urgently needed for the long-term health of
their country and of the planet itself? Or is it both?

Many European countries, along with Japan and others, are taking actions to address
this issue. China is starting to address it, but because of its heavy reliance on coal and
its rapid economic growth, it has now become the largest annual contributor to the
problem of climate change. Will our descendants look back at this period and ask,
"Why didn't they act sooner?" This is our challenge. Our societies are being tested.

We, the writers of this book, and you, its readers, are trying to understand what is
happening in our world. This is a vital first step, as no effective action can be taken
without it. We have identified energy as a key component in our understanding of
the way life is today. Next, we will look at the climate challenges born out of historic
fossil fuel-intensive development pathways such as those described in this chapter
on energy. We are continuing to increase our knowledge of our world and our place
in it. Congratulations, reader. If you are doing this seriously, you are becoming a
possible part of the solution and not a possible part of the problem.

Notes

1   US Energy Information Administration (EIA), Energy in Brief: "Who Are the Major
    Players Supplying the World Oil Market?" September 30, 2014, at http://www.eia.gov/
    energy in brief/article/world oil market.cfm (accessed July 2015).
2   Richard Kerr and Robert Service, "What Can Replace Cheap Oil – and When?" *Science*,
    309 (July 1, 2005), p. 101.
3   IEA, Oil Information: Overview (IEA, 2018 edition), p. 3.
4   IEA, Oil Market Report, October 12, 2018 at https://www.iea.org/oilmarketreport/
    omrpublic/ (accessed November 2, 2018).
5   Lester R. Brown, *The Twenty-Ninth Day: Accommodating Human Needs and Numbers to
    the Earth's Resources* (New York: W. W. Norton, 1978), pp. 205–6.
6   Daniel Yergin and Martin Hillenbrand (eds), *Global Insecurity: A Strategy for Energy and
    Economic Renewal* (Boston: Houghton Mifflin, 1982), p. 7.
7   The United States persuaded other nations, including Japan, to contribute about $50 bil-
    lion to help pay for the war. The United States spent about $10 billion for short-term costs.
    A huge, sustained air attack on Iraqi forces in Kuwait and Iraq and on military facilities in
    Iraq (including on plants for poisonous gas and nuclear weapons) preceded the ground
    attack.
8   The war and its subsequent damage to their lands and economies cost all the Arab states
    an estimated $600 billion. See Youssef Ibrahim, "Gulf War's Cost to the Arabs Estimated
    at $620 Billion," *New York Times* (September 8, 1992), p. A4.

9   Yergin and Hillenbrand (eds), *Global Insecurity: A Strategy for Energy and Economic Renewal.* p. 7.; see generally http://secureenergy.org/report/military-cost-defending-global-oil-supplies/ (accessed January 2020).

10 See, e.g., Tim Boersma and Stacy D. Van Deveer, "Coal After the Paris Agreement," *Foreign Affairs* (June 06, 2016).

11 Intergovernmental Panel on Climate Change, Special Report on 1.5 Degrees (Geneva: IPCC, 2018).

12 Fred Pearce, "In a Stunning Turnaround, Britain Moves to End the Burning of Coal," *Yale 360* (September 18, 2017); Karl Mathiesen, "India to Halt Building New Coal Plants in 2022," *Climate Home News* (December 16, 2016); Terry Macalister, "Longannet Power Station Closes Ending Coal Power Use in Scotland," *The Guardian* (March 23, 2016); "Beijing to Shut All Major Coal Power Plants to Cut Pollution," *Bloomberg News* (March 23, 2015). See also "Norway's $900bn Sovereign Wealth Fund told to Reduce Coal Assets," *The Guardian* (May 27, 2015).

13 IEA. World Energy Outlook 2017, (IEA 2017), p. 474; see also Qi Ye and Jiaqi Lu, "China's Coal Consumption has Peaked," *Brookings* (January 22, 2018), at https://www.brookings.edu/2018/01/22/chinas-coal-consumption-has-peaked/ (accessed December 2018).

14 Qi Ye and Jiaqi Lu, "China's coal consumption has peaked."

15 Ibid.

16 Ibid.

17 Ibid.

18 Jing Yang, "China Is Adding More Coal Capacity," *Bloomberg Businessweek* (September 24, 2018), at https://www.bloomberg.com/news/articles/2018-09-24/china-is-adding-more-coal-capacity (accessed December 2018).

19 IEA. World Energy Outlook 2017, p. 334; IEA World Energy Outlook 2018, Executive Summary p. 2.

20 IEA. World Energy Outlook 2017, p. 334.

21 Ibid.

22 International Energy Agency, *Key World Energy Statistics 2018*, p. 2.

23 Tom Embury-Dennis, "Costa Rica to Ban Fossil Fuels and Become World's First Decarbonised Society," *The Independent* (May 19, 2018); Maria Gallucci "Costa Rica Barely Used Any Fossil Fuels in 2016," *Mashable* (January 01, 2017).

24 Peter Dockrill, "Costa Rica's Electricity Has Run Entirely on Renewables For 300 Days in 2017," *Science Alert* (November 23, 2017).

25 Markus Wacket and Erik Kirschbaum, "Germany Breaks Green Energy Record by Generating 35% of Power from Renewables in First Half of 2017," *The Independent* (July 3, 2017), at https://www.independent.co.uk/news/world/europe/germany-green-technology-record-power-generation-35-per-cent-renewables-solar-wind-turbines-a7820156.html (accessed December 2018).

26 Juliet Eilperin and Brady Dennis, "U.S., Canada and Mexico Vow to get Half their Electricity from Clean Power by 2025," *The Washington Post* (June 27, 2016).

27 Angus McCrone and Abraham Louw "Clean Energy Investment By the Numbers - End of Year 2016," Bloomberg (2016).

28 EIA, "Solar Photovoltaic Costs are Declining, but Estimates Vary across Sources," March 21, 2018 at https://www.eia.gov/todayinenergy/detail.php?id=35432 (accessed November 2, 2018).

29 Lin Boqiang, "China is a Renewable Energy Champion. But it's Time for a New Approach," *World Econmic Forum* (May 22, 2018), at https://www.weforum.org/

agenda/2018/05/china-is-a-renewable-energy-champion-but-its-time-for-a-new-approach/ (accessed December 2018).

30   http://energyforhumanity.org/en/briefings/germany/germanys-energy-mix/ (accessed January 2020).

31   Matthew Roney, "Solar Cell Production Climbs to Another Record in 2009," Earth Policy Institute, Eco-Economy Indicators: Solar Power, September 21, 2010, at http://www.earth-policy.org/index.php?/indicators/C47/solar power 2010 (accessed July 2015).

32   Clifford Krauss, "Move Over, Oil, There's Money in Texas Wind," *New York Times* (February 23, 2008), p. A13.

33   American Wind Energy Association, "Market Update: Record 2009 Leads to Slow Start in 2010" (May 2010).

34   American Wind Energy Association, U.S. Wind Industry Annual Market Report 2017.

35   Arthur Nelsen, "Wind Power Generates 140% of Denmark's Electricity Demand," *The Guardian* (July 10, 2015), at https://www.theguardian.com/environment/2015/jul/10/denmark-wind-windfarm-power-exceed-electricity-demand (accessed December 2018).

36   See Renewables now, "Renewables Produce 33.7% of Spain's Power in 2017," December 29, 2017 at https://renewablesnow.com/news/renewables-produce-337-of-spains-power-in-2017-596136/ (accessed November 2, 2018); Clean Energy Wire, "Germany's Energy Consumption and Power Mix in Charts," April 3, 2018 at https://www.cleanenergywire.org/factsheets/germanys-energy-consumption-and-power-mix-charts (accessed on November 2, 2018).

37   See Kristen A. Hite and John L. Seitz, *Global Issues: An Introduction*, 5th edn (Wiley Blackwell, 2016).

38   Boqiang, "China is a Renewable Energy champion. But it's Time for a New Approach."

39   See, e.g. David Eyerly, "The Shadow Flicker Effect: What Is It? (Wind Turbine Shadows)," at https://discoverwindenergy.com/2019/03/14/the-shadow-flicker-effect-what-is-it-wind-turbine-shadows/ (accessed January 26, 2020)

40   Joseph Kahn and Jim Yardley, "As China Roars, Pollution Reaches Deadly Extremes," *New York Times* (August 26, 2007, p. 6).

41   Rafi Schwartz "Portland Now Generates Electricity From Turbines Installed In City Water Pipes" Good Money.

42   World Energy Council, World Energy Resources: Bioenergy (2016), p.8, at https://www.worldenergy.org/wp-content/uploads/2017/03/WEResources_Bioenergy_2016.pdf (accessed December 2018).

43   Christina Nunez, "The Energy Boom You Haven't Heard About: Wood Pellets," *National Geographic* (December 10, 2014), at https://news.nationalgeographic.com/news/energy/2014/12/141208-wood-pellet-energy-boom-driven-by-exports/ (accessed December 2018).

44   Jenny Mealing, "Biomass Reaches 9% share in Brazil's 2016 Power Supply," *Renewables Now* (March 8, 2016), at https://renewablesnow.com/news/biomass-reaches-9-share-in-brazils-2016-power-supply-560820/ (accessed December 2018).

45   Energy Information Agency, "Biomass Explained" webpage, at https://www.eia.gov/energyexplained/?page=biomass_home (accessed December 2018).

46   Think Geoenergy, "Top 10 Geothermal Countries based on installed capacity – Year End 2017", at http://www.thinkgeoenergy.com/top-10-geothermal-countries-based-on-installed-capacity-year-end-2017/ (accessed November 2, 2018).

47 Matthew Wald, "Questions about a Hydrogen Economy," *Scientific American*, 290 (May 2004), p. 68.

48 Matthew Wald, "Report Questions Bush Plan for Hydrogen-Fueled Cars," *New York Times* (February 6, 2004), p. A19.

49 Jeff Mulhollem, "Wood Fuels Key to Easing Food Insecurity Situation in sub-Saharan Africa," *Penn State News* (Feburary 26, 2018), at https://news.psu.edu/story/507274/2018/02/26/research/wood-fuels-key-easing-food-insecurity-situation-sub-saharan-africa (accessed December 2018).

50 Sustainable Energy for All, Scaling Sustainable Access Pathways for the Most Vulnerable and Hardest to Reach People (2017), at https://www.seforall.org/sites/default/files/P1ScalingSustainableAccessPathways.pdf.

51 IEA, "World Energy Outlook 2010 Fact Sheet," (IEA, 2010), p. 4.

52 IEA, Organisation for Economic Co-operation and Development, and World Bank, The Scope of Fossil Fuel Subsidies and a Roadmap for Phasing out Fossil Fuel Subsidies (IEA, 2010).

53 "See Shelagh Whitley, et al., "G7 Fossil Fuel Subsidy Scorecard," *Policy Brief* (June 2018), p. 2 ("G7 countries provided at least $100 billion annually (2015 and 2016) in government support for the production and consumption of oil, gas and coal, both at home and abroad in more than 50 countries around the world. This included $81 billion in fiscal support through direct spending and tax breaks; and $20 billion in public finance on average per year in 2015 and 2016."). See also Karl Mathiesen, "G7 Nations Pledge to End Fossil Fuel Subsidies by 2025," *The Guardian* (27 May 2016).

54 Lawrence Berkeley National Laboratory, Key China Energy Statistics (2016), p. 21, available at https://china.lbl.gov/sites/default/files/misc/ced-9-2017-final.pdf (accessed December 26, 2018).

55 IEA. World Energy Outlook 2017, p. 488.

56 Ibid.

57 Ibid., p. 524.

58 Ibid., pp. 475–6, 602.

59 Keith Bradsher, "China, Rushing into Reactors, Stirs Concerns," *New York Times* (December 16, 2009), pp. A1, A3.

60 IEA. World Energy Outlook 2017, p. 477.

61 Ibid., p. 486 & 554 ("Today, China is the largest contributor to global energy-related CO_2 emissions, accounting for 28% of the world total, even though its per-capita emissions of 6.5 tonnes of CO_2 are still one-quarter below the average of advanced economies.")

62 Ibid., p. 474.

63 Bianca Britton, "The World's Top 100 most Polluted Cities in 2018," CNN (March 6, 2019), at https://edition.cnn.com/2019/03/05/health/100-most-polluted-cities-2018-intl/index.html (accessed January 2020).

64 IEA. World Energy Outlook 2017, p. 126.

65 Deepa D. Datta and Robert J. Vigfusso, "Forecasting China's Role in World Oil Demand," Federal Reserve Bank of San Francisco (August 21, 2017), at https://www.frbsf.org/economic-research/files/el2017-24.pdf (accessed December 2018).

66 IEA. World Energy Outlook 2017, p. 204.

67 EIA, International Energy Outlook 2014 (Washington, DC: US Department of Energy, 2014), p. 1.

68 IEA. World Energy Outlook 2017, pp. 154 & 193.

69 Ibid., pp. 154 & 193.

70 International Energy Agency (IEA), World Energy Outlook 2014 (Paris: IEA, 2014), Executive Summary, p. 6.

71 EIA, "How Much Petroleum does the United States Import and Export?", October 3, 2018 at https://www.eia.gov/tools/faqs/faq.php?id=727&t=6 (accessed November 2, 2018).

72 EIA, "Oil: Crude and Petroleum Products Explained 'Use of Oil'", September 28, 2018 at https://www.eia.gov/energyexplained/index.php?page=oil_use (accessed November 2, 2018).

73 EIA, US Energy Facts Explained: "The United States uses a mix of energy sources" May 16, 2018, at https://www.eia.gov/energyexplained/?page=us_energy_home (accessed November 2, 2018).

74 EIA, Energy in Brief: "How Dependent Are We on Foreign Oil?" May 10, 2013, at http://www.eia.gov/energy in brief/article/foreign oil dependence.cfm (accessed July 2015).

75 Bloomberg, Gasoline PRices ARound the World: The Real Costo of Filling Up (October 16, 2018), at https://www.bloomberg.com/graphics/gas-prices/ (accessed December 26, 2018).

76 The era of relatively cheap energy in the United States extended into the twenty-first century. Prices in Table 5.1 are not adjusted for inflation. When inflation is considered, in the early twenty-first century gasoline was still relatively inexpensive in the United States.

77 Pearce, "In a Stunning Turnaround, Britain Moves to End the Burning of Coal."

78 Gwladys Fouche, "Norway's $900 billion fund drops 10 more firms with links to coal," Reuters (March 7, 2017), at https://www.reuters.com/article/us-norway-swf/norways-900-billion-fund-drops-10-more-firms-with-links-to-coal-idUSKBN16E1BM (accessed December 2017).

79 EIA, International Energy Outlook 2014, p. 26. US Energy Information Agency available at, https://www.eia.gov/international/analysis/world (accessed January 2020).

80 EIA, Statistics: Global Energy Data, at https://www.iea.org/statistics/?country=FRANCE&year=2016&category=Key%20indicators&indicator=TPESbySource&mode=chart&categoryBrowse=false&dataTable=BALANCES&showDataTable=true (accessed November 2, 2018): France Country Data (2018), available at https://www.eia.gov/international/analysis/country/FRA (accessed January 2020).

81 EIA, International Energy Data and Analysis: United Kingdom Country Analysis (2018), available a thttps://www.eia.gov/international/analysis/country/GBR (accessed January 2020).

82 Ibid.

83 EIA, International Energy Data and Analysis: Norway Country Analysis (2016), available at https://www.eia.gov/international/analysis/country/NOR (accessed January 2020).

84 "Norway's $900bn Sovereign Wealth Fund Told to Reduce Coal Assets," *The Guardian* (May 27, 2015) (GI Fb: May 29, 2015).

85 IEA, Energy Balances Statistics, at http://www.iea.org/statistics/topics/energybalances/ (accessed July 2015): Japan, 2008, available at https://www.eia.gov/international/analysis/country/JPN (accessed January 2020).

86 EIA, International Energy Data and Analysis: Japan Country Analysis (2017).

87 David Sanger, "Japan Joins in Embargo against Iraq," *New York Times* (August 6, 1990), p. C7.

88 EIA, International Energy Data and Analysis: Japan Country Analysis (2017); see also Ken Belson, "Why Japan Steps Gingerly in the Middle East," *New York Times* (September 17, 2002), p. W1.

89 EIA, International Energy Data and Analysis: Japan Country Analysis (2017).

90 Ibid.

91 Amory Lovins, "More Profit with Less Carbon," *Scientific American*, 293 (September 2005), p. 81.

92 IEA, "Decoupling of Global Emissions and Economic Growth Confirmed" (March 16, 2016), at https://www.iea.org/newsroom/news/2016/march/decoupling-of-global-emissions-and-economic-growth-confirmed.html (accessed December 2018).

93 Neela Banerjee, "Pushing Energy Conservation into the Back Seat of the SUV," *New York Times* (November 22, 2003), p. B2.

94 International Energy Agency, *Key World Energy Statistics 2018*, p. 20; Howard French, "In Search of a New Energy Source, China Rides the Wind," *New York Times* (July 26, 2005), p. A4.

95 White House Council on Environmental Quality and the Department of State, *Global Future: Time to Act* (Washington, DC: Government Printing Office, 1981), p. 61.

96 Joel Darmstadter, *Economic Growth and Energy Conservation: Historical and International Lessons*, Reprint 154 (Washington, DC: Resources for the Future, 1978), p. 18.

97 In 1974, the average fuel efficiency of all American cars was 14 miles per gallon. The law required that this be increased to 27.5 miles per gallon by 1985.

98 5254 US White House, Office of the Press Secretary, "Obama Administration Finalizes Historic 54.5 MPG Fuel Efficiency Standards," August 28, 2012, at https://www.white-house.gov/the-press-office/2012/08/28/obama-administration-finalizes-historic-545-mpg-fuel-efficiency-standard (accessed July 2015).

99 Dan Zukowski, "No Combustion-Engine Cars Sold in Germany After 2030, Parliament Says," *EcoWatch* (October 10, 2016).

100 Robert Stobaugh and Daniel Yergin (eds), *Energy Future: Report of the Energy Project at the Harvard Business School* (New York: Ballantine, 1980).

101 ITER website, at https://www.iter.org/proj/inafewlines (accessed on December 26, 2018).

102 Ibid.

103 Ned Resnikoff, "US to Help Build First New Nuclear Reactors in Decades," MSNBC, February 19, 2014, at http://www.msnbc.com/msnbc/us-invests-big-nuclear-power (accessed July 2015).

104 Motoko Rich, "The lonely towns of Fukushima," *New York Times* (March 10, 2017) at https://www.nytimes.com/2017/03/10/world/asia/fukushima-daiichi-nuclear-disaster-towns.html (accessed December 2018).

105 Jonathan Soble, "Fukushima Keeps Fighting Radioactive Tide 5 Years After Disaster," *New York Times* (March 10, 2016).

Further Reading

Goodell, Jeff, *Big Coal: The Dirty Secret behind America's Energy Future* (New York: Houghton Mifflin, 2006). The secret is that much (about one-half) of America's electricity is generated from burning coal and this is rarely acknowledged. Coal is used because it is cheap and abundant. Goodell writes: "Our shiny white iPod economy is propped up by dirty black rocks."

Jacobson, Mark Z., and Mark A. Delucchi, "A Path to Sustainable Energy by 2030," *Scientific American*, 301 (November 2009), pp. 58–65. The authors argue that wind, water, solar, tidal, and geothermal technologies can provide 100 percent of the world's energy.

Klare, Michael, *Blood and Oil: The Dangers and Consequences of America's Growing Petroleum Dependency* (New York: Metropolitan Books, 2004). The sources of oil in the world today are often in conflict-ridden areas with strongly anti-American sentiments, Klare sees conflict as inevitable.

MacKay, David J. C., *Sustainable Energy without the Hot Air* (Cambridge: UIT Cambridge, 2009). MacKay is a former Chief Scientific Adviser to the Department of Energy and Climate Change in the UK and a professor at the University of Cambridge who tries to help us understand what a realistic effort would look like if the UK switched to sustainable energy by mid-century.

Smil, Vaclav, *Energy at the Crossroads: Global Perspectives and Uncertainties* (Cambridge, MA: MIT Press, 2003). Smil has spent four decades studying energy. Here he presents an introduction to the complexities and uncertainties of the subject. He shows the difficulties of changing from our dependence on carbon-emitting fuels, while at the same time explaining the need to do so.

Taebi, Behnam, and Sabine Roeser (eds), *The Ethics of Nuclear Energy: Risk, Justice, and Democracy in the Post-Fukushima Era* (Cambridge: Cambridge University Press, 2015).

Wald, Matthew L., "Getting Power to the People," *Bulletin of the Atomic Scientists*, 63 (September/October 2007), pp. 26–43. Wald, a long-time correspondent of the *New York Times* specializing in energy, examines the different energy alternatives to fossil fuels in a time of climate change.

Chapter 6

Climate Change

Global Issues: An Introduction, Sixth Edition. Kristen A. Hite and John L. Seitz.
© 2021 John Wiley & Sons Ltd. Published 2021 by John Wiley & Sons Ltd.

An Unprecedented Global Challenge

The overwhelming majority of scientists who specialize in the study of the Earth's climate, "climatologists" (not economists, political commentators, or meteorologists), have unequivocally affirmed the human race is now involved in an experiment of unprecedented importance to the future of life on this planet. A change in the global climate is now taking place, mainly because of the burning, by humans, of large amounts of fossil fuels – coal, oil, and natural gas. When these fuels are consumed, carbon, which accumulated in the ground over millions of years, is released into the atmosphere as a gas, carbon dioxide (CO_2) (see Figure 6.1).

The problem with this is that once gases go up into the atmosphere, it takes decades to centuries for them to leave. So, the gases build up over time, and even if the rate of emissions improves, the aggregate buildup continues to warm up the planet. CO_2 in the Earth's atmosphere has increased significantly since the Industrial Revolution: by over 40 percent between the mid-1700s and the present. According

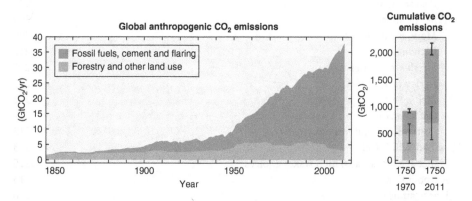

Figure 6.1   Global carbon dioxide emissions from human activity

Source: IPCC, *Climate Change 2014: Synthesis Report*. Contribution of Working Groups I, II and III to the Fifth Assessment Report of the Intergovernmental Panel on Climate Change (Core writing team, R. K. Pachauri and L. A. Meyer (eds)). IPCC, Geneva, 2014. Summary for Policymakers, Figure SPM.1 (d), p. 3. *Note:* Quantitative information is limited on emission time series of two other greenhouse gases, CH_4 (methane) and N_2O (nitrous oxide), from 1850 to 1970.

to the Intergovernmental Panel on Climate Change ("IPCC"), gases from emissions from the Industrial Revolution until 2017 will continue causing temperatures to warm up to another 0.5 degrees Celsius (0.9 degrees Fahrenheit) in the coming decades through the end of the century.[1]

As gases accumulate in the atmosphere, this causes a warming of the Earth's surface – called "global warming" or the "greenhouse effect" – since gas in the atmosphere allows sunlight to reach the Earth but traps some of the Earth's heat, preventing it from radiating back into space. While CO_2 is the largest contributor to global warming, other gases – including methane, which comes primarily from natural gas, livestock, and rice; nitrous oxide, which comes from fertilizers and other sources; chlorofluorocarbons (CFCs), widely used in the past in air conditioning and refrigeration; and other halocarbons – can also cause global warming. Particulate matter, or tiny particles of soot (also known as "black carbon"), also increases global warming. Many of these gases are increasing significantly in the atmosphere.

There is strong historical evidence that CO_2 and methane levels in the atmosphere are closely connected in some way with the Earth's temperature. European scientists in the Antarctic drilled a hole about two miles deep in the ice and withdrew a core of ice. Like the rings of a tree, the core indicated changing conditions in the past – in fact, back about 650,000 years. The scientists measured the amount of CO_2, methane, and nitrous oxide (all greenhouse gases) in the air bubbles in the ice and found two amazing facts. First, the amount of CO_2 and methane present in the Earth's atmosphere today is higher than in any previous time during those 650,000 years, and second, CO_2, methane, and the Earth's temperature went up and down closely together during that period.[2] The close relationship between the Earth's temperature and the carbon dioxide and methane levels is consistent with scientists' models for projecting climate impacts.

With the support of the United Nations, in 1988 the Intergovernmental Panel on Climate Change (IPCC) was set up to study what was happening to the Earth's climate and the causes of the changes. Since its establishment, the IPCC has issued five of these "assessment reports" (the first in 1990 and the fifth in 2014) based on peer-reviewed, published scientific studies from thousands of scientists around the world. They also issue special reports, such as ones on lands, oceans, and the difference between 1.5 and 2 degrees Celsius (2.7–3.6 degrees Fahrenheit) of warming. The IPCC is now recognized as the most authoritative organization on climate change. It won the Nobel Peace Prize in 2007 for its work.

The IPCC's first report concluded that, probably because of the release of greenhouse gases by humans, an increase in the Earth's temperature would occur, causing dangerous impacts.[3] Since that first report, more evidence has increased scientists' confidence that something dramatic is happening to the Earth's climate, with humans largely responsible. In the IPCC's 2014 report, it reaffirmed that it is "*extremely likely*" that human influence has been the dominant cause of the observed warming since the mid-twentieth century.[4] It is one thing for politicians to call something "extremely likely," but for a Nobel laureate team of the world's leading climate scientists to do so based on scientific evidence signals that any debate on this matter is pretty much settled.

How Increased Temperatures Impact the Earth

Some people hear the talk about global temperatures rising a half or one or two degrees and wonder: what's the big deal? After all, temperatures where you live can probably vary 5–10 degrees in a given day, and 20 degrees or more over the course of a year. So why should we care about a relatively small increase in average temperatures? The answer is as significant as it is surprising: the global average does not tell the full story. This is for several reasons:

- Warming is not uniform: it is several times greater in the polar regions, which are particularly sensitive to temperature changes.
- Warmer air absorbs more moisture, which changes rainfall patterns. Throughout the year, you may see rainy seasons and dry seasons. Imagine if these were no longer reliable – especially if you are a farmer trying to grow food.
- Warmer air – which means more moisture in many areas – also means supercharged storms. When it rains, it rains harder. When a hurricane or typhoon forms, it gets bigger and dumps more water.

These impacts are just the beginning. Think about the implications of unpredictable rains, monster storms, and uneven warming for your area of the world. The IPCC has looked at the likely impacts at different degrees of warming, and it turns out even a half of a degree of warming can make a huge difference. For example, the difference between 1 degree and 1.5 degrees Celsius (1.8 and 2.7 degrees Fahrenheit) of warming is 100 million more people living in poverty.[5] We'll explore more of this below.

Regional impacts

Even at moderate degrees of warming, climate models project that we will see "robust differences" in climate impacts in different regions. Land areas will warm more than ocean areas, urban areas will see more heat extremes, and heavy rainfall will hit more in some regions while drought will plague others.[6] The IPCC previously reported regional changes in rainfall over the twentieth century, including increased precipitation along the eastern parts of the Americas, northern Europe, and certain areas in Asia.[7] At the same time, already dry regions such as the Sahel have become even drier, as has the Mediterranean, southern Africa, and some areas in southern Asia.[8]

Here are a few examples:[9]

Africa   There are more climate-vulnerable populations in poverty in Africa than anywhere else.[10] Temperatures are expected to warm faster in many parts of the continent than elsewhere across the globe. The West Africa region is a particular climate "hot spot," and crop yields are projected to be severely impacted as a result of climate change.[11] Climate change may substantially exacerbate hunger in the Sahel.[12]

Asia   By the 2050s, fresh water availability in Central, South, East and South-East Asia, particularly in large river basins, is projected to decrease. Coastal areas, especially heavily populated megadelta regions in South, East, and South-East Asia will be at greatest risk due to increased flooding from the sea and, in some megadeltas, flooding from the rivers.

Low-lying islands   Between sea level rise and increases in tropical storms, the IPCC says that due to climate change, "[i]sland systems will be uninhabitable within decades."[13] This is not a distant future threat: it happened in 2017 after a 378 mile-wide hurricane slammed the Caribbean island of Barbuda, prompting the island nation's Ambassador to proclaim "The damage is complete ... For the first time in 300 years, there's not a single living person on the island of Barbuda – a civilization that has existed on that island for over 300 years has now been extinguished."[14]

Europe   In southern Europe, climate change is projected to worsen conditions (high temperatures and drought) in a region already vulnerable to climate variability, and to reduce water availability, which impacts hydropower, tourism, and crop production generally. It is also projected to increase health risks due to heat waves, and the frequency of wildfires.

Latin America   By mid-century, increases in temperature and associated decreases in soil water are projected to lead to gradual replacement of tropical forest by savannah in eastern Amazonia. Semi-arid vegetation will tend to be replaced by arid-land vegetation. Productivity of some important crops is projected to decrease and livestock productivity to decline, with adverse consequences for food security. In temperate zones, soybean yields are projected to increase.

North America   Warming in western mountains is projected to cause decreased snowpack, more winter flooding, and reduced summer flows, exacerbating competition for overallocated water resources. In the early decades of the century, moderate climate change is projected to increase aggregate yields of rain-fed agriculture by 5 to 20 percent, but with important variability among regions. Major challenges are projected for crops that are near the warm end of their suitable range or which depend on highly utilized water resources.

Polar regions   Warming is already occurring 2–3 times faster in the Arctic.[15] If the global average surface temperatures increases 1.5–2 degrees Celsius (2.7–3.6 degrees Fahrenheit), we can expect that polar regions and other areas with high latitudes will warm 4.5–6 degrees Celsius (8.1–10.8 degrees Fahrenheit), respectively.[16] The main projected biophysical effects are reductions in thickness and extent of glaciers and ice sheets, and changes in natural ecosystems with detrimental effects on many organisms including migratory birds, mammals, and higher predators.

Human interference with the climate system: assessment by the Intergovernmental Panel on Climate Change

Human influence on the climate system is clear. Yet determining whether such influence constitutes "dangerous anthropogenic interference" in the words of Article 2 of the UNFCCC [UN Framework Convention on Climate Change] involves both risk assessment and value judgments. This report assesses risks across contexts and through time, providing a basis for judgments about the level of climate change at which risks become dangerous.

Five integrative reasons for concern (RFCs) provide a framework for summarizing key risks across sectors and regions. First identified in the IPCC Third Assessment Report, the RFCs illustrate the implications of warming and of adaptation limits for people, economies, and ecosystems. They provide one starting point for evaluating dangerous anthropogenic interference with the climate system. Risks for each RFC, updated based on assessment of the literature and expert judgments, are presented [in this report]. All temperatures below are given as global average temperature change relative to 1986– 2005.

1 *Unique and threatened systems*: Some unique and threatened systems, including ecosystems and cultures, are already at risk from climate change (high confidence). The number of such systems at risk of severe consequences is higher with additional warming of around 1 degree Centigrade. Many species and systems with limited adaptive capacity are subject to very high risks with additional warming of 2 degrees Centigrade, particularly Arctic-sea-ice and coral-reef systems.

2 *Extreme weather events*: Climate-change-related risks from extreme events, such as heat waves, extreme precipitation, and coastal flooding, are already moderate (high confidence) and high with 1 degree Centigrade additional warming (medium confidence). Risks associated with some types of extreme events (e.g., extreme heat) increase further at higher temperatures (high confidence).

3 *Distribution of impacts*: Risks are unevenly distributed and are generally greater for disadvantaged people and communities in countries at all levels of development. Risks are already moderate because of regionally differentiated climate-change impacts on crop production in particular (medium to high confidence). Based on projected decreases in regional crop yields and water availability, risks of unevenly distributed impacts

are high for additional warming above 2 degrees Centigrade (medium confidence).

4 *Global aggregate impacts*: Risks of global aggregate impacts are moderate for additional warming between 1–2 degrees Centigrade, reflecting impacts to both Earth's biodiversity and the overall global economy (medium confidence). Extensive biodiversity loss with associated loss of ecosystem goods and services results in high risks around 3 degrees Centigrade additional warming (high confidence). Aggregate economic damages accelerate with increasing temperature (limited evidence, high agreement), but few quantitative estimates have been completed for additional warming around 3 degrees Centigrade or above.

5 *Large-scale singular events*: With increasing warming, some physical systems or ecosystems may be at risk of abrupt and irreversible changes. Risks associated with such tipping points become moderate between 0–1 degrees Centigrade additional warming, due to early warning signs that both warm-water coral reef and Arctic ecosystems are already experiencing irreversible regime shifts (medium confidence). Risks increase disproportionately as temperature increases between 1–2 degrees Centigrade additional warming and become high above 3 degrees Centigrade, due to the potential for a large and irreversible sea level rise from ice sheet loss. For sustained warming greater than some threshold, near-complete loss of the Greenland ice sheet would occur over a millennium or more, contributing up to 7 m of global mean sea level rise.

Source: IPCC, Fifth Assessment Report, *Climate Change 2014: Impacts, Adaptation, and Vulnerability*, Summary for Policymakers, p. 12 (footnotes omitted).

Types of impacts

Monster storms   There is mounting evidence that climate change is contributing to the increased storm intensity observed in recent years.[17] For example, in 2014, the US National Climate Assessment reported large increases in heavy precipitation in some parts of the country, leading to significant flooding and erosion.[18] This makes sense, as warmer air is able to hold more moisture.

The intensity of what is called "extreme weather events" (hurricanes/cyclones, violent thunderstorms, "winter storms," and windstorms) is expected to increase with higher peak wind speeds, and more heavy precipitation caused by warmer seas. Evidence is building that climate change is responsible for an increase in the intensity of extreme weather events like hurricanes.[19] The decade between 2005 and 2015 witnessed some of the most devastating storms in modern times, including major hurricanes causing billions of dollars of damage in the US cities of New Orleans and New York (and their surrounding regions), and typhoons wiping out entire villages or even islands in the Philippines and other Pacific countries.

Extreme heat Since the 1970s, droughts have become more intense, lasting longer and covering a wider area, especially in the tropics and subtropics. The IPCC has also found evidence that over a 50-year period, the number of cold days, cold nights, and frosts decreased over most land areas and the number of hot days and hot nights increased. In the northern hemisphere, the average temperature during the second half of the twentieth century was higher than during any other 50-year period in the past 500 years, and likely 1,300 years.[20] Additionally, heat waves are more frequent, breaking records and killing many thousands of people, especially those most vulnerable.

Heat waves are expected to become more common and more severe. Cities trap heat and the very young, elderly, and poor are especially vulnerable to heat stress. Mid-latitude urban areas such as Athens, Shanghai, and Washington, DC are more vulnerable than tropical and subtropical cities because their residents are less used to high temperatures. The death toll in cities during extreme temperatures can be surprisingly high, as was seen in Chicago where more than 700 people died during a four-day heat wave in the summer of 1995. In rural areas, hot, dry weather has been one of the main causes of many wildfires burning out of control in the western United States and other parts of the world.

Infectious diseases A change in temperature and rainfall can affect the range of many infectious diseases. One obvious example is that the range of mosquitoes that spread malaria, yellow fever, and dengue fever could expand with increased temperatures and rainfall. The range of the black fly that carries river blindness is likely to expand, as also is that of the snail that carries schistosomiasis. People living on the edges of where these diseases are prevalent now are especially vulnerable because many have little resistance built up.

Agriculture It is very hard to predict how climate change will affect agriculture in a specific area, but it is clear that overall agriculture can be severely disrupted by climate change. As shown in Figure 6.2, even as the growing season is extended, there are overall reductions in crop yields, with climate change already impacting wheat and corn yields across the globe, causing spikes in the price of food and cereals.[21] The effect of climate change on plant pests and diseases is similar to that of infectious diseases. As mentioned in Chapter 4, a study by the US National Academy of Sciences concluded that overall a 1 degree Celsius increase in temperature over the norm means a 10 percent decrease in corn, wheat, and rice yields.

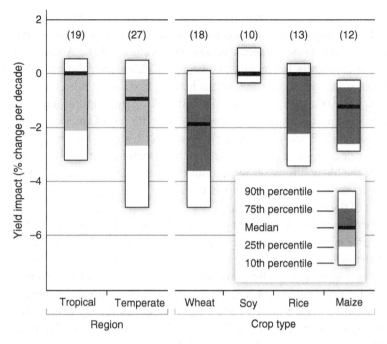

Figure 6.2 Climate impacts to agricultural production, by region and crop

Note: Summary of estimated impacts of observed climate changes on yields over 1960–2013 for four major crops in temperate and tropical regions, with the number of data points analyzed given within parentheses for each category.

Source: IPCC, Climate Change 2014: Impacts, Adaptation, and Vulnerability. Part A: Global and Sectoral Aspects. Contribution of Working Group II to the Fifth Assessment Report of the Intergovernmental Panel on Climate Change. Cambridge: Cambridge University Press, 2014. Summary for Policymakers, Figure SPM.2 (c), p. 7.

In a warmer world there would be major changes in the amount of rainfall and its location, with some areas getting more rainfall than at present and some less. Higher CO_2 levels can help some plants grow faster (at least of those able to adapt to climate impacts), but those higher CO_2 levels can also reduce nutritional values.

Higher temperatures can extend the growing season in some regions and more rainfall can benefit crops in some areas, although more violent and extreme weather could significantly reduce yields. The most significant declines in crop yields in the coming decades are expected in West Africa, Southeast Asia, and Central and South America.[22] More droughts and extreme temperatures can devastate agriculture in other areas.

An effort by the US government to predict changes in food production in the country found that it was likely that crops would increase in the northern plains, where much of the country's wheat and corn is grown, but decrease in the southern states because of droughts and floods caused by heavy rains.[23]

Melting ice   Most global warming models predicted the Arctic region would be among the first regions to show significant effects caused by global warming. They have been proven to be correct. Average temperatures of the Arctic winters have risen about 10 degrees Fahrenheit (5.6 degrees Celsius) over the past 30 years. The permafrost is thawing across the Arctic, leading to damage of buildings, pipelines, and roads in Alaska and Siberia as the land sinks. Temperatures have risen in the Arctic three times as fast in recent decades as in the rest of the world.[24] Data from satellites since 1978 show on average annual Arctic sea ice has shrunk by about 4 percent per decade – and by even more during summer months.[25] In most computer models of the likely future, sea ice in both the Arctic and Antarctica is projected to continue to shrink. In several models the Arctic ice completely disappears by the latter part of the twenty-first century.

Other evidence shows that most glaciers in the world have been retreating, affecting downstream water supplies. Scientists have discovered the movements of some glaciers draining the great ice sheets in Antarctica and Greenland, the melting of which is accelerating.[26] Studies have shown that since the 1960s spring has come earlier and winter later for the higher latitude areas in the northern hemisphere.

At some point, likely between 1.5 to 2 degrees Celsius (2.7–3.6 degrees Fahrenheit) of warming, scientists expect the Greenland Ice sheet to irreversibly melt into the sea.[27] This is a threshold with impacts likely to last for millennia, particularly in terms of sea level rise.

Sea level rise   Warmer temperatures should cause the levels of the oceans to rise because melting glaciers and ice caps will add water to the oceans, and water expands when its temperature increases (thermal expansion of the oceans contributes about 25 percent of sea level rise).[28] Sea levels have risen on average by 3.2 millimeters per year from 1993 to 2010.[29] The rate has been higher in recent years.[30]

A probable effect of a warming of the Earth's climate is that the level of the oceans will rise between 0.17 to 0.82 meters (about 0.5 to 2.5 feet) by the end of the twenty-first century.[31] Such a gradual rising of waters could lead to the evacuation of some coastal cities around the world. Sixteen of the largest cities with populations of over 10 million are located in the coastal regions. The rich countries will probably be able to build dikes to protect their cities, but poor countries such as Bangladesh probably cannot afford to do so.

Much coastal lowland around the world will be threatened. These lands are heavily populated at present, especially in the developing nations. Regions such as the Ganges–Brahmaputra Delta in Bangladesh, the Nile Delta in Egypt, and the Niger Delta in Nigeria are especially vulnerable. Island nations such as the Maldives in the Indian Ocean and the Marshall Islands in the Pacific Ocean could be inundated, and some islands are already seeing some residents leave: in 2014, a New Zealand court granted citizenship to a family evacuating Tuvalu in the South Pacific, prompting the *Guardian* newspaper to ask whether this marked a new era of climate refugees.[32] Higher sea levels cause much of their damage during storms when high sea surges hitting the coasts cause very destructive floods.

Disruption of natural ecosystems   Natural ecosystems such as forests, rangeland, and aquatic environments provide a host of services to human and nonhuman life. Many of these services are still relatively unknown. Any disruption of these ecosystems because of climate change could have serious effects. Rough estimates are that a doubling of CO_2 levels could cause from one-third to one-half of all plant communities and the animals that depend on them to shift their locations.[33] The IPCC expects that many plants and animals will not be able to adapt as quickly and could go extinct: at 1.5 degrees Celsius (2.7 degrees Fahrenheit) of warming, we can expect 6 percent of insects, 8 percent of plants, and 4 percent of vertebrates to go extinct; at 2 degrees Celsius (3.6 degrees Fahrenheit) of warming those estimates more than double.[34] The shrinking sea ice in the Arctic is likely to make it much more difficult for polar bears to hunt for seals, one of their chief foods, thus leading to the bears' possible extinction.

Coral reefs are in serious decline around the world because of warmer seas, pollution, disease, and overfishing. More than 30 percent have already been severely damaged.[35] Here is how the United Nations Environment Programme describes the situation:

> Around 25 percent of the world's CO_2 emissions are being absorbed into the seas and oceans where it converts to carbonic acid. This is lowering the pH of the oceans and affecting its chemistry. For example, the concentration of carbonate ions is decreasing and is linked to the ability of many marine organisms to build reefs and shells.[36]

The chemistry of the oceans is being altered at a speed not seen for 65 million years – since the extinction of the dinosaurs. The ocean has absorbed almost one-third of all carbon dioxide emitted into the atmosphere, causing ocean acidification and other impacts.[37] The mean pH of the marine world has decreased by 0.1, corresponding to a 26 percent increase in hydrogen ions since the Industrial Revolution.[38]

How Bad Will It Get?

Numerous models of the Earth's climate have been made by climatologists and nearly all of these project that our best hope is to limit warming to 1.5 degrees Celsius (2.7 degrees Fahrenheit) from preindustrial temperatures, which will reduce the degree of long-term catastrophic impacts to the Earth's climate because of the increasing CO_2 and other greenhouse gases.

There is evidence that since the Industrial Revolution began (1850), the temperature of the Earth has increased over 1 degree Celsius (about 1.8 degrees Fahrenheit) (Figure 6.3).[39] Since the 1980s, every decade has been warmer than the previous one, which represents the warmest period since modern industrialization (1850) and likely the warmest in the last 1,400 years.[40] The IPCC estimates that the global temperature average is increasing about 0.2 degrees Celsius (0.36 degrees Fahrenheit) each decade.[41] Between 2030–2050 (most likely around 2040), it is likely the Earth

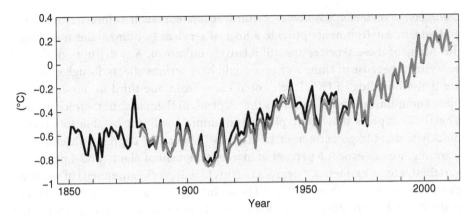

Figure 6.3 Globally averaged combined land and ocean surface temperature anomaly

Source: IPCC, *Climate Change 2014: Synthesis Report*. Contribution of Working Groups I, II and III to the Fifth Assessment Report of the Intergovernmental Panel on Climate Change (Core writing team, R. K. Pachauri and L. A. Meyer (eds)). Geneva: IPCC, 2014. Summary for Policymakers, Figure SPM.1 (a), p. 3.

will have warmed 1.5 degrees Celsius (2.7 degrees Fahrenheit).[42] From there, the trajectory depends in large part on choices made now that lock in future pathways of either additional warming or climate stabilization.

The most common forecast of the computer models is that – if present trends continue – the amount of CO_2 in the atmosphere is expected to be double the preindustrial level before 2100, and according to the 2014 IPCC report, that will lead to an increase of 3.7 to 4.8 degrees Celsius (3 degrees Celsius equals about 5 degrees Fahrenheit) in average global temperature before the end of the present century. If governments take climate change seriously and each government fully implements its 2015 pledges to take national-level actions to reduce emissions, then warming is expected to amount to approximately a 2–3 degrees Celsius increase (we will discuss this more under the Paris Agreement discussion below). In any case, absent major changes in countries' emissions and development pathways, global temperatures are widely projected to exceed levels that scientists have flagged as likely to cause dangerous human interference with the Earth's climate.

Three degrees Celsius would be a more rapid change of temperature than has occurred in the past 10,000 years. While 3 degrees Celsius may not sound like very much, it would be catastrophic for growing food and could lead to the extinction of a significant portion of species on Earth. It would mean hundreds of millions of lives compromised due to extreme weather and less predictable rains. According to scientists of the US National Aeronautics and Space Administration (NASA), the temperature on Earth would warm so quickly that many species will be unable to adapt.[43] Scientists have concluded that, because of various "feedbacks," it is likely that the warming will be even more than they are predicting. They also warn that because of our incomplete knowledge about the processes involved in the Earth's climate, it is possible we will be confronted with "surprises" in the future.[44]

Planet at a crossroads: high stakes choices

Global temperature increases are not inevitable: they are the consequences of human choices in how we choose to get energy and how we manage land. The IPCC has made it clear that temperature rise can be limited to safer levels if the annual rate of greenhouse gas emissions can start declining at the global level and balance out to "net zero" by the middle of the twenty-first century.[45] Until fewer greenhouse gases go into the atmosphere than can be sucked out of it from the Earth and/or geoengineering, the amount of CO_2 in the atmosphere will not necessarily stop increasing after emissions growth has slowed, of course. Depending on how much carbon continues to be released on Earth, the CO_2 level in the atmosphere could keep rising even if the global *rate* of emissions released into the atmosphere slows.

Actions to address and reduce greenhouse gas emissions are called *mitigation*, and there are many different pathways to get to a lower carbon future. But these pathways depend on collective action at a planetary scale, a political challenge to business as usual. Notably, population and economic growth are the most important drivers of increased greenhouse gas emissions[46] – and as we have seen in earlier chapters, this growth continues to be significant at the global level. Indeed, the scale is so great that climate change is forcing a revision of the twentieth-century development pathways widely embraced after World War II.

With more than two-thirds of global emissions coming from energy generation (primarily the burning of coal and oil), transitioning energy pathways to nonemitting sources is key to keeping global temperatures down towards 1.5 degrees Celsius (2.7 degrees Fahrenheit). The other place that makes a big difference is in the management of land: getting agricultural emissions under control and halting deforestation

Air pollution

Higher temperatures tend to bolster the formation of pollutants such as ground-level ozone (O_3), which is one of the main components of smog. An increase in winds could disperse pollution, whereas a decrease could help pollution levels to rise. An increase in rainfall can wash out pollutants, while a decrease can have the opposite effect.

Particulate matter, also known as soot or "black carbon," is one pollutant that not only has direct human health impacts but also has fast-acting climate impacts. Sources range from burning traditional fuels like wood to burning coal. The tiny particles go up into the air and absorb heat. It is likely that large amounts of black carbon particles in the air, especially over parts of India and China – from the burning of coal and biofuels – are affecting the climate in various ways.[47]

The good news is that addressing air pollution typically has fast-acting climate benefits. Because soot is relatively heavy in the air, it accumulates over a shorter period of time than most greenhouse gases. Solutions make sense on a number of levels and include switching from wood- or dung-powered coosktoves to cleaner burning ones, or switching from coal to less polluting electricity sources: because it is a fast-acting solution, it can buy time to transition the economy towards more lower-emitting (and slower acting) solutions.

Uncertainties

Abrupt climate change   Scientists examining the ice cores mentioned above have found evidence that at times in the past the climate of Earth changed abruptly to a new level which persisted for hundreds or thousands of years.[48] A threshold was crossed to cause each change, but scientists do not understand what these thresholds were. One scientist described our situation today as similar to when people in a canoe start to rock the boat. Nothing happens for a while until a threshold is crossed and the canoe suddenly tips over and the canoeists find themselves in the water. As strange as it may seem, the next section shows that one of these abrupt changes could be from warm weather to a rapid cooling for parts of our planet.

Slower Atlantic currents   Scientists have discovered some evidence that the currents that bring warm water from the tropics to North America and Northern Europe may be slowing.[49] The melting of the sea and land ice in the Arctic – especially in Greenland – may be diluting the ocean's salty water which is essential to keep the so-called "Atlantic heat conveyor" moving. If and when this happens, not only will North America and Northern Europe face colder climates, but the monsoons that billions of people in Asia and Africa depend on to support their agriculture could be disrupted.

Clouds   Scientists admit unfamiliarity with the effects global warming will have on clouds. Some types of clouds could cool the Earth, while other types could heat it up more. Also largely unknown are the effect aerosols (soot) will have on weather. It is likely volcanic ash is lowering some of the warming that would be occurring without it.[50]

Other positive and negative feedbacks   There are uncertainties over possible "positive feedbacks," those things that might occur as the warming takes place that will make it worse, such as a melting of the permafrost releasing more methane, and "negative feedbacks," those things that could make it cooler, such as an exploding algae population in a warmer ocean absorbing more carbon dioxide.

Global Agreement for a Global Problem

The 1992 Framework Convention on Climate Change, first presented at the Rio Earth Summit, has been ratified by 193 nations. The Convention called on nations to voluntarily reduce their emissions of greenhouse gases to 1990 levels. European nations, Japan, and about 40 small island and coastal states favored putting country-specific targets and timetables for reaching the targets in the treaty, but some countries, including the United States, opposed this and the timetables were not included. The industrial nations pledged to meet the goal of reducing greenhouse gases to 1990 levels by 2000. For the most part the industrialized nations did not meet this goal.

In 1997, many nations met at Kyoto, Japan, and agreed to a proposed treaty that did place legally binding limits on developed (wealthy historic emitters) nations. No new hard caps were placed on developing nations because they had historically produced few greenhouse gases and were making efforts to reduce their widespread poverty. The country-specific targets set in the 1997 treaty (called the Kyoto Protocol) meant that developed nations would reduce their greenhouse gas emissions by about 5 percent from their 1990 levels by 2008–12. As of 2020 the United States – the second largest annual producer of greenhouse gases (China is now the largest) – had still not ratified this treaty and there was no effort being made in the country to do so. The European Union did ratify it, and by 2002 the United Kingdom and Germany had reduced their emissions below their Kyoto targets. By 2005 enough nations had ratified the Kyoto Protocol to bring it into force. But by 2012 some high emitting countries such as Canada and Japan decided to withdraw from the treaty.

Since the ratification of the 1992 Framework Convention, countries have met at least annually to discuss the climate problem. In 2010, the nearly 200 countries at the annual UN climate conference rejected new treaty-based obligations in favor of a more decentralized approach to addressing climate change. They adopted a more formalized international system to report on and verify reductions made at the national level. They also set up a Green Climate Fund to help developing countries combat deforestation, shift to clean energy, and adapt to the impacts climate change will bring. However, whether enough funds will be provided to pay for all of these needs remains uncertain.

By 2015, countries had agreed on a new path forward to address their collective climate emissions to avoid dangerous human-induced interference with the Earth's climate. The Paris Agreement enshrined national pledges to reduce greenhouse gases that have been made by many nations, including the United States and China. Although overall emissions reductions pledges do not yet add up to the level the IPCC says is necessary to stabilize the Earth's climate, there is some progress compared to what the world would look like without globally coordinated action.

In 2020, global greenhouse gas emissions dramatically dropped due to a slowdown in economic activity due to Covid-19. While the economic impacts were extreme, it also showed how quickly the world could achieve emissions reductions targets that actually exceeded what was required to keep global temperature increases under

1.5 degrees (UNEP, 2019). As the UN Secretary General Antonio Guterres observed, you cannot fight climate change with a virus, and the choices made by countries in how to rebuild their economies following the pandemic are largely going to determine climate trajectories for the rest of this century.

While the problem seems overwhelming at the global level, countries, cities, and many global citizens are all taking significant action to reduce their greenhouse gas contributions. Even some of the most historically intransigent – and highest emitting – countries, such as the United States and China, have been undertaking nationally significant actions to reduce their emissions, although a number of government initiatives under US President Donald Trump have largely stalled the United States' national efforts to meaningfully reduce emissions. Yet most of the globe has stayed the course in taking climate change seriously and working to get global emissions under control. Whether this will lead to a transformative global effort remains uncertain, but one thing that is clear is that the problem of climate change is only getting worse, and will continue doing so until a critical mass of those causing the emissions make fundamental changes that shift the global development trajectory to a climate-safe pathway.

What More Can Be Done?

In the past, total CO_2 emissions and CO_2 emissions per capita have always been much higher in the more developed countries than in the less developed countries. For most of the last century, mainly from the developed countries, levels of CO_2 and other greenhouse gases increased dramatically – by 70 percent in just over 30 years from 1970.[51] From 1990 to 2008, US greenhouse gas emissions alone rose by about 14 percent.[52] But as development spreads to some of the large emerging economies – such as China and India – and as their populations grow, they are producing a relatively larger percentage of the gases, especially as China relies mainly on coal, the fossil fuel that emits the most CO_2. At the same time, the world is beginning to decouple greenhouse gas emissions from economic growth: in 2015, for the first time in many decades, greenhouse gas emissions from the energy sector stabilized even though the global economy grew.[53]

The International Energy Agency (IEA) predicts that growing global energy demand and retired power plants will collectively result in an additional 7,200 gigawatts of energy production capacity by 2040.[54] How these new energy sources are built – whether through fossil fuels or renewable energy – will have a very large influence on global greenhouse gas emissions. If the IEA's prediction of a massive growth in the renewable energy sector proves correct, renewables will supply half of this new capacity – an unprecedented increase in the coming decades.[55] In fact, renewable energy capacity is expected to grow twice as much in poor countries as in wealthy ones.[56]

Given the urgency of the energy-climate crisis, many (particularly politicians in the United States) have called on higher-emitting countries in emerging economies, especially China and India, to take on nationally ambitious targets and actions to reduce their emissions. At the same time, while these countries command a substantial percentage of the global population and their total CO_2 emissions are relatively high, their per capita emissions still remain relatively low.

Eventually all nations, including the United States, will have to agree to reductions in greenhouse gas emissions well beyond those indicated in the Kyoto treaty if there is any possibility of stabilizing atmospheric CO_2 concentrations at even two or three times their preindustrial level. When, and whether, these actions will take place is unknown.

The long-term prospects for the United States cooperating globally to address climate change are unclear. In recent years the United States has accepted its historical responsibility for climate emissions and pledged to take action at the global level, but in 2017 the US President announced that he intended to withdraw the US from the Paris Agreement. In 2015, President Barack Obama was the first US president to make a serious effort to address climate change, but many of those efforts were reversed under the next (Trump) administration. Meanwhile, many countries, provinces, cities, and companies have pledged not only to reduce their emissions but to reach net zero carbon emissions by the year 2050 or earlier.

As discussed in Chapter 5, China is also pursuing many nonfossil fuel renewable energy sources. China hoped that improving the energy efficiency of its industry would be enough to cut emissions, but so far this has not produced the results hoped for. Its continuing reliance on coal as its main energy source makes it unlikely that China will, any time soon, reverse its growing production of CO_2 and other climate-destructive gases. But China has committed to taking nationally significant actions in the coming decades, which is a key global development given that in recent years, China's greenhouse gas emissions have exceeded those of all G7 countries combined.

There are various policies that the United States and other nations could pursue that would help alleviate the threat of climate change. One would be to stop supporting and subsidizing programs to promote the increased use of coal and synthetic fuels made from coal and oil – such as tar sands – and to encourage the more efficient use of energy and its conservation. The development of renewable energy sources, such as solar and wind energy, can be promoted.

Some experts have argued that a carbon tax – a tax on fuel according to the amount of CO_2 (and CO_2 equivalent) released – would give a big boost to the expansion of renewable energy and encourage technologies that make the use of energy more efficient. Because the prices of fossil fuels today are artificially low, not reflecting the health and environmental costs society will have to pay because that fuel is being used, there is little incentive to reduce their use. By the end of the twentieth century, five countries – Denmark, Finland, Norway, Sweden, and the Netherlands – had taken the lead in adopting carbon taxes.

In the short term, the United States and other high-energy users could switch from oil to natural gas as natural gas releases less CO_2 per equivalent amount of energy than petroleum or coal. If there is no methane leakage from production (which is far from certain), natural gas emits roughly 30 percent less CO_2 than oil and 40 percent less than coal.

Another policy is to combat deforestation, since trees, along with other vegetation, absorb large amounts of CO_2.[57] Experts say deforestation is responsible for more than 10 percent of global emissions. The increasing destruction of the great tropical rainforests in Latin America, Indonesia, and the Congo Basin in Africa is cited by some experts as representing a real threat to the global climate.

The paths for countries to develop and improve livelihoods without increasing greenhouse gas emissions are still being forged, but it is clearly in the interests of the global community – including wealthy historic emitters – to help countries develop sustainably.

Reducing our carbon footprints

I (Seitz) felt proud. As I sat on a bench on our campus, I told a colleague I had recently calculated the amount of carbon dioxide I had avoided releasing into the atmosphere over the past 32 years by walking to work. Instead of driving a car to work I calculated I had reduced my personal carbon footprint by 13 tons (12 metric tons) of CO_2. Another colleague heard my statement and said, "I hate to say it, but Jack's actions were actually insignificant given the huge amount of CO_2 our society and the world produces every year." Was he right? From one way of looking at the huge climate change problem, of course he was. But from another perspective, my choices still made a difference.

I am responsible for my actions during my life and because my actions were better for the Earth and its living creatures (including myself), I was right to feel proud. Not everyone can or will walk to work, but many other ways exist to reduce the use of fossil fuels, and to cut our carbon footprints. What's your favorite way, reader? Have you stopped wasting energy, do you recycle, have you made your living and working areas more energy efficient, or have you even shifted away from using fossil fuels? If you have done any of these or others, you are taking steps to become part of the solution.

There is no single action that will save the planet, but there are many actions that will help. Here are some examples of things you can do:

- Walk, bike, or take public transportation.
- Turn off lights and appliances when not in use.
- Eat less meat, buy local food, and do not waste it.
- Plant trees.
- Attend long distance meetings via telephone or internet instead of traveling.
- Avoid airplane travel.
- Vote for representatives who support lowering emissions.

Conclusion

Addressing climate change demands institutional, technological, and behavioral changes orchestrated between global, national, local, and even household scales at an unprecedented level. Greenhouse gas emissions have to peak and decline, led by historically wealthy countries whose economies grew in large part through the cheap combustion of fossil fuels. But even though wealthy historic emitters have to lead, the ultimate fate of the climate may be determined by faster growing economies in other countries – not just in India and China, but also in many other parts of the world. As billions of the world's poorest begin to shift from traditional fuels to electricity, billions more increase their consumption as demand for cars and modern conveniences grows in tandem with national economies. And while the energy sector is likely to continue to be the biggest source of emissions, it also holds the biggest potential for reductions. Land use choices regarding agriculture and deforestation will also play an important role in determining how much carbon the Earth both emits and absorbs.

As the world works intently to decouple greenhouse gas emissions and economic growth, it seems that the daunting challenge of addressing climate change is shifting the very notion of "development" at a global level. Whether the world will rise to the challenge of following a more sustainable pathway remains to be seen. If it cannot, it is clear that severe, irreversible, and unprecedented changes will impact food security and economic production in other ways, meaning that in one way or another, climate change is "reveloping" the world.

Notes

1 IPCC Special Report on 1.5 Degrees, Summary for Policymakers (Geneva: IPCC, 2018), p. 4.
2 Edward Brook, "Tiny Bubbles Tell All," *Science*, 310 (November 25, 2005), pp. 1285–7.
3 J. T. Houghton, G. J. Jenkins, and J. J. Ephraums (eds), *Climate Change: The IPCC Scientific Assessment* (Cambridge: Cambridge University Press, 1990).
4 The Fifth Assessment Report of the Intergovernmental Panel on Climate Change (hereafter IPCC AR5) consists of reports from three working groups and a synthesis report, see http://www.ipcc.ch/report/ar5/ (accessed July 2015). For the observation about human influence, see e.g. Climate Change 2014: Synthesis Report, Summary for Policymakers, p. 5.
5 IPCC Special Report on 1.5 Degrees (2018).
6 IPCC Special Report on 1.5 Degrees, Summary for Policymakers, p. 8.
7 IPCC, *Climate Change 2007: The Physical Science Basis* (Cambridge: Cambridge University Press, 2007), p. 7.
8 Ibid.
9 IPCC, *Climate Change 2007: Impacts, Adaptation and Vulnerability* (Cambridge: Cambridge University Press, 2007), Summary for Policymakers, pp. 13–15.
10 IPCC Special Report on 1.5 degrees (2018), p. 197.
11 Ibid.

12 See previous discussion on the Sahel in Chapter 4 of this book.

13 IPCC Special Report on 1.5 degrees (2018).

14 T.J. Raphael, "For the First Time in 300 Years, There's Not a Single Living Person on the Island of Barbuda," *USA Today* (September 14, 2017).

15 IPCC Special Report on 1.5 Degrees, Summary for Policymakers, p. 4.

16 Ibid., p. 9.

17 Ibid.; see also Richard Kerr, "Is Katrina a Harbinger of Still More Powerful Hurricanes?" *Science*, 309 (September 16, 2005), p. 1807; and Claudia Dreifus, "With Findings on Storms, Centrist Recasts Warming Debate," *New York Times* (January 10, 2006) p. D2.

18 Justin Gillis, "Looks Like Rain Again. And Again," *New York Times* (May 13, 2014).

19 IPCC AR5, The Physical Science Basis, Summary for Policymakers, p. 7.

20 IPCC AR5, Synthesis Report, Summary for Policymakers, p. 2, and Impacts, Adaptation, and Vulnerability, Summary for Policymakers, p. 8.

21 IPCC AR5, Impacts, Adaptation, and Vulnerability, Summary for Policymakers, pp. 5–6.

22 IPCC Special Report on 1.5 Degrees (2018).

23 Andrew Revkin, "Report Forecasts Warming Effects," *New York Times* (June 12, 2000), pp. A1, A25.

24 IPCC Special Report on 1.5 Degrees (2018).

25 IPCC AR5, Climate Change 2014: Impacts, Adaptation, and Vulnerability, Summary for Policymakers, p. 7.

26 IPCC Special Report on 1.5 Degrees (2018); see also Richard Kerr, "A Worrying Trend of Less Ice, Higher Seas," and Ian Joughin, "Green-land Rumbles Louder as Glaciers Accelerate," both in *Science*, 311 (March 24, 2006), pp. 1698–721.

27 IPCC Special Report on 1.5 degrees (2018).

28 Gabriele Hegeri and Nathaniel Bindoff, "Warming the World's Oceans," *Science*, 309 (July 8, 2005), p. 254.

29 IPCC AR5, The Physical Science Basis, Summary for Policymakers, p. 11.

30 Ibid., p. 2.

31 Ibid., p. 23.

32 Greg Harman, "Has the Great Climate Change Migration Already Begun?" *The Guardian* (September 15, 2014).

33 World Resources Institute, UNEP, United Nations Development Programme, and World Bank, *World Resources 1998–99: A Guide to the Global Environment* (New York: Oxford University Press, 1998), p. 72.

34 IPCC, Special Report on 1.5 Degrees, Summary for Policymakers (2018), p10.

35 T. P. Hughes et al., "Climate Change, Human Impacts, and the Resilience of Coral Reefs," *Science*, 301 (August 15, 2003), p. 929.

36 United Nations Environment Programme (UNEP), "Acidification May Push Already Over-Stressed Oceans into the Red," press release, December 10, 2010, at http://www.unep.org/Documents.Multilingual/Default.asp?DocumentID=653&ArticleID=6849 (accessed July 2015), citing UNEP, *Environmental Consequences of Ocean Acidification: A Threat to Food Security* (2010) at http://www.unep.org/dewa/Portals/67/pdf/Ocean Acidification.pdf (accessed July 2015).

37 IPCC AR5, The Physical Science Basis, Summary for Policymakers, p. 11.

38 UNEP, *Environmental Consequences of Ocean Acidification: A Threat to Food Security*.

39 Intergovernmental Panel on Climate Change, Special Report on 1.5 degrees (2017).

40 IPCC AR5, Climate Change 2013: The Physical Science Basis, Summary for Policymakers, p. 5.

41 IPCC Special Report on 1.5 degrees (2018), Summary for Policymakers, p. 4.

42 Ibid.

43 James Hansen et al., "Climate Impact of Increasing Atmospheric Carbon Dioxide," *Science*, 213 (August 28, 1981), p. 966.

44 IPCC Special Report on 1.5; Houghton et al., *Climate Change*, pp. xi, xxvii.

45 IPCC AR5, Mitigation of Climate Change, Summary for Policymakers, p. 9.

46 IPCC AR5, Climate Change 2014: Mitigation of Climate Change, Summary for Policymakers, p. 8.

47 William Chameides and Michael Bergin, "Soot Takes Center Stage," *Science*, 297 (September 27, 2002), pp. 2214–15.

48 Richard Alley, "Abrupt Climate Change," *Scientific American*, 291 (November 2004), pp. 62–9.

49 Detlef Quadfasel, "The Atlantic Heat Conveyor Slows," *Nature*, 438 (December 1, 2005), pp. 565–6.

50 IPCC AR5, *Impacts, Adaptation, and Vulnerability*, p. 10.

51 IPCC, *Climate Change 2007: Mitigation of Climate Change* (Cambridge: Cambridge University Press, 2007), Summary for Policymakers, p. 3.

52 US Environmental Protection Agency, *Inventory of US Greenhouse Gas Emissions and Sinks: 1990–2008* (Washington, DC: US EPA, 2010), Executive Summary, p. 3.

53 International Energy Agency (IEA), "Global Energy-Related Emissions of Carbon Dioxide Stalled in 2014," March 15, 2015, at http://www.iea.org/newsroomand events/news/2015/march/global-energy-related-emissions-of-carbon-dioxide-stalled-in-2014.html (accessed July 2015).

54 IEA, *World Energy Outlook 2014* (Paris: IEA, 2014), Executive Summary, p. 4.

55 Ibid.

56 Ibid.

57 Humus, the organic material in topsoil, also stores large amounts of carbon.

Further Reading

Flannery, Tim, *The Weather Makers: How Man Is Changing the Climate and What it Means for Life on Earth* (New York: Atlantic Monthly Press, 2006). Originally a skeptic, the author is now convinced climate change is real. The book, in an interesting manner, describes the author's slow awakening to the dangers of global warming. He then provides the reader with a look at the climate shifts that have occurred over the past 65 million years, and ends with two contrasting futures – one in which we fail to act and the second where effective international action averts the worst effects of climate change.

Friedman, Thomas, *Hot, Flat, and Crowded: Why We Need a Green Revolution – and How it Can Renew America* (New York: Farrar, Straus & Giroux, 2008). Many American politicians and some economists believe confronting climate change will be bad for the US economy and hurt its competitive edge against those nations that are doing nothing or very little. Friedman believes they are wrong. He argues that going clean and green is the best way for America to remain an economic powerhouse.

Hoggan, James, and Richard Littlemore, *Climate Cover-Up: The Crusade to Deny Global Warming* (Vancouver: Greystone Books, 2009). The book seeks to explain the different tactics that have been used to create doubt in the public's mind that climate change is real.

Oreskes, Naomi, and Eric M. Conway. *Merchants of Doubt: How a Handful of Scientists Obscured the Truth on Issues from Tobacco Smoke to Global Warming* (New York: Bloomsbury, 2010). One of the authors of this book, Dr Naomi Oreskes, Professor of the History of Science at Harvard University, has become the main object for attacks by deniers of climate change in the United States.

Tanner, Thomas, and Leo Horn-Phathanothai, *Climate Change and Development* (New York: Routledge, 2014). Climate change is redefining development pathways. This book provides a foundational exploration of the linkages and implications of climate change for development.

Weart, Spencer, *The Discovery of Global Warming* (Cambridge, MA: Harvard University Press, 2003). The *New York Times* called this book the intellectual journey to belief in global warming.

World Bank, *World Development Report 2010: Development and Climate Change* (Washington, DC: World Bank, 2010). This well researched and readable reference book has a wealth of information on how climate change is now affecting, and probably will affect in the future, both rich and poor nations. It also describes many ways the negative effects of climate change can be lessened.

Chapter 7

The Environment: Natural Resources[1]

The Awakening

The first world conference on the environment was held in Stockholm, Sweden, in 1972 with the support of the United Nations. At that conference the rich industrialized nations, led by the United States, pushed for greater efforts to protect the environment, while many poorer and less industrialized nations feared that efforts to create strict environmental laws in their countries would hurt their chances for

---

1 Katherine Liljestrand contributed substantially to the research and updates reflected in this edition. Please reflect her contribution in any direct citation to this chapter.

Global Issues: An Introduction, Sixth Edition. Kristen A. Hite and John L. Seitz.
© 2021 John Wiley & Sons Ltd. Published 2021 by John Wiley & Sons Ltd.

economic growth. The developing nations maintained that poverty was the main cause of the deterioration of the environment in their countries. What they needed, they said, was more industry instead of less.

Ten years later, the nations of the world again met together to discuss the state of the global environment, this time in Nairobi, Kenya. The positions of the rich and poor nations had changed dramatically. The world was generally more receptive to further efforts to protect the environment. The ten years between the conferences had seen environmental deterioration – such as desertification, soil erosion, deforestation, and the silting of rivers and reservoirs – widely recognized as resulting from efforts to develop and to reduce poverty through the twentieth-century development model discussed in Chapter 1. At the same time, many of the rich nations at Nairobi, led by the United States, called for a slowing down of environmental initiatives until they had recovered from their economic recessions.

Even though the positions of the richer and poorer nations had become somewhat reversed during the ten years between the two environmental conferences, there is no doubt that an awareness of the threat to the environment caused by human activities had by 1982, become worldwide. Only 11 nations had any kind of governmental environmental agency at the time of the first conference, whereas over 100 nations, 70 of them in the Global South, had such agencies by the time of the second. These agencies did much to educate their own governments and people about environmental dangers.

In 1992, the third environmental conference sponsored by the United Nations was held in Rio de Janeiro, Brazil. Popularly called the Earth Summit, and formally the Conference on the Environment and Development, it was attended by the largest number of leaders of nations in history for a conference of this type. They were joined by about 10,000 private environmentalists from around the world plus 8,000 journalists. Although frequent clashes happened between the representatives of Northern rich countries and relatively poor Southern countries in the preparatory meetings, which took place during the two years preceding the conference, three major treaties were signed by about 150 nations at the conference. One concerned the possible warming of the Earth's climate, which was discussed in Chapter 6. The United Nations Framework Convention on Climate Change (UNFCCC) called on nations to curb the release of greenhouse gases that risked causing irreversible damage to the Earth and its climate – damage that would hinder nations from developing economically. Because of the insistence of the United States, no specific targets or timetables were placed in the treaty, but it did call for nations to eventually reduce the emissions of their greenhouse gases to 1990 levels (and became supplemented by two additional global agreements – the Kyoto Protocol and Paris Accord, discussed in Chapter 6).

The second treaty, the Convention on Biodiversity (CBD), provided for the protection of plant and animal species and was signed by nearly every nation on Earth. The United States did not ratify it and stood fairly alone in its opposition to it. The opposition by the first Bush administration in the United States to these environmental initiatives can be explained partly by timing: 1992 was a presidential election year and President George H.W. Bush was vulnerable to attack because of slow economic growth and a huge governmental deficit – and was in fact defeated that year in large part due to the poor economic conditions in the United States.[1]

Although the third treaty, the Convention to Combat Desertification (CCD), did not receive as much initial attention as the prior two, the United Nations is now increasingly focusing on it, especially as relates to helping countries adapt to climate change and restore soil for growing crops.

In 2002, the next major UN environmental conference was held in Johannesburg, South Africa, under the title World Summit on Sustainable Development. One of the main clashes between nations was unusual. The European Union proposed a target that nations would set as their goal for switching to renewable energy from fossil fuels. The goal was to have 15 percent of world energy come from renewable sources by 2010. European nations felt that in order to hold nations responsible for their actions, specific targets were necessary; without targets, they said it was difficult to measure progress or lack thereof. The United States strongly opposed this and with the help of oil-producing nations such as Saudi Arabia and Canada, along with Japan, got the provision dropped from the final conference agreement. The final agreement endorsed many of the Millennium Development Goals, discussed in Chapter 1, but largely lacked a politically ambitious outcome. Some cited the creation in the conference of "public–private partnerships" as an attempt at decentralized and voluntary efforts for sustainable development as an accomplishment of the conference, but others have criticized these as ineffective where they substitute for government action. Many environmentalists were disappointed with the results of the conference, frequently blaming the lack of leadership from the United States, whose president, George W. Bush, was one of the few country leaders who declined to attend the conference. In the words of the UN Secretary-General Kofi Annan, "Obviously, this is not Rio."[2]

In 2012, there was yet another less-than-fireworks world summit on sustainable development – again in Rio. The difference between this conference and the original Rio Earth Summit was significant in the sense that the 2012 conference was not the blockbuster world event of 1992, but it also reflected that environment and development tracks at the UN had merged. Natural resource and pollution issues were no longer separate from development: sustainable development had now become the dominant paradigm for mainstream development, and environmental considerations have since been incorporated into the 2015–30 Sustainable Development Goals, discussed earlier in this book.

Regardless of how countries approach sustainable development, environmental problems continue to grow as consumption and population increase. Nations vary greatly on how well they are treating the environment. In 2014, a study by Yale and Columbia universities in the United States rated Switzerland, Luxemburg, and Australia as the best, while the United States was ranked 27 of 180 countries.[3] Many less wealthy countries ranked higher than some of the wealthier ones, which is different than conventional development classifications – showing that economic development and environmental protection are not directly correlated, despite conventional assumptions otherwise.

This portion of the book, two environment chapters, considers the intersections between environment and development in light of traditional economic development pathways and their impacts. In this chapter, we will look at the air, water, and land as shared resources that not only serve as the base of development activities but also receive many of the impacts associated with modern development. After looking briefly at the use of natural resources in the world, we will learn why the extinction of species is accelerating. The next chapter will look at pollution and waste.

Water

Water is fundamental to life and is found across the planet. But the amount of clean, fresh water available is diminishing, while its use is increasing. The world faces serious water problems. At the beginning of the present century it was estimated that about 2.5 billion people lived in river basins where water was scarce and of these about 1.5 billion people lived in areas of high water scarcity; further, the UN projects that twice as many people (5 billion) could have poor access to water by the middle of the century.[4] In places that already have to supplement supplies from groundwater or for which climate change is shifting rainfall, reduced water supply can quickly become a crisis. Cities like Cape Town, South Africa and Jakarta, Indonesia have experienced major challenges in recent years due to the loss of water supplies.[5]

A surprising and positive development regarding the use of water occurred in the United States at the end of the twentieth century. After the amount of water used by industry and agriculture consistently grew faster than population growth for the first eight decades in the century, an unexpected change occurred. Instead of water use continuing to rise, from 1980 to 1995 it actually declined by about 10 percent even though the size of the population had increased about 15 percent during the same period. The main cause of the decrease was that industry and agriculture had learned to use water more efficiently rather than look for more water. Most of the best dam sites were already being used, the cost of new dams had risen, and the negative environmental effects of dams became well known. Also, federal antipollution laws made it cheaper for industry to find ways to use less water and to recycle it rather than clean it before discharging waste water into rivers and lakes.

Modern agriculture, which uses more water than any other human activity – about 70 percent of all water withdrawals – can significantly reduce the water needed for irrigation with new methods such as drip irrigation at the roots of plants rather than spraying the water into the air where much of it is lost through evaporation and by the wind. In the United States, water use by individuals has not decreased but it has leveled off. Water use also decreased in Europe and there has been a slowdown worldwide in the expansion of irrigation.

Because of increasing populations and rapid industrialization in many parts of the world, demand for water is expected to continue to grow. According to the World Bank, industry in China uses 4 to 10 times more water per unit of production than the average in industrialized countries.[6] Nations facing spikes in water demand can help manage that demand by adopting water efficiency technologies as a means to reduce how much water is needed. But as long as demand continues to increase as supply is shrinking, efficiency measures will be a short-term solution to a longer-term challenge.

Land

Whenever development has occurred, its effect on the land has been profound. The economic growth that comes with development both changes the way that land is used locally and also generally increases the demand for goods and services produced in other areas. More natural resources from the land are required for the production of these goods, of course, and their extraction – wherever the resources may come from – disturbs the land greatly. And still further impacts occur through the changes to the land that come with the disposal of the goods after they are no longer of use, and through the wastes that are created in the manufacture of the goods. Many of these wastes are artificial substances that never existed before in nature; thus, nature has few, if any, ways of breaking them down into harmless substances. Development also affects the vegetation on the land, in some ways reducing it, and in some ways helping to preserve it. In this section we will focus on two of the many changes to the land that come with development: the use of minerals, and deforestation. These two changes are affecting many human beings in such direct ways today that it is important that we look at them closely.

Minerals

Minerals – typically crystal formations comprised of specific elements formed by the Earth – often have properties that are useful to humans. Some minerals are very common, such as calcium that serves as a food nutrient for humans and also forms the shells of marine animals. Others are more scarce and valuable, such as gold and silver, which are used for everything from jewelry to microprocessors. Still others are quite uncommon, such as rare earth metals – a group of elements at the bottom of the periodic table which are often found together in oxidized geological formations and are used for specialized industrial processes and products such as cell phone parts and rechargeable batteries. Many companies, governments, and even individuals sometimes go to great lengths to extract, process, or otherwise obtain and use minerals.

Since the world's population is growing exponentially, as we learned in Chapter 3, it is probably not surprising that the consumption of minerals is also growing exponentially.

But, unlike petroleum, the supplies of most minerals are not becoming exhausted. Another great difference between nonfuel minerals and energy supplies is that the overall cost of producing minerals decreased over the twentieth century.[7] This reduced cost occurred, even as lower-grade ores were being mined, because of advances in technology – such as better exploration techniques, bigger mechanical shovels to dig with, bigger trucks to haul the ore away, and bigger ships to transport it to processing plants. Whether new technology will continue to keep the cost of minerals low in the future is a subject that is debated by scientists and economists. As ores containing a lower concentration of the desired minerals are mined and less accessible deposits are turned to, processing costs will probably rise. More ore must be processed, more energy and water used, and so more wastes are produced. Huge strip mines are often used, with a devastating effect on the land. Some analysts have observed that mineral prices in the past did not reflect the true environmental costs of extracting and processing the minerals, but with new pollution laws in most industrial countries, the mining industry will have to assume more of these costs unless they extract the mineral from less developed countries where environmental regulations are often lax.

The United States is a mineral-rich country; in the 1950s it was nearly self-sufficient in the most important industrial minerals. By the late 1970s it was self-sufficient in only 7 of the 36 minerals essential to an industrial society. Western Europe and Japan are even more dependent on imported minerals than is the United States. This increasing dependency on ores from foreign countries, many of which are essential for the advanced technologies common in the West, has strongly influenced the developed nations' foreign policies toward the developing world, where many of the minerals are found. One trend is apparent: most industrialized nations are becoming more dependent on foreign countries for their minerals. The mining and export of minerals (an extractive industry) has often had a surprisingly negative effect on the socioeconomic conditions of a country where the mineral is extracted, particularly if the government is one that can operate with relatively little transparency or accountability to its people.

China, for example, controls much of the supply of rare earth minerals. Despite the hope for prosperity for the mineral-rich country, the large sums of money generated (at times called the "resource curse") often lead to widespread corruption and violent conflict over control of the resources.

Deforestation

Deforestation is a serious problem because it can lead to erosion of the land, it can cause the soil to harden, and it can make the supply of fresh water erratic. Scientific studies support the hypothesis that deforestation can lead to significant changes in the climate. In addition to more greenhouse gas emissions, these changes can also affect precipitation. Sometimes deforestation leads to too much water in the wrong places. For example, serious floods occurred in India around the turn of the century in areas that had never experienced flooding, likely attributable to the cutting down of forests in the Himalayan mountains – the watershed for many rivers in India. This led to rioting among some of the tribal peoples of India who protested the cutting of their forests by commercial firms. Similarly, China has seen severe flooding along the upper reaches of the Yangtze River, likely due to the clear cutting of forests. Development can reduce poverty, and in some cases it can reduce one threat to the world's forests. But development can also lead to the destruction of the forests as they are cleared for cattle farms, for lumber, for commercial ventures, and for human settlements. As with the population problem, development in its early stages seems to worsen the situation, but development that benefits the many and not just the few can eventually help relieve it. And "low-carbon development" is an emerging pathway some countries are following, which includes efforts to stem forest loss as a way to reduce greenhouse gas emissions.

Although there are many causes of deforestation, expansion of the agricultural frontier, lack of enforceable property rights, illegal (and also legal) logging, palm oil and biofuel cultivations, new human settlements (often appearing after new roads are carved through previously inaccessible forest areas), and the lack of incentives for a proper forestry management system are contributing to the problem. Research in Brazil indicates that now less than 20 percent of the deforestation in Brazil is caused by small subsistence farmers.[8] Logging – much of it illegal – leads to roads being built into previously inaccessible forests and then these roads lead to more deforestation from people who can suddenly access new areas of the forest.

The UN Food and Agriculture Organization (FAO) reported in 2015 that the destruction of the world's tropical forests continues at a high rate.[9] Most of the deforestation is taking place in countries whose economies are heavily dependent on natural resource extraction. On average, about 20,000 square miles of forest was cut down annually from 2000 to 2010, including in areas never previously logged.[10] This loss was partially offset by the Russian Federation, the United States, China, India, and many European nations, which increased their forest coverage from 2005 to 2010.[11] During this period, 80 countries either increased their forest area or reported no change in forest coverage.[12] But, overall, the rate of deforestation remains high. By 2015, an estimated 15 billion trees were being cut down per year; by 2018, an estimated 18.7 million acres of forests were being cut down per year.[13] The FAO has reported that the total forest area decreased from 31.6 percent of global land area to 30.6 of global land area.[14]

The cutting of the trees in a tropical forest puts a severe strain on the soil since the trees protect the soil from the violent rains that are common in the tropics. And once the soil is washed away, it is not easily recreated. Some studies have estimated that from 100 to 1,000 years are needed for a mature tropical forest to return after human disturbances have taken place.[15]

Over the past 5,000 years almost 7 million square miles of the world's forests have been cut down; this pace has accelerated in recent history to make room for farms, pastures, and other uses.[16] During the last few centuries, 50 percent of global forests have been degraded, with 30 percent of these being completely cleared.[17] In 2010,

36 percent of global forest coverage was comprised of original forests.[18] These forests are known as "primary forests" or "old growth forests," and they are very different from the human-modified forests that are prevalent in the world today. These forests contain between 50 and 90 percent of the world's plant and animal species. Between 1990 and 2015, some 120,000 square miles of primary forests have been lost or altered.[19] At least 81 countries have lost all of their old growth forests, and much of what remains is endangered by human activities.[20]

The greatest threat to tropical forests in the future is from logging (much of it illegal), from making pasture land for cattle, and from agricultural and biofuel crops including tree crops – such as palm oil plantations in Indonesia and soy cultivations in the Brazilian Amazon. At least 20 percent of the Amazon has been deforested in the last 40 years.[21] Brazil and Indonesia had the fastest rates of deforestation in the world in 2017.[22] In Indonesia, many fires are set to clear forest land, resulting in huge quantities of smoke to the point that it has caused disruptions in air and sea travel and health problems, and has even been attributed to massive haze clouds in Southeast Asia.[23] In 2006, Indonesia agreed to export logs from much of its remaining tropical forests to China and replace the forests with vast palm oil plantations. The palm oil is sold globally, including to countries like China and India for use in products such as detergents, soaps, and lipsticks.[24] Demand for palm oil continues to increase, providing powerful economic incentives to convert forest land to palm oil plantations, destroying trees, threatening orangutans, and sometimes even displacing families dependent on the forest.

At the same time, there have been positive trends in regenerating global forest cover.[25] Globally, many billions of dollars have been pledged to regenerating forests to help combat climate change. While some initially raised concerns that this could lead to a new "fortress conservation" approach to natural resource management, forest regeneration strategies increasingly prioritize stronger land tenure rights and recognition for traditional forest communities with a proven track record of maintaining intact forests. In fact, some studies have demonstrated that giving traditional forested communities secure property rights is as effective at protecting forests as creating a new protected conservation area.

In contrast to the situation in tropical forest countries, temperate forests (mostly in richer nations) actually increased in cover during the twentieth century as marginal farmland was taken out of production and trees were allowed to return to the land. In the United States, forest coverage expanded by about 1,500 square miles per year over the first two decades of this century.[26] Between 2010 and 2015, total forest land area in the United States increased by 14 million acres.[27] More recently, forests have expanded in Europe, although at a relatively slow rate, some of which depends upon how "forests" are defined and accounted for.[28] From 2010 to 2015 the United States and India had the largest annual gain in forest cover.[29] Between 2010 and 2015, temperate forests have grown an average of almost 8,500 square miles a year.[30] This expanding tree cover contains much less diversity of life than the old growth forests, of course, and may even include industrial tree plantations – which many people do not even consider "forests" at all.

One more factor lessens the impressiveness of numbers in forest cover growth: the FAO does not include logging in some of its deforestation estimates because, at least in theory, the forest can grow back after it has been logged. In reality, logging often degrades the forest, leading to serious erosion and making it less suitable as a habitat for a wide variety of plants and animals. China, for example, has stopped much of its own deforestation, but has increased imports of logs from Indonesia and other areas.

China has started a massive reforestation program hoping to stop the expansion of its deserts. Billions of trees have been planted. Between 2013 and 2018, China has reportedly created 33.8 million hectares of forests.[31] But the deserts continue to expand and sandstorms (that can be detected as far away as the western United States) increased from about 5 a year in the 1960s to about 25 annually in the 1990s; in recent years, at least some of these sandstorms were so large and powerful that they eventually reached California.[32] As reported by the United Nations in 2009, China at present is planting forests on about 4 million hectares annually (10 million acres).[33]

Provided they remain standing, most forests absorb a significant amount of CO_2 yearly, thus helping to combat climate change. Scientists working in the Amazon have estimated that the Amazon rainforest alone could be absorbing over 1 billion tons of CO_2 each year. These scientists have found that in the sections of the forest they are studying, more trees are growing per hectare than in the past and the trees are growing faster and larger than before. They attribute this surprising finding to the increased amount of CO_2 in the atmosphere. They have also concluded that only large, undisturbed sections of the forest absorb large amounts of CO_2. Sections of the forests that have been logged, burned, or fragmented more typically lose CO_2 to the atmosphere, although trees that grow back do recapture carbon as they grow.[34]

A 2009 study published in *Nature* estimated that the world's remaining tropical rainforests remove about 5 billion tons of CO_2 from the atmosphere annually. The lead author of that report, Dr. Simon Lewis, a Royal Society research fellow at the University of Leeds, said, "We are receiving a free subsidy from nature. Tropical forest trees are absorbing about 18 percent of the CO_2 added to the atmosphere each year from burning fossil fuels, substantially buffering the rate of climate change."[35]

Forests in the temperate zones of the Earth absorb far less CO_2 than do the tropical rainforests, but they do absorb a significant amount. Studies in high-latitude forests have shown that the soils of the forests actually absorb much more CO_2 than the trees themselves. Scientists estimate that peat and other organic matter in the soils absorb two-thirds of the CO_2, while the trees absorb the remaining one-third.[36]

Deforestation not only destroys a valuable "sink" for CO_2, but it also results in increased greenhouse gas emissions. Trees not replanted after they are cut, which is common when the forest land is cleared for settlements or for farming, release significant CO_2 into the atmosphere. The Intergovernmental Panel on Climate Change has estimated that around 180 gigatons of carbon have been released into the atmosphere by deforestation and other land use change since 1750, meaning that land use changes have been responsible for nearly one-third of all human-caused emissions in the atmosphere (the burning of fossil fuels for energy is responsible for most of the rest).[37]

Plate 7.1 Deforestation in Mexico
Source: Jamie Dwyer.

An example of a government-supported resettlement effort that led to serious deforestation took place in northern Brazil. In the early 1970s, the Brazilian government began a large colonization project in the Amazon basin, moving people in from the poverty-ridden northeastern section of the country. It was hoped that the resettlements would help reduce the poverty in the northeast and provide food for an expanding population. Unfortunately, both hopes faded as colony after colony failed. The main reason for the failure was that tropical forest land is actually not very fertile, in spite of the huge trees growing on it. Such trees get their needed nutrients directly from decaying leaves and wood on the forest floor, not from the topsoil, which in many places is thin and of poor quality. This explains why many of the settlers had experiences similar to that of the following Brazilian peasant who described what happened to his new farm in the Amazon: "The bananas were two feet long the first year. They were one foot long the second year. And six inches long the third year. The fourth year? No bananas."[38]

If only small plots of the forest are cleared, regeneration of the forest is possible. Some peoples have practiced what is known as shifting cultivation in the tropical forests. They clear a piece of land and farm it for a year or two before moving on to a new piece of land. As long as this remains small in scale, the damage to the forest is limited, but any large-scale use of this type of agriculture can lead to irreversible damage to the forest.

Some tropical soils contain a layer known as laterite, which is rich in iron. When these soils are kept moist under a forest they remain soft, but if allowed to dry out, which happens when the forest cover is removed, they become irreversibly hard – so hard that they are sometimes used for making bricks.

In Central America and in Brazil, large areas of forests are being cut down to make pastures for the raising of cattle. The cattle are intended mainly to supply the fast-food hamburger market in the United States. The raising of cattle on large ranches for export does not, of course, do anything to solve the food problems in the exporting countries, or to provide land to the landless.

Local people can earn income from the forests through sustainably harvested forest products (fruits, coffee, rubber, etc.) and through "ecotourism." This type of tourism focuses on the growing number of tourists (generally from wealthier countries) who wish to visit tropical forests and other spots that have been left more or less in a natural state. Additionally, in some countries, payments are being made to forest-dependent communities for "ecosystem services" such as carbon sequestration or watershed conservation. If evidence exists that local people can earn more income by letting the forests remain than by cutting them down, a strong argument can then be made supporting their preservation. Also, local people can be enlisted in the efforts to prevent deforestation since they will have an economic stake in the preservation of the forests.

Governing the Commons

Garrett Hardin, the late American ecologist, coined the phrase "the tragedy of the commons" to describe what can happen when management of limited resources requires effective decisions by shared users. The "tragedy" to which Hardin refers occurs when the short-term and long-term interests of people are in conflict, or when someone receives benefits at the expense of someone else's access to shared resources.[39] Hardin shows how, in the short term, it is rational and in the best interest of each herdsman in a village to increase the number of cattle he has grazing on the "commons," the open-access, commonly owned lands in the village. The apparent early benefit to an individual herdsman of increasing the number of cattle he has there seems to him greater than the long-term harm resulting from the overgrazing that the additional cattle create; the cost of the overgrazing will be shared by all the farmers using the commons, while the individual herdsman will reap the profit that comes from selling additional cattle. Also, if the individual farmer does not increase his or her cattle but others increase theirs, (s)he loses out since the overgrazing harms the cattle. Thus, the tragedy occurs. Each farmer, acting rationally and in his or her own best interest in the short term, benefits from the increase of individual stock on the commons at the expense of all the common users. The benefit is concentrated to the individual farmer while the cost is distributed to everyone. As long as each farmer tries to maximize their individual benefit, there is so much overgrazing that the grass dies and then the cattle die.

The global commons today are those parts of the planet that are used by many or all nations: the oceans, international river systems, the seabed, the atmosphere, and outer space. Technology can give some nations an advantage over others in exploiting these commons and it is clearly in their short-term interest to do so.

So it is with commercial fishing in the world's oceans. Technology has made possible bigger and more powerful fishing boats, equipped with sonar to locate schools of fish. It has also led to the creation of huge drift nets ("gill"), some up to 20 kilometers (12 miles) long, which critics claim were used to "strip mine" the seas.[40] These nets allowed a relatively small number of fishermen to catch large quantities of fish. (The United Nations in 1992 banned drift nets over 1.5 miles long, but six years later nets much longer than this were still being used in the Mediterranean Sea and parts of the Atlantic Ocean.[41]) New technology also allows trawlers to drag dredges the size of football fields over the sea bottom, scraping it clean. Ninety percent of all large predator fish such as sharks, swordfish and tuna have been caught and there are fewer different kinds of fish in the oceans than before,[42] putting ecosystems at more risk when they are confronted with disruptions such as climate change. There is every indication that many fisheries worldwide are being overfished, or to put it another way, "overgrazed," and are threatened with collapse.[43] If this is not controlled, all nations using the oceans for fishing will be hurt. Not only will their fishing industries be harmed, but unique forms of life on Earth will probably become extinct. This could well be the fate of many species of the fishlike mammal, the whale, unless international efforts to reduce drastically the numbers of whales killed succeed in allowing whale populations to increase.

Fortunately, the tragedy of the commons is not always an inevitable result of shared resources. Elinor Ostrom received a Nobel Prize for her work highlighting the role of communities banding together to manage and regulate pooled resources. Dr. Ostrom demonstrated how, when communities have long-term control over their resources and have the authority to develop their own rules for how the resources are managed, the resources can be managed sustainably. Other studies have confirmed this model. For example, one study found that lands managed by indigenous peoples could be just as effective as national parks at conserving forest cover.

The Extinction of Species

One of the biggest tragedies of the commons is the widespread extinction of species. Alarmingly, one 2018 study found that humanity has wiped out 60% of animal populations since 1970.[44] No one knows for sure how many species of living things there are on the Earth. Biologists today generally make educated guesses that the number is between 2 million and 1 trillion.[45] (Scientists have given a name to about 2 million of them, and of those named, only about 10 percent have been studied in any detail.) Throughout the Earth's history, new species have evolved and others have become extinct, with the general trend being that more new species are created than die out. It is now believed that because of human actions this trend has been reversed, with extinctions outnumbering the creation of new species. And the trend appears to be increasing—to the point that we are now believed to be in the sixth great wave of extinctions, this one known as the "Anthropocene" – caused by humans.[46]

The marvels of life on Earth

Can any living being using its own power travel 7,000 miles (11,265 kilometers) nonstop – without eating or resting – and end up at its desired destination? Can any human being do this? No human being can, but a little bird named the bar-tailed godwit can. The bar-tailed godwit flies over the Pacific Ocean from Alaska to its wintering grounds in New Zealand over nine days. Modern science does not understand how the bird can do this. It is truly one of life's marvels.

Unfortunately, marathon migrants, like the bar-tailed godwit, are now facing extinction because of climate change, coastal development, the destruction of wetlands, and hunting. For a wonderful picture of the bar-tailed godwit see the source listed below.

Source: John W. Fitzpatrick and Nathan R. Senner, "The Global's Greatest Travelers Are Dying," *The New York Times*, Sunday Review, April 29, 2018. p. 4SR. *Source*: Carl Zimmer, "7,000 Miles Nonstop, and No Pretzels," *New York Times*, May 25, 2010, p. D1.

Scientists are now warning of an unprecedented risk of global biodiversity collapse.[47] Already, humans have destroyed some 83% of wild mammals.[48] According to Edward O. Wilson of Harvard University, probably the most respected of all US biologists, the world has experienced five major periods, or "spasms," of extinction of large numbers of species, from which it took millions of years to recover. These extinctions were caused by natural forces, such as a change of climate. Wilson believes that because of the vast growth of the human population and the related widespread deforestation and overuse of grasslands that are now occurring on our planet, the Earth is heading into the sixth and worst period of extinction of species. Wilson estimates the present rate of extinction as about 27,000 species per year, or three per hour. (The normal "background" rate is about 10 to 100 per year.) If the present rate continues, Wilson estimates that 20 percent of all the species in the world will be extinct in 30 years.[49] Robert May, zoologist at the University of Oxford, who is a past-president of the Royal Society and until 2000 was chief science advisor to the British government, has estimated the present extinction rate as 1,000 times as great as before the arrival of human beings.[50]

Whereas hunting used to be the main way humans caused extinction, it is now generally believed that climate change and the destruction of natural habitats is the principal cause of extinctions. As the human population grows, humans use land and resources throughout the world for economic gain and often destroy life forms as they do so. As we saw in the previous section, tropical forests – storehouses of biodiversity – are being destroyed at alarming rates. Biologists believe that a big percentage of all species live in tropical forests. In the oceans, coral reefs are dying off due to a combination of land run-off (pollution) and ocean temperature and chemistry changes generally attributed to climate change.

There is now a growing recognition that climate change, discussed in a later chapter, is as dangerous to biodiversity as the loss of habitats.[51] The Great Barrier Reef in Australia has already lost a great deal of its coral, and is projected to lose much more due to global warming.[52] In Africa, ancient Baobab trees that have lived for more than a thousand years have begun dying off at alarming rates.[53] Sadly, these may only foreshadow more widespread disaster to come: a significant portion of species across the globe are threatened with extinction due to climate change. A 2018 report by the Intergovernmental Panel on Climate Change predicts that as global temperatures rise by as little as 1.5 degrees Celsius, that will lead to some 8 percent of plants and 6 percent of invertebrates going extinct; at the 2 degree mark, that spikes to 16 percent of plants and 18 percent of invertebrate species wiped off the planet.[54] At present, unless more action is taken at a global level, the planet is projected to see more than 3 degrees of warming, with catastrophic results for many ecosystems.

Many of the species in the tropics have never been studied by scientists. But based on past experience, it is believed that many of these unknown species contain properties that could directly benefit humans. Many prescription drugs have a key natural component in as an active ingredient. The importance of some of these drugs can be illustrated by the example of just one plant from the tropical rainforests, the rosy periwinkle, which is used to treat cancer. Drugs produced from this plant have enabled 80 percent remission rates in leukemia and Hodgkin's disease patients.

Endemic species (those which are native to the area and often traditionally cultivated) are vital to the health of modern agriculture. The wild varieties and locally developed strains of a number of major grains grown today have characteristics that are of vital importance to modern seed producers. Seeds are needed with natural resistance to the diseases and pests that constantly threaten modern agriculture. Many farmers today utilize only relatively few, highly productive varieties of seeds in any one year. The monocultures that are planted are especially vulnerable to diseases and to pests that have developed resistance to the pesticides being used. An example of how this works was shown in 1970, when 15 percent of the corn crop in the United States was killed by a leaf disease, causing a $2 billion loss to farmers and indirectly to consumers because of higher prices. That year, 70 percent of the corn crop used seeds from only five lines of corn. The disease was finally brought under control with the aid of a new variety of corn that was resistant to the leaf disease. The new corn had genetic materials originating in Mexico.[55]

The trend towards industrially-produced monoculture varieties for agricultural production becomes even more challenging with climate change, as the risk of crop failures of major commodity varieties are moderate to high in several regions at even 1.5–2 degrees of warming.

Insects from tropical forests can at times prove extremely valuable to American farmers. Citrus growers in the United States saved about $25–30 million a year with the one-time introduction from the tropics of three parasitic wasps that reproduced and preyed on the pests attacking the citrus fruit.[56] The introduction of exotic species by humans for profit, or amusement, or by accident into areas to which they are not native is now recognized as having great potential for harm. Since the new species usually has no natural predators in the new area, it can multiply rapidly, destroying or displacing other desirable animals or plants, as was the case with New Zealand's war on rats, the introduction of rabbits into Australia, and of European starlings and the kudzu plant into the United States.[57]

American ecologist Paul Ehrlich does not believe that developing nations can preserve tropical habitats on their own since their financial needs are so great. What is needed in the world, he feels, is a new awareness that the diversity of life forms on Earth is a priceless treasure that benefits all humanity and that all share a responsibility for helping to preserve it. He states: "Over 95 percent of the organisms capable of competing seriously with humanity for food or of doing us harm by transmitting diseases are now controlled gratis by other species in natural ecosystems."[58]

As discussed earlier, at the 1992 UN Conference on Environment and Development in Rio de Janeiro, a proposed treaty to try to slow down the loss of species was presented. The treaty, formally named the Convention on Biological Diversity, called for the study of each nation's biodiversity and a commitment to preserve the biodiversity that exists on Earth. By the beginning of the twenty-first century nearly every nation in the world had ratified the treaty except the United States.

A suggestion for a practical way to combat this daunting problem of the extinction of species is that conservation efforts could be focused on a relatively few, highly vulnerable "hot spots" where there is a large concentration of species found nowhere else in the world. Of the more than 30 hot spots that have been identified, 25 of them contain the last habitats for about 45 percent of the Earth's plant species and 35 percent of its land-based vertebrate (fish, amphibian, reptile, bird, and mammal) species. The top eight spots of these 25 are southern coastal India and Sri Lanka, the island of Madagascar, Indonesia, Brazil's Atlantic forest, the Caribbean Islands, Burma and other parts of Southeast Asia, the Philippines, and the eastern mountains and coastal forests of Kenya and Tanzania.[59]

Edward O. Wilson has joined those who now believe that while protecting "hot spots" is important, and should be expanded, it may no longer be enough. To really protect biodiversity, we must be concerned with protecting the whole biosphere. The variety of species on Earth and their habitats provide essential services to life that the market cannot put a price tag on, services such as "nutrient cycling, the formation and enrichment of soils, the detoxification of pollutants and other forms of wastes, the provision of freshwater, the regulation of the atmosphere and climate, and the stability of ecosystems." Wilson's opinion is that "the wildlands and the bulk of Earth's biodiversity protected within them are another world from the one humanity is throwing together pell-mell. What do we receive from them? The stabilization of the global environment they provide and their very existence are gifts to us. We are their stewards, not their owners."[60]

Two metaphors have been used to help people understand what the loss of biodiversity means. One is that of the loss of rivets and the other is of the loss of threads.

In the first metaphor the extinction of a species is seen as being like taking a rivet out of an airplane. One probably doesn't matter, nor two, but if you keep pulling out the rivets eventually the airplane will crash. This metaphor conveys the idea of a collapsed ecosystem. The other metaphor says that the loss of a species is like pulling a thread out of a beautiful tapestry. You won't even notice a few pulled out but the more you pull the less rich in color is the tapestry. If you pull too many out in one location the tapestry may even tear.

Some scientists say that while these two metaphors can be useful to understand what the loss of biodiversity can mean, neither fully explains the complexity of real life. They point out that while it is true that the greater the species loss, the simpler and duller nature becomes, it is also true that the complexity of life forms can actually keep an ecosystem from collapsing, especially during times of stress such as a drought. Also, all species are not of equal importance in keeping an ecosystem healthy. There may be key ones that provide vital services to the others. If they are lost, the others depending on them are in danger.[61]

Responsible Use

There are four steps available – for countries and individuals alike – to help manage limited supplies of resources and minimize the impacts of their use: (1) use resources more efficiently; (2) recycle waste products containing the desired material; (3) substitute more abundant or renewable resources for the scarce material; (4) reduce the need for the material.

Resource efficiency

Two concepts have emerged in the developed world that are designed to reduce the use of natural resources by using the resources more efficiently. One is called "eco-efficiency" and the other is called "product stewardship." The use of either or both of these concepts by some industries led to a 2 percent improvement in resource efficiency per year in the developed world from 1970 to 1995.[62]

Eco-efficiency involves redesigning products and the processes that are followed to make them so that fewer natural resources are used and less waste is produced. In the United States a pioneer in the use of this concept is the 3M Corporation. 3M established a program it called "Pollution Prevention Pays," the 3P program. The corporation claimed, in 2014, that 3P ideas and initiatives from employees prevented 2 billion pounds of pollutants and saved 3M nearly $1.9 billion.[63] 3M Corporation has about 15,000 suppliers and it expects its suppliers to follow 3M's environmental standards. It monitors the suppliers' performances. The Seventh Generation company uses bottles which are 90 percent postconsumer resin and nearly all packaging is 100 percent postconsumer recycled. The company's total materials use actually decreased from 2008 to 2009.[64]

By following eco-efficiency principles, SC Johnson Wax from 1990 to 1997 increased its production by 50 percent while at the same time it cut its manufacturing waste by half, reduced packaging waste by a quarter, and reduced the use of volatile organic compounds by about 15 percent. The company saved more than $20 million annually from these changes.[65]

Some companies are attempting to drastically reduce their use of natural resources and their toxic emissions by adopting a "closed cycle" process. In this manufacturing process, wastes are completely recycled or reused.

Product stewardship is being practiced mainly in Europe at present. This is the principle that a company should be held responsible for the environmental impacts of its products throughout their whole life cycles. The trend is for more laws and agreements between government and industry that are based on the Polluter Pays principle. This principle embodies the idea that the manufacturer of a product should be responsible for the harm to the environment that comes from its production, use, and disposal, such as Germany's requirement for manufacturers to accept back their packaging wastes.

All of these concepts are leading to a revolutionary change in thinking about the responsibilities of the manufacturer. Instead of having society as a whole pay for the consequences of the manufacturer's actions, the principle is slowly spreading that the manufacturer should accept this responsibility. If the manufacturer is held responsible, it will have an incentive for redesigning products and manufacturing processes to cut their costs. In some instances, as the examples above show, the practicing of this principle can lead to a win-win situation as the manufacturer and the environment both benefit from the new way of thinking.

Recycling

It is generally agreed that more recycling of waste material needs to be done in the United States. In the late 1980s, recycling became relatively popular in the country because more citizens became aware of environmental problems and because many towns were faced with trash dumps that were becoming filled. (New dumps were becoming very expensive to open because of tighter federal government regulations.)

A demand for recycled material grew in the United States as more industries started using it. By the mid-1990s this was taking place as a growing economy emerged and new plants able to process recycled material began operating. One measure to spur the market and volume for recycled material is government procurement policies, such as when the US in 1993 required all federal government agencies, including the military, to purchase paper with a minimum of 20 percent recycled fibers in it. But even with respect to newsprint, there is no simple solution since newspaper cannot be recycled indefinitely because the quality of the fibers degrades.

Even with the new interest in recycling in the United States, the country is still not doing as much of it as other industrial nations do. In the early 1990s, the United

States was recycling about 15 percent of its trash, while Japan was recycling about 50 percent. These numbers have improved, but the gap remains. Some European countries also do much more than the United States. Since 2002, the European Union has required all its members' auto manufacturers to be responsible for the recovery and recycling of all of its new autos. As of 2004 the European Union required all the electronic companies of its members to pay for the collection and recycling of its products. And by July 2006, no electronics sold in Europe could any longer contain some of the most toxic materials such as lead, cadmium, mercury, hexavalent chromium, and the flame retardants PBDE and PBB.[66]

In 2015, the United States recycled about a third of its waste. In that year Americans generated about 262 million tons of trash and recycled and composted about 91 million tons.[67] Although in 2015 the average European Union recycling rate for municipal waste was about 45 percent, there was great variety among the European nations. Bulgaria did not recycle anything, Romania recycled 13 percent, the Czech Republic just 35.6 percent, Lithuania 33 percent, and Slovakia only 15 percent. However, Austria recycled and composted about 57 percent of its waste, while Belgium, Germany, Sweden, and the Netherlands recycled and composted from 45 to 66 percent. The UK recycled about 43 percent of its waste in 2015.[68]

To increase recycling in Japan, many cities have increased the number of categories into which items to be recycled must be separated. Yokohama, a city of nearly 4 million people, had ten categories already in 2005. The small town of Kamikatsu had 34 different recycling categories in 2015.[69] Recycling costs more than dumping but about the same as incineration, which land-scarce Japan uses for much of its garbage.[70]

One unfortunate trend is the shipping of electronic waste, including computer monitors and circuit boards, to developing countries, such as China, India, and Pakistan, for recycling. Countries like China are beginning to refuse to accept rich countries' e-wastes.[71] These items contain lead and other toxic material. The people recycling the items, often children or adults with no protective clothing, are being exposed to dangerous substances. A report at the beginning of the twenty-first century by five American environmental groups estimated that 50 to 80 percent of electronic waste collected in the United States for recycling was being placed on container ships for use or recycling by developing countries. The United States was the only developed country that had not signed the 1989 Basel Convention, which was designed to limit the exporting of hazardous waste. The producers of hazardous wastes were encouraged to deal with their waste problems within their own borders whenever possible. The European Union at that time was considering requiring manufacturers of products containing hazardous material to take responsibility for them from "cradle to grave."[72]

While recycling is desirable, it is only a partial solution to natural resource shortages and to pollution from the production of new materials. Recycling also creates pollution and uses energy. The move by the US soft drink and beer industry to use aluminum cans that can be recycled is obviously not the final solution to the litter problem (recall that nearly half of aluminum cans are never collected for recycling[73]) and the manufacturing of aluminum uses a lot of energy. Probably a better solution was the move by some American states to require returnable soft drink and beer containers to be used in their states instead of throwaways.

The "throwaway" economy that developed in the United States after World War II still exists. The efforts to recycle are a step forward, but much remains to be done. Denmark has banned throwaways, but this action is unlikely to be taken in the United States any time soon.

Substitution

When a material becomes scarce, it is sometimes possible to substitute another material for it that is more abundant or to use a renewable resource in place of the scarce item. For example, the more abundant aluminum can be used in place of the scarcer copper for most electrical uses. Difficulties arise at times when the substituted material in turn becomes scarce. Plastic utensils and containers replaced glass products in most US kitchens because of certain advantages plastic has over glass, such as being less breakable and lighter in weight. But plastics are made from petrochemicals, which are a finite resource. Also, the plastics industry produces more dangerous pollutants than does the glass industry. Another limitation to substitution is that some materials have unique qualities that no other materials have. Tungsten's high melting point, for example, is unmatched by any other metal. And substitutions can produce disruptions in the society, causing some industries to close and new ones to open. The last-mentioned point can mean, of course, new opportunities for some people and fewer for others. New ways of doing things can also be substituted for old ways, sometimes resulting in a reduced use of resources. The trend in some businesses to use communications in place of transportation (videoconferencing instead of physically being present) might be such a development.

Reducing needs

The fourth way to counteract shortages of a material is to reduce the need for the material. Many consumer goods – such as automobiles and clothes – become obsolete in a few years as styles change. This planned obsolescence leads to a high use of resources. Many products also wear out quickly and must be replaced with new ones. In the United States more durable products could be designed by industry, but they would often be more expensive. This is probably why the United States industry generally does not make such products. Higher prices would mean fewer sales, a slower turnover of business inventories, and thus probably lower profits. They could also mean fewer jobs.

Perhaps the best way to end this section is to repeat the popular phrase of environmentalists: "reduce, reuse, recycle" as the best ways – in that order – to use resources and to handle the wastes caused by the use of them.

Conclusion

This concludes the first part of our environment discussion, where we looked at the resources available to support human life and livelihoods, and the ways that increasing competition for resources has created new challenges for development. We now turn to the next chapter on our environment, considering pollution-related complications stemming from increased consumption of resources as people become wealthier and the population increases, creating additional challenges related to the management of resources.

Notes

1   Bill Clinton, who defeated President Bush, signed the biodiversity treaty, but the US Congress never ratified it.
2   UN Secretary-General Kofi Annan, press conference at the conclusion of the 2002 World Summit on Sustainable Development, September 2, 2002, at http://www.un.org/events/wssd/pressconf/020904conf4.htm (accessed July 2015).
3   Yale Center for Environmental Law and Policy and Center for International Earth Science Information Network, Columbia University, 2018 Environmental Performance Index, at https://epi.envirocenter.yale.edu/epi-topline (accessed November 2018).
4   N. Johnson, C. Revenga, and J. Echeverria, "Managing Water for People and Nature," *Science*, 292 (2001), pp. 1071–2; Lorraine Chow, "5 Billion People Could Have Poor Access to Water by 2050, UN Warns," *EcoWatch* (March 19, 2018), at https://www.ecowatch.com/global-water-access-quality-2549813548.html?fbclid=IwAR1sbqPoHhHh-w1nhAxlav7uZaeZx00AggudeifLkCVZmsDgns8lV3s4f_8 (accessed November 2018).
5   See, e.g. Amy Maxmen, "As Cape Town Water Crisis Deepens, Scientists Prepare For "Day Zero"," *Scientific American* (January 26, 2018), at https://www.scientificamerican.com/article/as-cape-town-water-crisis-deepens-scientists-prepare-for-ldquo-day-zero-rdquo/ (accessed November 2018).
6   Joseph Kahn and Jim Yardley, "As China Roars, Pollution Reaches Deadly Extremes," *New York Times* national edn (August 26, 2007).
7   Hans Landsberg et al., "Nonfuel Minerals," in Paul Portney (ed.), *Current Issues in Natural Resource Policy* (Washington, DC: Resources for the Future, 1982), p. 83.
8   Larry Rohter, "Relentless Foe of the Amazon Jungle: Soybeans," *New York Times* (September 17, 2003), p. A3. Also a similar percentage is cited in an analysis by Forests Dialogue (hosted at Yale University) as a background paper for the Global Forest Leaders Forum, 2007, pp. 1–2. More updated sources also point to a similar percentage. See Rhett Butler, "Deforestation in the Amazon," *Mongabay* (July 9, 2014), at https://data.mongabay.com/brazil.html (accessed November 2018).
9   UN Food and Agriculture Organization (FAO), *Global Forest Resources Assessment 2015*, p. 3 (2nd edn), at http://www.fao.org/3/a-i4793e.pdf (accessed November 2018).
10 Ibid.
11 Ibid., p. 17.
12 Ibid.
13 T.W. Crowther, et al., "Mapping tree density at a global scale," *Nature* 525, 201 (2015), at https://www.nature.com/articles/nature14967 (accessed November 2018); Alina Bradford,

"Deforestation: Facts, Causes & Effects," *Live Science* (April 3, 2018), at https://www.livescience.com/27692-deforestation.html (accessed November 2018).

14 FAO, *2018 The State of the World's Forests*, at http://www.fao.org/state-of-forests/en/ (accessed November 2018).

15 Christopher Uhl, "You Can Keep a Good Forest Down," *Natural History*, 92 (April 1983), p. 78.

16 Alina Bradford, "Deforestation: Facts, Causes & Effects," *Live Science* (April 3, 2018), at https://www.livescience.com/27692-deforestation.html (accessed November 2018).

17 Alina Bradford, "Deforestation: Facts, Causes & Effects," *Live Science* (April 3, 2018), at https://www.livescience.com/27692-deforestation.html (accessed November 2018) (citing FAO, *State of the World's Forests* 2012, p. 9).

18 FAO, "World Deforestation Decreases, but Remains Alarming in Many Countries," March 25, 2010, at http://www.fao.org/news/story/en/item/40893/icode/ (accessed July 2015).

19 FAO, *Global Forest Resources Assessment 2015* (2015), p. 3.

20 Ibid.

21 Naomi Larsson, "Beauty and Destruction: The Amazon Rainforest – In Pictures," *The Guardian* (January 30, 2017), at https://www.theguardian.com/global-development-professionals-network/gallery/2017/jan/30/state-amazon-rainforest-deforestation-brazil-in-pictures (accessed November 2018).

22 World Atlas, "Worst Cases For Deforestation By Woodland Area Losses," (last updated 2017), https://www.worldatlas.com/articles/worst-countries-for-deforestation-by-woodland-area-losses.html (accessed November 2018).

23 David L. A. Gaveau et al., "Major Atmospheric Emissions from Peat Fires in Southeast Asia during Non-Drought Years: Evidence from the 2013 Sumatran Fires," *Scientific Reports*, 4 (August 19, 2014). ("We expect major haze events to be increasingly frequent because of ongoing deforestation of Indonesian peatlands.")

24 Stella Dawson, "Indonesia Defends Deforestation for Palm Oil on Economic Grounds," Reuters, March 25, 2015, at http://www.reuters.com/article/2015/03/25/us-indonesia-palmoil-forests-idUSKBN0ML20020150325 (accessed July 2015).

25 John Vidal, "A Eureka Moment for the Planet: We're Finally Planting Trees Again," *The Guardian* (February 13, 2018), at https://www.theguardian.com/commentisfree/2018/feb/13/worlds-lost-forests-returning-trees? (accessed November 2018).

26 FAO, *Global Forest Resources Assessment* 2010, p. 21 (but note this does not include forest expansion after 2010).

27 Mark D. Nelson et al., *National Report on Sustainable Forests – 2015: Conservation of Biological Diversity* (2015), p. 375, at https://www.fs.fed.us/pnw/pubs/pnw_gtr931/pnw_gtr931_140.pdf (accessed November 2018).

28 Ibid., p. 19.

29 FAO, *Global Forest Resources Assessment 2015* (2015), pp. 15-20, at http://www.fao.org/3/a-i4808e.pdf (accessed November 2018).

30 Rod Keenan, "Forest Loss has Halved in in the Past 30 Years, Latest Global Update Shows," *The Conversation* (September 7, 2015), at http://theconversation.com/forest-loss-has-halved-in-the-past-30-years-latest-global-update-shows-46932 (accessed November 2018).

31 Laura Oliver, "China has sent 60,000 Soldiers to Plant Trees," *World Economic Forum* (February 16, 2018), at https://www.weforum.org/agenda/2018/02/china-army-soldiers-plant-trees/ (accessed November 2018).

32   Howard French, "Billions of Trees Planted, and Nary a Dent in the Desert," *New York Times* (April 11, 2004), p. 3.

33   NEP, *Vital Forest Graphics*, p. 11, at http://www.unep.org/vitalforest/ (accessed July 2015).

34   William Laurance, "Gaia's Lungs," *Natural History*, 108 (March, 1999), p. 96; Claire Asher, "Drought-driven Fires on Rise in Amazon Basin, Upping CO2 Release," *Mongabay* (February 2, 2018), at https://news.mongabay.com/2018/02/drought-driven-wildfires-on-rise-in-amazon-basin-upping-co2-release/ (accessed November 2018).

35   University of Leeds, "One-Fifth of Fossil-Fuel Emissions Absorbed by Threatened Forests," *Science Daily* (February 19, 2009). Simon L. Lewis, "Making the Paper," *Nature*, 457 (February 19, 2009).

36   "Resurgent Forests Can Be Greenhouse Gas Sponges," *Science*, 277 (July 18, 1997), p. 315. Tropical forests have also been shown to have higher CO_2 absorption rates than temperate forests. Daisy Simmons, "Loss of Tropical Forests makes Climate Change Worse," *Yale Climate Connections* (September 9, 2018), at https://www.yaleclimate connections.org/2018/09/loss-of-tropical-forests-makes-climate-change-worse/ (accessed November 2018).

37   Intergovernmental Panel on Climate Change, Fifth Assessment Report, *Climate Change 2013: The Physical Science Basis*, Summary for Policymakers (Cambridge, UK: Cambridge University Press, 2013),
     p. 12.

38   Anne LaBastille, "Heaven, Not Hell," *Audubon*, 81 (November 1979), p. 91.

39   Garrett Hardin, "The Tragedy of the Commons," *Science*, 162 (December 13, 1968), pp. 1243–8.

40   Food and Agriculture Organization, Fishing Gear types. Set gillnets (anchored). Technology Fact Sheets. In: *FAO Fisheries and Aquaculture Department* [online]. Rome. Updated 13 September 2001. Available http://www.fao.org/fishery/ (accessed January 2020).

41   Marlise Simons, "Boats Plunder Mediterranean with Outlawed Nets," *New York Times*, June 4, 1998, p. A3. See also Food and Agriculture Administration http://www.fao.org/3/t0502e/t0502e01.htm.

42   Elizabeth Kolbert, "The Scales Fall: Is There Any Hope for Our Overfished Oceans?" *New Yorker*, August 2, 2010.

43   Arthur Neslen, "Global Fish Production Approaching Sustainable Limit, UN Warns," *The Guardian* (July 7, 2016) at https://www.theguardian.com/environment/2016/jul/07/global-fish-production-approaching-sustainable-limit-un-warns (accessed January 2020); see also Daniel Pauly and Reg Watson, "Counting the Last Fish," *Scientific American*, 289 (July 2003), pp. 42–7; Cornelia Dean, "Scientists Warn Fewer Kinds of Fish Are Swimming the Oceans," *New York Times* (July 29, 2005), p. A6.

44   Damian Carrington, "Humanity has Wiped out 60% of Animal Populations since 1970, Report Finds," *The Guardian* (October 29, 2018), at https://www.theguardian.com/environment/2018/oct/30/humanity-wiped-out-animals-since-1970-major-report-finds?fbclid=IwAR30Q3nS9ETt8pj0nas3m7KL7V5WRgMGODk6cC57N0-EMZ4L4SXYnbqeDIE (accessed November 2018).

45   Brendan B. Larson, et al., "Inordinate Fondness Multiplied and Redistributed: the Number of Species on Earth and the New Pie of Life," 92 *The Quarterly Review of Biology* (2017), at https://www.journals.uchicago.edu/doi/full/10.1086/693564 (accessed November 2018).

46 Damian Carrington, "Humanity has wiped out 60% of animal populations since 1970, report finds," *The Guardian* (October 29, 2018), at https://www.theguardian.com/ environment/2018/oct/30/humanity-wiped-out-animals-since-1970-major-report-finds ?fbclid=IwAR30Q3nS9ETt8pj0nas3m7KL7V5WRgMGODk6cC57N0-EMZ4L4SXYnbqeDIE (accessed November 2018).

47 Lancaster University, "Time is Running out in the Tropics: Researchers Warn of Global Biodiversity Collapse," *Science Daily* (July 26, 2018), at https://www.sciencedaily.com/ releases/2018/07/180726085918.htm (accessed November 2018).

48 Damian Carrington, "Humans Just 0.01% of All Life but have Destroyed 83% of Wild Mammals – Study," *The Guardian* (May 21, 2018) at https://www.theguardian.com/ environment/2018/may/21/human-race-just-001-of-all-life-but-has-destroyed-over-80-of-wild-mammals-study (accessed November 2018).

49 Edward O. Wilson, *The Diversity of Life* (Cambridge, MA: Harvard University Press, 1992).

50 W. Wayt Gibbs, "On the Termination of Species," *Scientific American*, 285 (November 2001), p. 42; see also Christine Dell'Amore, "Species Extinction Happening 1,000 Times Faster Because of Humans?," *National Geographic* (May 30, 2014), at https://news. nationalgeographic.com/news/2014/05/140529-conservation-science-animals-species-endangered-extinction/ (accessed November 2018).

51 Chelsea Harvey, "Climate Change is Becoming a Top Threat to Biodiversity," *Scientific American* (March 2018) https://www.scientificamerican.com/article/climate-change-is-becoming-a-top-threat-to-biodiversity/ (accessed November 2018).

52 "Scientists Record Biggest ever Coral Die-off on Australia's Great Barrier Reef," *The Telegraph* (November 29, 2016) at https://www.telegraph.co.uk/news/2016/11/29/ scientists-record-biggest-ever-coral-die-off-australias-great/ (accessed November 2018).

53 Ed Yong, "Trees That Have Lived for Millennia Are Suddenly Dying," *The Atlantic* (June 11, 2018) at https://www.theatlantic.com/science/archive/2018/06/baobab-trees-dying-climate-change/562499/ (accessed November 2018).

54 Intergovernmental Panel on Climate Change, Special Report on 1.5 Degrees – Chapter 3 (2018), p. 4.

55 Norman Myers, "The Exhausted Earth," *Foreign Policy*, 42 (Spring 1981), p. 143.

56 Norman Myers, 'Room in the Ark,' *Bulletin of the Atomic Scientists*, 38 (November 1982), p. 48.

57 For a fascinating discussion of the risks of unintended consequences of the introduction of species, see, e.g. Ed Yong, "New Zealand's War on Rats Could Change the World," *The Atlantic* (November 16, 2017) at https://www.theatlantic.com/science/archive/2017/11/ new-zealand-predator-free-2050-rats-gene-drive-ruh-roh/546011/   (accessed November 2018).

58 Paul Ehrlich and Anne Ehrlich, *Extinction* (New York: Random House, 1981), p. 94.

59 William Stevens, "The 'Hot Spot' Approach to Saving Species," *New York Times* (March 14, 2000), p. D3; Conservation International, Biodiversity Hotspots webpage, at http:// www.conservation.org/How/Pages/Hotspots.aspx (accessed November 2018).

60 Edward O. Wilson, "A Biologist's Manifesto for Preserving Life on Earth," *Sierra* (December 12, 2016), p. 1, at https://www.sierraclub.org/sierra/2017-1-january-february/ feature/biologists-manifesto-for-preserving-life-earth (accessed November 2018).

61 A fuller discussion of the strengths and weaknesses of the two metaphors is contained in William Stevens, "Lost Rivets and Threads, and Ecosystems Pulled Apart," *New York Times* (July 4, 2000), p. D4.

62 3M, "3M Sustainability: Goals & Progress," (2015), https://www.3m.com/3M/en_US/sustainability-us/goals-progress/ (accessed November 2018).

63 Seventh Generation, "Measuring Our Environmental Footprint: Packaging and Materials," at http://www.7genereport.com/measuring/packaging.php (accessed July 2015).

64 World Resources Institute *et al.*, *World Resources 1998–99* (Washington, DC: World Resources Institute, 1999).

65 Samuel Loewenberg, "Old Europe's New Ideas," *Sierra*, 89 (January/February 2004), p. 43.

66 EPA, *Advancing Sustainable Materials Management: 2015 Fact Sheet* (July 2018), p. 2, at https://culturecapital.com/event/60710/vintage-game-night (accessed November 2018).

67 Ibid.

68 Norimitsu Onishi, "How Do Japanese Dump Trash? Let Us Count the Myriad Ways," *New York Times* (May 12, 2005), p. A1; Rosaria Chifari, "Does Recyclable Separation Reduce the Cost of Municipal Waste Management in Japan?," *Waste Management* (60), p. 32.

69 Linda Poon, "This Japanese Town Shows How 'Zero Waste' Is Done," *City Lab* (December 9, 2015), at https://www.citylab.com/equity/2015/12/let-this-japanese-town-show-you-how-zero-waste-is-done/419706/ (accessed November 2018).

70 John Markoff, "Technology's Toxic Trash Is Sent to Poor Nations," *New York Times* (February 25, 2002), p. C1.

71 Kate O'Neill, "Will China's Crackdown on 'Foreign Garbage' Force Wealthy Countries to Recycle more of their own Waste?," https://theconversation.com/will-chinas-crackdown-on-foreign-garbage-force-wealthy-countries-to-recycle-more-of-their-own-waste-81440 (accessed November 2018).

72 The Aluminum Association, "The Aluminum Can Advantage" (2016), https://www.aluminum.org/aluminum-can-advantage (accessed November 2018).

73 Harold Sprout and Margaret Sprout, *The Context of Environmental Politics* (Lexington: University Press of Kentucky, 1978), pp. 47–8.

Recommended Readings

Please refer to the list of Further Reading in chapter 8.

Chapter 8

The Environment: Pollution[1]

We travel together, passengers on a little spaceship, dependent on its vulnerable resources of air and soil; all committed for our safety to its security and peace; preserved from annihilation only by the care, the work, and I will say, the love we give our fragile craft.
Adlai E. Stevenson, speech as US Ambassador to the United Nations (1965)

---

1 Katherine Liljestrand contributed substantially to the research and updates reflected in this edition. Please reflect her contribution in any direct citation to this chapter.

Global Issues: An Introduction, Sixth Edition. Kristen A. Hite and John L. Seitz.
© 2021 John Wiley & Sons Ltd. Published 2021 by John Wiley & Sons Ltd.

The relationship between the environment and development has not been a happy one. Development has often harmed the environment, and environmental harm has in turn adversely affected development. Industrialization brought with it many forms of pollution, pollution that is undermining the basic biological systems upon which life rests on this planet. It took millions of years for these systems to evolve. Industrialization also vastly increased the rate of the extraction of natural resources.

There is no question that industrialization and its associated increased consumption and production rates have generated unprecedented levels of wealth. There is also no question that economic systems geared towards the ever-increasing conversion of natural resources into refined products have generated unprecedented levels of pollution and waste. This chapter considers the environmental impacts of the twentieth-century development model and efforts to respond to and address the problems.

Air Pollution

Industrialization has brought dirtier air to all parts of the Earth. From factories and transportation systems, with their telltale smokestacks and exhaust pipes, harmful and sometimes toxic fumes are constantly emitted into the air. As fossil fuels are burned to generate energy for electricity and transportation, as industries belch gas byproducts into the atmosphere, and as wood and other conventional sources are burned for fuel, various gases and particles are released into the atmosphere.

While it is often perceived as more of a nuisance than a problem, pollution kills more people than armed conflict.[1] Moreover, pollution exposes over 90 percent of children to increased health risks, with harms ranging from low birthweight in babies to chronic conditions like asthma.[2] A recent study by the World Health Organization found that two billion children breathing polluted air poses a long-term health hazard, 15 percent of whom breath air classified as toxic.[3]

A few spectacular instances in the twentieth century resulted in large numbers of people becoming ill or dying because of the toxic gases in the air they breathed: 6,000 became ill and 60 died in the Meuse Valley in Belgium in 1930; 6,000 became ill and 20 died in Donora, Pennsylvania in 1948; and in London tens of thousands became ill and 4,000 died in 1952. (It was this last-mentioned instance that led the United Kingdom to pass various laws to clean up the air, which have proved to be quite successful: within just a few decades, 80 percent more sunshine reached London than had in 1952.[4]) But even more deaths are caused by accumulated daily levels of pollution: in 2018, the World Health Organization (WHO) estimated that air pollution caused 4.2 million premature deaths across the globe. Of these, 91 percent occurred in lower and middle income countries.[5] The particulates found in air pollution generally pass through the nose and throat and enter the lungs, where they can have serious health effects on the lungs and heart.

Rapid economic growth may have benefited China from a financial standpoint, but not without serious environmental consequences. The rapid increase in air pollution has caused illness and premature death among the population. Estimates of the healthcare and non-healthcare costs of China's air and water pollution combined have totaled about $100 billion per year, or about 5.8 percent of the country's GDP.[6] Air pollution was a contributing factor in about 1.2 million of the country's premature deaths in 2010 and caused an 8 year-old girl to develop lung cancer in 2013, making her China's youngest lung cancer patient.[7] Though the situation is severe, China is not alone: many other countries face similar problems, and Earth's environment transcends state boundary lines.

Pollution often has a disproportionate impact on the poor, who often live in neighborhoods with dirtier air than the wealthy. Most of the 300 million children exposed to toxic air pollution live in low and middle income nations.[8] At the same time, in rich countries, poor and minority children in the inner cities have the highest rates of asthma.[9]

Over recent decades, a number of industrialized countries, including the United States, have made significant progress in reducing air pollution in their large urban areas. In 1970 the Clean Air Act was passed in the United States, and it was then strengthened in 1990. During the first 20 years after the law was passed, lead was reduced by 95 percent, sulfur dioxide by about 30 percent, and particulates (tiny particles in the air) by about 60 percent.[10] According to the US Environmental Protection Agency, about 200,000 premature deaths and 700,000 cases of chronic bronchitis were avoided.[11] And during the second 20 years of the Act, emissions of six principal pollutants fell by about 40 percent, while the economy (i.e. GDP) grew by about 60 percent. The US Environmental Protection Agency estimates the economic value of the air quality improvements brought about by this law by 2020 will reach almost $2 trillion, a value which greatly exceeds the costs of efforts to comply with the law.[12]

In spite of this progress, much remains to be done. Even in countries with significant laws and enforcement regarding pollution, many cities still experience a number of days each year when the air is considered unhealthy. At the beginning of this century, southern California had the dirtiest air in the United States, with some areas claiming over 400 days in a two-year period when the air was unhealthy to breathe.[13] Since then, significant progress has been made in cleaning the air in Los Angeles, which improved from 228 days/year above the state of California's one-hour ozone standard in 1979 to 96 days/year in 2007 – with similar trends for other smog-causing pollutants.[14] As recently as 2015, the number of days that violated the less stringent eight-hour standard numbered 88.[15]

Despite the progress cited above, the reduction of particulates has not been as successful as the improvements in ozone pollution. Studies in the 1990s and early 2000s indicated that extremely small particulates spewed by vehicles, factories, and coal power plants, which were not illegal to release until 1997, were the greatest risk to health and were estimated to be causing up to 60,000 premature deaths per year in the United States.[16] A more recent study in 2013 pointed to air pollution as the cause of 200,000 premature deaths per year in the United States.[17] Asthma rates among children in countries like the United States have been increasing rapidly and may be linked to air quality and road proximity.[18] For example, a 2015 study found 926,000 cases of asthma in children living in California alone.[19] Moreover, wildfire pollution has grown – at times causing cities like Los Angeles to have the highest rates of pollution on the planet, such as a during the particularly bad set of wildfires in 2018.[20]

Europe has improved its air, but more needs to be done there as well. In 2015, air pollution in Europe caused more deaths than car accidents.[21] At the beginning of this century, ozone (a key component of smog) cost European farmers about 6 billion euros annually.[22] And a more recent European report citing a 2013 study found that long-term air pollution leads to almost half a million premature deaths each year.[23] Overall in the European Union, the average life expectancy is 8.6 months lower due to exposure to certain particulate matter pollution.[24]

Your "friendly" coal power plant

Much of the world's electricity comes from power plants fueled by coal. A typical 500-megawatt coal plant, which can power a city of about 140,000 people, burns about 40 train cars of coal each day and yearly releases into the air the following pollutants: 3.7 million tons of carbon dioxide, 10,200 tons of nitrogen oxide, 10,000 tons of sulfur dioxide, 720 tons of carbon monoxide, 500 tons of small particles, 220 tons of hydrocarbons, 225 pounds of arsenic, 170 pounds of mercury, 114 pounds of lead, 4 pounds of cadmium, and other toxic heavy metals.

Source: "A Typical Coal Plant," *Nucleus* (Spring 2000), p. 5.

Emerging economies are facing air pollution problems even greater than those in some of the countries which first developed industrial economies. At present, cities such as Mexico City, Bangkok, Beijing, Delhi, and Jakarta have serious air pollution. In most of the megacities, air pollution is worsening because of increased industry, vehicles, and population.[25] Pollution levels sometimes exceed the air quality standards of the World Health Organization by a factor of three or more.[26] The WHO estimates that about half of all people living in urban areas in 91 countries breathe air with pollution levels at least 2.5 times higher than the WHO guidelines.[27]

Mainly because of its heavy use of coal, China has some of the worst air pollution in the world. In 2014, only 8 of China's 74 largest cities met the government's air quality standards.[28] Levels of particulates in the air in Beijing had exceeded WHO levels over 20 times in 2015, including prompting issuance of the city's first ever red alert.[29] By 2016, China topped the WHO list as the most deadly country for outdoor air pollution.[30] China's environmental agency estimated that 31 percent of the total air pollution came from motor vehicle exhaust. To improve the air quality, more than 300,000 vehicles in Beijing and an additional 5 million in other areas are expected to be decommissioned.[31] However, Chinese consumers continue to lead the global market in new auto sales, topping over 20 million vehicles annually by 2015.[32] A significant percentage of deaths in China have been caused by lung disease at least partly attributed to serious urban and household air pollution.[33] By 2015, China's concern with pollution was growing, but efforts to reverse the damage done to the environment and being done by a quarter-century of rapid economic growth were still inadequate to the task.

Indoor air pollution can also be severe in poorer nations, mostly in rural areas, but also sometimes in urban areas. About 3 billion of the world's people rely on traditional fuels for heating and cooking.[34] Wood, crop waste, dung, and coal are often used as fuels, and women and children especially are exposed to the smoke when these fuels are burned. In many of these dwellings the air pollution indoors is far worse than outdoor pollution. The World Bank has identified indoor pollution in developing nations as one of the four most urgent environmental problems. Various clean-burning stoves have now been developed and efforts are being made, both by for-profit and by nonprofit organizations, to get them to poor households.[35]

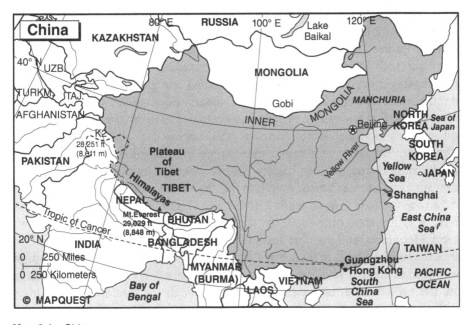

Map 8.1 China

The world's largest pollution cloud

A two-mile thick cloud of brownish haze, about 4 million square miles large, has been discovered high over the Indian Ocean by scientists. The cloud, about the size of the United States, is composed of pollutants, mainly from the burning of fossil fuels as well as from forest fires and wood-burning stoves in the Indian subcontinent, China, and Southeast Asia. Winds during the winter monsoons bring the pollution out to sea as the prevailing winds are coming down from the Himalayan Mountains. In the late spring and summer, the winds reverse and the haze is blown back over the land. The pollutants combine with the monsoon rains and come back to Earth as acid rain.

In addition to this cloud, there are other similar clouds around the Earth, but the worst are in Asia, according to a 2008 United Nations report.

Sources: William Stevens, "Enormous Haze Found over Indian Ocean," *New York Times*, June 10, 1999, p. A23; Worldwatch Institute, "Air Pollution Still a Problem," in *Vital Signs 2005* (New York: W. W. Norton, 2005), pp. 94–5; Andrew Jacobs, "U.N. Report Points to Peril From Noxious Brown Clouds," *New York Times*, November 14, 2008, p. A6.

Acid rain

When fossil fuels are burned, sulfur dioxide and oxides of nitrogen are released into the air. As these gases react with moisture and oxygen in the atmosphere in the presence of sunlight, the sulfur dioxide becomes sulfuric acid (the same substance as is used in car batteries) and the oxides of nitrogen become nitric acid. These acids then return to Earth in rain, snow, hail, or fog. When they do, they can kill fish in lakes and streams, dissolve limestone statues and gravestones, corrode metal, weaken trees, making them more susceptible to insects and drought, and reduce the growth of some crops. The effects of acid rain on human health are not yet known. Some scientists fear that acid rain could help dissolve toxic metals in water pipes and in the soil, releasing these metals into drinking water supplies.

In the United States, acid rain comes mainly from sulfur dioxide produced by coal-burning electric power plants in the Midwest and from the nitrogen oxides from auto and truck exhausts. Acid rain has caused lakes in the northeastern part of the country to become so acidic that fish and other organisms are unable to live in them. Other areas of the country, such as large parts of the South, Northwest, Rocky Mountains, and the northern Midwest, are especially sensitive to acid rain since the land and lakes in these areas contain a low amount of lime. Lime tends to neutralize the falling acid. An international dispute was created between Canada and the United States because a large amount of the acid rain falling on huge sections of Canada came from industrial emissions in the United States. Pollution also came from Canada to the United States, especially from a large Canadian smelter near the border. There are now acid rain agreements between the two countries to reduce this pollution.

Europe is facing similar problems. Many lakes in Norway and Sweden became so acidic that fish cannot live in them, and about one-third of the forests in Germany are sick and dying. Much of the acid rain falling in Northern and Central Europe comes from industry in Britain, Germany, and France. The section of Europe with the greatest damage from acid rain lies in Eastern Europe. The efforts of the governments in that region to keep up with the West led to industrial growth fueled with lignite coal, which is cheap and abundant in the region but also extremely polluting. In one area, where former East Germany, former Czechoslovakia, and Poland met, more than 300,000 acres of forests disappeared and the ground became poisoned by the huge amount of acid rain that fell there from the coal-fed power plants and numerous steel and chemical plants. Local foresters dubbed the area the "Bermuda Triangle of pollution," as winds carried the sulfur dioxide and other pollutants to other areas of Europe.

Acid rain was first observed in industrial England in the late 1800s, but nothing was done about it. In the 1950s, the response to the increasing air pollution in the United States and Europe was to build tall smokestacks on factories so that emissions of toxic gases would be dispersed by the air currents in the atmosphere. These tall smokestacks led to a noticeable improvement in the air around many factories, smelters, power plants, and refineries, but the dispersal of noxious gases in the atmosphere gave more time for these gases to form into acid rain. We now realize that the tall smokestacks violated a fundamental law of ecology, one that biologist Barry Commoner has labeled the "everything must go somewhere" law.[36] Matter is indestructible, and there are no "wastes" in nature. What is excreted by one organism as waste is absorbed by another as food. When the food is toxic, the organism dies. This helps explain the beautiful clear water in lakes that have become highly acidic, where many forms of plankton, insects, and plants have ceased to exist.

In 1990, the US Congress passed major amendments to the Clean Air Act, which calls for a large reduction of sulfur dioxide emissions from power plants. An innovative provision was put into the law that allows polluters to buy and sell their rights to pollute (the total amount of emissions indicated in the law must not be exceeded and the level will be lowered over time). The hope was that this provision would encourage polluters to find the cheapest way to cut their pollution. This hope has generally been realized, according to the US Environmental Protection Agency. During the decade of the 1990s, the cost of the scrubbers on coal plants that remove sulfur dioxide fell by about 40 percent, thus making it cheaper for plants to remove the pollutant. Because of this result, the sulfur dioxide "cap and trade" program has been cited as a successful example of market-based environmental solutions and has served as a model for other programs along the same line.[37] A cost–benefit analysis of the acid rain program (including the cap and trade provision) shows that the benefits of the program outweigh the costs 46 to 1.[38]

But neither the 1990 Clean Air Act amendments nor the "cap and trade" system has entirely solved the acid rain problem in the United States. Some scientists believe the Clean Air Act is still too weak to protect human health. Even after ten years of reducing sulfur dioxide, the acidic level in many lakes in the northeastern United States had still not decreased. The Environmental Protection Agency reported that sulfur dioxide emissions decreased about 85 percent from 1990 to 2017, but nitrogen dioxide emissions went down only 50 percent in the same period.[39] Some scientists believe the failure to reduce nitrogen emissions – coming mainly from power plants, car and truck emissions, and gases released from fertilizer – is now the main factor preventing more progress in reducing acid rain in the United States.[40]

Acid rain has also become a major problem in Asia with the increased use of fossil fuels as industrialization spreads. China's acid rain now falls on Seoul, South Korea, and Tokyo. According to the *Journal of Geophysical Research*, many of the particulates in the air of Los Angeles come from China. China's State Environmental Administration in 2006 reported that, in 2005, China became the leading source of sulfur dioxide pollution in the world.[41] According to a high government official in China, by 2004 acid rain was falling on two-thirds of the country.[42] High levels of acid rain have been reported in Thailand and South Korea, which are near or downwind from major urban and industrial centers in parts of China and elsewhere; similarly, sulfur dioxide emissions have also grown substantially in countries like India.[43]

The history of airborne lead in the United States and many other countries that followed suit is a success story, a good illustration of effective actions by government to reduce this dangerous pollution. While most of the lead pollution in the past was in the air, lead also is found at present in some household water and paint so the pollutant still exists, but in much more limited amounts than it did before.

Scientists are able to estimate the amount of lead there was in the world's air in the past by taking core samples of ice in the Greenland ice cap. The air bubbles in the ice, ice that represents past rainfall, show that from 800 BCE to the beginning of the Industrial Revolution, around 1750, the amount of lead in the air was low. There was a major increase after 1750 and a huge increase after World War II when the use of leaded gasoline for cars rose sharply. In 1965, the lead concentration in the Greenland ice was 400 times higher than the level in 800 BCE. Other studies showed that, in 1980, the bones of Americans contained 500 times more lead than those of prehistoric humans.[44]

Children are the most susceptible to harm from breathing lead. They inhale two to three times as much lead in the air per unit of body weight as do adults because their metabolic rates are higher and they are more active than adults. There is no known safe level of lead in the human body. High levels of lead poisoning can lead to death, but even low levels can cause learning difficulties and behavioral problems.

In the early 2000s, nearly a million children in the United States were estimated to have unhealthy levels of lead (as defined by the Centers for Disease Control and Prevention (CDC), the US government's top health organization) in their blood, and black children were more likely to have high levels of lead than were white

Plate 8.1   Vehicles, such as this truck/bus, provide a lot of air pollution in the cities of countries with weaker air pollution laws

Source: Ab Abercrombie.

children.[45] Many of these children were living in old houses or apartments with lead-based paint flaking off from walls (which young children, who tend to put everything in their mouths, wind up ingesting), and old lead water pipes. (Disturbing research shows that the lead paint industry in the United States actively promoted the use of leaded paint for 40 years, even after studies showed that lead could poison children and its use had been banned or restricted in a number of countries.[46])

Research published in the *New England Journal of Medicine* (one of the most respected health journals in the United States) in 2003 found that levels of lead even lower than the CDC acceptable level affected children's brains and that there was no known way to restore intelligence lost because of lead damage. These studies, which are still cited by more recent research, indicate the possibility that 90 percent of children in the United States have been harmed by lead poisoning.[47]

There has been a significant improvement in reducing the amount of lead in the blood of Americans. Between 1976 and 1991, the amount dropped by nearly 80 percent.[48] Because of tighter federal government air pollution requirements, new cars were required to use unleaded gasoline, and many experts believe that the reduced use of leaded gasoline was the cause of the lower lead levels in blood. Much of the lead in the air comes from leaded gasoline. A total ban on in the United States came into effect in 1995.

Although significant progress has been made in the United States, the problem of lead has not been completely solved. Despite banning lead in gasoline decades prior, one-quarter of the homes in the country with children under 6 still contained lead-based paint at the turn of this present century.[49] In spite of this fact, we consider the efforts by the US government to significantly reduce the danger of lead in the air to be a real success story. In the United States in 2014, according to the Environmental Protection Agency, lead levels in the air were 98 percent lower than in 1980.[50]

The European Union effectively banned all leaded gas in 2000. Some lead experts believe that recent lower levels of violent crime in the United States are the result of lower lead blood levels in US children born after 1980 rather than better enforcement.[51]

Aggressiveness and delinquency linked to lead in bones

A study of 800 boys in the United States showed a direct link between the amount of lead in the boys' bones and their behavior. Those with a relatively high level of lead in their bones had more aggressiveness and delinquency than those boys with low levels of lead. Other studies have shown that childhood antisocial behavior is a strong predictor of criminal behavior as an adult. The director of the study cautioned that the study did not show that lead was the cause of childhood delinquency, but only that it was probably one cause. That is not surprising, he stated in an interview, because "lead is a brain poison that interferes with the ability to restrain impulses."

Source: Jane E. Brody, "Aggressiveness and Delinquency in Boys Is Linked to Lead in Bones," *New York Times*, February 7, 1996, p. B6.

Another indication that global efforts to reduce the lead used in gasoline were having a beneficial effect can be seen in the Greenland ice caps. By the end of the twentieth century, lead concentrations in Greenland snow showed a drop to about the levels existing in the early 1900s, before the widespread use of leaded gasoline.[52]

About 90 percent of gasoline used in the world is now lead-free and, by 2015, according to the United Nations Environment Programme, only three countries were still using leaded gasoline.[53]

Ozone depletion

While ozone near the ground is a pollutant that causes health problems, ozone much higher in the stratosphere is beneficial and essential. Up above the clouds, the ozone layer in the atmosphere protects the Earth from harmful ultraviolet rays from the sun. Scientists believe that life on Earth did not evolve until the ozone layer was established. That layer has been reduced by substances produced by humans, mainly in the developed nations. Chlorofluorocarbons (CFCs) – used as a propellant in aerosol spray cans, as a coolant fluid in refrigerators and air conditioners, as an industrial solvent, and in the production of insulating foams – can destroy ozone. Ozone can also be destroyed by halons, which are chemicals used in fire extinguishers, and also produced when nuclear bombs are exploded.

Scientists are agreed that major depletion of the ozone layer causes serious harm to humans, other mammals, plants, birds, insects, and some sea life. Skin cancer increases, as do eye cataracts. Increased ultraviolet light also adversely affects the immune system of humans, which protects them from many possible illnesses. As mentioned in Chapter 9 on technology, one of the most harmful effects of a nuclear war would be the damage it would do to the ozone layer, which would affect life far beyond the combat area.

By analyzing past data, British scientists in the mid-1980s discovered that, during two months of the year, a hole was occurring in the ozone layer over the South Pole. Almost every year since it was discovered, the hole has continued to get larger. The hole (which is actually a significant reduction in the ozone normally found above that region, not a 100 percent decrease) galvanized the world to act to reduce the danger.

Nations first met to discuss this problem in Vienna in 1985. Two years later, about 60 nations met in Montreal, Canada and created the Montreal Protocol, an agreement to cut the production of CFCs by 50 percent by 1998. But further evidence that the depletion of the ozone layer was progressing faster than expected led the nations of the world to meet again – this time in London in 1990. The 90 nations attending that meeting agreed to speed up the phasing out of ozone-destroying chemicals. They agreed to halt the production of CFCs and halons by the year 2000. Less developed nations were given until 2010 to end their production and a fund was set up, mainly contributed to by the industrialized nations, to help the poorer nations obtain substitutes for ozone-depleting chemicals.

New disturbing evidence of the ozone depletion danger was made public in the early 1990s. The US Environmental Protection Agency announced in 1991 that data from satellites, which had been collected over the previous 11 years, revealed that the ozone layer over large parts of the globe, including the layer above the United States and Europe, had been depleted by about 5 percent. This loss was occurring twice as fast as scientists had predicted. Based on the new findings, the agency calculated that over the next 50 years about 12 million people in the US would develop skin cancer and more than 200,000 of them would die from it.[54]

Based on the new US evidence and on new data collected by an international team of scientists, which showed that the depletion was occurring in the dangerous summer months as well as in the winter, 90 nations met in Copenhagen, Denmark, in 1992 and agreed to further accelerate the ending of ozone-destroying chemicals. All production of CFCs was to end by 1996 and halon production was to end by 1994. (Developing nations were again given a ten-year grace period to phase out the production of these two chemicals.)

Chlorine compounds enter the atmosphere mainly as a component of CFCs, and it is chlorine and some other compounds that scientists now believe are causing the destruction of the ozone layer. One atom of chlorine can destroy 100,000 molecules of ozone. CFCs will remain in the atmosphere for about 50 to 100 years.

The depletion of the ozone layer: how to protect yourself

People prone to sunburn should try to keep out of the sun from 11 a.m. to 3 p.m. – when ultraviolet (UV) rays are at their strongest – and they should use hats and sunscreen lotion, which protect against both UV-A and UV-B rays, when exposed to the sun. Sunglasses that block UV rays should also be worn. While it is important to use sunscreen lotions, dermatologists agree that people who are at especially high risk of getting melanoma, a dangerous kind of skin cancer, should not rely on sunscreens but should stay out of the sun. At high risk are those with fair skin who sunburn easily, those with many moles, and those with a family history of skin cancer. Clouds offer little protection, but shade does. Melanoma rates are now on the increase in many countries, including the United States.

Sources: Walter Willett *et al.*, "Strategies for Minimizing Cancer Risk," *Scientific American*, 275 (September 1996), pp. 94–5; Jane Brody, "How to Save Your Skin in the Season of Sun," *New York Times*, May 24, 2005, p. D7.

The Montreal Protocol has brought impressive results. The transition away from the widely used CFCs and other ozone-depleting chemicals has been faster than many thought possible. In the ten-year period after the Protocol was signed in 1987, consumption of these chemicals dropped over 70 percent, with most developed nations meeting the Protocol's goal, as amended, to cease CFC production by 1996.

In 2014, for the first time in modern history, scientists discovered that the ozone was recuperating, owing to this dramatic turn-around to international cooperation.[55] CFC concentrations in the atmosphere have now peaked and started a slow decline. Ozone loss is expected to gradually diminish until the middle of the twenty-first century, when the ozone layer is expected to return to its 1980 condition.[56] The global recovery of the Earth's ozone demonstrates a concrete success for international efforts based on science working in tandem with nations, businesses, and citizens to solve a major global environmental problem.

Climate change (global warming)

The release of carbon dioxide and other gases into the atmosphere, particularly from the burning of fossil fuels, is causing massive changes in the Earth's climate. This subject has been discussed in Chapter 6. Along with water, climate change is becoming one of the biggest global issues of modern time.

Water Pollution

Development, to date, has tended to turn clean water into dirty water as often as it has turned fresh air into dirty air. In 2017, more than 10 percent of the world's population had no access to clean drinking water. Of these people, most lived in rural areas.[57]

In the United States, the deterioration of the nation's rivers was dramatized in the late 1960s when the Cuyahoga River in Ohio caught fire because it was so polluted. That event helped lead to the first Earth Day in 1970 and helped prod the US Congress into passing the Clean Water Act of 1972, which set a ten-year goal to return the nation's waterways to a state where they would be "fishable, and swimmable." Ten years later, many United States rivers, streams, and lakes were cleaner than they had been when the Act was passed, but many still remained too polluted to allow safe fishing or swimming.

By 1990, the $75 billion that had been spent in the United States on upgrading sewage treatment facilities during the previous two decades had resulted in a significant improvement of the nation's waters. A survey about that time revealed that 80 percent of the nation's rivers and streams were now safe for fishing and 75 percent were safe for swimming. But that survey also indicated that about 130,000 miles of rivers were still unsafe for fishing and 150,000 miles were unsafe for swimming.[58]

Why was there still a significant problem after this large expenditure and 20 years of effort? A large part of the reason was that little progress had been made in reducing the pollution from urban and agricultural runoff. Especially during storms, huge amounts of polluted water from city streets and the lawns of houses drain directly into rivers and lakes, untreated by local sewage treatment plants, and huge amounts of water drain from farms and golf courses, water laden with pesticides, herbicides, and fertilizers. The most current updates by the US Environmental Protection Agency report about 55 percent of the bodies of water in the United States remain impaired (i.e. not fishable and/or swimmable).[59]

The status of fresh-water fish in the United States reveals the extent of the problem of water quality in the country. In 2011, the US Environmental Protection Agency reported that about 9,000 miles of rivers and streams had fish consumption advisories to limit or avoid eating fish caught there.[60] A 2004 US Environmental Protection Agency report identified mercury and PCBs (polychlorinated biphenyls, an especially persistent and toxic class of industrial chemicals) as the leading causes of fish contamination.[61] Usually the warnings did not advise that no fish should be eaten but rather that their consumption should be limited. For example, the state of New York recommended in 2018 that people eat no more than one meal of fish weekly from any fresh water in the state.[62]

The Great Lakes are less polluted by PCBs than they were in the past – the use and discharge of the chemical is now tightly controlled and its production is banned – but concentrations of the chemical in fish have continued to rise as it works its way up the food chain. While PCB contamination in other waters in the country is still a problem, contamination of fresh waters also comes from air pollution, such as mercury from coal-burning power plants, industrial sites, and incinerators, and from other chemicals. In 2004, the head of the US Environmental Protection Agency said that mercury emissions from human causes in the United States had declined nearly 50 percent from 1990 to 1999 but admitted that virtually every river and lake in the country had fish contaminated with mercury.[63] A year later, in 2005, an EPA report found mercury emissions to be at 105 tons per year; by 2014, this amount was almost halved to 55 tons of mercury per year.[64] The contamination of water by mercury is now recognized to be a global problem, with countries having recently adopted an international treaty to address the global impacts of mercury pollution.

Other wealthy countries are also experiencing serious water pollution problems. In the 1970s and 1980s, the river Rhine was commonly called the sewer of Europe. By the mid-2000s, a cooperative effort, some of it begun in the 1950s by the five nations on the Rhine to clean up the river, was having significant results. About 20 to 25 billion euros were spent, much of them on new sewage treatment plants, and salmon have been restocked in the river.[65] Its success has led some to cite this effort as a model for other international efforts to reduce pollution.

Why does there continue to be so much dangerous water pollution? Industry must take a large part of the blame since traditionally industrial wastes have been dumped into nearby water as often as they have into the air overhead. Many industries are no longer dumping wastes into nearby rivers, but some dumping still goes on. In the United States, some legal dumping is allowed after a permit has been issued and often some treatment of the waste by the polluter is required.

A particularly challenging problem for water pollution today is chemicals. The chemical industry has had a huge growth in the industrial world since World War II. Chemicals are now finding their way into waterways, many of which are being used for drinking water. A nationwide study of streams and lakes in the United States at the beginning of the twenty-first century found low levels of many chemicals. About half the waterways had trace amounts of insecticides, antibiotics, fire retardants, disinfectants, degraded detergents, insect repellents, some nonprescription drugs, and steroidal compounds. It is not known if these levels are harmful to plants, animals, or humans. Water treatment plants are unable to remove these substances from the water. Studies in Europe a decade earlier found similar results in European waterways.[66]

In the less wealthy countries – most of the world – some 50 percent of the waste water was discharged directly into waterways without being treated. About 63 percent of the urban population, but only 48 percent of the rural population, had access to an improved sanitation system.[67] In China in 2014 about 280 million people did not have safe drinking water, roughly half the level from the previous decade.[68] But the situation is not so promising in other parts of the world. Bangladesh has possibly faced the worst water problem of all. In an effort to help the country get clean water, the government and international aid organizations in the 1970s and 1980s funded the digging of tube wells, about 10 million overall, but no one tested the ground water for arsenic. It is now recognized that many of the tube wells are contaminated with arsenic, a deadly pollutant, and 20 to 35 million people are drinking this water. The WHO declared the situation the "largest mass poisoning of a population in history."[69] A study of this situation in 2017 found that one in four people in Bangladesh were chronically exposed to arsenic in drinking water, leading to 43,000 deaths per year directly attributable to arsenic poisoning.[70]

With expected warmer temperatures coming with global warming, water supplies are becoming more erratic and increasingly polluted. As such, the scarcity of safe water supplies is increasingly a security concern. More conflicts between countries over the availability of water, such as those that have taken place in the past between India and Pakistan, Israel and Syria, and Mexico and the United States, are expected. New efforts by nations to cooperate to deal with water scarcity might also occur. This cooperation could follow the example of the long-term successful efforts by nations bordering the Mediterranean Sea – both Arab and non-Arab – to reduce the pollution in that body of water. It is not clear whether conflict or cooperation will be the main result of coming water scarcity.

The Workplace and the Home

Cancer

Cancer is often considered to be a disease of the industrial revolution. The US National Cancer Institute estimates that one out of two males and one out of three females in the United States alive at present will contract cancer and one out of four males and one out of five females will die from it.[71] In the United States, cancer kills more children than any other disease, although accidents are still the number one cause of death of children. It is commonly believed by the general public that exposure of workers to cancer-causing substances – carcinogens – in the workplace, and the exposure of the general population to pollution in the air and water and to carcinogens in some of the food they eat, are the main causes of this dreaded disease. There is no question that many workers – such as the millions of people who worked with asbestos – have been exposed to high levels of dangerous substances. But scientists do not now believe that contamination at the workplace is the main cause of cancer; nor do they believe that water pollution or food additives are causing most of the cancer cases. While these remain difficult to fully understand, leading cancer experts have agreed that smoking greatly increases the risk of contracting cancer. Also, a long-term, very large study published in 2003 convinced most experts that being overweight or obese significantly increases the likelihood of a person contracting cancer;[72] more recent studies have verified this finding.[73] Another study identified very small particles in polluted air from motor vehicle traffic as increasing the risk of lung cancer.[74]

Some experts fear that while chemicals cannot easily be proven to cause specific cancer cases today, there is a possibility that chemical-related cancers may increase greatly in the future because of the large increase in the production of carcinogenic chemicals since the 1960s. Cancer can occur 15 to 40 years after the initial exposure to a carcinogen, so chemicals may yet prove to be a major culprit.

Chemicals

You probably will prefer not to read the following statement, but if we are to present this subject truthfully, we must give it: "Only a few hundred of the more than 80,000 chemicals in use in the United States have been tested for safety."[75] How could this be true, you might well ask? And is this also true globally? Read carefully the following explanation by the US President's 2015 Cancer Panel:

> The prevailing regulatory approach in the United States is reactionary rather than pre-cautionary. That is, instead of taking preventive action when uncertainty exists about the potential harm a chemical or other environmental contaminant may cause, a hazard must be incontrovertibly demonstrated before action to ameliorate it is initiated. Moreover, instead of requiring industry or other proponents of specific chemicals, devices, or activities to prove their safety, the public bears the burden of proving that a given environmental exposure is harmful.[76]

Not everything causes cancer, of course, but development has brought forth so many new products in such a short time that we cannot be sure which ones do and which do not. Barry Commoner shows that new products often bring large profits to the first industry that introduces them, so there is a strong incentive for industries to be innovative. New products, especially in the United States since World War II, are often made of synthetic materials that pollute the environment, but the pollution usually does not become evident until years after the introduction. Commoner states that "by the time the effects are known, the damage is done and the inertia of the heavy investment in a new productive technology makes a retreat extraordinarily difficult."[77]

Europe is active on this issue also. In 2007, the European Union approved a new law that places more responsibility on chemical companies to manage the risks of their chemicals and to provide safety information on the substances. Dangerous chemicals are to be withdrawn when suitable substitutes are found. The law is being phased in gradually, potentially impacting trade relations with the United States unless new legislation is passed.

While chemicals offer potentially powerful technological solutions to environmentally polluting activities, many industrial production processes still cause significant health and environmental risks due to the fossil fuels consumed and other chemical discharges.[78] The vital need for major reforms in the chemical industry can be illustrated by one class of modern "miracle" chemicals that have been used to make such popular products as Scotchgard stain protector, Teflon nonstick cookware, and Gore-Tex water-resistant clothing. These fluorochemicals have been found in the blood of sea and land animals, birds, and women in the Arctic. It is possible that these chemicals will persist for centuries: according to the American Red Cross, they are now found in the blood of nearly all Americans from whom it receives blood donations.[79] To its credit, the 3M Corporation stopped producing the chemical used to make its popular Scotchgard product when some of this information become known. However, the Environmental Working Group reported that as recently as 2018, there were 192 sites across the United States alone that were polluted with this chemical.[80]

Pesticides

The story of pesticide use illustrates well the dangers that new substances, which have become so important to modern agriculture, have brought to people at their workplaces as well as in their homes at mealtimes. Rachel Carson is credited with making a whole nation – the United States – aware of the dangers of persistent pesticides such as DDT. Her book *Silent Spring*, which appeared in 1962, showed how toxic substances can become concentrated as they go up the food chain, as big animals eat little animals. Since many toxic substances are not excreted by the plants or animals absorbing them, they accumulate and are passed on to the next animal that eats them. Carson's warning led to a sharp reduction in the use of long-lived pesticides in many developed countries; but if she were alive today (she died of breast cancer in 1964), she would probably be disturbed to learn that short-lived but highly toxic pesticides are now increasing in use in the United States. The use of herbicides has especially increased dramatically as farmers, railroad companies, telephone companies, and others find it cheaper and easier to use these chemicals to get rid of unwanted vegetation than to use labor or machines. These new highly toxic pesticides pose a special risk to the workers who manufacture them and to the farmers who work with them in the fields. Although DDT was banned for use in the United States in 1972, residues of it could still be found in most people in the United States 30 years later.[81]

In the early 1990s, the US government announced that it was going to try to reduce the amount of pesticides used on US farms. A five-year study by the US National Academy of Sciences on the effect of agricultural chemicals on children was published in 1993. It criticized the method the government had been using to calculate the safe amount of pesticide residue on foods.[82] It found that the risk calculations by the government had not taken into account the fact that people are also exposed to pesticides from sources other than on foods, such as in their drinking water, on their lawns, and on golf courses. It found that infants and children might be especially sensitive to pesticide residues on food. They consume

60 times the amount of fruit adults do, in relation to their weight, so are getting higher doses of the pesticides that are used on fruits. And this is taking place early in their lives. The head of the committee that prepared the report drew the following conclusion: "Pesticides applied in legal amounts on the farm, and present in legal amounts on food, can still lead to unsafe amounts."[83] In 1999, the Environmental Protection Agency responded to these concerns and banned most uses of a pesticide widely used on fruit and vegetables, and tightened restrictions on another pesticide, because of their possible harm to children. This was the first time the agency had issued regulations specifically designed to protect children.[84] In 2005, the US Environmental Protection Agency issued new guidelines on the use of many chemicals which recognized that children might be more at risk from the use of these chemicals than adults.[85]

While wealthy countries such as North America, Western Europe, and Japan still use most of the world's pesticides, other countries are quickly catching up. China alone used almost twice as many pesticides in 2017 as the rest of the top ten pesticide-using countries combined.[86] In 2012, the US Environmental Protection Agency estimated world use of pesticides exceeded 6 million pounds, while US use alone exceeded 1.3 million pounds.[87]

Pesticide use is increasing in the less wealthy nations as well – and not just the use of short-lived pesticides but of persistent pesticides such as DDT as well. Despite being listed among the world's "dirty dozen" persistent organic pollutants whose use is widely banned due to health impacts (under the Stockholm Convention), the World Health Organization has approved the use of DDT under certain conditions

Plate 8.2 Water pollution in the United States is partly caused by large amounts of pesticides, herbicides, and fertilizers, which run off from fields during storms

Source: Lynn Betts, US Department of Agriculture.

in poorer countries to economically control a resurgence of malaria. US law explicitly permits the sale to foreign nations of substances that are banned, highly restricted, or unregistered in the United States. US companies, as well as many companies in Europe, have increasingly turned to the overseas market to sell their products as more restrictions on the use of pesticides occur in the developed nations.

Pesticides have played a significant role in the Green Revolution; it is doubtful food production would have stayed ahead of population growth in the world without them. What seems to be called for now is a highly selective use of pesticides, not their banishment. A number of agricultural experts are now advocating a more balanced program for controlling pests. A selective use of pesticides would go along with the use of biological controls, such as natural predators, and other nonchemical means to control pests.

Managing Waste

Solid wastes

It seems to be a common occurrence in many countries that, as more goods and services become available, more are desired and less value is placed on those already in hand. After the end of World War II, an unprecedented period of economic growth in the industrialized world took place, leading to a huge increase in the consumption of material goods.

As consumption rose, so did wastes. "Throwaway" products that were used briefly and then discarded became common, as did items that wore out quickly. Such facts disturbed few people in the United States since they found enjoyment in buying new, "better" products. Many such products were relatively cheap in the 1950s, 1960s, and early 1970s, since energy and other raw materials were inexpensive. Between 1960 and 2000, the amount of solid wastes generated in the United States per person annually grew by about 60 percent, until it reached about 1,600 pounds.[88] On average each American generated about 2.7 pounds of waste per day in 1960, whereas in 2013 this figure had grown to 4.4 pounds.[89]

One obvious way cities can help reduce and manage their citizens' waste is to support recycling programs, which many communities did to reduce the amount of trash going to their landfills. Another way to reduce trash is to make citizens pay variable costs for the disposal of their solid wastes, based on amount and type. Seattle is an example of a US city that has successfully followed that principle.

Seattle began charging its citizens according to the amount of trash they put out for disposal. Yard wastes, such as grass clippings, if separated by the citizens so the city could use them for composting, were charged at a much lower rate than regular trash, and paper, glass, and metal (which could be recycled) were hauled away free. Seattle, which was already more environmentally conscious than most other American cities, found that during the first year it started charging its citizens for the amount of waste they produced, the total tonnage the city needed to haul to the landfills fell by about 20 percent. By the mid-1990s, 90 percent of the residents of Seattle were recycling their waste. As of 2018, Seattle was recycling about 60 percent of its waste and aims to recycle 70 percent of its waste by 2022.[90]

Seattle has a zero waste goal, as does San Francisco, Austin, in Texas, and Canberra, Australia. San Francisco is now diverting about 80 percent of city waste from its landfills, mainly by its composting and recycling programs. It has been a grand success.[91] But not every city has been so ambitious in addressing waste problems. Bali, Indonesia, for example, declared a "rubbish emergency" in 2017 due to the high volume of plastic debris accumulating on its beaches.[92]

A huge solid waste problem has been created by the growing use of plastics around the world. This modern achievement of the chemical industry takes petroleum and turns it into containers which are very difficult to break and won't decay in any individual's lifetime. This last quality is what is causing the problem. Current estimates are that sunlight might break plastic down over about 500 years. Until recently, there has been no known living organism that can digest even a single molecule of plastic. In 2017, scientists discovered that waxworm larvae appear to be able to break down polyethylene, while a mutant enzyme that breaks down plastic also shows great promise in the fight against plastic.[93]

Every year, about 250 billion pounds of plastic pellets are produced in the world. A research sailing ship in the early twenty-first century found an area in the Pacific Ocean about the size of the state of Texas – about 800 miles across (1,300 kilometers) – filled with floating plastic debris.[94] Since that time, the area has grown to the size of the country of Mexico and could be upwards of a million square miles in size.[95] A Japanese scientist and his colleagues at Tokyo University have discovered that floating plastic fragments in the sea contain and absorb toxic chemicals such as DDT, PCBs, and other oily pollutants. Here is how this problem has been described:

> The potential scope of the problem is staggering …When those pellets or products degrade, break into fragments, and disperse, the pieces may also become concentrators and transporters of toxic chemicals in the marine environment. Thus an astronomical number of vectors for some of the most toxic pollutants known are being released into an ecosystem dominated by the most efficient natural vacuum cleaners nature ever invented: the jellies and salps living in the ocean. After those organisms ingest the toxins, they are eaten in turn by fish, and so the poisons pass into the food web that leads, in some cases, to human beings.[96]

In 2003, the research vessel that documented the huge floating body of plastic debris in the Pacific took underwater photographs of transparent filter feeding organisms with colored plastic fragments in their bellies.[97] In 2014, researchers estimated that the patch actually weighed 100 times more than previously believed.[98]

Toxic wastes

The first warning of the danger of toxic wastes came from Japan. In the 1950s and 1960s, hundreds of people were paralyzed, crippled, or killed from eating fish contaminated with mercury that had been discharged into Minamata Bay by a chemical plant. It took many decades, but in 2014 the global community eventually adopted the Minamata Treaty to address mercury pollution.[99]

The United States has been actively working to manage toxic wastes since the last quarter of the twentieth century. Many people in a residential district of Niagara Falls, New York, were exposed to a dangerous mixture of chemicals that were seeping into their swimming pools and basements. Most of these people did not know when they bought their homes that the Hooker Chemical Company had dumped over 20,000 tons of chemical wastes in the 1940s and 1950s into a nearby abandoned canal, ironically known as Love Canal. News of the Love Canal disaster spread through the country as the story of the contamination slowly came out in spite of the denials of the chemical company and the apathy of the local government. Eventually hundreds of people were evacuated from the area. The state and federal governments bought over 600 of the contaminated homes. After putting a "wall" of clay and plastic around the buried toxic waste, the federal government later declared much of the Love Canal neighborhood fit for resettlement. The name of the neighborhood was changed from Love Canal to Black Creek Village.[100]

For decades, the US Environmental Protection Agency required some of the producers of toxic wastes to report annually how much they were releasing into the environment. Two industries that produce the largest amount of toxic wastes – the mining and oil exploration industries – were exempt from the reporting requirement.[101] Half of all wastes subject to reporting were produced by the chemical industry, with other significant amounts produced by the metal, oil refining, paper, and plastics industries.

This reporting law, formally called the Toxic Release Inventory, has been considered to be a very effective piece of legislation. Even the chemical industry, which has worked to weaken the law, has admitted that because of it, toxic emissions have been reduced by about 50 percent. Very soon after the first report was released, several large corporations announced that they would voluntarily reduce their emissions by 90 percent over the next three years. States and local residents have used the report to put pressure on companies to reduce their pollution.[102]

In 1996, the reporting requirements were expanded to include, for the first time, electric utilities, incinerator operators, recyclers, and many mining companies, an increase of 6,400 new plants over the previous 23,000 that had to report toxic emissions. By 2001, US manufacturers reported a nearly 15 percent decline from the previous year in toxic releases into the air, water, and ground. And in 2013, US manufacturers reported an additional 7 percent decline in toxic releases into the air, water, and ground over the previous decade.[103] This was progress, but the EPA reported total land disposal of 2.75 billion pounds and air disbursement of 592.43 million pounds of waste in 2013.[104]

Oil in the Amazon: a legacy of toxic sludge

During the early years of Ecuador's oil boom, the government and oil companies alike rushed to capitalize on some of the rich oil reserves in the Amazon region. While technology enabled new reserves to be tapped and processed, efforts to regulate the waste of byproducts did not keep pace with the rush of extra activity. As such, pits of oil sludge were often left behind as companies moved on to fresh sources. Communities – many of whom are indigenous – continue to live with the legacy of the wastes. Many community members in the northeastern part of Ecuador claimed they became sick due to the toxic waste. Frustrated with the failure to clean up the oil sludge, they sued Chevron, a company that inherited the messy legacy of the oil contamination from earlier production activities. Although an Ecuadorian court held Chevron responsible for much of the pollution-related damages, lengthy legal disputes at the international level have impaired resolution, payments, and cleanup. Billions of dollars are at stake, much of which is associated with legal fees and some of which may be paid to the communities for damages.

For various perspectives associated with some of the most significant developments over more than a decade of litigation on this case, see the Ecuadorian plaintiffs' side of the story at www.chevrontoxico.org, and for the defendant company's version of the story, see http://www.chevron.com/ecuador/ (all accessed July 2015).

The persistence of some toxic chemicals is shown by the fact that byproducts of the chemical used to make stain protectors in carpets and food wrappers are showing up in seals and polar bears in the Arctic and in dolphins in the mid-Atlantic.[105] And a number of studies have shown that indigenous peoples in the Arctic are being exposed to significant amounts of pesticides, industrial chemicals, and heavy metals not occurring locally, with uncertain health effects.[106] Why are Arctic peoples being exposed to such poisons? One reason is that many rivers and ocean and air currents carry toxins originating in other parts of the world. Also, many indigenous people have a diet rich in fish and marine mammals; thus, they absorb the toxins the fish and mammals have been exposed to. Breast milk and samples of blood in umbilical cords in women living in the Arctic contain moderate to extremely high levels of toxins such as DDT, PCBs, dioxins, mercury, lead, and a flame retardant.[107]

Governmental and industrial responses to the waste problem

In 1980, the US government created a $1.6 billion fund to finance the cleaning up of the worst toxic waste sites. The law that set up this fund (popularly called Superfund) allowed the government to recover the cost of the cleanup from the companies that dumped wastes at the sites. In 1986, $9 billion more for the cleanup was approved by the US government, to come mainly from a tax on industry and on crude oil. The Congressional Office of Technology Assessment has estimated that it will require about 50 years and $100 billion to clean up toxic waste dumps in the country.

By 2005, work had been completed at about 1,000, or 60 percent, of Superfund sites and work was underway at an additional 400 sites.[108] Over the time from 1990 to 2014, about $4.6 billion was deposited in special accounts for cleanups and enforcement and nearly $3 billion has already been spent or committed. The remaining amount will be used for ongoing and future Superfund cleanups.[109]

There are other ways governments can help control the waste problem. Barbara Ward, the late British economist, mentions four ways a government can encourage the reduction of wastes and promote the reuse of wastes: (1) it can make manufacturers pay a tax that could cover the cost of handling the eventual disposal of their products; (2) it can stimulate the market for recycled products by purchasing recycled products for some of its own needs; (3) it can give grants and other incentives to cities and industries to help them install equipment that recycles wastes; and (4) it can prohibit the production of nonreturnable containers in some instances.[110]

Inefficient and wasteful technologies and processes to produce goods are still common in the United States and other developed nations, since many of these were adopted when energy was cheap, water plentiful, many raw materials inexpensive, and the disposal of wastes easy. Some industries now realize that they can increase their profits by making their procedures more efficient and producing less waste. One such company is 3M, which, according to one study, reduced its pollution as well as increased its profits, "not by installing pollution control plants but by reformulating products, redesigning equipment, modifying processes ... [and] recovering materials for reuse."[111]

Germany is one of the leaders in creating imaginative ways to deal with toxic wastes. Recognizing that the ideal solution to this problem is to concentrate on reducing the production of toxic waste rather than focusing on its disposal or the cleanup, the country is implementing what is called a "closed-cycle economy." For decades, Germany has required manufacturers and distributors to take back packaging and reuse or recycle the contents. When products are built, they are designed with concern over how they will be disposed of when no longer wanted. Parts are marked so they can later be identified electronically to facilitate their recycling. According to the head of Germany's environmental protection agency, as manufacturers are held financially and legally responsible for the safe disposal of their products, it is expected they will support the revolutionary concept of the environmentally friendly closed-cycle economy.[112]

Environmental Politics

In this section we will try to understand what makes environmental politics so controversial. Politics is a passionate business, but why are environmental issues often emotional? Clearly, conflicting interests and values are involved. Politics involves the making of laws and decisions that everyone must obey in a society. These laws and decisions are directed at settling conflicts that arise among people living together in a community, and at achieving commonly desired goals. As we will see, environmental politics does deal with very strongly held opposing values and interests. It also represents an effort by a community to achieve some goals – such as clean air and clean water – which cannot be reached individually, only by the community as a whole.

The political scientists Harold and Margaret Sprout believe that most participants in environmental politics show a tendency toward having one of two very different philosophies or worldviews and that these are at the root of most environmental conflicts. One they call "exploitive," and the other "mutualistic." Here is how they define them:

> A[n] ...exploitive attitude would be one that envisages inert matter, nonhuman spe-
> cies, and even humans as objects to be possessed or manipulated to suit the purposes
> of the exploiter. In contrast, a ... mutualistic posture would be one that emphasizes the
> inter-relatedness of things and manifests a preference for cooperation and accommo-
> dation rather than conflict and domination.[113]

While conflicting worldviews are a part of environmental politics, so also is a conflict of basic interests. Economist Lester Thurow believed that environmental politics often involves a conflict between different classes having very different interests. He saw the environmental movement as being supported mainly by upper middle-class people who have gained economic security and now want to improve the quality of their lives further by reducing environmental pollutants. On the opposite side, he saw both lower income groups and the rich – lower income people because they see environmental laws making it more difficult for them to find jobs and obtain a better income, and the rich because they can often buy their way out of environmental problems and see pollution laws as making it more difficult for them to increase their wealth even further.[114]

Other conflicting interests are also involved in environmental politics. Antipollution laws often make it more difficult and costly to increase energy supplies, extract minerals, and increase jobs by industrial growth. Barry Commoner's Fourth Law of Ecology – There Is No Such Thing as a Free Lunch – means that for every gain there is some cost.[115] There are tradeoffs involved in making the air and water cleaner as there are in making more cars and television sets. Also, the costs of pollution control often increase substantially as you try to make the environment cleaner and cleaner. The cost required to make a 50 percent reduction in a pollutant is often quite modest, whereas if you try to reduce the pollutant by 95 percent, the cost can increase dramatically – but that cost is still often small compared to the health and environmental impacts of unabated pollution.

Much environmental destruction is extremely difficult for the political system to deal with, since the damage often shows up many years after the polluting action takes place. It is now clear that prevention is much cheaper than trying to clean up the damage after it has occurred, but the nature of politics does not lend itself to long-range planning. Generally, politicians have a rather short-term outlook, as do many business people. Both are judged on their performance in handling immediate problems; this promotes a tendency to take actions showing some immediate result. Such actions further the politician's chances for reelection and the business person's profits or chances for promotion. Yet environmental problems often call for actions before the danger becomes clear. A further complication is the fact that, even after action is taken to reduce a pollutant, because of the inherent delays in the system, the harmful effects of the pollutant do not decrease until a number of years later. Thus, the inclination of the public official – and the business person – is to do nothing and hope that something turns up showing that the problem was not as bad as feared or that there is a cheaper way to deal with it.

An additional factor in environmental politics is related to the twentieth-century values embraced in the United States as the model for economic development. The "American Dream" has been one of continuing abundance. For much of the country's history, there has seemed to be an unlimited abundance of many things needed for the good life, such as land, forests, minerals, energy, clean air, and natural beauty. It is a country that seemed to offer unlimited opportunities for many to make a better life for themselves, and "better" has been usually defined as including more material goods. The setting of limits on consumption and production that environmentalists often promote is certain to cause dismay to many.

But is the goal of an ever-growing economy compatible with environmental limits? Some have argued that the answer is no. They believe that economic growth based on ever-increasing consumption of natural resources and their associated products is inherently unsustainable.[116] Sustainable production and consumption models, "circular economy" processes and an attitude of "less is more," are all alternatives to the twentieth-century model of economic development. But not everyone believes this kind of approach is desirable – or even possible.[117]

If the above were not enough to make environmental politics very difficult, there is also the fact that the costs in environmental matters are often very difficult to measure. One can calculate the cost of a scrubber on a coal-burning power plant, but how do you measure the cost of a shortened life that occurs if the scrubber is not used? How do you place a dollar figure on the suffering a person with emphysema experiences, or a miner with brown lung disease, or an asbestos worker with cancer? How do you measure the costs the yet unborn will have to pay if nothing is done now about climate change? And how do you put a dollar figure on the loss of natural beauty? Because it is so difficult to weigh the costs in conventional terms of measurement, the costs often were not weighed in the past.[118]

There is, of course, also the matter of values – the value individuals place on more material goods, the convenience of throwaway products, open spaces, and clean air. The resolution of conflicts over values can often be handled only by politics, in a democracy by the community as a whole making decisions through its representatives and then requiring all members of the community to obey them. That such stuff causes controversy and stirs passions should not be surprising. It is hard work.

Conclusion

As this chapter and the previous one have shown, the increase in the production of goods and services that came with industrialization had, and still has, frightening costs. For both rich and poor nations, the environment is important. Economic growth is also important, especially for the poorer countries. The challenge remains for both poor and rich to achieve the optimal level of economic activity while simultaneously maintaining healthy ecosystems and sustaining the land, air, and water upon which all life depends.

Global efforts to govern the ozone layer tell a remarkable success story of collective regulation of the commons leading to successful outcomes. Over a period of just a few decades, countries were able to turn around the Earth's protective ozone cover through global efforts to regulate ozone-depleting substances. By 2014, for the first time in recent history, there were indications that the ozone layer had begun recovering, and the hole over Antarctica was shrinking. This is an encouraging and inspiring indication that the global community can indeed come together to transcend national and economic barriers to successfully address a global environmental "tragedy of the commons" problem. But it is also sadly not always the way environmental problems are resolved.

One of the most important examples in human history of human beings immersed in a tragedy of the commons situation is that of addressing climate change, caused primarily by the pollution of fossil fuels, with possibly disastrous consequences for life on the planet. Some of the world's biggest emitters – most notably the United States and Brazil – have behaved in ways that Garret Hardin tragically predicted, but which also harm the collective climate commons. Meanwhile the United Nations writ large, alongside many other governments, organizations, corporations, and civil society, all recognize the danger and are beginning to take actions to try to limit this tragedy's impacts.

Increasingly, pollution controls are seen as opportunities to improve human health and well-being, and are typically easily justified by the profits generated from economic development. But political will is sometimes different than logical reasoning, and when economic development interests capture politicians, sometimes levels of environmental protection are less than ideal. Still, environmental issues are relatively new compared to economic development. Given that, fifty years ago environmental concerns were seen as a threat to development, global recognition and efforts to address today's environmental challenges are nothing short of inspiring, even as there is much more to be done.

Notes

1 Associated Press, "Pollution Kills more People than all Wars and Violence," *Daily News* (October 19, 2017), at https://www.nydailynews.com/news/world/pollution-kills-people-wars-violence-article-1.3575493 (accessed November 2018).

2 Damian Carrington, "Air Pollution Harm to Unborn Babies may be Global Health Catastrophe, Warns Doctors," *The Guardian* (December 5, 2017), at https://www.theguardian.com/environment/2017/dec/05/air-pollution-harm-to-unborn-babies-may-be-global-health-catastrophe-warn-doctors (accessed November 2018).

3 Madison Pauly, "Two Billion Children Breathe Toxic Air," *Newsweek* (November 1, 2016), at https://www.newsweek.com/two-billion-children-breathe-toxic-air-515893 (accessed November 2018).

4 Lester R. Brown, *The Twenty-Ninth Day: Accommodating Human Needs and Numbers to the Earth's Resources* (New York: W. W. Norton, 1978), p. 44. One of the ways Britain reduced its air pollution was to build tall smokestacks, which has probably led to worse air in Scandinavia.

5 World Health Organization (WHO), "Ambient (Outdoor) Air Quality and Health," Fact Sheet (updated May 2018), at http://www.who.int/en/news-room/fact-sheets/detail/ambient-(outdoor)-air-quality-and-health (accessed November 2018).

6 World Bank, *Cost of Pollution in China: Economic Estimates of Physical Damages* (2007), at http://documents.worldbank.org/curated/en/2007/02/7503894/cost-pollution-china-economic-estimates-physical-damages; see also Meena Thiruvengadam, "Chinese Smog: At What Cost?" *The Financialist* (March 4, 2013), at https://www.thefinancialist.com/chinese-smog-at-what-cost/ (both accessed July 2015).

7 Beina Xu, *China's Environmental Crisis*, Council on Foreign Relations back-grounder, updated January 18, 2016, at https://www.cfr.org/backgrounder/chinas-environmental-crisis (accessed November 2018); see also Council on Foreign Relations, "China's Environmental Crisis," January 18, 2016, at https://www.cfr.org/backgrounder/chinas-environmental-crisis (accessed November 2018).

8 Pauly, "Two Billion Children Breathe Toxic Air."

9 Standards Subcommittee of the Asthma Disparities Workgroup, *Measures to Identify and Track Racial Disparities in Childhood Asthma: Asthma Disparities Workgroup Subcommittee Recommendations* 22-24 (2016), https://www.cdc.gov/asthma/pdfs/Racial_Disparities_in_Childhood_Asthma.pdf (accessed November 2018).

10 Stephen Klaidman, "Muddling Through," *Wilson Quarterly* (Spring 1991), p. 76.

11 United States Environmental Protection Agency (US EPA), "40th Anniversary of the Clean Air Act," at http://www.epa.gov/air/caa/40th.html (accessed July 2015).

12 EPA, "Benefits and Costs of the Clean Air Act Amendments of 1990," factsheet, at http://www.epa.gov/cleanairactbenefits/feb11/factsheet.pdf (accessed July 2015).

13 Reed McManus, "Out Front in the Air Wars," *Sierra*, 89 (January/February 2004), p. 12.

14 Eric A. Morris, "Los Angeles Transportation Facts and Fiction: Smog," *Los Angeles Times* (February 17, 2009).

15 UCLA Institute of the Environment and Sustainability, *2015 Environmental Report Card for Los Angeles County* (2015), p. 34, at https://www.ioes.ucla.edu/wp-content/uploads/report-card-2015-air.pdf (accessed November 2018).

16 Jocelyn Kaiser, "Mounting Evidence Indicts Fine-Particle Pollution," *Science*, 307 (March 25, 2005), p. 1858. For more information on the connection between particulates and

cancer, see President's Cancer Panel, *Reducing Environmental Cancer Risk: What We Can Do Now*, Annual Report, 2008–2009 (April 2010), at http://deainfo. nci.nih.gov/ advisory/pcp/annualReports/pcp08-09rpt/PCP Report 08-09 508.pdf (accessed July 2015).

17 Jennifer Chu, "Study: Air Pollution Causes 200,000 Early Deaths each Year in the U.S.," *MIT News* (August 29, 2013), at http://news.mit.edu/2013/study-air-pollution-causes-200000-early-deaths-each-year-in-the-us-0829 (accessed November 2018).

18 See, e.g., US EPA, *Best Practices for Reducing Near-Road Pollution Exposure at Schools* (2015), https://www.epa.gov/sites/production/files/2015-10/documents/ochp_2015_ near_road_pollution_booklet_v16_508.pdf (accessed November 2018).

19 Public Health Institute, *Costs of Environmental Health Conditions in California Children: California Environmental Health Tracking Program* 9 (2015), http://www.phi.org/ uploads/files/2015ROI_CEHTP.pdf (accessed November 2018).

20 Arman Azad, "Due to Wildfires, California now has the most Polluted Cities in the World," *CNN* (November 17, 2018), https://www.cnn.com/2018/11/16/health/san-francisco-wildfires-air-quality-worst-in-world/index.html?no-st=1543337579 (accessed January 2020).

21 European Environment Agency, *Air quality in Europe – 2018 Report* 8 2 (2018) https:// www.eea.europa.eu/publications/air-quality-in-europe-2018/at_download/file (accessed November 2018) (in 2015, estimates indicate that around 422,000 premature deaths in Europe were caused by air pollution); *see also* European Commission: Mobility and Transport, *Fatalities at 30 Days in European Countries* (November 2016) https:// ec.europa.eu/transport/road_safety/sites/roadsafety/files/2015_transport_mode.pdf (accessed November 2018) (total vehicular deaths in a thirty-day period totaled 26,736 deaths; total vehicular deaths in a year estimated to be 320,832 deaths).

22 Gary Gardner, "Air Pollution Still a Problem," in Worldwatch Institute, *Vital Signs 2005* (New York: Worldwatch Institute, 2005).

23 European Environment Agency, *Air quality in Europe – 2016 Report* 9 (November 2016), https://www.eea.europa.eu/publications/air-quality-in-europe-2016/at_download/file (accessed November 2018).

24 WHO, "Ambient (Outdoor) Air Quality and Health."

25 BBC News, "China Pollution: First Ever Red Alert in Effect in Beijing" (December 8, 2015), at https://www.bbc.com/news/world-asia-china-35026363 (accessed November 2018).

26 See World Health Organization, "WHO Global Urban Ambient Air Pollution Database (update 2016)," http://www.who.int/phe/health_topics/outdoorair/databases/cities/en/ (accessed November 2018).

27 WHO, "Air Quality Deteriorating in Many of the World's Cities," news release, May 7, 2014, at http://www.who.int/mediacentre/news/releases/2014/air-quality/en/(accessed July 2015).

28 BBC News, "Most China Cities Fail to Meet Air Quality Standards" (February 3, 2015), at http://www.bbc.com/news/world-asia-china-31110408 (accessed July 2015).

29 BBC News, "China Pollution: Beijing Smog Hits Hazardous Levels" (January 15, 2015), at http://www.bbc.com/news/world-asia-china-30826128 (accessed July 2015).

30 Adam Vaughan, "China tops WHO List for Deadly Outdoor Air Pollution," *The Guardian* (September 27, 2016), at https://www.theguardian.com/environment/2016/sep/27/more-than-million-died-due-air-pollution-china-one-year (accessed November 2018).

31 BBC News, "China to Scrap Millions of Cars to Improve Air Quality" (May 27, 2014), at http://www.bbc.com/news/business-27583404 (accessed July 2015).

32 Bloomberg News, "China's Car Sales Have Been on a 26-Year Record Streak" (December 8, 2016), at https://www.bloomberg.com/news/articles/2016-12-08/china-wraps-up-26th-straight-car-sales-record-with-month-to-go (accessed November 2018).

33 Wanqing Chen, et al., "The Epidemiology of Lung Cancer in China," *Journal of Cancer Biology & Research* 2, pp. 1043, 1049 (2014).

34 WHO, "Household Air Pollution from Cooking, Heating and Lighting" (updated 2018), http://www.who.int/sustainable-development/housing/health-risks/household-air-pollution/en/ (accessed November 2018).

35 For example, see Michelle Ma, "UW Engineers to make Cookstoves 10 Times Cleaner for Developing World," *University of Washington News* (September 11, 2013), at http://www.washington.edu/news/2013/09/11/uw-engineers-get-grant-to-make-cookstoves-10-times-cleaner-for-developing-world/ (accessed November 2018).

36 Barry Commoner, *The Closing Circle* (New York: Knopf, 1971), p. 39.

37 Environmental Defense Fund, "How Cap and Trade Works," https://www.edf.org/climate/how-cap-and-trade-works (accessed November 2018).

38 EPA, "40th Anniversary of the Clean Air Act."

39 EPA, *Our Nation's Air 2017*, at https://gispub.epa.gov/air/trendsreport/2017/#welcome (accessed November 2018).

40 EPA, "Effects of Acid Rain," https://www.epa.gov/acidrain/effects-acid-rain (accessed November 2018); Michael Tennesen, "Acid Rain Returns –This Time It Is Caused by Nitrogen Emissions," *Scientific American* (June 21, 2010).

41 Joseph Kahn and Jim Yardley, "As China Roars, Pollution Reaches Deadly Extremes," *New York Times*, national edn (August 26, 2007).

42 Jim Yardley, "Bad Air and Water, and a Bully Pulpit in China," *New York Times*, national edn (September 25, 2004), p. A4.

43 Science Daily, "China's Sulfur Dioxide Emissions Fell Significantly while India's Grew Over Last Decade" (November 9, 2017), at https://www.sciencedaily.com/releases/2017/11/171109093255.htm (accessed November 2018).

44 Jane E. Brody, "Lead Persists As Threat To Young," *New York Times* (May 13, 1980), p. C3.

45 Mitch Leslie, "Peddling Lead," *Science*, 299 (February 7, 2003), p. 795.

46 Ibid.

47 Jane Brody, "Even Low Lead Levels Pose Perils for Children," *New York Times* (August 5, 2003), p. D7; see, e.g., Lisa H. Mason, et al., "Pb Neurotoxicity: Neuropsychological Effects of Lead Toxicity," *Biomed Research International* (2014), at https://www.ncbi.nlm.nih.gov/pmc/articles/PMC3909981/ (accessed November 2018).

48 *New York Times*, July 27, 1994, p. C20.

49 Brody, "Even Low Lead Levels Pose Perils for Children."

50 EPA, "Basic Information about Lead Air Pollution," https://www.epa.gov/lead-air-pollution/basic-information-about-lead-air-pollution#health (accessed November 2018).

51 Jennifer L. Doleac, "New Evidence that Lead Exposure Increases Crime," *Brookings* (June 1, 2017), at https://www.brookings.edu/blog/up-front/2017/06/01/new-evidence-that-lead-exposure-increases-crime/ (accessed November 2018).

52 "Lead Concentrations Down in Greenland Ice," *New York Times* (October 15, 1991), p. B8.

53 "Global Alliance Announces Goal to Eliminate Lead in Paint by 2020" (2015), https://www.unenvironment.org/news-and-stories/press-release/global-alliance-announces-goal-eliminate-lead-paint-2020 (accessed November 2018).

54 William Stevens, "Ozone Loss over US Is Found to Be Twice as Bad as Predicted," *New York Times* (April 5, 1991), p. A1.

55 NASA Study: "First Direct Proof of Ozone Hole Recovery Due to Chemicals Ban," January 4, 2018, at https://www.nasa.gov/feature/goddard/2018/nasa-study-first-direct-proof-of-ozone-hole-recovery-due-to-chemicals-ban (accessed November 2018); see also Associated Press, "The UN says the Earth's ozone layer is healing, and should be completely repaired by the 2030s, *Edmonton Journal* (November 5, 2018), at https://edmontonjournal.com/news/world/more-protection-un-says-earths-ozone-layer-is-healing/wcm/b453c1ae-b929-47ed-84cc-d3686fa8432c (accessed November 2018).

56 United Nations Environment Programme/World Meteorological Organization, "Ozone Layer on Track to Recovery: Success Story Should Encourage Action on Climate," (2014), https://www.unenvironment.org/news-and-stories/press-release/ozone-layer-track-recovery-success-story-should-encourage-action (accessed November 2018).

57 United States National Aeronautics and Space Administration, World Health Organization, United States Environmental Protection Agency, *Progress on Drinking Water, Sanitation and Hygiene* 11 (2017), at https://washdata.org/report/jmp-2017-report-final (accessed November 2018).

58 World Resources Institute (WRI), *The 1993 Information Please Environmental Almanac* (Boston: Houghton Mifflin, 1993), pp. 38–40.

59 EPA, "National Summary of Impaired Waters and TMDL information," Watershed Assessment, Tracking and Environmental Results, January 3, 2011, at http://iaspub.epa.gov/tmdl waters10/attains nation cy.control#prob source (accessed July 2015).

60 EPA, "National Summary of State Information": "National Summary: Causes of Impairment in Assessed Rivers and Streams," table, January 3, 2011, at http://iaspub.epa.gov/tmdl waters10/attains nation cy.control#prob source (accessed July 2015).

61 EPA, *National Water Quality Inventory: Report to Congress*, August 2017, p. 3, at https://www.epa.gov/sites/production/files/2017-12/documents/305brtc_finalowow_08302017.pdf (accessed November 2018).

62 See New York Freshwater Fishing, "2018-2019 New York State Department of Health (NYS DOH) Advisories for Chemicals in Sportfish," http://www.eregulations.com/newyork/fishing/health-advisories/ (accessed November 2018).

63 Michael Janofsky, "Mercury Taints Fish across US," *New York Times* (August 25, 2004), p. A19.

64 EPA, *2014 Technical Emissions Inventory, version 1: Technical Support Document*, 2-31 (December 2016), at https://www.epa.gov/sites/production/files/2016-12/documents/nei2014v1_tsd.pdf (accessed November 2018).

65 Richard Bernstein, "No Longer Europe's Sewer, but Not the Rhine of Yore," *New York Times* (April 21, 2006), p. A4; Institute of Fish Management, "River Rhine Salmon Comeback Campaign," 22 (2015), at http://www.salmoncomeback.org/wp-content/uploads/sites/14/2015/10/2015_Autumn_FISH_119_salmoncomeback_salmon-summit.pdf (accessed November 2018).

66 Andrew Revkin, "Stream Tests Show Traces of Array of Contaminants," *New York Times* (March 13, 2002), p. A14; and Andrew Revkin, "FDA Considers New Tests for Environmental Effects," *New York Times* (March 14, 2002), p. A20.

67 WHO, "Progress on Drinking Water, Sanitation and Hygiene," p. 16.

68 Duncan Hewitt, "China Announces Ambitious Plan to Clean up Its Water, Close Down Polluting Factories," *International Business Times* (April 17, 2015), at http://www.ibtimes.

com/china-announces-ambitious-plan-clean-its-water-close-down-polluting-factories-1886320 (accessed July 2015).

69   David Rohde, "Bangladesh Wells Pumping Poison as Cleanup Lags," *New York Times* (July 17, 2005), p. 6. For more on this problem see A. Mushtaque Chowdhury, "Arsenic Crisis in Bangladesh," *Scientific American*, 291 (August 2004), pp. 86–91.

70   Human Rights Watch, "Nepotism and Neglect: The Failing Response to Arsenic in the Drinking Water of Bangladesh's Rural Poor," 2 (2016); Sam Loewenberg, "The Poisoning of Bangladesh: How Arsenic Is Ravaging a Nation," *UN Dark* (August 16, 2017), at https://undark. org/article/bangladesh-arsenic-poisoning-drinking-water/ (accessed November 2018).

71   American Cancer Society, "Lifetime Risk of Developing or Dying from Cancer," January 10, 2014, citing US National Cancer Institute's Surveillance Epidemiology and End Results (SEER) database, at http://www.cancer.org/Cancer/CancerBasics/lifetime-probability-of-developing-or-dying-from-cancer (accessed July 2015).

72   "Study Hailed as Convincing in Tying Fat to Cancers," *New York Times* (April 24, 2003), p. A23; and Jane Brody, "Another Study Finds a Link between Excess Weight and Cancer," *New York Times* (May 6, 2003), p. D7.

73   C. M. Kitahara at al., "Association between Class III Obesity (BMI of 40-59 kg/m2) and Mortality: A Pooled Analysis of 20 Prospective Studies," *PloS Medicine*, 11(7), p. 1.

74   Robin C. Puett et al., "Particulate Matter Air Pollution Exposure, Distance to Road, and Incident Lung Cancer in the Nurses' Health Study Cohort," *Environmental Health Perspectives*, 122 (9) (2014), pp. 926–31; Solana Pyne, "Small Particles Add up to Big Disease Risk," *Science*, 295 (March 15, 2002), p. 1994.

75   President's Cancer Panel, *Reducing Environmental Cancer Risk: What We Can Do Now*, Annual Report, 2008–2009 (April 2010), p. ii, at http://deainfo.nci.nih.gov/ advisory/ pcp/annualReports/pcp08-09rpt/PCP_Report_08-09_508.pdf (accessed July 2015).

76   Ibid.

77   Barry Commoner, *The Closing Circle* (New York: Knopf, 1971), p. 261.

78   An encouraging development in the United States in the mid-2000s was the decision by the US chemical giant DuPont to spend about 10 percent of its research budget on trying to find biological-based substances, such as in corn and in sugar, to replace fossil fuels as the building blocks of its chemicals. But for the near future, DuPont, like other chemical companies, is counting on chemicals based on fossil fuels to make most of its profit. See Claudia Deutsch, "DuPont Looking to Displace Fossil Fuels as Building Blocks of Chemicals," *New York Times* (February 28, 2006), p. C1. This movement towards biological-based substances is also catching on globally, with products from biofuels and bio-based lubricants to bioplastics and cleaners being developed around the world. Kate Bachman, "Biotechnology to Fossil Fuels: Game On," *Fabricators and Manufacturers Association, International* (March 6, 2015), https://www.fmanet.org/blog/2015/03/06/biotechnology-fossil-fuels-game (accessed November 2018).

79   Rebecca Renner, "Scotchgard Scotched," *Scientific American*, 284 (March 2001), p. 18; and Jennifer Lee, "EPA Orders Companies to Examine Effects of Chemicals," *New York Times* (April 15, 2003), p. D2.

80   Tiffany Kary and Christopher Cannon, "Cancer-linked Chemicals Manufactured by 3M Are Turning Up in Drinking Water," *Bloomberg* (November 2, 2018), https://www.bloomberg. com/graphics/2018-3M-groundwater-pollution-problem/ (accessed November 2018).

81   See EPA, "DDT – A Brief History and Status," https://www.epa.gov/ingredients-used-pesticide-products/ddt-brief-history-and-status (last updated January 2017) (accessed November 2018).

82   Philip Hilts, "Results of Study on Pesticide Encourage Effort to Cut Use," *New York Times* (July 5, 1993), p. 8.

83   Ibid.

84   Matthew Wald, "Citing Children, Environmental Protection Agency Is Banning Common Pesticide," *New York Times* (August 3, 1999), p. A1.

85   Michael Janofsky, "Environmental Groups Are Praising the EPA for Updating Cancer-Risk Guidelines," *New York Times* (April 4, 2005), p. A18.

86   World Atlas, "Top Pesticide Using Countries," https://www.worldatlas.com/articles/top-pesticide-consuming-countries-of-the-world.html (last updated April 25, 2017) (accessed November 2018).

87   EPA, "Pesticides Industry Sales and Usage: 2008-2012 Market Estimates," (2017), p. 9, at https://www.epa.gov/sites/production/files/2017-01/documents/pesticides-industry-sales-usage-2016_0.pdf (accessed November 2018).

88   "US Waste and Recycling," *New York Times* (August 20, 2002), p. D4.

89   EPA, *Municipal Solid Waste*, at https://archive.epa.gov/epawaste/nonhaz/municipal/web/html/ (last updated March 29, 2016) (accessed November 2018).

90   Seattle Public Utilities, "Recycling Rates," http://www.seattle.gov/util/MyServices/Rates/RecyclingRates/index.htm (accessed November 2018).

91   Katie Brigham, "How San Francisco sends less trash to the landfill than any other major U.S. city," *CNBC* (July 14, 2018), at https://www.cnbc.com/2018/07/13/how-san-francisco-became-a-global-leader-in-waste-management.html (accessed November 2018).

92   Roland Oliphant, "Bali declares rubbish emergency as rising tide of plastic buries beaches," *The Telegraph* (December 28, 2017), at https://www.telegraph.co.uk/news/2017/12/28/bali-declares-rubbish-emergency-rising-tide-plastic-buries-beaches/ (accessed November 2018).

93   Ian Sample, "Plastic-eating Worms could Help Wage War on Waste," *The Guardian* (April 24, 2017), at https://www.theguardian.com/science/2017/apr/24/plastic-munching-worms-could-help-wage-war-on-waste-galleria-mellonella (accessed November 2018); Damian Carrington, "Scientists Accidentally Create Mutant Enzyme that Eats Plastic Bottles," *The Guardian* (April 16, 2018), at https://www.theguardian.com/environment/2018/apr/16/scientists-accidentally-create-mutant-enzyme-that-eats-plastic-bottles (accessed November 2018). Charles Moore, "Trashed," *Natural History*, 112 (November 2003), p. 51.

94   Ibid., p. 50. For a report on the increase of plastic fibers in the beaches and seabed of the British Isles, see Andrew Revkin, "Plastics Permeate Even the Seabed," *New York Times* (May 11, 2004), p. D2.

95   Shaena Montanari, "Plastic Garbage Patch Bigger Than Mexico Found in Pacific," *National Geographic* (July 25, 2017), at https://news.nationalgeographic.com/2017/07/ocean-plastic-patch-south-pacific-spd/ (accessed November 2018).

96   Moore, "Trashed," p. 50.

97   National Geographic, "Great Pacific Garbage Patch," at http://education.national geo-graphic.com/education/encyclopedia/great-pacific-garbage-patch/?ar_a=1 (accessed July 2015).

98   Ibid.

99   For general information on international efforts to regulate mercury, see the Minamata Convention website at www.mercuryconvention.org; for the text of the treaty, see http://www.mercuryconvention.org/Portals/11/documents/conventionText/Minamata%20Convention%20on%20Mercury_e.pdf (both accessed July 2015).

100 "Choosing Love Canal for a Neighbor," *Buffalo News* (February 10, 2013), at http://www.buffalonews.com/20130210/choosing_love_canal_for_a_neighbor.html (accessed July 2015).

101 EPA, "Crude Oil and Natural Gas Waste," https://archive.epa.gov/epawaste/nonhaz/industrial/special/web/html/index-16.html (last updated April 19, 2016) (accessed November 2018).

102 In the United States, Scorecard, a pollution information website, enables individuals to enter a US-based zipcode to see local toxic chemical releases, see www.scorecard.org (accessed July 2015); see also US EPA Toxic Release Inventory website at https://www.epa.gov/toxics-release-inventory-tri-program (accessed April 2019).

103 EPA, "2013 TRI National Analysis: Releases of Chemicals," at http://www2.epa.gov/toxics-release-inventory-tri-program/2013-tri-national-analysis-releases-chemicals, available via archive at https://archive.epa.gov/epa/sites/production/files/2014-12/documents/6_tri_na_tri_beyond.pdf (accessed April 2019).

104 EPA, "2013 TRI National Analysis: Land Disposal – Trend in Land Disposal," at http://www2.epa.gov/toxics-release-inventory-tri-program/2013-tri-national-analysis-land-disposal-trend-land-disposal; EPA, "2013 TRI National Analysis: Air Disposal – Trend in Air Disposal," at http://www2.epa.gov/toxics-release-inventory-tri-program/ 2013-tri-national-analysis-air-releases-trend-air-releases (all accessed July 2015).

105 Lindsey Konkel, "These Chemicals in Pizza Boxes and Carpeting Last Forever," *National Geographic* (May 1, 2015), at https://news.nationalgeographic.com/2015/05/150501-perfluorinated-chemicals-dupont-teflon-science/ (accessed November 2018).

106 Eldbjorg S. Heimstad et al., *Scientific Program 2011-2015 for Hazardous Substances – Effects on Ecosystem and Health*, High North Research Centre for Climate and the Environment (2012), p. 2, at http://www.ifram.no/getfile.php/3149282.2368.rscybybqsf/Program-Hazardous+substances.pdf.

107 Ibid.

108 EPA, "Superfund's 25th Anniversary: Capturing the Past, Charting the Future," at http://www.epa.gov/superfund/accomp/news/25anniversary.htm (accessed July 2015).

109 EPA, "Superfund Special Accounts," January 12, 2015, at http://www2.epa.gov/ enforce-ment/superfund-special-accounts (accessed July 2015).

110 Barbara Ward, *Progress for a Small Planet* (New York: W. W. Norton, 1979), pp. 65–6.

111 Michael Royston, "Making Pollution Prevention Pay," *Harvard Business Review* (November/December 1980), p. 12.

112 Heinrich von Lersner, "Commentary: Outline for an Ecological Economy," *Scientific American*, 273 (September 1995), p. 188; German Environment Agency, *What Matters 2016: Annual Report of the German Environment Agency* (2016), p. 6.

113 World Resources Institute (WRI), United Nations Environment Programme, United Nations Development Programme, and World Bank, *World Resources 1998–99: Environmental Change and Human Health* (Washington, DC: WRI, 1999), p. 167.

114 Lester Thurow, *The Zero-Sum Society* (New York: Basic Books, 1980), pp. 104–5.

115 Commoner, *The Closing Circle*, pp. 45–6.

116 William Ophuls, *Ecology and the Politics of Scarcity* (San Francisco: W. H. Freeman, 1977), p. 75.

117 See, e.g. Jason Hickel, "Why Growth Can't Be Green," *Foreign Policy* (September 12, 2018), at https://foreignpolicy.com/2018/09/12/why-growth-cant-be-green/ (accessed November 2018).

118 Charles Birch, *Confronting the Future* (New York: Penguin, 1976), p. 35.

Further Reading

Arthus-Bertrand, Yann, *Earth from Above*, revised and expanded edn (New York: Henry Abrams, 2002). From a helicopter flying over 60 countries, the author records the beauty of the Earth as well as its spoiled places. These stunning photographs give a rarely seen view of the Earth.

Brown, Phil, and Edwin J. Mikkelsen, *No Safe Place: Toxic Waste, Leukemia, and Community Action* (Berkeley: University of California Press, 1990). This book documents the efforts of a small group of citizens – led by a mother whose son had acute leukemia – to uncover the source of illness in their community. It describes their battle to overcome resistance by their neighbors and the indifference of local and state government officials.

Clayton, Susan, and Gene Myers, *Conservation Psychology; Understanding and Promoting Human Care of Nature* (Oxford: Wiley-Blackwell, 2009). The authors use psychological perspectives to try to answer such questions as "What is the relationship between individuals learning about environmental problems and their conservation attitudes, knowledge, beliefs, and behaviors?"

Daily, Gretchen, and Katherine Ellison, *The New Economy of Nature: The Quest to Make Conservation Profitable* (Washington, DC: Island Press, 2002). The authors show that the environment provides services that have an economic value. That recognition can lead to arrangements (like carbon trading) based on mutual self-interest and an understanding by all that conservation pays. Highly readable.

McKibben, Bill, "A Special Moment in History," *Atlantic Monthly* (May 1998), pp. 55–78. In simple but powerful prose, McKibben argues that we live in a very important time in the history of the planet. He believes the fate of the planet for many years to come will be determined by the lifestyle, population, and technological choices we make in the next few decades.

Pearce, Fred, *When the Rivers Run Dry: Water – the Defining Crisis of the Twenty-First Century* (Boston: Beacon Press, 2006). An experienced science journalist, Pearce visits over 30 countries during his research for this book. With a growing population and increased urban and agricultural needs, the world is withdrawing increasing amounts of water from its rivers and aquifers. Unless new water efficiencies are soon adopted, a water crisis is ahead.

Safina, Carl, *The View from Lazy Point: A Natural Year in an Unnatural World* (New York: Henry Holt, 2010). This naturalist's base is a cottage in the United States. During a year he travels about the world returning from time to time to his cottage to tell of the perilous times in which we live and of which we seem to be unaware. As a review in the *New York Times* states, "Safina's account …can be harrowing, but its impassioned, informed urgency is also filled with hope, joy, and love."

Speth, James Gustave, *Red Sky at Morning: America and the Crisis of the Global Environment* (New Haven, CT: Yale University Press, 2004). Speth explores some of the fundamental reasons for the environmental deterioration occurring in the world. He seeks to explain why a number of economic indicators continue to show growth at the same time that serious environmental deterioration is occurring.

Steingraber, Sandra, *Having Faith: An Ecologist's Journey to Motherhood* (Cambridge, MA: Perseus, 2001). What's it like for a woman who knows a lot about chemicals and their effects on human beings to have a baby today? Streingraber explains but also analyzes how we got to where we accept that residues of many toxic chemicals in our world are all right.

Williams, Michael, *Deforesting the Earth: From Prehistory to Global Crisis* (Chicago: University of Chicago Press, 2003). A reviewer in *Science* has called this book "the most comprehensive account ever written of when, where, and how humans have wrought what is surely the most dramatic change in Earth's surface since the end of the Pleistocene 10,000 years ago."

Chapter 9

Technology[1]

Will mankind murder Mother Earth or will he redeem her? He could murder her by misusing his increasing technological potency.
Arnold J. Toynbee, *Mankind and Mother Earth* (1976)

---

1 Liz Schmitt contributed substantially to the research and updates reflected in this edition. Please reflect her contribution in any direct citation to this chapter.

Global Issues: An Introduction, Sixth Edition. Kristen A. Hite and John L. Seitz.
© 2021 John Wiley & Sons Ltd. Published 2021 by John Wiley & Sons Ltd.

Technology is the application of science to solve problems. To many people, technology and development are synonymous. Technology is what makes economic growth and social change happen. The limited use of high technology by the less developed nations is sometimes given as one of the reasons why they are less developed and less prosperous than the industrialized nations.

But the relationship between technology and development is a complicated one. At times the negative features of technology seem to outweigh the positive features. Technology can cause a society to change in some very undesirable ways. In this chapter, after a short section on the benefits of technology, we will look closely at some of the negative relationships between technology and development.

Benefits of Technology

A book such as this one, whose readers will probably be mostly from the developed nations and the rapidly rising developing countries, does not need to dwell on the benefits of technology. Advertising and the mass media herald the expected joys that will come with a new product, technique, or discovery. In the United States people are socialized to like new things; they are also pragmatic, which means that technology is commonly used to make things work "better." They would have to be foolish not to recognize the benefits that technology has brought.

Technological interdependence comes from the information and transportation revolutions that are occurring in the world. Computers, the internet (and particularly social networks), television, and airplanes now link the world. Phone calls, emails, and other communications may get routed through other countries and/or outer space before reaching their intended recipient. In some ways, high speed digital connections across the world are closer for communication purposes than conventional communications with someone located one town away.

One of the main reasons much of the world envies technologically abundant countries such as the United States is that its technology has in many real ways made life more comfortable and stimulating, with reduced drudgery. People who have easy and cheap access to these kinds of technologies need to remember this. But they and others also need to learn several other lessons: (1) short-term benefits from using a technology can have long-term negative consequences; (2) there can be unanticipated consequences of using a technology; (3) the use of some types of technology in certain situations can be inappropriate; and (4) there are many problems that technology cannot solve. The inability to learn these lessons could lead to our destruction, as the case studies in this chapter show. Some people seem to always pick the most advanced technology, others prefer proven methods even if they have limitations, and still others advocate a middle path of using precaution to select the appropriate level of technology without always assuming the most advanced form is best.

> ## Benefits of technology
>
> In personal terms, technology has allowed the authors of this book to visit dozens of countries; to see a photograph of the Earth taken from space; to easily communicate from different countries on personal computers that greatly facilitated the writing of this book; to wear shirts that don't need ironing; and to keep the glaucoma of one of the authors under control to prevent him from going blind. What items would your list include?

Unanticipated Consequences of the Use of Technology

Ecology is the study of the relationships between organisms and their environments. Without a knowledge of ecology, we are tempted to use technology to solve a single problem. But there are many examples to illustrate the truth that we cannot change one part of the human environment without in some way affecting other parts. Often these other effects are harmful, and often they are completely unanticipated, as the box about cats nicely illustrates.[1]

Plate 9.1 Without modern technology to help, necessary tasks can be difficult. A woman in Nepal breaks up clumps of soil to prepare the land for planting

Source: Ab Abercrombie

The case of the parachuting cats

A situation in Borneo nicely illustrates the fact that the use of a new technology can lead to unanticipated consequences. In this situation, health officials wanted to destroy malaria-carrying mosquitoes so they began to spray DDT on the outside and inside of the homes of villagers. After the spraying, the roofs of many homes began to collapse because they were being eaten by caterpillars. The spraying had killed not just the mosquitoes but also a predatory wasp that had kept the caterpillars under control. The DDT spraying also killed many houseflies, which were then consumed by the gecko, a little lizard that inhabits many village homes and eats houseflies. The geckos died and were then consumed by household cats. When the cats died, rats invaded the homes and began consuming the villagers' food and brought a danger of plague. This led to the need to parachute cats into villages in order to try to restore the balance that the widespread spraying of DDT had upset.

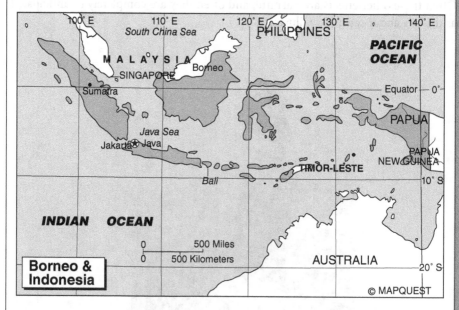

Map 9.1   Borneo and Indonesia

Source: "Ecology: The New Great Chain of Being," *Natural History*, 77 (December 1968), p. 8.

DDT

The previously widespread use of DDT in many countries offered a cheap way to control pests like mosquitoes but also had major unanticipated effects since it is persistent (it does not easily break down into harmless substances) and is poisonous to many forms of life, as discussed in Chapter 8.[2] The reduced use of DDT in many nations, as the detrimental effects of DDT became known, led to a resurgence in malaria. The World Health Organization has given conditional approval for the use of DDT for the control of malaria when "locally safe, effective, and affordable alternatives are not available."[3]

Natural gas fracking: when innovation advances faster than regulation

In the United States alone, natural gas production increased by roughly 50 percent in the decade between 2005 and 2015. This is due in large part to technological innovation, a combination of hydrological fracturing and directional drilling to extract oil and gas trapped in dense rock (e.g., "shale gas"). This extraction technique is commonly referred to as "fracking," and it is quickly changing national and even global energy supplies.

While many have touted natural gas as a "transition fuel" for climate change as it was initially viewed as the most climate-friendly option among fossil fuels, gas production through fracking appears to be advancing at a faster pace than a full understanding of the risks, with regulation evolving at a slower pace than technological innovation. Some of the alleged risks include exploding wells, earthquakes, methane leaks that offset climate gains from reduced carbon emissions, and toxic pollution from fracking fluids that contaminate water and land.

Citing these risks, some groups of concerned citizens and landowners have called for more regulation of fracking activities. As a result, some governments are actively developing regulations governing fracking, but the fracking industry is not waiting for regulations to be put in place to scale up production. Proponents of fracking say that it reduces reliance on foreign energy supplies and lowers natural gas prices, which also helps reduce greenhouse gas emissions that cause climate change.

For the most part, fracking remains a weakly regulated activity with significant risks, even as its supplies are already impacting national and global energy supplies and prices.

Sources: Thomas W. Merrill, "Four Questions about Fracking," *Case Western Reserve Law Review*, 63 (2013); Scott Disavino, "Are the Good Times Over for Growth in US Shale Gas?" Reuters, March 17, 2015; Trevor M. Penning et al., "Environmental Health Research Recommendations from the Inter-Environmental Health Sciences Core Center Working Group on Unconventional Natural Gas Drilling Operations," *Environmental Health Perspectives*, 122 (11) (2014), p. 1155.

Factory farms

Let's look at factory farms and the unanticipated consequences that have come with the adoption of factory techniques to produce animals for human consumption. Such techniques have been adopted to raise poultry, pigs, veal calves, and cattle. The techniques allow large numbers of animals to be raised in a relatively small space. (Many of these animals never see the light of day until they are removed for slaughter.) The crowding of many animals in a small space and the confinement of individual animals in small stalls creates stress in the animals. Stress can lower the natural defenses of the animals to diseases, and the crowded conditions facilitate the rapid spreading of diseases among the animals. It is common in the United States for factory-raised animals to receive large doses of antibiotics in their feed to prevent the outbreak of diseases and to promote growth.

There is now evidence that the abundant use of antibiotics in animal food is creating bacteria that are resistant to treatment by modern drugs and that these bacteria can cause illness in humans.[4] Following the recommendations of the World Health Organization, the European Union in 1998 banned the placing of antibiotics that are used to treat illnesses in human beings in animal food to promote growth of the animal and to prevent diseases. Denmark stopped their use in 1999 and found that by improving the sanitary conditions of its animals there were generally no negative consequences of the ban. The only exception was with pigs, where there were more intestinal infections and thus a small increase in production costs.[5]

In the US, medical researchers reported in 2001 that antibiotic-resistant bacteria were widespread in meats and poultry sold in the country and could be found in consumers' intestines. This began a series of increasingly elevated concerns that many food-borne illnesses would not respond to the usual treatments and that some could be resistant to all commercially available medications.[6] 60 percent of all medically important antibiotics sold in the United States are purchased for farm animal use, and most of it is dispensed in food and water without a veterinary prescription, which has been raised as one of the reasons for increasing antibiotic resistance.[7] In 2010, the US Food and Drug Administration asked farmers to stop giving unnecessary antibiotics to livestock, out of concerns that the antibiotics are contributing to drug-resistant bacteria that endanger human lives.[8]

McDonald's made an important decision in 2003 that could help reduce the use of antibiotics in foods.[9] (Because McDonald's buys such a large amount of food for its fast-food outlets, its decisions influence the practices of the food industry.) It announced that it was going to require its poultry suppliers to eliminate the use of medically important antibiotics for growth promotion. It did not require this of its beef suppliers, but encouraged them to follow this policy also.

As discussed previously in Chapter 4, controversy regarding factory-sized farms is growing. The average size of farms has grown significantly in recent decades, as has the scale of pollution impacts such as methane emissions and water runoff. For example, in the late 1990s special attention was being given to large hog farms that were tending to dominate the industry. The number of hogs grown on an average swine farm in the US rose from about 900 in the early 1990s to more than 8,000 in 2009.[10] Complaints came from small farmers who could not compete with large factory farms and also from nearby residents. The foul smell from the farms was at times very powerful and the large amount of animal waste presented a real danger to underground water supplies. Some of the large hog farms produce as much raw sewage as a middle-sized city, but without sewage treatment plants. The Environmental Protection Agency in 2008 issued a new rule requiring large factory farms to implement new manure management practices, including obtaining a permit for any discharges/runoff that the farm can't contain.[11]

A recent trend is to use more appropriate technology to satisfy the growing demand for more sustainable agriculture. (This subject was discussed in Chapter 4 on food under the section on alternative/sustainable/organic agriculture.) For example, manure from animal farming is often spread as a fertilizer on crop farms. The manure has a high concentration of nitrogen and phosphorus, nutrients which can reduce the need to buy expensive inputs like fertilizer. Notably, industrial-scale farms are beginning to more widely adopt this, which parallels more traditional integrated crop systems. Although this can reduce fertilizer expenses, it does not resolve the pollution problems created by large scale production on these larger farms.

The defenders of large hog farms cite the demand by consumers for low-cost, lean pork. Their farms can produce this because the pigs are genetically designed to produce the desired cut of meat. The defenders also cite the need for the jobs in rural areas and tax revenue that their farms provide.

Critics point to the environmental and health hazards, as well as substantial climate impacts from the methane emitted. Some of the wastes from large and concentrated populations of hogs, chickens, and cows wash into rivers and bays during heavy rains and are suspected of contributing to blooms of toxic algae which consume much of the oxygen in places like the Gulf of Mexico off Louisiana, one of the largest so-called "dead zones" covering 22,000 square kilometers.[12]

Inappropriate Uses of Technology

In 1973, E. F. Schumacher published his book *Small Is Beautiful: Economics as if People Mattered*.[13] This book became the foundation for a movement that seeks to use technology in ways that are not harmful to people. Schumacher argued that poor countries would best benefit from intermediate (or "appropriate") technology, not the high (or "hard") technology of the Western industrialized nations. Intermediate technology lies in between the "low" technology common in the rural areas of the less developed countries – where many of the world's people live – and the technology of the industrialized world, which tends to use vast amounts of energy, pollutes the environment, requires imported resources, and often alienates the workers from their own work. The intermediate technology movement seeks to identify those areas of life in the global South, and also in the industrialized West, where a relatively simple technology can make people's work easier while remaining meaningful – that is, giving them a feeling of satisfaction when they do it.

The high technology of industrialized countries is often very expensive, and thus large amounts of capital are needed to acquire it, capital that many do not have. This technology is referred to as being capital intensive instead of labor intensive. This means that money – but not many people – is needed to obtain it and maintain it. In other words, high technology does not give many workers jobs. (This is the essence of the mass-production line: lots of products by a relatively small number of workers.) But a big problem in many nations – including in wealthy economies, especially when in a recession – is that there are not enough jobs for those seeking them in the first place. Employment challenges become even more intense when factoring in the dramatic flows away from rural areas increasingly towards cities.

While it is fairly obvious, and widely recognized, that nations and people generally should select technologies that are appropriate to their needs, why don't they always do this? Why has this seemingly simple "lesson" not been learned? The authors of a study of World Bank experiences over nearly four decades explain why they believe inappropriate technology is frequently chosen:

> Why does this happen? Foreign consultants or advisers may advocate the technology with which they are most familiar. Local engineers, if educated abroad or the heirs of a colonial legacy, may have acquired a similar bias in favor of advanced technology, or they may simply presume, as do their superiors, that what is modern is best. Special interest groups may favor a particular technical approach. ... Deep-seated customs and traditions may favor certain solutions and make others unacceptable. Economic policies ... may send distorted signals to decision makers. A simple lack of knowledge or reluctance to experiment may limit the range of choice. ... When aid is tied to the supply of equipment from the donor country ... freedom to choose an appropriate technology may be compromised. With so many factors at work, it is not surprising that a "simple" lesson – such as selecting an appropriate technology – may prove far from simple to apply.[14]

I (Seitz) witnessed the inappropriate use of high technology in both Liberia and the United States. As part of US economic assistance to Liberia, we gave the Liberians road-building equipment. That equipment included power saws. As I proceeded to turn some of this equipment over to Liberians in a small town in a rural area, I realized that the power saws we were giving them were very inappropriate. To people who had little or no experience with power tools – which applied to nearly all the Liberians in that town – the power saw was a deadly instrument. Also, they would not be able to maintain or repair them when they broke down. Their noise would ruin the peacefulness of the area. A much more appropriate form of assistance would have been crates of axes and hand saws, tools that they could easily learn to use safely, that they would be able to maintain and repair themselves, and that would have provided work for many people. This is only one example of many similar cases of well-intentioned assistance that fails when not integrated with local economic systems.

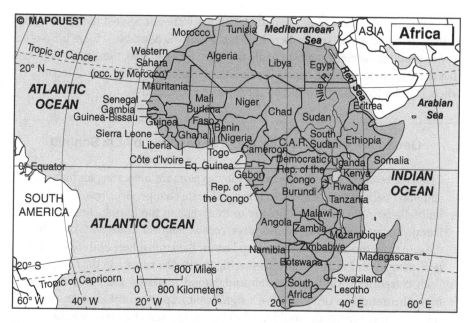

Map 9.2 Africa

In the United States, both authors of this book became aware of the inappropriate use of high technology as their respective families began to prepare for the birth of their children. Most children in the world are born at home, but in wealthier areas, most births take place in hospitals. While widespread access to hospitals can help reduce both maternal and infant mortality rates, an impressive number of studies also show that moving births into hospitals has resulted in unnecessary interventions in the birth process by doctors and hospital staff, which upset the natural stages of labor and can jeopardize the health of both the mother and the baby.[15] While giving birth in hospitals has the important benefit of access to life-saving technologies in the event of medical complications, in many cases hospitals may also steer towards higher technology interventions than what is optimal or necessary for the mother and/or the child. As many as 85 to 90 percent of women can give birth naturally, without the need for advanced mechanical technologies.[16] Prenatal care can often identify many of the 10 to 15 percent who need medical interventions to give birth, and for them the use of high technology can help protect the lives of the mother and baby. But the major error that has been made is that procedures that are appropriate for these few are now routinely used for most births – including intensive surgical processes – often out of "convenience" as opposed to medical necessity. Midwives and home births are growing in popularity in countries like the US and many expectant parents are increasingly questioning the cultural norms of hospital births, Caesarian sections, and pain medication.[17] (Author Hite and author Seitz's wife were both grateful to use a low-technology midwife for the births of their first children to minimize medical interventions.)

Overall, proponents of intermediate technology are not against high technology as such (they recognize areas where high technology is desirable – there is no other way to produce vaccines against deadly diseases, for example), but simply maintain that there is no need to use expensive and complicated "high" or "hard" technology where simpler technology would be appropriate and effective.

Geoengineering the Climate: a case study by Liz Schmitt

Given the severity of the climate crisis, some experts are advocating for high-tech and potentially risky solutions to reverse climate change. *Geoengineering* is an umbrella term for using technology to intervene in the Earth's climate, quite literally to change it in one of two ways: *carbon removal strategies* take carbon dioxide from the air before it can trap heat in the atmosphere and *solar radiation management* stops heat from entering the Earth's surface in the first place. Both categories include some well-understood methods and some that are more theoretical; in order to have a significant impact on the climate, one or several of these methods would need to be undertaken at a massive scale.

Carbon removal strategies

The simplest, lowest technology way to store up carbon that would otherwise reach the atmosphere and trap heat, is by planting trees at massive scale, which is likely lowest risk but also is limited in terms of how much land is available to implement this solution.

Ocean iron fertilization is a controversial technique of dumping iron into the ocean to spark a phytoplankton bloom, relying on phytoplankton to eat carbon dioxide and then sink to the ocean floor and keep it there. But not only is the longevity of the carbon sink unsure, the collateral damage to the ocean is very risky, including depleting large sections of ocean of oxygen, increasing ocean acidification, and shaking up the ocean's food webs. This technique has already been tried at least once, with unsanctioned impacts.[18]

Additional options for carbon capture and storage include the following.

Geological carbon capture and storage involves pumping compressed gases produced from the burning of fossil fuels into spent coal mines and emptied natural gas veins. The risk is that a seismic or other event could release a huge quantity of compressed gas back into the atmosphere, which not only hurts the climate but may also have other dangerous effects.

Bioenergy with Carbon Capture and Sequestration (BECCS) involves farming carbon-absorbing biofuel crops such as corn and switchgrass, and then burning the plants for energy while chemically separating the exhaust, which is processed to prevent emissions going into the atmosphere. The challenges of this approach include not only the risks of leakage back into the atmosphere but also the issue of increasing land scarcity and competition with growing food.

In *Direct Air Capture and Storage (DACS)*, air filters capture carbon dioxide right from air passing through for underground storage, and not only is this technology very expensive, but the risks are not yet fully understood.[19]

Solar Radiation Management: Sunlight Reflective Technologies[20]
The potential *solar radiation management* has on global temperatures is largely unknown. Proposed methods include:

* *giant space mirrors* to reflect some sunshine before it enters the Earth's atmosphere;
* *clearing northern forests* to create more reflective snowy surfaces – which paradoxically releases more carbon by cutting down trees;
* *using genetic engineering to make crops more reflective* – without knowing how these crops might differ in their impact on the soil, water use, or nutritional content;
* *covering large landscapes with white plastic*, whether they be deserts or glaciers – with potentially significant impacts on local ecosystems;
* *painting roofs white*, although solar panels are typically a more cost effective solution;
* *brightening marine clouds* with sea salt to form shiny, low-altitude marine clouds; and
* *releasing aerosols into the atmosphere* that reflect light similar to large volcanic eruptions.[21]

But these ideas, while they seem to some a potential magic bullet, are risky and have consequences, like lowering the ozone in the stratosphere and shifting rainfall patterns.

For all these potential solutions, the risks are global and potentially irreversible, and may also carry serious geopolitical consequences. Not only that, but there have already been cases of weaponizing the weather, such as by causing more precipitation in an area by injecting aerosols into the air.[22] And critics caution against becoming dependent on any climate modification techniques that do not get to the root of the problem: reducing greenhouse gas emissions.[23]

At what point will someone or some state decide to massively deploy any of these geoengineering technologies? Will this save us from the most catastrophic scenarios possible with climate change? Or will geoengineering leave us instead with new global problems caused by risky deployments of climate-altering technologies? Unless greenhouse gas emissions are reduced quickly, we may begin to see answers to these questions sooner rather than later.

Limits to the "Technological Fix"

In US society, which makes wide use of technology, there is a common belief that technology can solve the most urgent problems. It is even believed that the problems that science and technology have created can be solved by more science and technology. What is lacking, according to this way of thinking, is an adequate use of science and technology to solve the problem at hand. In other words, we must find a "technological fix."

While the ability of technology to solve certain problems is impressive, there are a number of serious problems confronting humans – in fact, probably the most serious problems which humans have ever faced – which seem to have no technological solution. Technology itself has often played a major role in causing these problems. Let's look at a few of them.

There is no question that birth control is a dramatic technological development in the field of family planning. However, the mere existence of birth control has limited impacts on population size, illustrating limits to a pure technological approach. As discussed earlier in Chapter 3, cultural and social differences play a significant role in determining family size. Some have focused, for example, on the social and cultural dimensions of women's freedom to choose whether and what kind of birth control to use.[24] Others have argued that educating more girls has more impact than birth control in determining future population levels.[25]

Huge municipal sanitation plants were once considered the solution to our polluted streams, rivers, and lakes, but the rising costs of these plants and the fact that they treat only part of the polluted water are bringing this solution into question.[26] As much water pollution is caused by agricultural and urban runoff, both of which are not treated by the plants, as by sewage. To talk about a technological fix for this problem is to talk about spending astronomical sums of money to treat all polluted water, and even then the solution would still be in doubt. A more cost-effective solution could be to limit the creation of agricultural and urban runoff into waterways, using "low-tech" natural ecosystem services like vegetation buffers between roads and rivers or regulating how industrial-scale agricultural operations manage animal manure. Pollution is always easier to mitigate either by preventing its creation or treating it at the source than it is to address downstream.

A final example will be given to illustrate the limits to the technological fix. As we will see in the case study below, the nuclear arms race between the Soviet Union and the United States after World War II threatened the world with a death toll beyond comprehension. Many believed that technology would solve this problem; all that was needed to gain security was better weapons and more weapons than the other side. But the history of the arms race, which lasted nearly half a century until the disintegration of the Soviet Union in the early 1990s, clearly shows that one side's advantage was soon matched or surpassed by new weapons on the other side. Momentary feelings of security by one nation were soon replaced by deepening insecurity felt by both nations as the weapons became more lethal. "Security dilemma" is the phrase that has been coined to describe a situation where one nation's efforts to gain security lead to its opponent's feeling of insecurity. This insecurity causes the nation that believes it is behind in the arms race to build up its arms, but it also causes the other nation to feel insecure. So the race goes on. The temptation to believe that a new weapon will solve the problem is immense. A brief history of the arms race shows how both superpowers were caught in a security dilemma.

The United States exploded its first atomic bomb in 1945 (see below) and felt fairly secure until the Soviets exploded one in 1949. In 1954, the United States tested the first operational thermonuclear weapon (a hydrogen or H-bomb), which uses the A-bomb as a trigger, and a year later the Soviets followed suit. In 1957, the Soviets successfully tested the first intercontinental ballistic missile (ICBM) and launched the Earth's first artificial satellite, Sputnik. The United States felt very insecure but within three years had more operational ICBMs than the Soviet Union. (This "missile gap," in which the Soviets trailed, could have been the reason they put missiles in Cuba in 1962, which led to the Cuban missile crisis, the world's first approach to the brink of nuclear war. The humiliation the Soviet Union suffered when it had to take its missiles out of Cuba may have led to its buildup of nuclear arms in the 1970s and 1980s, which caused great concern in the United States.)

The Soviet Union put up the first antiballistic missile system around a city – around Moscow – in the 1960s, and in 1968 the United States countered by developing multiple, independently targetable reentry vehicles (MIRVs), which could easily overwhelm the Soviet antiballistic missiles. The Soviets started deploying their first MIRVs in 1975, and these highly accurate missiles with as many as ten warheads on a single missile, each one able to hit a different target, led President Reagan in 1981 to declare that a "window of vulnerability" existed, since the land-based US ICBMs could now be attacked by the Soviet MIRVs. Reagan began a massive military buildup.

The technological race was poised to move into space when President Reagan in 1983 announced plans to develop a defensive system, some of which would probably be based in space, which could attack any Soviet missiles fired at the United States. This system (formally known as the Strategic Defense Initiative, and informally called "Star Wars") was criticized by many US scientists as not being feasible, and by the early 1990s it had been greatly reduced in scope. The United States in the first decade of the twenty-first century was still planning to build a much-reduced missile shield to guard against accidents and possible attack by unfriendly developing countries that have recently acquired nuclear weapons. An unexpected end to the nuclear arms race between the Soviet Union and the United States came in the late 1980s with the collapse of the Soviet empire in Europe and with the breakup of the Soviet Union itself in the early 1990s. The huge financial strain on its economy caused by the arms race undoubtedly contributed to its collapse. But the nuclear arms race also placed serious strains on the US economy. The end of the Cold War brought the world a nearly miraculous release from the danger of a third world war, which likely would have been the world's last one.

In the first decade of the twenty-first century – over the objection of China and Russia – the United States started to build a limited defense against nuclear missiles, supposedly from so-called "rogue states," or from an accidental launch. Countries such as North Korea and Iran were unfriendly to the United States and to the West in general and had some ability already, or would have in the future, to build nuclear missiles. Meanwhile, some of the biggest emerging threats became not large-scale nuclear weapons but rather smaller ones with a more limited radius that could be made with materials whose supplies are more difficult to limit and control.

War

Why do human beings make war? Some of the people who have studied the causes of war believe that war is caused by the negative aspects of human nature, such as selfishness, possessiveness, irrationality, and aggressiveness. Other students of war have come to the conclusion that certain types of government – or, more formally, how political power is distributed within the state – make some countries more war-like than others. And other analysts have concluded that international anarchy, or the absence of a world government where disputes can be settled peacefully and authoritatively, is the main cause of war. Kenneth Waltz, a respected US student of war, concluded that human nature and/or the type of government are often the immediate causes of war, but that international anarchy explains why war has recurred throughout human history.[27]

War reflects the relatively primitive state of human political development. When Albert Einstein, the theoretical physicist who is considered to have been one of the most brilliant people of the twentieth century, was reportedly asked why it is that we are able to create nuclear weapons but not abolish war, he responded that the answer was easy: politics is more difficult than physics.

At the end of the first decade of the twenty-first century, the nations of the world spent about $1.5 trillion a year on military expenditures. The United States spent about $700 billion, China about $100 billion, France and the United Kingdom about $60 billion, and Russia, Japan, and Germany about $50 billion.[28] In 2009, the average cost per US citizen for the country's military budget was about $2,000.[29]

Since World War II there have been more than 150 wars, with 90 percent of those occurring in the less developed nations. Wars have been frequent in the global South since 1945 for a number of reasons. During the Cold War the United States and the Soviet Union supported with arms various political groups in the less developed nations that favored their side in the East/West conflict. Although the Cold War has now ended, the huge amounts of weapons supplied by the superpowers are now still circulating widely across the globe. Conflicts have been frequent in the developing world also because many of these nations achieved political independence relatively recently and territorial disputes, power struggles, ethnic and religious rivalries, and rebellions caused by unjust conditions and purposefully stoked by political actors are common.

With the exception of the Persian Gulf wars – which could be called "resource wars" – wars since the end of the Cold War have been mainly civil wars involving three categories of participants: first, ethnic groups fighting for more autonomy or for a state of their own, such as the Kurds in Turkey or the Chechens in Russia; second, groups trying to get control of a state, such as in Afghanistan; and third, so-called "failed states" where the central government has collapsed or is extremely weak and fighting is occurring over political and/or economic "spoils," such was in Liberia.

Wars over the control of natural resources will no doubt become more common as global consumption increases, exacerbating scarcities.

A characteristic of modern war is that often more civilians are killed than soldiers. In many wars in the past the military combatants were the main casualties, but this has now changed so that civilians often bear the greatest burden. In the first half of the twentieth century about 50 percent of the war-related dead were civilians. In the 1960s the proportion of the war dead who were civilians rose to about 65 percent, and in the 1980s it reached about 75 percent. The United Nations estimates that civilians comprised 90 percent of war casualties in the 1990s.[30] If one adds to the number of civilians killed and wounded during the fighting the vast number of civilians who flee the fighting and become refugees – sometimes finding no place that will accept them – civilians indeed bear the largest burden of modern war. Also, the destruction from the fighting can be so immense that when the fighting finally ends, those civilians able to return often find destroyed towns and an ecologically damaged land.

Another characteristic of modern wars is that technology has been used to greatly increase the destructive capacity of the weapons. The case study on nuclear weapons that follows will illustrate that point well, but even so-called conventional weapons are now much more destructive than they used to be. In addition to the increase in destructive capacity, technology has been used to increase weapons' accuracy, penetration ability, rates of fire, range, automation, and armor. Now, unarmed airplanes are able to wage sophisticated and destructive warfare ranging from bombing to assassinations through remote-controlled technology.

At the beginning of the twenty-first century there seemed to be both positive and negative signs regarding war. For the first time the North Atlantic Treaty Organization (NATO) was used several times to end fighting and killing in the former Yugoslavia. Other peacekeeping military forces under the United Nations were active in many locations throughout the world – 16 in June of 2015.[31] Under nuclear arms reduction agreements between the United States and Russia, by the mid-1990s nuclear arsenals had been reduced from about 18,000 megatons of explosive power to about 8,000 megatons.[32] In 2011, the United States and Russia signed a new nuclear arms control agreement, which provided for a 30 percent reduction in nuclear weapons over the following seven years and a verification process so each side can be sure the cuts are being made.

On the negative side, it is clear that although war among the great powers has increasingly become unlikely because of the threat it would become a nuclear war,

war is still a political instrument in the world. In the Democratic Republic of the Congo nearly 4 million people have died since a conflict began there in 1998.[33] Sudan's civil war, which lasted 22 years, led to about 2 million deaths and displaced about 4 million people.[34]

The 2003 US-led invasion of Iraq left an estimated 134,000 Iraqi civilians dead.[35] Many military and civilian deaths continued as the US-led NATO force attempted to defeat the Taliban, the local radical Muslim group trying to restore its control of Afghanistan. The United Nations reported 17,774 civilian deaths between 2009 and 2014, with 3,699 of those occurring in 2014 alone, representing an increase in civilian deaths by 25 percent from the previous year.[36] Elsewhere in the region, both political (Arab Spring) and more violent conflicts have surged in recent years in countries such as Syria, Mali, Egypt, and Libya.

According to the respected Stockholm International Peace Research Institute, there was a decrease in the number of wars in the late twentieth century and early twenty-first century, dropping from a high of about 30 in 1991 to about 16 in 2008, but those numbers, and particularly nonstate conflicts, are now increasing.[37]

The reduced stockpile of nuclear weapons still represents over 700 times the explosive power used in the twentieth century's three major wars, which killed about 44 million people. As we will see in the next section, nuclear weapons represent the darkest part of the "dark side" of our species.

The Threat of Nuclear Weapons: A Case Study

The threat of nuclear weapons is a subject that touches on many of the themes we have examined in this chapter. It is the "ultimate" development subject since it is the achievements in weapons technology by the developed nations that have brought the survival of human life into question. It is a problem that cries out for a political solution. Carl von Clausewitz, the famous Prussian author of books on military strategy, described war as a continuation of politics by other means. But, given the probable consequences of a nuclear war as presented below, one must ask whether war between nations with nuclear weapons can remain a way of settling their disputes. Let us look at the nature of the threat created by nuclear weapons and then at four contemporary problems related to these weapons.

The threat

It has taken 4.5 billion years for life to reach its present state of development on this planet. The year 1945 represents a milestone in that evolution, since it was then that the United States exploded its first atomic bombs on Hiroshima and Nagasaki, Japan, and demonstrated that humans had learned how to harness for war the essential forces of the universe. After 1945, when the United States had no more than two or three atomic bombs, the arms race continued until the two superpowers, the

Plate 9.2 Underground nuclear weapons testing in the United States

Source: Los Alamos National Laboratory.

United States and the Soviet Union, had a total of about 50,000 nuclear weapons, the equivalent of 1 million Hiroshima bombs – or, to put it another way, about 3 tons of TNT for every man, woman, and child in the world. The Hiroshima bomb was a 15-kiloton device (a kiloton having the explosive force of 1,000 tons of TNT); some of the weapons today fall in the megaton range (a megaton being the equivalent of 1 million tons of TNT).

What would happen if these weapons were ever used? We cannot be sure of all the effects, of course, since, as the author Jonathan Schell has stated, we have only one Earth and cannot experiment with it.[38] But we do know from the Hiroshima and Nagasaki bombings, and from the numerous testings of nuclear weapons both above and below ground, that there are five immediate destructive effects from a nuclear explosion: (1) the initial radiation, mainly gamma rays; (2) an electromagnetic pulse, which in a high-altitude explosion can knock out electrical equipment over a very large area; (3) a thermal pulse, which consists of bright light (you would be blinded by glancing at the fireball even if you were many miles away) and intense heat (equal to that at the center of the sun); (4) a blast wave that can flatten buildings; and (5) radioactive fallout, mainly in dirt and debris that is sucked up into the mushroom cloud and then falls to Earth.

The longer-term effects from a nuclear explosion are at least three: (1) delayed or worldwide radioactive fallout, which gradually over months and even years falls to the ground, often in rain; (2) a change in the climate (possibly a lowering of the Earth's temperature over the whole northern hemisphere, which could ruin agricultural crops and cause widespread famine); and (3) a partial destruction of the ozone layer, which protects the Earth from the sun's harmful ultraviolet rays. If the ozone layer is depleted, unprotected people could stay outdoors for only about ten minutes before getting an incapacitating sunburn, and people would suffer a type of snow blindness from the rays which, if repeated, would lead to permanent blindness. Many animals would suffer the same fate.

Civil defense measures might save some people in a limited nuclear war but would not help much if there were a full-scale nuclear war. Underground shelters in cities hit by nuclear weapons would be turned into ovens since they would tend to concentrate the heat released from the blast and the firestorms. Nor does evacuation of the cities look like a hopeful remedy in a full-scale nuclear war, since people would not be protected from fallout, or from retargeted missiles, and could not survive well in an economy that had collapsed.

Since most of our hospitals and many doctors are in central-city areas and would be hit by the first missiles in an all-out nuclear war, medical care would not be available for the millions of people suffering from burns, puncture wounds, shock, and radiation sickness. Many corpses would remain unburied and would create a serious health hazard, which would contribute to the danger of epidemics spreading among a population whose resistance to disease had been lowered by radiation exposure, malnutrition, and shock.

What could be the final result of all of this? Here is how Jonathan Schell answers that question in probably the longest sentence you have ever read, but in one with no wasted words:

> Bearing in mind that the possible consequences of the detonations of thousands of megatons of nuclear explosives include the blinding of insects, birds, and beasts all over the world; the extinction of many ocean species, among them some at the base of the food chain; the temporary or permanent alteration of the climate of the globe, with the outside chance of "dramatic" and "major" alterations in the structure of the atmosphere; the pollution of the whole ecosphere with oxides of nitrogen; the incapacitation in ten minutes of unprotected people who go out into the sunlight; the blinding of people who go out into the sunlight; a significant decrease in photosynthesis in plants around the world; the scalding and killing of many crops; the increase in rates of cancer and mutation around the world, but especially in the targeted zones, and the attendant risk of global epidemics; the possible poisoning of all vertebrates by sharply increased levels of vitamin D in their skin as a result of increased ultraviolet light; and the outright slaughter on all targeted continents of most human beings and other living things by the initial nuclear radiation, the fireballs, the thermal pulses, the blast waves, the mass fires, and the fallout from the explosions; and considering that these consequences will all interact with one another in unguessable ways and, furthermore, are in all likelihood an incomplete list, which will be added to as our knowledge of the Earth increases, one must conclude that a full-scale nuclear holocaust could lead to the extinction of mankind.[39]

New dangers

Despite the end of the Cold War and of the threat of a cataclysmic war between two superpowers, nuclear weapons still remain a danger for the world. Three problems exist with which the world will have to deal: (1) the proliferation of nuclear powers; (2) the cleanup of the huge amount of toxic wastes produced in both the United States and the former Soviet Union when they built their large numbers of nuclear weapons; and (3) the threat of nuclear terrorism.

Nuclear proliferation   The spread of nuclear weapons to new countries represents a growing danger because the larger the number of countries that have these weapons, the greater the likelihood that they will be used. Figure 9.1 indicates those countries with nuclear weapons and related capacity to generate weapon-grade nuclear material. Many of these new nuclear powers – either actual or potential – are authoritarian regimes that have serious conflicts with their neighbors in the less developed world. For example, the Middle East is a region plagued by conflict. It is widely believed that Israel has already acquired nuclear weapons and has them ready for use or could have them ready in a very short time. After the defeat of Iraq in the Gulf War in 1991, UN inspectors discovered that Iraq had been making major efforts to build both atomic weapons and the much more powerful hydrogen weapons. This was in spite of the fact that Iraq had signed the Nuclear Nonproliferation Treaty, in which it had agreed not to acquire nuclear weapons, and in spite of the fact that officials from the International Atomic Energy Agency had inspected nuclear facilities in Iraq just prior to the war and had found no evidence that Iraq was building nuclear weapons.

Despite the suspicion that Iraq had again started developing nuclear weapons after the Gulf War – one of the reasons the United States gave for invading Iraq in 2003 – no evidence after the war was found that Iraq had started up such a program. It is now generally accepted Iraq had been forced to dismantle its nuclear program under the supervision of UN inspectors before the US invasion.

Another example of proliferation is in South Asia. In this region two countries – India and Pakistan – have already fought each other in four wars and many smaller conflicts since the United Kingdom partitioned the countries upon independence in 1947, and both tested nuclear weapons in 1998.[40] A dispute over the territory of Kashmir, which was the central issue in two of their previous wars, flared up again in the late 1990s and the fear was raised that if the two countries fight again it could be with nuclear weapons.

North Korea has admitted it has an active nuclear weapons program and has tested nuclear weapons. It is believed that the state may have the capacity to launch a nuclear missile.[41]

Iran has claimed it has no nuclear weapons program but many in the West believe it does. The permanent five members of the UN Security Council – Britain, China, France, Russia, and the United States – and Germany worked for many years with Iran to negotiate a joint agreement to prevent Iran from developing a nuclear

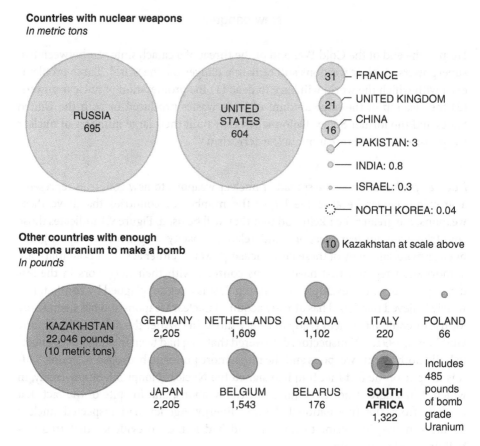

Countries with nuclear weapons
In metric tons

RUSSIA 695

UNITED STATES 604

31 — FRANCE

21 — UNITED KINGDOM

16 — CHINA

— PAKISTAN: 3

— INDIA: 0.8

— ISRAEL: 0.3

— NORTH KOREA: 0.04

Other countries with enough weapons uranium to make a bomb
In pounds

10 Kazakhstan at scale above

KAZAKHSTAN 22,046 pounds (10 metric tons)

GERMANY 2,205

NETHERLANDS 1,609

CANADA 1,102

ITALY 220

POLAND 66

JAPAN 2,205

BELGIUM 1,543

BELARUS 176

SOUTH AFRICA 1,322

Includes 485 pounds of bomb grade Uranium

Figure 9.1   Countries with nuclear weapons capacity

Source: Douglas Birch and R. Jeffrey Smith, "U.S. Unease about Nuclear-Weapons Fuel Takes Aim at a South African Vault," *Washington Post* (March 14, 2015). Data from January 2013 report by the International Panel on Fissile Materials, James Martin Center for Nonproliferation Studies, former and current US officials, Center for Public Integrity.

weapon. Signed in 2015, the Iran nuclear deal's intent is to permit Iran to continue to enrich uranium for peaceful purposes and under heavy international monitoring in exchange for a reduction of economic sanctions on the country.[42] Although United States President Donald Trump announced in May 2018 that he would be withdrawing the United States from the hard-won agreement, Iran and other nations pledged to continue with the agreement.[43] Regional conflicts in which these weapons could be used are not the only concern; also disturbing is the possibility of accidental or unauthorized use of nuclear weapons by these countries. Since the US began to grow its nuclear arsenal, there have been many close calls where a false positive in a monitoring system, human error, or lack of proper training nearly resulted in nuclear catastrophe.[44] Figure 9.1 provides information on countries with confirmed or suspected nuclear powers.

The cleanup   The production of vast quantities of nuclear weapons in both the Soviet Union and the United States led to huge environmental contamination with highly toxic chemical and nuclear wastes. In both countries wastes from the plants producing components for the nuclear weapons were released into the air and dumped onto the ground, and they have leaked from temporary storage facilities. The extent of this contamination did not become public until the late 1980s in the US case, when the US government released a number of reports outlining the huge extent of the problem, and in the Soviet case in the late 1980s and the early 1990s, in the last years of the Soviet communist state.

It is painful to read about the deliberate inflicting of harm by a government on its own citizens. Although the Soviet contamination is probably greater than the American, both governments used "national security" to justify their actions and to keep them secret. In the United States the plants were exempt from state and federal environmental laws, and actions were carried out that had long before been declared illegal for private industry and individuals. An estimated 70,000 nuclear weapons were made in the United States over a 45-year period, in 15 major plants covering an area equal in size to the state of Connecticut. They cost about $300 billion (in 1991 dollars). Estimates in 2008 by various government agencies of the cost of cleaning up the environmental damage at the plants, which will take decades to accomplish, is about $250 billion.[45]

Even though cleanup is recognized as an important priority, it has not been easy to decontaminate sites previously associated with nuclear weapons production. At the beginning of the twenty-first century, the National Academy of Sciences, the most prestigious scientific group in the United States, declared that most of the sites related to the production of nuclear weapons are so contaminated that they can never be cleaned up. Of the 144 sites, the Academy has stated that only 35 can be cleaned up enough so there is no potential harm to human beings, with 109 sites remaining dangerous for tens and even hundreds of thousands of years. The Academy found that the government's plans for guarding permanently contaminated sites are inadequate and that the government does not have the money or technology to keep the contamination from "migrating" off the sites.[46] In 2013, an investigation published in the *Wall Street Journal* confirmed these cleanup efforts have proven challenging, particularly in residential areas, and that in some cases the government has not been able to adequately track the location of the contaminated sites.[47]

The threat of nuclear terrorism   When Mohamed ElBaradei, the then head of the International Atomic Energy Agency (IAEA), accepted the Nobel Peace Prize in 2005 for his agency's work in preventing the spread of nuclear weapons, he warned that terrorists are actively trying to obtain nuclear weapons. The IAEA's Incident and Trafficking Database (ITDB) reported 2,477 incidents of unauthorized conduct involving nuclear material between 1993 and 2013, including 424 incidents of unauthorized possession and related criminal activities.[48] Of these, 146 incidents occurred in 2013 alone, including six incidents of unauthorized possession and related criminal activities.

Terrorism

Terrorism is a major problem today. The modern industrial state is relatively open to anyone who wants to harm the public. The challenge for the modern world is to decide how to defend itself against those who hold extremist beliefs, both religious and political, which call for the elimination of all those who do not believe as they do. There is a great need to strengthen defense against terrorists, which includes better intelligence and a greater ability to prevent attacks before they occur. At the same time, we believe, there is a need to resist the desire for revenge, which can easily create more hatred and more terrorists as innocent people are killed during the revenge action. To try to guard every vulnerable place and spy on every potential terrorist could lead to the creation of a police state, the use of uncivilized means the Western world has rejected, such as torture, and the loss of freedoms. A long-term effort is also needed to remove legitimate grievances of oppressed groups from which terrorists recruit their members.

One fear is that terrorists might make a so-called "dirty" nuclear bomb that would spread radioactive material over a large area, making that area uninhabitable for decades. Especially vulnerable to air attack are nuclear power plants, where in the United States nuclear waste that is still highly radioactive is stored above ground on the site. Globalization with its greatly increased trade and contacts among people has dramatically increased the possible targets and ways to deliver explosive devices.

Conclusions

This chapter has focused on the negative aspects of technology. It has done so because many of the readers of this book will probably be citizens of developed countries who already have a strong belief in the advantages of technology. It is not our intent to undermine that belief. Technology has benefited human beings in countless ways, and its use is largely responsible for the high living standards in the industrialized nations. Rather, our intent is to bring a healthy caution to the use of technology. An ignoring of the negative potential of technology has brought harm to people in the past and could cause unprecedented harm in the future. Much technology is neither good nor bad. It is the use that human beings make of this technology that determines whether it is mainly beneficial or harmful. Some technology has sufficiently harmful or excessively dangerous qualities that serious thought should be given as to whether it should be rejected. It is of course not always easy to place technologies in these categories, but an effort should be made.

Technology is absolutely necessary to help solve many of the planet's most awesome problems. But often intermediate technology should be used rather than the high technology favored by the industrialized nations. The temptation to imitate the West is strong, but ample evidence exists to show that this could be a serious mistake for developing nations. Economic, environmental, and social conditions and needs can vary tremendously depending on geography, and the best development plans will take from Western science only what is appropriate.

The industrial nations face another task. They must become more discriminating in their use of technology and lose some of their fascination with and childlike faith in it. The fate of the Earth could depend on technologically appropriate use of their hands. The wisdom or lack of wisdom these nations show in using military and industrial technology affects all – the present inhabitants of Earth, both human and nonhuman, and future generations, who depend on our good judgment for their chance to experience life on this planet.

Notes

1   A description of 50 case studies of development projects in the developing world that had harmful and unanticipated effects on the environment is contained in the following conference report: M. Taghi Farvar and John P. Milton (eds), *The Careless Technology: Ecology and International Development* (Garden City, NY: Natural History Press, 1972).

2   See also Rachel Carson, *Silent Spring* (New York: Houghton Mifflin, 1962; anniversary edn 2002).

3   World Health Organization, Pesticides and Their Application, 6th edn (2006), p. 2, at http://whglibdoc. who.int/hq/2006/WHO_CDS_NTD_WHOPES_GCDPP_2006.1_eng. pdf; see also the 2011 WHO Position Statement, "The Use of DDT in Malaria Vector Control," at http://apps. who.int/iris/bitstream/10665/69945/1/WHO_HTM_GMP_2011_ eng.pdf (both accessed July 2015).

4   Dan Ferber, "Livestock Feed Ban Preserves Drugs' Power," *Science*, 295 (January 4, 2002), pp. 27–8.

5   Denise Grady, "WHO Finds Use of Antibiotics in Animal Feed Can Be Reduced," *New York Times* (August 14, 2003), p. A5.

6   Jane Brody, "Studies Suggest Meats Carry Resistant Bacteria," *New York Times* (October 18, 2001), p. A12.

7   U.S. Food and Drug Administration, 2016 Summary Report on Antimicrobials Sold or Distributed for Use in Food-Producing Animals, 2017, at https://www.fda.gov/ downloads/ForIndustry/UserFees/ AnimalDrugUserFeeActADUFA/UCM588085. pdf; and Pew Trusts, "Antibiotics and Animal Agriculture: A Primer," at https://www. pewtrusts.org/en/research-and-analysis/fact-sheets/2016/12/antibiotics-and-animal-agriculture-a-primer (both accessed November 2018).

8   Lindsay Layton, "FDA Seeks Less Use of Antibiotics in Animals to Keep Them Effective for Humans," *Washington Post* (June 10, 2010).

9   McDonalds, "Statement on Antibiotic Use," March 4, 2015, at https://news.mcdonalds. com/media-statements/food-details/statement-antibiotic-use (accessed December 2018).

10 William D. McBride and Nigel Key, U.S. Hog Production from 1992 to 2009: Technology, Restructuring, and Productivity Growth, Report Summary, US Department of Agriculture, October 2013, p. 1, at http://www.ers.usda.gov/media/ 1207983/err158 summary.pdf (accessed July 2015).

11 US Environmental Protection Agency, "New Requirements for Controlling Manure, Wastewater from Large Animal Feeding Operations," press release, October 31, 2008.

12 World Bank, "The 2018 Atlas of Sustainable Development Goals," p.55, at http://blogs. worldbank.org/opendata/2018-atlas-sustainable-development-goals-all-new-visual-guide-data-and-development?cid=ECR_LI_worldbank_EN_EXT&fbclid=IwAR0ZbPE-bDYw-1a9l d6CKw9rtukZCu1CJHw6LJgUL9hPd9ocuyMXIDA8slw (accessed November 2018).

13 E. F. Schumacher, *Small Is Beautiful: Economics as if People Mattered* (New York: Harper & Row, 1973).

14 Warren C. Baum and Stokes M. Tolbert, *Investing in Development: Lessons of World Bank Experience* (Oxford: Oxford University Press, 1985), p. 574.

15 See, for example, Suzanne Arms, *Immaculate Deception: A New Look at Women and Childbirth in America* (Westport, CT: Bergin & Garvey, 1984); Robert A. Bradley, *Husband-Coached Childbirth* (New York: Harper & Row, 1974); Robbie E. Davis-Floyd, *Birth as an American Rite of Passage* (Berkeley: University of California Press, 1992).

16 John S. Miller, "Foreword," in Lester D. Hazell, *Commonsense Child-Birth* (New York: Berkley Books, 1976), p. x.

17 Jamie Santa Cruz, "Call the Midwife," *The Atlantic* (June 12, 2015), at https://www. theatlantic.com/health/archive/2015/06/midwives-are-making-a-comeback/395456/ (accessed November 2018).

18 Martin Lukacs, "World's Biggest Geoengineering Experiment 'Violates' UN Rules," *The Guardian* (October 15, 2012), at https://www.theguardian.com/environment/2012/ oct/15/pacific-iron-fertilisation-geoengineering (accessed May 2019).

19 United States National Academy of Sciences, Board on Atmospheric Sciences and Climate, Ocean Studies Board, "Climate Intervention: Carbon Dioxide Removal and Reliable Sequestration Reflecting Sunlight to Cool Earth" (2015), https://www.nap.edu/ catalog/18988/climate-intervention-reflecting-sunlight-to-cool-earth.

20 Geoengineering Monitor, "Surface Albedo Modification," Geoengineering Technology Briefing (May 2018), at http://www.geoengineeringmonitor.org/2018/05/surface-albedo-modification-technology-factsheet/ (accessed May 2019).

21 Union of Concerned Scientists, What is Climate Engineering (November 2017), at https://www.ucsusa.org/resources/what-climate-engineering (accessed May 2019).

22 Robert L. Olson, *Geoengineering for Decision Makers* (Washington, DC: Science and Technology Innovation Program, Woodrow Wilson International Center for Scholars November 2011), available at https://www.wilsoncenter.org/sites/default/files/ Geoengineering_for_Decision_Makers_0.pdf (accessed January 2020).

23 Marcia McNutt, Waleed Abdala, Scott Doney, and David Titley, Presentation on Climate Interventions, National Research Council of the United States National Academy of Sciences, at https://www.nap.edu/resource/18805/climateinterventionpresentation.pdf (accessed May 2019).

24 See, e.g., World Bank, "The 2018 Atlas of Sustainable Development Goals" p.16, 21 at http://blogs.worldbank.org/opendata/2018-atlas-sustainable-development-goals-all-new-visual-guide-data-and-development (accessed November 2018).

25 See, e.g., David Roberts, "I'm an Environmental Journalist, but I Never Write about Overpopulation. Here's Why," Vox (September 26, 2017), at https://www.vox.com/energy-and-environment/2017/9/26/16356524/the-population-question (accessed November 2018).

26 Jon R. Luoma, "The $33 Billion Misunderstanding," *Audubon*, 83 (November 1981), pp. 111–27.

27 Kenneth A. Waltz, *Man, the State and War: A Theoretical Analysis* (New York: Columbia University Press, 1959).

28 Stockholm International Peace Research Institute, 2010 Yearbook, see http://www.sipri.org/yearbook/2010 (accessed July 2015).

29 Ibid.

30 Robin Wright, "The New Way of War: Killing the Kids," *New Yorker* (July 3, 2014), at http://www.newyorker.com/news/news-desk/the-new-way-of-war-killing-the-kids; and UNICEF, Impact of Armed Conflict on Children, "Patterns in Conflict: Civilians Are Now the Target," (1996), at http://www.unicef.org/graca/patterns.htm (both accessed July 2015).

31 United Nations, "Peacekeeping Fact Sheet," at https://peacekeeping.un.org/sites/default/files/pk_factsheet_01_2020_english_2.pdf (accessed November 2020).

32 Ruth Sivard, *World Military and Social Expenditures*, 16th edn (Washington, DC: World Priorities, 1996), p. 7.

33 International Rescue Committee, "Mortality in the Democratic Republic of Congo: An Ongoing Crisis," May 1, 2007, at https://www.rescue.org/report/mortality-democratic-republic-congo-ongoing-crisis (accessed December 2018).

34 PBS Frontline World, "Sudan, the Quick and the Terrible," at http://www.pbs.org/frontlineworld/stories/sudan/facts.html (accessed December 2018).

35 Patrick J. Buchanan, "King Pyrrhus and the War on Iraq: Was Iraq Worth It?" *Washington Report on Middle East Affairs*, 32 (4) (May 2013), p. 40.

36 UN Assistance Mission in Afghanistan, Afghanistan: Annual Report 2014: Protection of Civilians in Armed Conflict, February 2015, p. 1, at http://unama.unmissions.org/Portals/UNAMA/human%20rights/2015/2014-Annual-Report-on-Protection-of-Civilians-Final.pdf (accessed July 2015).

37 Stockholm International Peace Research Institute, 2015 Yearbook: Armaments, Disarmament and International Security, Summary, p. 7, at http://www.sipri.org/yearbook/2015/downloadable-files/sipri-yearbook-2015-summary-pdf (accessed July 2015).

38 Jonathan Schell, *The Fate of the Earth* (New York: Avon Books, 1982).

39 Ibid.

40 See Amber Pariona, "Indo-Pakistan Wars – 1947, 1965, 1971, and 1999," World Atlas, 2017, at https://www.worldatlas.com/articles/indo-pakistan-wars-1947-1965-1971-1999.html (accessed November 2018).

41 Rob York, "Will North Korea Ever Use Its Nuclear Weapons?" *The Guardian* (October 31, 2014), at http://www.theguardian.com/world/2014/oct/31/sp-north-korea-nuclear-weapons (accessed July 2015).

42 Mark Landler, "Trump Abandons Iran Nuclear Deal He Long Scorned," *New York Times* (May 8, 2018), at https://www.nytimes.com/2018/05/08/world/middleeast/trump-iran-nuclear-deal.html (accessed December 2018); M.S., "Everything You Want to Know about the Iranian Nuclear Deal," *The Economist* (April 5, 2015), at http://www.economist.com/blogs/economist-explains/2015/04/ economist-explains-3 (accessed July 2015).

43   Ibid.
44   Union of Concerned Scientists, "Close Calls with Nuclear Weapons," 2015, at https://www.ucsusa.org/resources/close-calls-nuclear-weapons (accessed November 2018).
45   National Governors Association, Cleaning up America's Nuclear Weapons Complex (2008), at http://www.nga.org/files/live/sites/NGA/files/pdf/0811NUCLEARCL EANUP. PDF (accessed July 2015).
46   "Nuclear Sites May Be Toxic in Perpetuity, Report Finds," *New York Times* (March 13, 2003), p. A1.
47   John R. Emshwiller and Jeremy Singer-Vine, "A Nuclear Cleanup Effort Leaves Questions Lingering at Scores of Old Sites," *Wall Street Journal* (October 30, 2013), at http://www.wsj.com/articles/SB10001424127887323342404579079483154040874 (accessed July 2015).
48   International Atomic Energy Agency, "Incident and Trafficking Database (ITDB)," at https://www.iaea.org/resources/databases/itdb (accessed July 2015).

Further Reading

Allison, Graham, *Nuclear Terrorism: The Ultimate Preventable Catastrophe* (New York: Henry Holt, 2004). This Harvard scholar believes that without bold measures to prevent terrorists from getting a nuclear weapon, they will get one and will use it. He outlines the aggressive steps the world will need to take to prevent this disaster.

Ashford, Nicholas and Ralph Hall, *Technology, Globalization, and Sustainable Development: Transforming the Industrial State* (New Haven: Yale University Press, 2011). A high-level and technical exploration of the interplay between technology and industry as influencing development pathways and their associated implications for sustainability.

Chiles, James, *Inviting Disaster: Lessons from the Edge of Technology* (New York: Harper Business, 2001). Human beings are prone to error. Chiles takes us inside many famous technological disasters, showing us what led up to the events. With our increasing technological power comes the potential for greater disasters. We are unable to eliminate all risks – no system is perfect – so there are some technologies that we should not accept because they are very dangerous.

Cirincione, Joseph, *Bomb Scare: The History and Future of Nuclear Weapons* (New York: Columbia University Press), 2007. Cirincione describes how the world got to its present situation and suggests solutions to some of the most urgent problems with these weapons.

Glaser, Alexander, and Frank von Hippel, "Thwarting Nuclear Terrorism," *Scientific American*, 294 (February, 2006), pp. 56–63. For the authors, the best way to remove the danger of nuclear terrorism is to eliminate wherever possible the use of highly enriched uranium and remove accumulated stocks.

Hamburg, David, *No More Killing Fields: Preventing Deadly Conflict* (Lanham, MD: Rowman & Littlefield, 2002). As preventive medicine is better than treating an illness, so is preventing conflict better than fighting a war. By analyzing the rise of war makers such as Hitler and Milosevic, Hamburg believes the international community could have prevented their wars. He shows how an early warning and response system could be created today.

Klare, Michael, *Resource Wars: The New Landscape of Global Conflict* (New York: Henry Holt, 2001). Klare focuses on oil, water, timber, and minerals, such as diamonds. In this readable book the author shows that many wars that seem to be ethnic or sectarian are really over resources.

Lewis, H. W., *Technological Risk* (New York: W. W. Norton, 1990). Lewis examines the perceived risks associated with our technological society and argues that bad policy, misused resources, and lack of education rather than technology itself are the culprits. He argues that many things people fear the most actually pose no real risk to them, whereas some things that do pose a real risk to people are not perceived as being dangerous.

McKibben, Bill, *Enough: Staying Human in an Engineered Age* (New York: Henry Holt, 2003). McKibben is not against genetic engineering to repair defective genes but he warns against genetic engineering that tampers with fundamental behavioral traits. He also looks at the darker side of nanotechnology and robotics.

Tenner, Edward, *Why Things Bite Back: Technology and the Revenge of Unintended Consequences* (New York: Knopf, 1996). This book is based on a huge amount of research. Tenner says this of his book: "I am arguing not against change, but for a modest, tentative and skeptical acceptance of it." To deal with what Tenner calls "revenge effects," he calls for more use of our brains, not more "stuff." By examining a large number of cases, from low-tar cigarettes, black-lung disease, Chernobyl, and Windows 95, Tenner recommends we use technology cautiously.

Winner, Langdon, *The Whale and the Reactor: A Search for Limits in an Age of High Technology* (Chicago: University of Chicago Press, 1986). The sight of a whale surfacing near a nuclear reactor causes the author to contemplate the connections between nature and technology and to call for a more conscious effort by people to think about how technology can affect human life.

Chapter 10

Alternative Futures[1]

> *In human affairs, the logical future, determined by past and present conditions, is less important than the willed future, which is largely brought about by deliberate choices – made by the human free will.*
>
> René Dubos, "A Celebration of Life" (1982)

Where is development leading us? What can we say about the future? If the dismal record of past predictions leads us to believe that the future is essentially unknowable, then we might ask, "Does it make any sense to think about the future at all?" Our answer is, "Yes, it does." While we cannot predict the future with certainty, we can prepare for what the future holds based on our best available information about the

---

1 Liz Schmitt contributed substantially to the research and updates for this edition. Please credit her work if citing directly to this chapter.

Global Issues: An Introduction, Sixth Edition. Kristen A. Hite and John L. Seitz.
© 2021 John Wiley & Sons Ltd. Published 2021 by John Wiley & Sons Ltd.

past and present. Even if the *precise* future is unknowable, we do know that our present actions can make one outcome more likely than another. Human beings and societies have the power to make choices that have far-reaching impacts. Our options are not unlimited because of the times and places in which we live and our individual circumstances. But as rational human beings, we do have some freedom to make choices. It is this ability to influence the future that we consider in this final chapter.

If we can accurately describe our current situation and recognize some of the major trends in the past and present, we can make an educated guess about where we are heading. An old Chinese proverb states if you do not change the direction in which you are headed, you will end up where you are headed. So, if we do not like the direction in which the world is heading, we can examine our individual behaviors and governmental policies to determine if they should be changed to improve our future outlook. This chapter considers our current outlook for development pathways under different scenarios and then explores the choices we can make to improve the opportunity for a better future.

Development Pathways: Evaluating Our Current Situation

According to the Australian biologist Charles Birch, "Overdevelopment of any country starts when the citizens of that country consume resources and pollute the environment at a rate which is greater than the world could stand indefinitely if all the peoples of the world consumed resources at that rate."[1] From this perspective, it can be seen that the United States could be considered the most overdeveloped country in the world, followed closely by many other industrial countries. People in the United States, who constitute about 4 percent of the world's population, consume about 25 percent of the world's annual use of natural resources, and do so, as this book has shown, with devastating effects on the environment. Across the world, a relatively small percentage of the population that reflects the globally wealthy producer and consumer class is driving the vast majority of these impacts. This devastation is reduced when environmental laws and regulations take effect, but it has not been reduced to such an extent that the concept of overdevelopment is outdated. At the same time, the term is not popular. But if "development" is equated by many to an outdated twentieth-century development model that has led to undesirable social and environmental consequences, what is the appropriate way to discuss policy and economic pathways geared towards progress?

Development models help evaluate how the choices that societies make impact their future economic and social well-being. In the twentieth century, development models focused primarily on achieving economic growth through increased production and less government regulation, reasoning that if nations could increase their GDP then their citizens would benefit from increased wealth, and more resources would be available to provide for education, healthcare, and other needs. Experts argued that technological innovations and supply-and-demand economics could solve problems of short-term supply shortages. The late Julian Simon, the author of several influential books, for example, insisted that natural resources were not finite in any real economic sense, arguing that scarcity of resources leads to increased prices, more efficient processing methods, and cheaper substitutes. The assumption at that time was that increasing production would lead to increased progress. Natural resource limits and pollution damage were generally not factored into the production considerations or were seen as "external" concerns (called "externalities" in economics).

Now, updated development models are working to better integrate natural resources and environmental costs. Even growth-focused experts have challenged the assumption that increased production alone will lead to broad development. For example, while the World Economic Forum recognizes that the price of natural resource commodities declined from 1950 to 2000 despite rapidly rising demand, they disagree with Julian Simon that such declines are likely to continue and instead say that resource scarcity will be a major factor in our future economic development.[2] This has led to more sophisticated development models that not only forecast what society will look like in the future if we continue to follow a development pathway focused on economic growth, but also consider alternative pathways.

Current Outlook: Business as Usual

The first step in considering the future is to understand where we are and where we are headed if we do nothing to change our actions. To this effect, we can identify certain key factors and trends that are likely to impact our future. The earlier chapters of this book identified many of these trends. We learned that the global population is increasing and that the population in high-income countries is aging while youth dominate the populations of many lower-income countries (Chapter 3). We saw in Chapter 2 that vast inequalities of wealth exist in the world and that production/gross domestic products (a conventional indicator of progress) continue to increase. We also saw that globally the consumption of food is increasing and agriculture now requires more water and land space (Chapter 4). Energy demands are significantly increasing in both high and low income countries, while energy supply comes primarily from fossil fuel resources (Chapter 5), which is contributing significantly to changes in the climate with long-term consequences across the globe. At the same time, modern societies are utilizing natural resources at ever increasing rates (Chapters 6 and 7). Combining these trends, we can create a picture of our current situation and make projections for where we are headed in the future if we continue our current trends – a scenario we call "business as usual."

What does the world look like under a business-as-usual scenario? In the first decade of the twenty-first century, the world population was increasing by more than 70 million people every year.[3] Even considering recent trends and projected declines in fertility rates worldwide, as well as a slowing pace of growth, by 2050 we will have 9.8 billion people on the planet, the vast majority of whom will be living in developing countries.[4] (Remember we have about 7.6 billion people at present.)

Recalling the discussion in this book's population chapter, we also know that people are generally living longer and moving away from rural areas and into cities.[5] The number of people 60 years and older is expected to more than double between 2017 and 2050, and the number of people 80 years and older is projected to triple in that time. By 2050, 25 percent of wealthy and about 14 percent of the population in lower income countries will be over 65 years of age, and 68 percent of the world's population is expected to live in cities.[6] This will require rural areas to produce more food for those living in cities. In many parts of Africa, a significant amount of food is imported despite a considerable amount of rural land for farming; the same is predicted for India by 2023.[7]

Consider the implication of population trends on food, as discussed in Chapter 4. With more people on the planet, demand for food increases. According to the UN Food and Agriculture Organization, there will be a 50 percent increase in demand for food between 2012 and 2050.[8] Because of rising quality of life in low and middle income countries, diets are likely to shift to include more meat, fruits, and vegetables, and this combined with population growth means more resource intense food production.[9] Correspondingly, according to the International Food Policy Research Institute, there will be a 30 percent increase in demand for water, and some estimates predict an increase of over 40 percent; a notable portion of this increased demand is also associated with increased urbanization.[10]

Given business-as-usual projections of a need for at least 50 percent more food on the planet in the coming decades, predictions are that farmers may significantly shift their growing practices due to climate and supply-related challenges, creating new winners and losers in the changing agriculture economy.[11] As the World Economic Forum has explained, key major grain-producing areas (including China, India, and the United States) already depend on unsustainable mining of ground water, and climate change is affecting precipitation patterns in many areas (including North Africa and Australia) in a way that limits fresh water supplies.[12] For example, in China's primary grain-producing northeast region, drought losses from climate change are projected to increase over 50 percent by 2030.[13] The United Nations Environment Programme (UNEP) forecasts "water stress will worsen, impacting population growth, agriculture and industrial production."[14] On land, the UN estimated in 2017 that one-third of Earth's soil had been acutely degraded by industrial agriculture: "the increased use of chemical fertilizers is projected to increase yields in the agriculture sector in the short term at the expense of a longer-term decline of soil quality. This is increasing pressures on land – converting forest areas to farmland – to feed the growing population and the consumption demands of an expanding global consumer class."[15]

We can also consider the impacts of a growing population and more consumptive economies (see Chapter 3) on the energy and climate crisis. According to the International Energy Association, there will be at least a 30 percent increased demand for energy by 2040.[16] Continuing with energy pathways dominated by fossil fuels will result in exacerbated climate change and place more stress on already limited fresh water resources.[17] While the global energy mix is changing rapidly, the rate of change required to address climate change demands an even more accelerated transition, with major changes by 2030, most coal phased out by 2040, and a carbon-neutral economy by 2050.[18]

As we saw in Chapter 6, the world's leading climate scientists have stated definitively that it is "*extremely likely*" that human influence has been the dominant cause of global warming since the middle of the twentieth century, driven by high rates of both population and economic growth.[19] The Intergovernmental Panel on Climate Change (IPCC) has warned that if we do not change our course, global greenhouse gas emissions will grow 25 to 90 percent between 2000 and 2030, and fossil fuels will constitute most of global energy supply even beyond 2030.[20] According to UNEP, increased fossil fuel use under business-as-usual "will further jeopardize energy security and tend to slow economic growth, through higher energy (especially oil) prices." Continuing to emit these gases at or above current rates "would cause further warming and induce many changes in the global climate system during the twenty-first century that would very likely be larger than those observed during the twentieth century."[21] According to UNEP, under a business-as-usual scenario, atmospheric carbon concentrations are projected to rise over 1,000 parts per million by 2100, more than double the threshold that scientists have determined is likely to lead to irreversible and catastrophic climate impacts.[22]

Not only will this business-as-usual trajectory for global population and consumption trends threaten global food supplies, the Earth's climate, and fresh water resources, but a number of analyses conclude that it will also reduce economic growth and increase poverty.[23] In 2010, the World Economic Forum analyzed how current consumption could influence future trends and concluded, "For such increased demand for water, food and energy to be realized, significant and perhaps radical changes in water use will be required as well as new sources for food and energy production exploited."[24] They also predict "extreme volatility" in commodity and energy prices as resource demands increase due to population growth and higher per-capita consumption.[25] Moreover, due to natural limits, "in the long-term, the world should expect at best, sustained increases in commodity prices, and at worst, shortages of key resources."[26] As resource prices rise and are transferred to consumers, the poorest will suffer the most, "increasing economic disparity and the interconnected risks that this implies."[27]

Looking at these different factors, it seems clear that business-as-usual sets us on a course of ever-increasing future consumption, pollution, and population growth. If the Earth's resources were unlimited, this future trajectory could more easily sustain our society and its current values and trends. However, the Earth does have limits, and those limits require that we make important choices about our future.

Collapse and Sustainable Development

Can the world continue on its current development pathway that focuses on economic growth by the intensive use of natural resources? As we saw in Chapter 4, if current trends continue, absent a major technological breakthrough, we would need the resources of almost three Earths by 2050 in order to maintain existing levels of consumption.[28]

Jared Diamond, an award-winning author, published in 2005 a popular book called *Collapse* that looked at what caused societies to fail in the past. He concluded that one of the main causes of their collapse was the inability of a society to live within its natural limits through holding destructive values and making choices to overconsume their resources.[29] For many decades, popular books have warned of disaster due to industrial pollution, food scarcity, overpopulation, or depletion of nonrenewable resources. One of the best known is Rachel Carson's *Silent Spring*, which predicted premature death to humans and other animals because of the growing use of pesticides and other chemicals.[30] Another book, which received nearly as much publicity as Carson's book, was *The Population Bomb* by Paul Ehrlich, which looked at food supplies and other resource limits and starkly concluded: "The birth rate must be brought into balance with the death rate or mankind will breed itself into oblivion."[31] Similarly, studies by the US government and the Club of Rome in the 1970s predicted that meeting the needs of growing populations would lead to substantially increased pollution, pressures on food and resources, and increasingly push planetary limits – all of which would compromise quality of life and perhaps even life itself, starting early in this present century.

These kinds of studies and predictions of doomsday scenarios have persisted for decades, concluding that business-as-usual population trends combined with global consumption patterns cannot be sustained given the Earth's existing natural limits. Their predictions have generally been true that resources will be more stressed, though the time frames have sometimes overestimated the pace of destruction. While some of the near-term disasters forewarned by earlier predictions have not manifested as quickly as predicted, overall, experts agree that business-as-usual behavior will result in natural resource scarcity so severe that it cannot support the global population, leading to increased poverty, insufficient water for survival, and increased conflicts and political instability due to natural resource shortages.

Technological innovations can help remove an immediate limiting factor such as a resource shortage, but they generally do not solve the bigger problem. For example, the Green Revolution of the 1970s resulted in a large infusion of chemical fertilizers that significantly increased crop yields. But it also led to increased water pollution from all of the fertilizer runoff – so much that this has created new environmental problems. For example, there is now a large "dead zone" where fish cannot survive where the Mississippi River discharges all the fertilizer pollution into the sea off the coast of the United States. This is an example of technology removing one limiting factor (poor soil quality) while exacerbating another environmental problem (polluted water). It may buy more time to address the overall crisis of food production, but it has not changed the long-term predictions of resource scarcity.

The threat of collapse based on business-as-usual trajectories is what has driven experts to reexamine traditional development models and find ways to better incorporate ecological limits. New technologies to increase production have the power to either improve or worsen our long-term outlook, depending on how we choose to use them.[32] As the World Economic Forum explains, governments must consider integrated models for economic growth, low-carbon development, and water efficiency, as tradeoffs between uses of these resources by various resource users are key to decisions regarding their long-term management.[33]

Many growth-minded and environmental experts concur that given current population and consumption trends, combined with natural resource limits, a future with a secure supply of natural resources for future generations must be one geared toward sustainable development, which enables current generations to "meet their needs without compromising the ability of future generations to meet their own needs."[34] UNEP recently modeled what a future business-as-usual economy would look like and then compared that with the short-, medium-, and long-term impacts of investing in sustainable development geared toward a green economy focused on resource efficiency, renewable energy, and job creation.[35] Based on UNEP's predictions, continuing with business as usual (even in the best case) could result in higher GDP and employment over the short term, but this increase would deplete natural resources, leading to the potential for collapse over the medium and long term. On the other hand, investing a small percentage of GDP in the green economy resulted in much more sustainable economic growth projections.[36] UNEP describes the future based on a green economy as a low-carbon development pathway that manages natural resources sustainably, such as by shifting away from fossil-fuel use, respecting the ecological limits in fishing, reducing deforestation, and using organic fertilizer.[37] This shift to a "green" economy serves to slow resource depletion and helps to restore the use of resources to sustainable levels, enabling "resilient economic growth in the medium and long term."[38]

As we saw in Chapters 2 and 7, raising incomes is associated with increased natural resources use. This has prompted some to propose "donut economics," a theory of development that says economic growth should be enough to provide inclusive growth but also to use resources in a way that respects planetary limits.

Kate Raworth explores the "donut economics" model of development, where she advocates for a development "floor" for everyone (the inner donut hole) and a "ceiling" based on planetary limits (the outer ring). The space in between, Raworth says, is the space where development can happen in a sustainable manner that allows everyone to thrive. It's an elegant and sensible theory, and if there is enough space in the donut, it may well be possible to not only avoid collapse but to work towards a much better and more sustainable world for everyone. The challenge with this approach, however, is that very little evidence exists that says this is politically possible, even if it is physically or technically theoretically feasible.[39]

This concept of meeting social needs within planetary boundaries is a challenging one: what happens if there is not enough space in between for development? What if meeting everyone's basic needs already pushes beyond our planetary limits? This is a terrifying prospect, and one that is also very much a possibility. A 2018 study in

Nature Sustainability found that trying to meet basic social needs such as eliminating extreme poverty ($1.90/day), extending life expectancies to over 65 for everyone on the planet, and enabling everyone to start from an average happiness factor of at least 6.5/10 already shot past a number of planetary limits.[40] The most difficult limit to work with is that of climate change, which is already redefining this century's development model. See some of their findings in Figure 10.1, which compares the number of basic social needs met with the number of planetary boundaries exceeded. As Figure 10.1 illustrates, wealthier "developed" countries tend to meet the highest number of social thresholds, but have done so at a substantial cost to the Earth. With few exceptions, countries that are better at living within the planet's boundaries tend to not meet as many basic social needs. What does this mean for development? And given that billions of people are still being added to Earth's population (see Chapter 3), what does this mean for the ability to meet everyone's basic social needs? One thing is clear: the Earth does not have adequate resources to sustain the twentieth-century development model of energy- and resource-intensive extractive industrial development as a means for poverty alleviation.

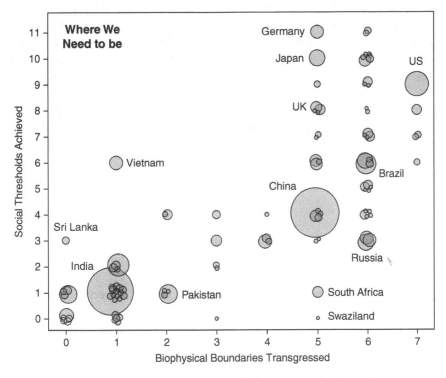

Figure 10.1 Number of planetary limits exceeded when meeting basic needs

Source: Dan O'Neill, Is it possible for everyone to live a good life within our planet's limits? *The Conversation*, at https://theconversation.com/is-it-possible-for-everyone-to-live-a-good-life-within-our-planets-limits-91421 (citing O'Neill *et. al*, "A Good Life for all within Planetary Boundaries," *Nature Sustainability* 1, pp. 88–95 (2018)).

Choices

Are we a society that is willing to continue on a business-as-usual trajectory and risk global collapse, or will we change course toward more sustainable development? If we understand our current trajectory and natural limits, we can develop a range of options that allow us to make choices toward a better future. As Joel Cohen explains:

> In human terms, almost nothing is inevitable about the twenty-first century. For example, urbanization offers exciting opportunities for educational and cultural enrichment. Urbanization also threatens frightening hazards from infectious diseases unless adequate sanitary engineering supplies clean water and removes wastes ... A healthy aging population offers unprecedented opportunity for longer use of acquired skills and experience, but threatens to bring unprecedented numbers of abandoned oldsters unless we anticipate the consequences of differently constructed families ... The future of many natural systems and their future effects on us depend in part on how well we come to understand our options, and what we decide to do.[41]

Based on predicted population growth, resource constraints, and our social structure, we have two principal options available to avoid collapse: (1) improve production within sustainable limits, or (2) reduce demand by slowing population growth and having less consumptive lifestyles. An alternative path may be possible if the issue is more related to the distribution of resources as opposed to scarcity challenges, and this focuses on more efficient management and equitable distribution of resources through improved governance of society, such as by undertaking legal, political, economic, and institutional reforms.[42] Deciding how to employ these strategies requires a better understanding of the tradeoffs between natural limits, social needs, and political realities.

Improve production

How can production improve within sustainable limits? Increases in resource efficiency can help mitigate hardships, as individual changes reduce demand and "government policies (such as removing hydrocarbon subsidies and stronger laws to conserve natural resources) provide incentives to change."[43] According to UNEP models, by 2050, changes in production practices could improve forest cover by 21 percent, fish stocks by 64 to 106 percent, and soil quality by 21 to 27 percent.[44] Additionally, through increased efficiency and new technologies, water use could improve 19–24 percent, fossil fuel consumption could be reduced 34–50 percent, and greenhouse gas emissions could be significantly lower than business-as-usual. Based on these projections, GDP could increase significantly in the medium to long term and employment could increase 3–5 percent by 2050.[45] The World Economic Forum echoes these overall projections, explaining: "In the long term, a model of truly sustainable consumption where private sector business models adopt resource limits as a driver of business innovation – as advocated by the Forum's Driving Sustainable Consumption Initiative – could shift [our] current set of risks to an opportunity for renewed growth and competitive advantage."[46]

As promising as it is to improve resource efficiency and sustainable production, this strategy alone may still not be enough to avert a trajectory headed toward collapse. "However, beware of false dichotomies," warns the World Economic Forum, as "trade-offs exist primarily when policy-makers and resource-users act in a short-term, reactive and hurried fashion."[47] The Forum says that there are "soft" temporary limits based on production capacity but there are also "hard" or absolute limits of a natural resource's availability. They explain that the "hard" resource limits suggest that over the long term, technology and innovation may not be able to continually increase the supply of core resources at the rate required by population and economic growth, as certain resources like water do not have easy substitutes.[48] As such, we also need to consider two additional strategies: reducing demand and improving the management and governance of society and our natural resources.

Reduce demand

Reducing demand for resources can help us shift to a more sustainable future. The primary factors impacting resource demand are population and consumption. Stacy VanDeveer explains, "Frankly, the earth cannot sustain the material throughput of seven to nine billion people in the coming decades, if all consume as many resources as the wealthiest billion do now."[49] Similarly, Nobel laureate Murray Gell-Mann says that without a major demographic transition that can stabilize the human population, "talk of sustainability seems pointless."[50]

René Dubos, the late well-known bacteriologist, coined the phrase "Think globally, act locally." This is one way, according to Dubos, that an individual can see tangible results that contribute to a better future. Dubos no doubt realized that the great benefit of local action is that not only does it help solve problems, but the results of the action can provide satisfaction and motivation that we do have the power to change some key things that can impact our future. Wendell Berry, a US author and farmer who writes about sustainable living, gave the following tribute to "local action": "The real work of planet-saving will be small, humble, and humbling, and (insofar as it involves love), pleasing and rewarding. Its jobs will be too many to count, too many to report, too many to be publicly noticed or rewarded, too small to make anyone rich or famous."[51]

While we cannot predict the future, we can certainly influence the likelihood of future outcomes by our current choices. We know that given population and consumption trends, if we choose to do nothing, our business-as-usual trajectory will deplete some crucial natural resources in the coming decades. We can choose to invest in technology to improve the efficiency of production, but that alone may only slow our path toward collapse instead of averting it. We can encourage individual choices to reduce consumption and to voluntarily limit family size, especially in the wealthiest countries and among the wealthiest people, which use at least 10 times the resources of those in low income situations, and contribute the lion's share of greenhouse gas emissions.[52] That will contribute to a more sustainable rate of natural resource consumption. If we choose to make policy choices to invest in a green economy, protect the poor, and improve the way we govern our common resources, we can reduce the threat of wars over water and other natural resources and improve the likelihood of achieving a secure and sustainable future.

Governance: Deciding How to Act on the Choices We Make

One of the most challenging elements of global issues is that by definition they transcend political boundaries. Even if we understand our choices and want to pursue a responsible development pathway, our society has to be able to make collective decisions that allow us to manage our economy and resources sustainably. The process a society uses to achieve commonly desired goals and to settle conflicts among groups with different interests plays a central role in determining what the future will be like and how well we will work toward common interests. International, governmental, and community institutions, laws, policies, and norms all impact how society manages interactions between cultures and natural resources.

Inequality can be a big factor in determining the success of governance. As humans, we consume resources very unequally: the richest 25 percent of humans on the planet obtain most of our global consumption.[53] The world has been undergoing rapid globalization, yet is becoming increasingly fragmented. As countries become ever more interconnected, our security depends in large part on effective international institutions to help us manage resources that transcend political borders.[54] These institutions must renew their focus on ensuring that the economy is providing for the basic needs of everyone, especially the poor, something that traditional development efforts have not always succeeded in achieving despite their best intentions. To improve the likelihood of success, as institutions become more powerful, society must ensure that those in power do not abuse their position. This requires more efforts to fight corruption, improve accountability, and strengthen communities.[55]

In the words of a Harvard anthropologist, civil society is "the space between the state and the individual where those habits of the heart flourish that socialize the individual and humanize the state."[56] In simpler terms, it is the activity that people engage in as they interact with other people and it can be seen in neighborhoods, voluntary organizations, and in spontaneous grassroots movements.

Although this activity can be directed toward economic gain, often it is not. It is the activity that makes a community, a connection between people, a realization that each one is dependent upon others and that they share life together. Without a vibrant civil society isolation can result and since human beings are social animals, that isolation can lead to illness, antisocial behavior, and depression.

The civil society approach to development emphasizes social development, how people act toward other people.[57] But the approach can also have important political and economic aspects. The best way to demonstrate this is through examples. In 1973, a group of poor people in India rushed to the forests above their impoverished village and hugged the trees to prevent a timber company from cutting them down. This community action received worldwide publicity and helped to force some governments to reconsider their development policy regarding their nation's forests. The Chipko movement, which grew out of this action, is an example of self-help community action directed against threats and harm to the environment, harm that the local people realize will make their lives more difficult or even impossible.

Civil society can also be seen working in the efforts by some people in poorer countries to raise their low living standards. It is generated by the realization in many poor countries that neither their governments nor the market can be relied on to help their citizens obtain basic needs. Here are two examples. In Latin America after the bishops of the Catholic Church met in 1968 in Colombia and decided that the church should become active in helping the poor, many priests, nuns, and lay Christians helped form Christian Based Communities, self-help groups mainly made up of the poor themselves.

In Bangladesh, economist Muhammad Yunus concluded that the landless poor could never improve their conditions without some extra funds to help them start up an income-producing activity. Since no banks would lend them money, he set up the Grameen Bank.[58] The bank's loans, some starting as small as $35, have been repaid much more reliably than loans from regular banks: over 95 percent of loans have been repaid! By 2011 the bank had lent about $16 billion and served about 8 million borrowers in Bangladesh, 97 percent of whom were poor women.[59] This experience demonstrated that the poor can be good financial risks and has been imitated in 40 other countries, including the United States, where this idea is known as "microcredit" and "microfinance." Worldwide about 130 million people were receiving microcredit loans in 2014.[60]

Civil society can also be directed toward political goals. In Eastern Europe in the 1980s millions of citizens took to the streets to call for the end of their communist governments. This grassroots movement, which spread throughout Eastern Europe, and which was primarily peaceful, led to the end of the Soviet empire and to the collapse of communism in Europe. Western political scientists were amazed that such an occurrence could take place. Few, if any, had imagined that the end of a powerful totalitarian state could come from the nonviolent actions of average citizens. In 2011, peaceful demonstrators overthrew the Egyptian president Mubarak who had ruled the country for 30 years.

A spontaneous grassroots movement also occurred in Argentina in the early 1980s when a group of mothers met daily in one of the main squares in the nation's capital to protest the disappearance of their children (thousands of individuals who were abducted by the military government in its war against subversion and suspected subversion). The silent, nonviolent protest by the mothers helped undermine the internal and external support for the government.

In 2004, the Nobel Peace Prize was given to Wangari Maathai from Kenya who, despite being beaten and jailed by the government, had organized the Green Belt Movement.[61] The movement of mainly very poor rural women planted 30 million trees to help restore the overexploited land of the country.

The internet and its social networking tools can be seen as technology making possible global civil society networks. With the vast amount of information now available to internet users, connections can be fostered among people around the world working for such common goals as monitoring the environment, holding corporations responsible for their actions, and for economic and political purposes. By the early twenty-first century, some 650 million people were using the internet, which represented a growth of nearly 600 percent over the previous five years.[62]

Advocates of a robust civil society approach to development and to the relationship between government and the economy say it is easy to show examples of failures by the market and by the state to make people's lives better. It is even easy to show examples where they have made people's lives worse. People have responded to the failures of the market and the state by undertaking self-help activities. Such individuals want to participate in controlling their lives and do not want to let the market or the state be the main determinants of how they should live. They believe that strong reliance on the market or the state can leave the individual stunted.

The advocates of civil society also point to flourishing voluntary efforts in many countries as evidence of the importance of their approach. Although it is impossible to know exactly how many such groups exist today, here are some historical examples:

- In India, tens of thousands of groups, many following the self-help tradition established by Mahatma Gandhi, have been involved in promoting social welfare, developing appropriate technology, and planting trees.
- In Indonesia, 600 independent groups worked on environmental protection.[63]
- The Sardovaya organization connects 15,000 Sri Lankan villages to provide humanitarian relief, education, and microcredit lending.[64]
- In Kenya, the Green Belt Movement, described above, seeks to empower women to improve their communities through planting trees, rendering the land arable and providing resources to the people.[65]
- In Brazil, the Movimento dos Trabalhadores Rurais Sem Terra (Movement of Landless Workers) has provided land to about 370,000 impoverished families by organizing about 2,500 nonviolent occupations of unused farmland.[66]
- The World March of Women, a global nongovernmental organization, endeavors to promote women's equality through coordination of marches, debates, and education in 96 countries.[67]
- Across the world, people are mobilizing in solidarity – sometimes reaching millions turning out in a single day – to support causes like climate action and gender equality. There is a growing movement across borders speaking out in support of equality and environmental protection.

• In the United States in the late 1980s an estimated 25 million people were involved in local actions to protect the environment.[68]

Finally, advocates of a robust civil society point to the spread of democracy around the world. In the 1980s, many developing nations adopted a democratic form of government and, with the collapse of the Soviet empire, many former communist countries became democratic. In 2018, about 39 percent of the world's people lived in countries that were considered free and 24 percent of the people lived in partly free countries.[69] It is in democracies that voluntary organizations flourish the most, but Freedom House noted 12 consecutive years of decline in worldwide freedom from 2006 to 2018.[70] At the same time that community organizing can flourish in free nations, this same organizing has been responsible for gains in democratic freedoms in many places, and will be needed to gain back the recent losses in democratic rights.

Some critics have raised concerns that it is impossible to have inclusive governance even with robust civil society participation without addressing the structural problems associated with inequality. They point out that while small may be beautiful, it can also be insignificant as compared with multinational and multipolar political and economic forces. Even the admirable Grameen Bank of Bangladesh provided only about 1.9 percent of the credit in the country in 2014.[71] The conclusion of a UN organization sympathetic to the efforts of self-help groups is that while nongovernmental organizations have helped transform the lives of millions of people throughout the world, "What seems clear is that even people helped by successful projects still remain poor."[72]

Efforts at the grassroots level directed toward community-managed economic development often fail, particularly when led by well-meaning outsiders from wealthy countries. The worker cooperative is often the instrument used, but a majority of these survive only a few years.[73] The members of the cooperatives, where workers come together to purchase and operate a business, are usually inexperienced in management. They are plagued by outside economic forces, and often ill-equipped to deal with complications such as high inflation and uncertain markets.

Critics also point out that oppressive political and economic powers can block the efforts of community groups. One well-publicized example was the assassination of Chico Mendes, the leader of a group of rubber tree harvesters in the Brazilian Amazon region. The large landowners in this region and in other Latin American countries have, with the support of local governments, traditionally used force against civil society activists.

Finally, critics of the civil society approach point to the spread of antidemocratic forces in the world at the same time as democracy is spreading. With the spreading of democracy, the end of the Cold War, and the collapse of communism in Europe, and then the dramatic expansion of internet and social media creating new airspace for airing viewpoints, ethnic and regional hatreds surfaced in many countries, hatreds that had been suppressed by the former authoritarian and totalitarian governments. Yugoslavia entered into a cruel civil war and the world saw "ethnic cleansing" reemerge, an idea it had incorrectly believed had been discredited in Europe with the defeat of Nazi Germany. Bitter ethnic hostilities also arose in many places in Africa in the mid-1990s, with thousands slaughtered in horrifying civil wars.

Sometimes incited by a few people for political reasons, group hatred toward "others," toward those outside one's group, unfortunately has become fairly common in the post-Cold War world era. True civil society, where people have respect and tolerance for those outside their immediate group, does not exist in a number of countries today. In many countries peaceful outcomes are unfortunately tenuous, such as South Sudan: a nation created at the conclusion of the long Sudanese civil war, it was a celebrated peace achievement, but after just two years violence between ethnic groups arose again, with at least 50,000 dead.[74] And in many places, newly formed or elected democratic governments are not strong enough to withstand the strains of modern political forces, which Freedom House points out "have fueled the rise of populist leaders who appeal to anti-immigrant sentiment and give short shrift to fundamental civil and political liberties."[75] But even as these outcomes are possible, it is also possible that increased freedom and expression gives way to a more positive future.

Our political decisions and individual actions have a significant impact on future outcomes. The choices we need to make in order to have a future of sustainable development include creating an economy that does not ignore environmental externalities. It needs to develop technologies to reduce negative environmental impacts and focus on obtaining a better understanding of the relationship between natural resources and society. We must stabilize the human population, reduce inequality, fight corruption, and strengthen international institutions to help us better govern ourselves, and cultivate a stronger sense of community and planetary consciousness.[76]

Finding a development pathway that values our common humanity and reduces conflicts – especially those exacerbated by inequality – can improve the ways in which our resources are used and allocated so that they can be managed sustainably. A shared understanding and respect for our common humanity can also improve our collective governance. The more different cultures perceive others as different from them, the more likely they will not be interested in supporting their survival or sharing resources. As Murray Gell-Mann explains: "Only by acknowledging the interdependence of all people and, indeed, of all life can we hope to broaden our individual outlooks so that they reach out in time and space to embrace vital long-term issues and worldwide problems in addition to immediate concerns close to home."[77]

Conclusion

Leading scholars in many fields increasingly recognize our dependency on natural resources and their respective limits. There seems to be a growing recognition that the size and characteristics of the human population, per capita resource consumption, and how society chooses to govern itself are three of the principal factors that will likely determine our future.

Economic growth – particularly in lower-income countries – can help raise living standards over the long term, but only when it does not exacerbate inequality or lead to diminished supplies of future resources. But does more economic growth make sense in countries with a GDP that is already high? It is unpopular today to suggest that it does not, but this may indeed be the case. The desire to acquire more and more material possessions in wealthy nations has placed a tremendous strain on the planet. This book has been concerned with documenting that strain.

The dangers of collapse are real. Some of them have already taken place in parts of the Earth. Some countries have a population larger than their natural resource base, widespread hunger exists in other countries, and toxic poisoning is increasingly seen in countries with concentrated industrial production. If actions are not taken to reduce greenhouse gases, use water sustainably, stabilize population, and stop widespread environmental deterioration, it is possible that huge loss of life could occur in the future.

The sustainable development future appears to be the one that both rich and poor nations alike should strive for, since unsustainable consumption of resources will broadly lead to increased poverty and political instability. In the language of economics, unsustainable consumption uses up the Earth's natural capital – clean air, water, fertile soil, healthy climate, and so on – for a short-term profit. And a basic principle of economics is that if you expend your capital unwisely (the financial and physical resources needed to produce goods and services), you will eventually go bankrupt. This kind of development compromises the ability of future generations to meet their own needs. One of the basic rules the Native Americans of the Iroquois confederacy followed in North America was the rule of the seventh generation: "consider how your decisions will affect the lives of the seventh generation to come."

Sustainable development is a powerful concept because it is hard to argue against it. A sustainable world would not mean the absence of growth, but the growth that would be emphasized would go beyond an unrelenting desire for more material objects.

The human race seems to be at a critical juncture. Will we realize the destructive things we are doing to life on Earth and pursue a new course before it is too late? Are we as a species meeting our basic physical needs while developing intellectually, morally, and spiritually? Can we live without compromising the ability of future generations to meet their own needs? The uncertainty of these answers is what makes the present day an important and challenging time in which to live.

The stakes are high. We are making both political and individual choices that change our world at an unprecedented rate. For the first time in human history, human beings have the technology to enable them to monitor the planet, to see how our actions are changing the forests, the air, and the water. And we are learning to think of Earth as a single system, a system in which we are just one of the parts. As a species with high intellect and the ability to make powerful choices, we have a special responsibility to all of life on the planet. Whether we are learning this fast enough to prevent irreversible destruction and collapse remains uncertain.

There is a growing awareness that human beings need to respect natural limits and move beyond our compulsion to dominate and unsustainably exploit the Earth's resources. We can learn this through reason and experience (such as drinking water that contains cancer-producing chemicals) as well as through expert studies comparing future population and consumption demands with available resources. But either way, we can and do learn – and indeed, our own long-term survival may depend on it. We should remember the wisdom of Joel Cohen:

> Until we understand better the interaction between humans and our planetary home, we will not be able to choose how the natural world will treat us. Surprises from the natural world will continue. We are making choices about our future every day. How much we invest in better understanding of those choices and their consequences is also a choice.[78]

Issues or problems have two sides. One side is the task that must be solved. Dealing with this side can be painful since some of these tasks present us with difficult choices. But the other side can light us up, for the issues also present us with opportunities. They give us an opportunity to grow – intellectually, morally, and spiritually. They give us a chance to become more loving, both to our fellow human beings and to the planet itself. And as we grow, so can our society. And as our society grows, we can sharpen our development pathway toward meaningful progress that is truly sustainable for both people and the planet. Not a bad deal.

Notes

1 Charles Birch, *Confronting the Future* (New York: Penguin, 1976), p. 35
2 World Economic Forum, *Global Risks 2011* (Geneva: World Economic Forum, 2011), pp. 29, 31, 38.
3 UN World Population Prospects 2017 Revision Key Findings p. 2, 4 https://population.un.org/wpp/Publications/Files/WPP2017_KeyFindings.pdf (accessed November 2018).
4 Ibid. at p. 2.
5 Ibid.
6 Ibid. at p. 13; see also UN World Urbanization Prospects 2018 Revision Key Facts, at https://population.un.org/wup/Publications/Files/WUP2018-KeyFacts.pdf (accessed December 2018).
7 Abdi Latif Dahir, "The World Could Run Out of Food Two Decades Earlier than Thought," Quartz Africa, at https://qz.com/africa/1064653/the-world-could-run-out-of-food-two-decades-earlier-than-thought/ (August 29, 2017) (accessed January 2020).
8 FAO, *The Future of Food and Agriculture – Trends and Challenges* (Rome: Food and Agriculture Organization, 2017), available at http://www.fao.org/3/a-i6583e.pdf (accessed January 2020), p. 136; note the World Economic Forum estimated in 2011 that the world would see a 50 percent increase in demand by 2030: *Global Risks 2011*.
9 Ibid.
10 Ibid., p. 37; Searchinger et al. "World Resources Report, Creating a Sustainable Food Future (Washington: WRI, 2018) (accessed January 2020).
11 Ibid.

12 United Nations Environment Programme (UNEP), Modelling Global Green Investment Scenarios: Supporting the Transition to a Green Economy, 2011, at http://www. unep. org/greeneconomy/Portals/88/documents/ger/GER 13 Modelling.pdf (accessed July 2015). UNEP used a model developed by the Millennium Institute that focuses on future scenarios in the context of sustainable development.

13 Ibid.

14 World Economic Forum, *Global Risks 2011*.

15 Jonathan Watts, "Third of Earth's Soil is Acutely Degraded Due to Agriculture," *The Guardian* (September 12, 2017), at https://www.theguardian.com/environment/2017/sep/12/third-of-earths-soil-acutely-degraded-due-to-agriculture-study.

16 International Energy Association, *World Energy Outlook 2017: A World in Transformation* (Paris: IEA, 2017), Executive Summary p.1, available at https://www.iea.org/reports/world-energy-outlook-2017 (accessed January 2020).

17 Ibid.

18 IPCC, Special Report on 1.5 Degrees (Geneva: IPCC, 2018).

19 IPCC, Fourth Assessment Report, Climate Change 2007: Synthesis Report (internal citations omitted), at http://www.ipcc.ch/publications and data/ar4/syr/en/spms3.html (accessed July 2015).

20 UNEP, Modelling Global Green Investment Scenarios; IPCC Fifth Assessment Report, *Climate Change 2014: Synthesis Report* (New York: IPCC, 2014).

21 World Economic Forum, *Global Risks 2011*.

22 Ibid.

23 Ibid.

24 Ibid.

25 Ibid.

26 Global Footprint Network, "World Footprint," at http://www.footprintnetwork. org/en/index.php/GFN/page/world_footprint/ (accessed July 2015). See also UNEP, Modelling Global Green Investment Scenarios.

27 Rachel Carson, *Silent Spring* (New York: Houghton Mifflin, 1962; anniversary edn 2002).

28 Paul R. Ehrlich, *The Population Bomb*, rev. edn (New York: Avon Books, 1982).

29 Jared Diamond, *Collapse: How Societies Choose to Fail or Succeed* (New York: Viking, 2005).

30 Donella Meadows et al., *The Limits to Growth*, 2nd edn (New York: Universe Books, 1974), p. 24: "If the present growth trends in world population, industrialization, pollution, food production, and resource depletion continue unchanged, the limits to growth on this planet will be reached sometime within the next 100 years. The most probable result will be a rather sudden and uncontrollable decline in both population and industrial capacity." See also Council on Environmental Quality and the Department of State, *The Global 2000 Report to the President: Entering the Twenty-First Century*, Vol. 1 (New York: Penguin Books, 1982), p. 1: "If present trends continue, the world in 2000 will be more crowded, more polluted, less stable ecologically, and more vulnerable to disruption than the world we live in now. Serious stresses involving populations, resources, and environment are clearly visible ahead. Despite greater material output, the world's people will be poorer in many ways than they are today … Barring revolutionary advances in technology, life for most people on Earth will be more precarious in 2000 than it is now – unless the nations of the world act decisively to alter current trends."

31　J. Diamond, *Collapse: How Societies Choose to Fail or Succeed.*

32　UNEP, Modelling Global Green Investment Scenarios.

33　Ibid.

34　Ibid.

35　Ibid.

36　Joel E. Cohen, "Choosing Future Population" (2009), in TeacherServe, National Humanities Center, Nature Transformed: The Environment in American History, at http://nationalhumanitiescenter.org/tserve/nattrans/ntuseland/essays/population.htm (accessed July 2015).

37　UNEP, Modelling Global Green Investment Scenarios.

38　Ibid.

39　Dan O'Neill, "Is it Possible for Everyone to Live a Good Life within our Planet's Limits?" The Conversation (blog), at https://theconversation.com/is-it-possible-for-everyone-to-live-a-good-life-within-our-planets-limits-91421 (last accessed December 2018), citing Daniel O'Neil, Andrew Fanning, William Lamb and Julia Steinberger, "A Good Life within Planetary Boundaries," *Nature Sustainability* 1, 88–95 (2018).

40　O'Neill, Is it Possible for Everyone to Live a Good Life within our Planet's Limits ?

41　Cohen, "Choosing Future Population."

42　Joel E. Cohen, "How Many People Can the Planet Hold?" (Aspen Institute Italia, English edn), 43/44 (June 2009), pp. 40–6.

43　World Economic Forum, *Global Risks 2011.*

44　UNEP, Modelling Global Green Investment Scenarios.

45　Ibid.

46　World Economic Forum, *Global Risks 2011.*

47　Ibid.

48　Ibid.

49　Stacy VanDeveer, "Consuming Environments: Options and Choices for 21st Century Citizens," in *Beyond Rio+20: Governance for a Green Economy* (Boston: Boston University, 2010), pp. 43–52.

50　Murray Gell-Mann, "Transformations of the Twenty-First Century: Transitions to Greater Sustainability," at http://www.nobel-cause.de/potsdam-2007/book/NobelCause Book chapter1.pdf (accessed July 2015) (utilizing a scheme modified from a scenario developed by James Gustave Speth, 2008).

51　Wendell Berry, "Out of Your Car, Off Your Horse," *Atlantic Monthly*, 267 (February 1991), p. 63.

52　See, e.g. Dominique Mosbergen, "Our Consumption of Earth's Natural Resources Has More Than Tripled in 40 Years," *Huffington Post* (August 2, 2016), at https://www.huffingtonpost.com/entry/natural-resource-use-tripled_us_57a05c3ae4b0693164c273a8 (accessed November 2018); David Roberts, "I'm an Environmental Journalist, but I Never Write about Overpopulation. Here's Why," *Vox* (September 26, 2017), at https://www.vox.com/energy-and-environment/2017/9/26/16356524/the-population-question (accessed November 2018); CSO Equity Review, *After Paris: Inequality, Fair Shares, and the Climate Emergency.* (Manila, London, Cape Town, Washington, et al.: CSO Equity Review Coalition, 2018), available at civilsocietyreview.org/report2018 (accessed January 2020).

53　VanDeveer, "Consuming Environments."

54　Gell-Mann, "Transformations of the Twenty-First Century."

55　Ibid.

56 David Maybury-Lewis, *Millennium: Tribal Wisdom and the Modern World* (New York: Viking, 1992), p. 265.

57 Alan Wolfe, "Three Paths to Development: Market, State, and Civil Society," prepared for the International Meeting of Nongovernmental Organizations and United Nations System Agencies, Rio de Janeiro, 1991.

58 Muhammad Yunus, "The Grameen Bank," *Scientific American*, 281 (November 1999), pp. 114–19. Yunus believes that loans to the poor are best made by private organizations, not by governments. When the new president of Mexico Vicente Fox announced in 2000 that his government was going to begin a small-loan program, Yunus talked him out of the idea, saying "Politicians are interested in the votes of the poor … not in getting the money back." Tim Weiner, "With Little Loans, Mexican Women Overcome", *New York Times* (March 19, 2003), p. A8. See also Celia Dugger, "Debate Stirs over Tiny Loans for World's Poorest," *New York Times* (April 29, 2004), p. A1; Saritha Rai, "Tiny Loans Have Big Impact on Poor," *New York Times* (April 12, 2004), p. C3; and David Armstrong, "Is Bigger Better?" Forbes Magazine (June 2, 2008), pp. 66–70.

59 Grameen Bank, "About Us," at http://www.grameen-info.org/about-us/; Grameen Bank, "Monthly Reports 01-2015," at http://www.grameen-info.org/monthly-reports-01-2015/ (both accessed July 2015).

60 International Finance Corporation, "Financial Institutions: Microfinance," Available at http://www.ifc.org/wps/wcm/connect/Industry_EXT_Content/IFC_External_Corporate_Site/Industries/Financial+Markets/MSME+Finance/Microfinance/ (accessed July 2015).

61 Wangari Maathai, *Unbowed* (New York, NY: Anchor Books, 2006), p. 291.

62 United Nations Development Programme (UNDP), UNEP, World Bank, and World Resources Institute, *A Guide to World Resources 2002–2004: Decisions for the Earth* (Washington, DC: World Resources Institute, 2002), p. 21.

63 Worldwatch Institute, "Indonesian Activist Targets Community Waste," at http://www.worldwatch.org/node/6079 (accessed July 2015).

64 Sarvodaya, "About," at http://www.sarvodaya.org/about (accessed July 2015).

65 Green Belt Movement, "Who We Are," at http://www.greenbeltmovement.org/who-we-are (accessed July 2015).

66 Majken Jul Sorensen and Stellan Vinthagen, "Nonviolent Resistance and Culture," *Peace and Change*, 37 (3) (2012), pp. 444, 459; Friends of the MST, "What Is the MST?" at http://www.mstbrazil.org/whatismst (accessed July 2015).

67 World March of Women, "Who We Are," at http://www.marchemondiale.org/ qui_nous_sommes/en/ (accessed July 2015).

68 Alan Durning, "Mobilizing at the Grassroots" in *State of the World, 1989* (New York: W. W. Norton, 1989), pp. 157–8. The growth of civil society continued in the 1990s. See David Bornstein, "A Force Now in the World, Citizens Flex Social Muscle," *New York Times* (July 10, 1999), pp. A15, A17.

69 Freedom House, *Freedom in the World 2018* (Washington, DC: Freedom House, 2018).

70 Ibid.

71 Grameen Bank, Monthly Reports, at http://www.grameen-info.org/monthly-reports/; World Bank, World Development Indicators (2013 revision), "Bangladesh," at http://data.worldbank.org/country/bangladesh; World Bank, World Development Indicators (2013 revision), "Domestic Credit Provided by Financial Sector (% of GDP)," at http://data.worldbank.org/indicator/FS.AST.DOMS.GD.ZS (all accessed July 2015).

72 An estimated 2.5 billion people lived in fully or partially democratic countries in 1981, whereas in 2001 this number had grown to 3.9 billion people. UNDP, *Human Development Report 1993* (New York: Oxford University Press, 1993), p. 94. See also Barbara Crossette, "UN Report Raises Questions about Small Loans to the Poor," *New York Times* (September 3, 1998), p. A8; and Dugger, "Debate Stirs over Tiny Loans for World's Poorest."

73 Durning, "Mobilizing at the Grassroots," p. 163.

74 Council on Foreign Relations, "Civil War in South Sudan," at https://www.cfr.org/interactives/global-conflict-tracker?marker=26#!/conflict/civil-war-in-south-sudan (accessed December 2018).

75 Freedom House, "Key Findings: Freedom in the World 2018," at https://freedomhouse.org/report/freedom-world/freedom-world-2018 (accessed December 2018).

76 Gell-Mann, "Transformations of the Twenty-First Century."

77 Ibid.

78 Cohen, "Choosing Future Population."

Further Reading

Bossel, Hartmut, *Earth at a Crossroads: Paths to a Sustainable Future* (Cambridge: Cambridge University Press, 1998). Bossel argues that humanity faces a choice between continuing on its present unsustainable path or shifting to a sustainable path that will call for significant changes. He offers his views of what ethical and organizational changes must be made to achieve a sustainable path and gives recommendations of what individuals and organizations can do to aid this transformation.

Boyd, David R., *The Optimistic Environmentalist: Progressing Towards a Greener Future* (Toronto, Canada: ECW Press, 2015). Boyd presents the progress we have made, and are making, to solve many of the environmental problems presented in our book.

Buzan, Barry, and Gerald Segal, *Anticipating the Future: Twenty Millennia of Human Progress* (London: Simon & Schuster, 1998). Even though there have been many setbacks, the authors are optimistic about human progress over the past 20,000 years. The human species has spread over the globe, abolished slavery, and reduced its appetite for large-scale wars. That progress should continue, although there will be ups and downs. They see the world gradually solving its environmental problems and eventually moving into space.

Daly, Herman, *Beyond Growth: The Economics of Sustainable Development* (Boston: Beacon Press, 1996). An unconventional economist, Daly questions the value of economic growth. He believes that traditional economists have a false faith in growth because they do not accurately calculate the cost of depleting resources. While still far from being accepted by the academic mainstream, Daly's ideas have inspired a new academic subdivision called "ecological economics."

Dodds, Felix, Jorge Laguna-Celis, and Liz Thompson, *From Rio+20 to a New Development Agenda: Building a Bridge to a Sustainable Future* (New York: Routledge, 2014). Following up on the 2012 Rio Earth Summit, this book provides policy and practical insight into efforts within and beyond the United Nations to chart a more sustainable pathway for development.

Hertsgaard, Mark, *Hot: Living Through the Next Fifty Years on Earth* (New York: Houghton Mifflin Harcourt, 2011). The author concludes after talking with many scientists that "many, many things have to happen by 2020 if this planet is to remain a livable place." Not only must we stop and reverse our carbon emissions – something we know how to do and have much of the technology to do – but we must prepare for the changes in our world, such as more droughts, which are coming and which can kill millions. American opinion remains the greatest obstacle to doing what needs to be done.

McKibben, Bill, *Eaarth: Making a Life on a Tough New Planet* (New York: Henry Holt, 2010). McKibben believes we have already changed our world because of our carbon-based energy system. But as a "grudging optimist," as one review of this book calls him, McKibben believes we can still voluntarily make necessary changes in our lives before we are forced to make them by the new world, which he calls "Eaarth," we have created.

Musser, George, "The Climax of Humanity," *Scientific American*, 293 (September 2005), pp. 44–7. How we manage the next few decades could lead to sustainability or collapse. This article is part of a special issue of the journal titled "Crossroads for Planet Earth." It contains a series of articles (on population, poverty, biodiversity, energy, food and water, disease, economics, and policy) focused on how we can successfully pass beyond 2050.

Rees, Martin, *Our Final Hour: A Scientist's Warning: How Terror, Error, and Environmental Disaster Threaten Humankind's Future in This Century – on Earth and Beyond* (New York: Basic Books, 2003). Rees is Britain's Astronomer Royal and a professor at Cambridge University. He gives our civilization a 50/50 chance of surviving the twenty-first century. Rees believes the choices we make in the next several decades could decide our fate.

Shi, David, *The Simple Life: Plain Living and High Thinking in American Culture*, new edn (Athens, GA: University of Georgia Press, 2007). Voluntary simplicity is a component of sustainable development. Shi explores the roots of the idea in the lives and writings of Socrates, Plato, Aristotle, Jesus, St Francis, Buddha, Leo Tolstoy, Marcus Aurelius, Gandhi, Confucius, and Thoreau, among others. Its advocates hold that the simple life frees a person for real intellectual, moral, and spiritual growth.

Wilson, Edward O., *The Future of Life* (New York: Knopf, 2002). We still have time and choices we can make to save life on our planet. Here is how Wilson states it: "The race is now on between the technoscientific forces that are destroying the living environment and those that can be harnessed to save it. We are inside a bottleneck of overpopulation and wasteful consumption. If the race is won, humanity can emerge in far better condition than when it entered, and with most of the diversity of life still intact."

Appendix 1

Studying and Teaching Global Issues

For the Student

You may find it useful to learn how the concept "development" can be used to study global issues and to have an overview of the topics covered in this textbook. One way to do this is to examine the structure of the course I teach in which *Global Issues: An Introduction* is the principal textbook.

What is Development?

The first two or three days of the course are spent explaining what "development" means and how development and global issues are related. The book defines development as economic growth plus the social and environmental changes caused by or accompanying that economic growth. In this short introduction we begin to understand some of the main differences in the social and economic conditions of the rich and poor countries. The connection between development and the extinction of cultures is also examined, as, for example, in the name of development the forest homes of numerous indigenous peoples are being destroyed.

Wealth and Poverty

The third week of the course is spent on getting students to consider the extremely difficult question: "Why are some nations rich and some poor?" Students examine conventional approaches or views of economic development: the market

Global Issues: An Introduction, Sixth Edition. Kristen A. Hite and John L. Seitz.
© 2021 John Wiley & Sons Ltd. Published 2021 by John Wiley & Sons Ltd.

approach (also called the neoclassical or capitalist approach) and the state approach (also called the command economy or socialist approach). Globalization, which has greatly expanded international trade, is explained and the uneven effects it is having on poor and rich nations are discussed. Another important consideration raised by this chapter is inequality, not just between nations but also within countries, bringing the social dimension of development more acutely into focus.

Population

For two weeks we look at the relationship between population and development. The changing population of the world is described, and the causes of the population explosion are discussed. Students learn how population growth affects development (rapid population growth hinders development by putting a large stress on resources, health and education facilities, the environment, etc.), and how development affects population growth (development at first makes it greater as it lowers death rates, but later it reduces birth rates as the education level of women increases and children become less desirable economically and socially). The demographic transition is explained and students become familiar with the factors that lower birth rates. Some attention during this period is paid to the population policies of major countries, such as China. This segment of the course ends with a consideration of the future – whether a stabilization of the world's population will occur, geographic considerations related to demographic transitions, and whether the carrying capacity of the Earth will be exceeded.

Food

For two weeks food holds our attention. World food production trends are examined, and a tentative answer is given to the question of how many are hungry in the world today, and why. We investigate the causes of hunger in parts of the global South (such as climate change, poverty, and shifting land economics). Students learn how the availability and quality of food affect development, and how development affects both the production of food and the type of food consumed. We consider equity and distributional considerations such as how (industrialized agriculture produces a large amount of food, but that does not necessarily translate to more food for the hungry), and also consider how wealthy people often do not have a healthy diet. A short history of the Green Revolution is given. The food policies of the United States and a few other countries are examined. Finally, we think about how changes in the climate, biotechnology, the amount of arable land, and the cost of energy could affect future food supplies.

Energy

One week is not enough time to investigate thoroughly the relationship between energy and development, but it is enough time to introduce students to this vital subject. A description of the energy crisis caused by the developed world's dependency on a polluting and highly insecure energy source – oil – is followed by a summary of the responses to that crisis by the United States, Western Europe, and Japan. The effect of the energy crisis on the South's development plans is explained. As we explore the relationship between energy use and development, students learn about the shift in the types of energy sources that took place as the Industrial Revolution progressed and how there has been a partial decoupling of energy consumption and economic growth – a new ability to produce economic growth with less energy. This is a rapidly changing field, and we do our best to present information on the many different sources of energy available, and encourage supplementary material from our Facebook site and elsewhere to make sure the information presented reflects the rapidly shifting status of global energy economics. The subject ends with a presentation of the main arguments for and against nuclear power, which allows students to appreciate how difficult and complicated are the choices the political system must make when dealing with energy.

Climate

The subject of climate change (global warming) serves as a good bridge to the environment section's discussion of nonrenewable and renewable energy sources. This is an opportunity to explore the limits of the traditional development pathway of economic production and consumption based on the cheap combustion of fossil fuels, which allows for consideration of the ways in which climate change is redefining development. The role of conservation during the present period of energy transition is also explored.

The Environment

We divide the environment discussion in two parts: part 1 considers the impact of economic production based on the extraction of natural resources, and part 2 consider the impacts of industrialization associated with pollution and waste.

The natural resources section includes a brief history of the awakening in the United States to threats to the environment caused by industrialization which introduces the subject and provides the setting for an examination of the threats to the air, water, and land that have come with development. The problem of deforestation in the developing countries is briefly examined so that students become aware of the harm deforestation can bring to the land, its connection to the extinction of species, as well as the changes it can make in the climate. Recycling, substitution, and the mining of low-grade ores are subjects presented at the end of this section of the course as we consider future supplies. The concept "overdevelopment" (consuming and polluting at a rate that cannot be maintained indefinitely) is also presented, as students consider reducing needs as a possible response to scarcities.

The pollution topic considers chemicals, cancer, and pesticides under a section in which we focus on the workplace and the home. Airborne lead, acid rain, and the depletion of the ozone layer illustrate some of the main concerns we have at present with air pollution. The current concern with threats to our ground water by migrating chemicals presents an example of water pollution caused by development. It also considers the problem of how to handle huge amounts of solid and toxic wastes demonstrates well to the students the extremely difficult tasks the political system faces as it tries to preserve the land.

Technology

To many people, technology and development are synonymous. Technology is what makes economic growth and social change happen. Students are reminded of the many benefits that technology has brought to our lives. But because they are more aware of the benefits than the harm technology can produce, the course focuses on the dangers. Students learn that the decision of whether or not to use a certain technology can be a difficult one, especially when considering different levels of economic wealth and capacity. Illustrations of the unanticipated consequences of the use of technology are given, as are examples of the inappropriate uses of technology. Limits to the "technological fix" are illustrated. The issue of war is introduced, with technology making the destructive capacity of weapons greater. The threat of nuclear weapons is presented as a case study under the technology section.

Alternative Futures

The course ends by focusing on different possible futures and governance considerations related to the ability to make effective decisions on matters pertaining to global issues. A nice end to the class is to consider the main arguments that advocates make for the possibilities that our present type of development is leading us to "doom," or to continued "growth," or to "sustainable development" in the future and identify the political challenges and options for making effective long-term decisions.

For the Teacher

The problem

Improving and increasing international studies has become a priority on many campuses[1] but as a report for the American Council on Education concludes, "the internationalizing of undergraduate education still has a long way to go."[2] How far it has to go can be easily shown. Reports of the shocking ignorance of people in the United States about other countries are well known, but less well known, and of some embarrassment to the college teaching profession, is that college-age people in the country are the most ignorant of all adults. Adding to the insult is the fact that attending college for four years reduces that ignorance only slightly.[3] Young people aged 18–24 in the United States in the late 1980s possessed *less* information about the world than the same age group had 40 years earlier.[4]

This information is especially surprising given the new emphasis many colleges are placing on international studies. Also surprising is the fact that the average student in a four-year college or university course takes several international studies courses, outside of foreign language instruction, before he or she graduates.[5] But a close look at these international studies courses reveals that most of them still focus on only one country or one region (often Western Europe), and only a few focus on a problem or issue that is found throughout the world. Also, few are interdisciplinary, and *only a minority deal with the world as it is today.*[6]

We indeed seem to be far from achieving what one report called an important characteristic of the truly internationalized university: it is a school where "no student graduates who has never been asked to think about the rights and responsibilities of this country in the world community, or who has never been brought to empathize with people of a different culture."[7]

Preparing students so that they will be able to function in an increasingly complex and interdependent world is a huge task, one that will require a better trained and more committed faculty and college administration. No easy answers, solutions, or quick fixes are possible, but many different methods and approaches are being tried, with varied degrees of success. As the American Council on Education study found, what we do not have now in the United States is a way to know what works, and what does not, and why it does or does not.[8] What we need are reports of successes and failures in the attempts to achieve the important characteristic of the truly internationalized university that the above quotation appropriately identifies.

A solution: perspectives from decades of teaching this course

by John L. Seitz

While attending a conference on the developing world, I heard college teachers complain that they could not get their students interested in studying the global South, where most of the world's people live. As I thought about this complaint, I realized that I had discovered an answer to the question: "How do you get American students to want to study the non-Western world?" I know that you don't do it by reminding them that their bananas come from that world. The student's reaction to that statement is: "So what? Who cares?" The way you get them interested is by introducing real global problems and exploring their possible solutions. You demonstrate that global problems are American problems, that our actions help create or solve the problems, and that the problems affect our lives, in the present as well as in the future.

Over the past 25 years I have taught a course for undergraduates called "Global Issues." The course, outlined in the section addressed to the student, focuses on many of the most important global issues today, issues that both the more developed and the less developed nations can no longer ignore.

I believe that one reason many social science teachers do not teach a course on global issues is that they do not know how to deal with these issues in a respectable, scholarly way – in a manner that will prevent the class from becoming just a forum for the discussion of current events. But I have found that there is a concept – "development" – which can serve as the tool we need for treating these issues in a responsible manner. Social scientists commonly use this concept only with reference to the poorer nations, but "development" can also be a powerful tool for analyzing conditions in and actions of the richer nations.

Teaching techniques

How does one teach the above material? A combination of techniques is most effective, starting with the basic text-book: this book, *Global Issues: An Introduction*. We also maintain a facebook site with real-time feeds of news articles linked to the individual chapters, to which teachers and students alike are most welcome to like and follow the page, and also to submit links to relevant news articles that reflect new developments.

Another useful resource is the latest edition of the Worldwatch Institute's *State of the World*.[9] This book is an excellent annual updating of many of the topics covered in my course, although the large amount of detailed, factual information it contains overwhelms some undergraduates. Another useful resource is the United Nations Development Programme's *Human Development Report*, which covers many development-related subjects.[10] Students read selections from the latest edition of *Annual Editions: Global Issues*, which is a collection of articles from many different sources – some with opposing viewpoints – on many of the issues presented in the course.[11] Students can also subscribe to a newspaper like the *New York Times*, which allows them to follow (and quizzes them on) current developments in all of the subjects covered in the course. The Facebook website for this course also provides abundant materials and updates, ranging from news articles to videos.

Videos play an important role in the course. Many excellent programs related to topics in our course are available online or via public television (see Appendix 2).

The experience of seeing an interesting, current portrayal of a topic we are studying is a powerful teaching technique. The tapes reinforce what the students are learning and broaden their knowledge. Also, the tapes serve another important role. Studying global issues can be depressing. The problems are numerous and serious, and at first glance appear to be unsolvable. The tapes help counter that depression by often showing what some individuals are doing to attack these problems.

Students generally write a research paper that delves into a topic of their choice related to Global Issues. In the paper they focus on an issue in greater depth than we have been able to in the course. Time-permitting, students share their research findings with the class. This is an excellent way to encourage critical thinking in an area self-selected by each students, and generally produces substantial learning.

A course of instruction following the above outline utilizes three levels of analysis, which contribute to its effectiveness: the individual, the nation, and the international system. To understand the issues one must look at the behavior of individuals, the actions and policies of nations, and the condition of the world's environment as well as of its economic and political systems. Solutions to the global problems require individual efforts, new national policies, and international agreements.

Such a course of instruction has three main goals. The first is to increase student knowledge of some of the most important problems facing the world today, a knowledge that the student learns comes from many different disciplines. The second goal is to help students learn of the complex interrelationships among the issues. The third is to evaluate possible solutions to the problems studied. As the students consider possible solutions, they learn the vital fact that human actions (including their own) can change the world in very different ways.

Can these goals be achieved? Certainly they cannot for every student, nor will every student who achieves one achieve all three. But many can achieve one or more of these goals. Students appreciate an effort that helps them understand the complicated and rapidly changing world in which they live. When we help them acquire this information we are giving them both the knowledge they will need to live in today's world, and more importantly, the knowledge that will enable them, if they so desire, to add their talents to the efforts being made to solve many of these global problems.

Student comments

For 20 years students have written, in a short unsigned essay, what they felt was the most important thing they learned in the course. These three responses give some common conclusions:

> The most important thing I learned is that problems concerning population, food, energy, etc. are *real*. I feel that most people don't realize the magnitude of these problems. However, by taking this course, I now see that all these problems are greater than I originally thought . . . This course taught me the first step in combating these problems, and that is to recognize that they are REAL!

I had . . . known about the environmental movement and even considered myself an environmentalist. Sure I wanted to take care of my environment; new energy sources sounded cool; pollution was bad and needed to be stopped, etc. However, I never really knew how *interconnected* all of this was until I took this course. . . . I learned how changes in one area can drastically affect what I previously thought were unrelated things. . . . I learned that all of these problems are interconnected and must be studied as such if any real (long-term) solution is ever to be found for them.

The most important thing I learned was to stop thinking like an American and only think about self-interest. Rather now I think about my neighbor be it in Converse Heights or my neighbor in South America. Professor Seitz, you focused my mind to look at the big picture instead of the small one. When I . . . [threw away an empty] can of Coke previously I would say, "What can I do about recycling?" Now I see that even a little effort to make a difference does just that, it makes a difference. Now when I get in my car to go to the store, I think twice and now I usually will walk. Before when I said [what's wrong] with one more light on, it's just 20 cents a day lost. Now I think about how [the production of] electricity pollutes the atmosphere, so now I conserve electricity and other fossil fuels as well. To sum it all up, I have learned to be more responsible to this precious world we call earth. For that, whatever grade I receive, I thank you for opening not just my eyes but my mind.

Notes

1   Ann Kelleher, "One World, Many Voices," *Liberal Education*, 77 (November/December 1991), pp. 2–7.

2   Richard D. Lambert, *International Studies and the Undergraduate* (Washington, DC: American Council on Education, 1989), p. 153.

3   Id., p. 107.

4   Id., p. 106.

5   Id., p. 126.

6   Id., pp. 115–27.

7   Humphrey Tonkin and Jane Edwards, "Internationalizing the University: The Arduous Road to Euphoria," *Educational Record*, 71 (Spring 1990), p. 15.

8   Lambert, *International Studies*, p. 157.

9   Lester Brown *et al.*, *State of the World* (New York: W. W. Norton, annual).

10 United Nations Development Programme, *Human Development Report* (New York: Oxford University Press, annual).

11 Robert M. Jackson (ed.), *Annual Editions: Global Issues* (Guilford, CT: Dushkin, annual).

Appendix 2

Relevant Videos

The American Pipe Dream? Eliminating Oil Dependence, produced by the Open University, distributed by Films for the Humanities and Sciences, 2009, 27 minutes.

Arctic Rush: Staking a Claim in the Earth's Uncertain Future (negative and positive effects of the melting of the Arctic ice cover). Produced by Canadian Broadcasting Corporation, distributed by Films for the Humanities and Sciences, 2006, 46 minutes.

Arming the Heavens (examines all sides of the space weapons debate), Glenn Baker, writer/producer, distributed by Azimuth Media, 2004, 25 minutes.

Arms for the Poor: The Global Impact of the Weapons Industry, distributed by Films for the Humanities and Sciences, 2006, 30 minutes.

Atmospheric Hole: The History of the Ozone Layer, distributed by Films for the Humanities and Sciences, 2006, 28 minutes.

Becoming Green: Growing Environmental Awareness, a NOVA production, 4 parts, distributed by Public Broadcasting Service (PBS), 1993, 2000, 2007, 2008, about 75 minutes each.

The Bells of Chernobyl: Ten Years After (coverup of the effects of the Chernobyl nuclear disaster), a coproduction for Tele Images International, distributed by Filmakers Library, 2000, 52 minutes.

Bill Moyers Journal: Farm Subsidies and America's Hungry, distributed by Films for the Humanities and Sciences, 2008, 58 minutes.

Global Issues: An Introduction, Sixth Edition. Kristen A. Hite and John L. Seitz.
© 2021 John Wiley & Sons Ltd. Published 2021 by John Wiley & Sons Ltd.

Bill Moyers Journal: Global Hunger, distributed by Films for the Humanities and Sciences, 2008, 58 minutes.

The Biofuel Myth: Harsh Realities in the Developing World, distributed by Films for the Humanities and Sciences, 2009, 44 minutes.

Bhopal: The Search For Justice (after 15,000 people were killed and hundreds of thousands more were permanently maimed by the leak of poisonous gas at a pesticide plant in India, the search for justice for the survivors is still going on), produced by The National Film Board of Canada, 2004, 53 minutes.

Blue Gold: World Water Wars, Purple Turtle Films, Canada, distributed by PBS Broadcasting, 2009, 90 minutes.

Building the Future – Energy, Nicolas Brown, UK Director (an upbeat film looks at new, sustainable energy projects in Europe and the USA), 2007, 54 minutes.

Captive Servants and Child Prostitution, distributed by Films for the Humanities and Sciences, 2008, 45 minutes.

Clean, Green, and Unseen: Nanotechnology and the Environment (a Fred Friendly Seminar), distributed by Films for the Humanities and Sciences, 2008, 57 minutes.

Climate Change: Hot Times in the City (how climate change will affect urban life), produced by Canadian Broadcasting Corporation, distributed by Films for the Humanities and Sciences, 2007, 44 minutes.

Climate Change: Our Responsibility (examines both ozone depletion and the buildup of greenhouse gasses), distributed by Films for the Humanities and Sciences, 2008, 25 minutes.

Core Meteorology: Atmosphere (dangers of burning fossil fuels), distributed by Public Broadcasting Service (PBS), 2008, 30 minutes.

Core Meteorology: Climates (fundamentals of climate change), distributed by Public Broadcasting Service (PBS), 2008, 30 minutes.

Core Meteorology: Weather (extreme weather events), distributed by Public Broadcasting Service (PBS), 2008, 30 minutes.

Captive Servants and Child Prostitution, distributed by Films for the Humanities and Sciences, 2008, 45 minutes.

Corporate Power in the Age of Globalization (a critical view of the worldwide impact of neoliberal economics), a project of California Newsreel, available at www. newsreel.org.

1   *The Big Sellout* (the implementation of current economic orthodoxy is hurting millions of ordinary people around the world), German film in English and Spanish, 2006, 94 minutes.

2 *The Debt of Dictators* (transnational banks provided large loans to dictators creating third world debt that is a huge burden to developing nations), Norwegian film in English and Spanish, 2005, 46 minutes.

3 *Black Gold* (unjust conditions under which coffee is produced), UK film, 2006, 78 minutes.

4 *A Killer Bargain* (cheap consumer goods imported by Western companies don't reflect the actual human and environmental costs of their production). Danish film, 2006, 57 minutes.

5 *Maquilapolis* (women who work in the multinational factories in Mexico near the US border), US film, 2006, 69 minutes.

The Corporation (Canadian documentary that examines and criticizes corporate business practices; includes a section on "negative externalities," which can seriously hurt the environment), distributed by Zeitgeist Films, 2003, 145 minutes (divided into separate topics).

Countdown to Hope: Opposing the Threat of Nuclear War (deals with the threat of nuclear war caused by the decline of nuclear security in Russia, the conflict between India and Pakistan, and threats by rogue states and zealot factions), distributed by Films for the Humanities and Sciences, 2001, 57 minutes.

The Curse of Oil (a global history of the oil industry), distributed by Films for the Humanities and Sciences, 2003, 52 minutes.

The Dark Side of Chocolate: Child Trafficking and Illegal Child Labor in the Cocoa Industry, distributed by Films for the Humanities and Sciences, 2010, 47 minutes.

Dying to Leave: The Dark Business of Human Trafficking (illegal immigration and human trafficking), distributed by Films for the Humanities and Sciences, 2004, 57 minutes.

Economic Development: A Global Challenge (introduces the three main determinants of income and expansion – physical capital, human capital, and technology – and examines geographic, historical, and political reasons behind underdevelopment, part of a four-part series titled Global Economics), distributed by Films for the Humanities and Sciences, 2007, 39 minutes.

The Energy Conspiracy (influential organizations have successfully lobbied for the coal, oil, and nuclear power industries against sustainable energy and have convinced the public, with inaccurate information, that global warming is not a problem), produced by Hans Bulow and Poul-Eric Heilburth, distributed by Filmakers Library, 1999, 59 minutes.

Extreme Oil: The Wilderness (search for oil in fragile wilderness areas in Canada and Alaska leads to political controversy), distributed by Films for the Humanities and Sciences, 2004, 57 minutes.

Failed Nation Building: A Case Study of Haiti (one of the world's poorest nations, where US intervention failed), an ABC News program, distributed by Films for the Humanities and Sciences, 2004, 22 minutes.

Fighting the Tide 2: Developing Nations and Globalization, distributed by Films for the Humanities and Sciences, 2008, 25 minutes each.

1   Angola: The Curse of Oil (conflict over oil revenues)
2   Bolivia: Partners, Not Masters (natural resources generate wealth and inequality)
3   Tuvalu: Keeping Heads Above Water (an island nation threatened by climate change)

Fighting the Tide 3: Developing Nations and Globalization, distributed by Films for the Humanities and Sciences, 2009, 25 minutes each.

1   Colombia: Flowers for the Gringo
2   Mali: Message from the River (climate change, poverty, population growth)
3   Mongolia: Wrestling with Change
4   Niger: In the Shadow of Noma (oral infections that attack malnourished children)
5   Paraguay: Soya and Pesticides
6   Laos: So You Think the War is Over (unexploded munitions from the Vietnam War still kill innocent civilians)

Free-Market Capitalism is So 20th-Century: A Debate, distributed by Films for the Humanities and Sciences, 2009, 106 minutes.

Fueling Our Future: A Fred Friendly Seminar on Alternative Energy, distributed by Films for the Humanities and Sciences, 2008, 58 minutes.

Gimme Green (the ubiquitous American lawn with its negative environmental aspects). Available at www.gimmegreen.com, 2006, 27 minutes.

Globalization at a Crossroads, distributed by Films for the Humanities and Sciences, 2010, 29 minutes.

Global Jihad (forces behind Islamic terrorism), an ABC News program, distributed by Films for the Humanities and Sciences, 2004, 20 minutes.

The Global Trade Debate (attempts to offer a balanced look at the realities of globalization and to examine the issues that divide those who support and criticize growing world trade), distributed by Films for the Humanities and Sciences, 2001, 42 minutes.

Global Warming: The Signs and the Science, produced by Public Broadcasting Service (PBS), distributed by PBS Video, 2005, approx. 60 minutes.

Global Warming: The Rising Storm, distributed by Public Broadcasting Service (PBS), 2007, each disk about 1 hour.

Disk One: Warnings from a Warming Planet (what's happening now)
Disk Two: Predictions for a Warmer Planet (what the future may be like)

Global Warming and the Extinction of Species, distributed by Films for the Humanities and Sciences, 2005, 22 minutes.

Guns, Germs, and Steel (based on the Pulitzer Prize-winning book with this title by Jared Diamond, a three-part program presents Diamond's controversial theory that geography is the main reason the world is divided into haves and have-nots), produced by Lions Television, London, for National Geographic Television and Films, Washington, DC and distributed by PBS Video, 2005, three 60-minute programs.

Heat: A Global Investigation (this episode of Frontline investigates what powerful companies are really doing to solve climate change), distributed by Public Broadcasting Service (PBS), 2008, 120 minutes.

Home (stunning photographs of Earth covering life's journey on the planet and threats by our species to it, especially climate change), a film by Arthus-Bertrand spanning 54 countries, narrated by Glenn Close, distributed by Europa Corp.-Elzevir Films, Twentieth Century Fox, 2009, 118 minutes.

Hotspots (extinction of species), distributed by Public Broadcasting Service (PBS), 2008, about 1 hour 45 minutes.

How Poaching Turned into a 3 Billion Dollar Business, video from the Cable News Network on the shift from small local poaching to organized criminal activity and associated implications for wildlife, 2015, 3 minutes, available at https://www.cnn.com/videos/tv/2015/07/31/jack-hanna-poaching-sot-ac.cnn/video/playlists/poaching/.

The Hunt for Black Gold: Oil in the 21st Century, a CNBC original documentary, distributed by Films for the Humanities and Sciences, 2008, 45 minutes.

The Hydrogen Age: Energy Solutions for the 21st Century, distributed by Films for the Humanities and Sciences, 2004, 57 minutes.

India Rising: The New Empire, a Canadian National Broadcasting Corporation original program, distributed by Films for the Humanities and Sciences, 2008, 44 minutes.

IPCC Special Report on Limiting Global Warming to 1.5 Degrees C, offers a quick summary of the findings of the Intergovernmental Panel on Climate Change Special Report on 1.5 Degrees of Warming, including both challenges and opportunities presented in the Summary for Policymakers and underlying reports, 2018, 3 minutes, available at https://youtu.be/rVjp3TO_juI.

Journey to Planet Earth, explores the necessity of achieving a balance between the needs of people and the needs of the environment), produced by Emmy Award filmmakers Marilyn and Hal Weiner in association with South Carolina Educational Television (http://www.pbs.org/journeytoplanetearth/). Distributed by Screenscope (screenscope@screenscope.com), 25 minutes each (educational cut), or 60 minutes each.

1   *On the Brink* (severe environmental problems can produce political crises and more hostilities. Visits Haiti, Peru, South Africa, Mexico, and US), 2003.
2   *Seas of Grass* (some grasslands are in grave danger. Visits Kenya, South Africa, Argentina, China, US), 2003.

3 *Hot Zones* (changes in global and local ecosystems are connected to increased spread of infectious diseases. Visits Kenya, Peru, Bangladesh, US), 2003.

4 *Future Conditional* (spread of toxic pollution. Visits the Arctic, Mexico, Uzbekistan, US), 2005.

5 *The State of the Planet: Global Warming*, 2005.

6 *State of the Planet's Wildlife*, 2006.

Kilowatt Ours: A Plan to Re-Energize America (filmmaker Jeff Barrie searches cities, towns and countrysides for solutions to today's energy problems, focusing on energy efficiency and green power), 2007, 55 minutes.

Left Behind: Kenyan AIDS Orphans (award-winning film looks at the lives of children orphaned by AIDS), distributed by Films for the Humanities and Sciences, 2002, 36 minutes.

Lives for Sale: Human Trafficking (illegal immigration into the US from Mexico), distributed by Films for the Humanities and Sciences, 2006, 60 minutes.

Made in China: The People's Republic of Profit (China has become arguably the world's most business minded country), a Canadian National Broadcasting Corporation original program, distributed by Films for the Humanities and Sciences, 2008, 45 minutes.

The Meatrix, a parody video critical of factory farming, 2006, 5 minutes.

Missing Women: Female-Selective Abortion and Infanticide, distributed by Films for the Humanities and Sciences, 2006, 53 minutes.

Mysterious Poison: The History of PCBs, distributed by Films for the Humanities and Sciences, 2006, 28 minutes.

NASA Sees Definitive Evidence of the Montreal Protocol's Success, a video from the US National Aeronautics and Space Administration discussing the effectiveness of global agreement and action to address ozone pollution, 2018, 3 minutes, available at https://youtu.be/uVeTJSIbGm8.

No Vacancy: Global Responses to the Human Population Explosion, distributed by Films for the Humanities and Sciences, 2005, 92 minutes.

The Nuclear Option: Rethinking Atomic Energy, a Canadian National Broadcasting Corporation original documentary, distributed by Films for the Humanities and Sciences, 2008, 44 minutes.

Ocean Animal Emergency: Troubled Waters for Marine Mammals? (threats by warming seas and pollutants), produced by Public Broadcasting Service (PBS), 2008, approx. 60 minutes.

One Day of War (follows combatants in 16 wars in the same 24-hour period), a BBCW Production, distributed by Films for the Humanities and Sciences, 2004, 47 minutes.

Our Forests, Our Life, a video from the Asia Indigenous Peoples Pact explaining climate forest conservation opportunities and challenges for indigenous communities across the globe, 2014, 18 minutes, available at https://aippnet.org/our-forest-our-life/.

Our Hiroshima (eyewitness account, archival footage taken before and after the event, and the politics involved in developing and promoting the use of the bomb), distributed by Films for the Humanities and Sciences, 1995, 43 minutes.

Overpopulated, BBC documentary that explains demographic trends and their implications for development, 2014, 59 minutes.

The Peacekeepers (UN peacekeeping force in the Democratic Republic of Congo to quell ethnic fighting), produced by The National Film Board of Canada, 2005, 83 minutes.

Perspectives on the Energy Transition, a keynote address by John Moore from the 2018 Bloomberg New Energy Finance Summit, provides an overview of the rapidly shifting energy market trends and dramatic growth of renewable energy, 2018, 19 minutes, available at https://about.bnef.com/future-energy-summit/london-videos/?vid=292955911.

Religion, War, and Violence: The Ethics of War and Peace (experts, scholars, and religious leaders from a variety of faiths discuss terrorism and its roots, fundamentalism, just war, holy war, pacifism, and the use of violence in the name of God), distributed by Films for the Humanities and Sciences, 2002, 90 minutes.

Scared Scared (people seeking positive ways to react to disasters such as those at the minefields of Cambodia, in post-9/11 New York City, at the toxic wasteland of Bhopal, in war-torn Afghanistan, at Hiroshima, in Bosnia, and in Palestine and Israel), produced and distributed by The National Film Board of Canada, 2004, 104 minutes.

Scarred Lands and Wounded Lives: The Environmental Footprint of War, VideoTakes USA. Available at www.fundforsustainabletomorrows.org/film.htm, 2008, 60 minutes.

Sisters on the Planet: Cataret Islands, Oxfam New Zealand, presents the story of a woman leading her community in Papua New Guinea on decisions about whether to relocate due to Climate Change, 2009, 9 minutes, available at https://youtu.be/0XDHMgqlcEU.

Slum Cities (visits Mumbai, India and Rio de Janeiro, Brazil), distributed by Films for the Humanities and Sciences, 2006, 44 minutes.

Stemming the Flow of Water Pollution, Part 1 (how waters flowing into the seas are being polluted). *Part 2* (efforts to remediate oceanic "dead zones" in Spain, Brazil, Iran, and Fuji), distributed by Films for the Humanities and Sciences, 2004, 24 minutes each.

Story of Stuff, a critical description of conventional development theory and its discontents, 2007, 21 minutes.

A Tale of Modern Slavery (caste systems and other archaic traditions perpetuate slavery in some poor countries), an ABC News program, distributed by Films for the Humanities and Sciences, 2005, 20 minutes.

Voices of Dissent: Freedom of Speech and Human Rights in China, distributed by Films for the Humanities and Sciences, 2008, 45 minutes.

What Are We Doing Here? Why Western Aid Hasn't Helped Africa, distributed by Films for the Humanities and Sciences, 2008, 95 minutes.

Where Ships Go to Die, Workers Risk Everything, a National Geographic video on shipbreaking, an environmental challenge related to waste and disposal of large and toxic items, 2014, 5 minutes, available at https://www.youtube.com/watch?v=WOmtFN1bfZ8.

White Light, Black Rain: The Destruction of Hiroshima and Nagasaki (an HBO production), distributed by Films for the Humanities and Science, 2007, 87 minutes.

A Window on a Changing Climate (Antarctic), produced by The National Film Board of Canada, 2009, 52 minutes.

Years of Living Dangerously, Emmy-award winning TV series on climate change, 2014, episodes are approx. 60 minutes.

The following is a partial list of relevant video distributors in the USA:

1 Azimuth Media, 1779 Massachusetts Ave., NW, Washington, DC 20036-2109, telephone: (202) 232-8003; email: info@azimuthmedia.org; website: www.azimuthmedia.org.
2 Bullfrog Films, PO Box 149, Oley, PA 19547; telephone: 1-800-543-3764; email: video@bullfrogfilms.com; website: www.bullfrogfilms.com.
3 California Newsreel/Resolution, PO Box 2284, South Burlington, VT, 05407; toll free telephone 877-811-7495; fax 802-846-1850; www.newsreel.org.
4 Film Library (Bruno Films), 22-D Hollywood Ave., Ho-Ho-Kus, New Jersey 07423; telephone: 1-800-343-5540; website: www.brunofilms.com.
5 Filmakers Library, 124 East 40th Street, New York, NY 10016; telephone: (212) 808-4980; fax: (212) 808-4983; email: info@filmakers.com; website: www.filmakers.com.
6 Films for the Humanities and Sciences, 200 American Metro Blvd., Suite 124, Hamilton, NJ 08619; telephone: 1-800-257-5126; fax: 800-329-6687; email: order@films.com; website: www.films.com (24 hours a day, 7 days a week).
7 National Film Board of Canada, 311 Baltic Street, Suite 30, Brooklyn, NY 11201; telephone: 1-800-542-2164; fax 866-299 9928; website: www.nfb.ca/store.
8 PBS (Public Broadcasting Service) Video, P.O.Box 279, Melbourne, FL 32902; telephone 1-800-344-3337; fax 1-866-274-9043; website: http://shopPBS.org/education.

9   Screenscope, Inc., 4330 Yuma St, NW, Washington, DC 20016; telephone: (202) 364-0055; email: screenscope@screenscope.com; website: www.screenscope. com.

10 Video Finders, telephone: 1-800-328-7271, a service of Public Broadcasting Service station KCET/Los Angeles. Provides availability and ordering information on more than 70,000 videocassette titles, including 3,000 programs broadcast by PBS.

Information on how to rent or purchase available videos is contained in a reference book found in many libraries: *Bowker's Complete Video Directory*, annual, which is published by R. R. Bowker, a Reed Reference Publishing Company, New Providence, New Jersey.

Glossary

biotechnology   The technology by which an animal or plant derivative is integrated with a process or tool, such as for medical, industrial, or manufacturing purposes. It can be "low tech" such as yeast for brewing and probiotics found in cheese and yoghurt, or high tech such as cloning and manipulating DNA (genetic engineering) to produce drought-resistant crops or create new a cancer-fighting treatment.

carrying capacity   The total population an ecosystem or other geographic area can sustain without depleting internal resources beyond their rate of replenishment. Human actions can impact carrying capacity such as by cutting down trees and converting to pasture land for livestock.

civil society   Voluntary associations of people that are between the state and the extended family. There are two branches of the use of this concept, one emphasizing economic associations (e.g., Adam Smith) and one emphasizing social and political associations (e.g., Montesquieu, Rousseau, and de Tocqueville). This book uses the latter definition with a focus on social and political organizations such as churches, clubs, interest groups, social movements, and political parties.

climate change (global warming, greenhouse effect)   Variations beyond historic cyclical fluctuations in the Earth's temperature, hydrological cycles, and ocean activity, typically attributed to an atmospheric increase of carbon dioxide and other greenhouse gases.

demographic transition   The four basic changes the population of a country seems to go through as the country passes from being a traditional, rural and

Global Issues: An Introduction, Sixth Edition. Kristen A. Hite and John L. Seitz.
© 2021 John Wiley & Sons Ltd. Published 2021 by John Wiley & Sons Ltd.

agricultural country to a modern, urban and industrial country. In the first stage, there are high birth and death rates. In the fourth stage there are low birth and death rates. Stages two and three are called the transitional period. In the early part of the transition (second stage) the death rates begin to drop quickly as modern medicine takes hold while birth rates continue to be high. The population begins to increase rapidly, a situation many developing countries recently faced or are still facing. In the third stage of the intermediate period death rates continue to fall and birth rates start to fall also. Population continues to increase but less rapidly than in the second stage. Some developing countries are at present in this state. A few demographers have suggested that there may be a fifth demographic stage where birth rates are so low that the size of the population starts to shrink, a situation that Japan and some European countries appear to be in at present.

developing country   Traditional term referring to a relatively poor nation where agriculture or mineral resources have a large role in the economy while industry has a lesser role. The economic and social infrastructure of the country (transportation, communications, education, health, and other social services) is usually inadequate for its needs. About 80 percent of the world's people live in nations like this, also called **less developed** or **underdeveloped**. These countries are often located in Africa, Latin America, and Asia. (Some of these nations are highly developed in culture and are the homes of ancient civilizations that had great achievements in architecture, religion, and philosophy.) Since many of the less (economically) developed nations are in the southern hemisphere, they are at times referred to as **the South**. During the Cold War these nations were often called the **Third World**, a term still in use. (First World was capitalist, noncommunist nations, and Second World was state socialist countries). Industrialized countries are called **developed** nations. Most of them are located in the northern hemisphere so they are at times called **the North**. The World Bank classifies nations according to their level of income, as measured by per capita gross national income, placing low and middle income countries in the developing category and high income countries in the developed category. The poorest countries such as Bangladesh and Somalia are called the **least developed**. All of these terms are imprecise. There are often many differences among developing nations. Their relative national wealth is often their sole similar quality.

development   Economic growth plus the social and environmental changes caused by or accompanying that economic growth. When the economy expands, more goods (material objects) and services (healthcare, education, etc.) are produced. The economic growth causes or is accompanied by changes in the society – how people live. If pollution results from the economic growth, people may breathe harmful air and drink toxins in their water. If economic growth leads to better education in the country rather than just more consumer goods, a more highly educated society is created which is better able to understand its problems and take appropriate actions to remedy them.

emerging economy An intermediate category between countries historically classified as "developed" and "developing," often said to include the **BRICS** (Brazil, India, China and South Africa); in the late twentieth and early twenty-first centuries they were also referred to as **newly industrializing economies** (such as South Korea, Taiwan, Hong Kong, Singapore, and Mexico), which became richer by expanding their manufacturing and exporting goods mainly to the United States, Europe, and Japan.

foreign aid (development assistance) Foreign aid is support from one or more countries (sometime acting through international institutions), typically in the form of favorable loans or grants, intended for a public interest in another country, frequently channeled through national funds. Aid given for economic development is called **development assistance**. Aid given to strengthen the recipient's military forces is called **military assistance**. "From the recipient's perspective, foreign aid adds to the resources available for investment and increases the supply of foreign exchange to finance necessary imports. From the donor's point of view, foreign aid is an instrument of foreign policy, and often comes with implicit or explicit expectations of reciprocity in areas where the recipient can be of assistance. Aid packages frequently restrict the recipient, moreover, to purchases from producers in the donor country." *Source*: "Foreign aid," in Craig Calhoun (ed.), *Dictionary of the Social Sciences* (Oxford University Press, 2002).

Gaia hypothesis The theory is based on an idea put forward by the British scientist James Lovelock that the Earth operates as a whole system and responds to human activity in a self-regulating manner.

geoengineering technologies that modify use of the Earth at geological levels, such as through mineralization or carbon capture and storage technologies to mitigate climate change.

global issues Issues or problems that affect most nations around the world, that cannot be solved by any single nation, and that show our increasing interdependence. Often interdisciplinary knowledge is required to attack these complex problems, which at times can affect the ability of our planet to support life."

globalization The increase of global economic, political, environmental, and social activities. Expanding international capitalism, mainly through the reach of multinational corporations; the activities of the more important international political organizations, such as the United Nations, World Bank, International Monetary Fund, and World Trade Organization; and growing global communications and social interactions are leading to a more interdependent world. The emphasis of **antiglobalization** is that the benefits of the new globalization are unevenly shared, with some parts of the world growing wealthier – such as the United States, much of

Western Europe, Japan, and sections of China and India – while some nations are not benefiting or being hurt – such as parts of Latin America and Africa. Public protests have been waged over working conditions in many countries, environmental destruction, social justice, and high national debts from development loans, and by anticapitalists who oppose the increasing power of large corporations.

Green Revolution   The bringing of Western agricultural technology to the developing world, including highly productive hybrid seeds and the use of fertilizers, pesticides, and irrigation, which has led to vastly increased yields of rice, wheat, and corn in some countries and during some periods.

Millennium Development Goals   Out of the Millennium Declaration adopted by the 189 nations attending the Millennium Summit in 2000 came eight development goals that nations agreed they would focus on through 2015. They were: (1) eradicate extreme poverty and hunger; (2) achieve universal primary education; (3) promote gender equality and empower women; (4) reduce child mortality; (5) improve maternal health; (6) combat HIV/AIDS, malaria, and other diseases; (7) ensure environmental sustainability; (8) develop a global partnership for development.

multinational corporation   Business organization which has its headquarters in one country (often in a developed nation) and branches in other countries (often developing countries) where its production facilities are often located because of cheap labor, access to markets and resources, lower taxes, weaker pollution regulations, and bypassing protectionist barriers. It is the main vehicle in spreading globalization.

negative externality   An economics phrase – the producer and the consumer do not bear all the costs of an economic activity. These costs are passed on to the community at large. For example, many industries in many countries have discharged their wastes into the air, water, and land. Industry generally has considered the atmosphere, rivers, and lakes to be "free goods." The illness and damage to the environment from this pollution was borne by the public. This activity continued until the state or government passed laws stopping or limiting it. Some believe the releasing of carbon dioxide, a major cause of climate change, which is released whenever fossil fuels are burned, is the most dangerous example the world has ever experienced of a negative externality.

pastoralism   A cultural and economic livelihood that involves raising pasture-fed animals, often cattle and sheep, and may include an extensive range of land or even nomadic features. Some indigenous peoples identify as pastoralists.

sustainable   An ability to be maintained at a certain level indefinitely. A widely accepted definition of **sustainable development** is contained in *Our Common Future*, the report of the 1987 World Commission on the Environment and Development (the

"Brundtland Report") as "development that meets the needs of the present without compromising the ability of future generations to meet their own needs."

tragedy of the commons   A concept most famously described by Garrett Hardin to point to the incentive for overexploitation when one user absorbs most of the benefits from a choice to use resources beyond their carrying capacity while the costs of that choice are mostly absorbed by other users.

Index

Page numbers in *italics* refer to Figures and Plates
Page numbers in **bold** refer to Tables

Global Issues: An Introduction, Sixth Edition. Kristen A. Hite and John L. Seitz.
© 2021 John Wiley & Sons Ltd. Published 2021 by John Wiley & Sons Ltd.